WATER
NO LONGER TAKEN FOR GRANTED

D1418454

ISSN 1536-5212

WATER
NO LONGER TAKEN FOR GRANTED

Sandra M. Alters

INFORMATION PLUS® REFERENCE SERIES
Formerly Published by Information Plus, Wylie, Texas

GALE
CENGAGE Learning·

Detroit • New York • San Francisco • New Haven, Conn • Waterville, Maine • London

GALE
CENGAGE Learning™

Water: No Longer Taken for Granted

Sandra M. Alters

Paula Kepos, Series Editor

Project Editors: Kathleen J. Edgar, Elizabeth Manar

Rights Acquisition and Management: Aja Perales, Jhanay Williams

Composition: Evi Abou-El-Seoud, Mary Beth Trimper

Manufacturing: Cynde Lentz

Gale
27500 Drake Rd.
Farmington Hills, MI 48331-3535

ISBN-13: 978-0-7876-5103-9 (set)   ISBN-10: 0-7876-5103-6 (set)
ISBN-13: 978-1-4144-3383-7   ISBN-10: 1-4144-3383-2

ISSN 1536-5212

This title is also available as an e-book.
ISBN-13: 978-1-4144-5765-9 (set)
ISBN-10: 1-4144-5765-0 (set)
Contact your Gale sales representative for ordering information.

Printed in the United States of America
1 2 3 4 5 6 7 13 12 11 10 09

TABLE OF CONTENTS

PREFACE

Water: No Longer Taken for Granted is part of the *Information Plus Reference Series*. The purpose of each volume of the series is to present the latest facts on a topic of pressing concern in modern American life. These topics include the most controversial and studied social issues in the 21st century: abortion, capital punishment, care for senior citizens, crime, the environment, health care, immigration, minorities, national security, social welfare, women, youth, and many more. Even though this series is written especially for high school and undergraduate students, it is an excellent resource for anyone in need of factual information on current affairs.

By presenting the facts, it is the intention of Gale, Cengage Learning to provide its readers with everything they need to reach an informed opinion on current issues. To that end, there is a particular emphasis in this series on the presentation of scientific studies, surveys, and statistics. These data are generally presented in the form of tables, charts, and other graphics placed within the text of each book. Every graphic is directly referred to and carefully explained in the text. The source of each graphic is presented within the graphic itself. The data used in these graphics are drawn from the most reputable and reliable sources, such as from the various branches of the U.S. government and from major independent polling organizations. Every effort has been made to secure the most recent information available. Readers should bear in mind that many major studies take years to conduct and that additional years often pass before the data from these studies are made available to the public. Therefore, in many cases the most recent information available in 2009 is dated from 2006 or 2007. Older statistics are sometimes presented as well, if they are of particular interest and no more-recent information exists.

Even though statistics are a major focus of the *Information Plus Reference Series*, they are by no means its only content. Each book also presents the widely held positions and important ideas that shape how the book's subject is discussed in the United States. These positions are explained in detail and, where possible, in the words of their proponents. Some of the other material to be found in these books includes historical background, descriptions of major events related to the subject, relevant laws and court cases, and examples of how these issues play out in American life. Some books also feature primary documents or have pro and con debate sections that provide the words and opinions of prominent Americans on both sides of a controversial topic. All material is presented in an even-handed and unbiased manner; readers will never be encouraged to accept one view of an issue over another.

HOW TO USE THIS BOOK

Water is one of the most vital resources on Earth. Most of the human body consists of water, and any person who is deprived of water for a significant period will die. The same can be said of all the animals and plants that people rely on for food. Only the air we breathe is more essential to human life, but while there is no shortage of air around the world, there are many regions where drinkable water is in short supply, such as the western United States. Furthermore, even where water is available, human activities may have contaminated it with diseases and chemicals, with serious consequences for the people and wildlife that use or live in it. As a result, the use and care of the water that is available is a controversial topic in the United States and around the world. This book explores all of the major issues relating to water in the United States, from water usage rights to pollution control to safe drinking water.

Water: No Longer Taken for Granted consists of eight chapters and three appendixes. Each chapter is devoted to a particular aspect of water in the United States. For a summary of the information covered in each chapter, please see the synopses provided in the Table of Contents at the front of the book. Chapters generally begin with an overview of the basic facts and background information on the chapter's topic, then proceed to examine subtopics of particular interest. For example, Chapter 4: Groundwater, begins with an overview of groundwater by describing where it can be found within Earth and by providing an estimate of the amount of fresh groundwater at all depths. The chapter then profiles groundwater, such as how water collects within the unsaturated and saturated zones, how it flows through the soil, and the various types of aquifers and springs. Next, the natural characteristics of groundwater are outlined, followed by an examination of current groundwater use, and then a look at contamination. Specifically, the chapter looks at how the quality of groundwater can be affected by pollution from various sources and the types of contaminants that result from those sources. The chapter concludes with a discussion about the challenges of cleaning up and protecting groundwater. Readers can find their way through a chapter by looking for the section and subsection headings, which are clearly set off from the text. They can also refer to the book's extensive Index, if they already know what they are looking for.

Statistical Information

The tables and figures featured throughout *Water: No Longer Taken for Granted* will be of particular use to readers in learning about this topic. These tables and figures represent an extensive collection of the most recent and valuable statistics on water and related issues—for example, graphics cover distribution of the world's water, groundwater use in the United States, the number and types of waterborne-disease outbreaks associated with recreational water use, the types of drinking water systems, industrial water use by state, and what percentage of the public is concerned about the pollution of drinking water. Gale, Cengage Learning believes that making this information available to readers is the most important way to fulfill the goal of this book: to help readers understand the issues and controversies regarding water in the United States and to reach their own conclusions.

Each table or figure has a unique identifier appearing above it for ease of identification and reference. Titles for the tables and figures explain their purpose. At the end of each table or figure, the original source of the data is provided.

To help readers understand these often complicated statistics, all tables and figures are explained in the text. References in the text direct readers to the relevant statistics. Furthermore, the contents of all tables and figures are fully indexed. Please see the opening section of the Index at the back of this volume for a description of how to find tables and figures within it.

Appendixes

Besides the main body text and images, *Water: No Longer Taken for Granted* has three appendixes. The first is the Important Names and Addresses directory. Here, readers will find contact information for a number of government and private organizations that can provide further information on water. The second appendix is the Resources section, which can also assist readers in conducting their own research. In this section, the author and editors of *Water: No Longer Taken for Granted* describe some of the sources that were most useful during the compilation of this book. The final appendix is the Index.

ADVISORY BOARD CONTRIBUTIONS

The staff of Information Plus would like to extend its heartfelt appreciation to the Information Plus Advisory Board. This dedicated group of media professionals provides feedback on the series on an ongoing basis. Their comments allow the editorial staff who work on the project to make the series better and more user-friendly. The staff's top priorities are to produce the highest-quality and most useful books possible, and the Advisory Board's contributions to this process are invaluable.

The members of the Information Plus Advisory Board are:

- Kathleen R. Bonn, Librarian, Newbury Park High School, Newbury Park, California

- Madelyn Garner, Librarian, San Jacinto College, North Campus, Houston, Texas

- Anne Oxenrider, Media Specialist, Dundee High School, Dundee, Michigan

- Charles R. Rodgers, Director of Libraries, Pasco-Hernando Community College, Dade City, Florida

- James N. Zitzelsberger, Library Media Department Chairman, Oshkosh West High School, Oshkosh, Wisconsin

COMMENTS AND SUGGESTIONS

The editors of the *Information Plus Reference Series* welcome your feedback on *Water: No Longer Taken for Granted*. Please direct all correspondence to:

Editors
Information Plus Reference Series
27500 Drake Rd.
Farmington Hills, MI 48331-3535

CHAPTER 1
WHAT IS WATER?

Most people living in the United States assume they will have plenty of clean, safe water for drinking, that crops and gardens can be regularly irrigated, and that sewage will be taken care of by their local treatment plant. In many parts of the world, however, the availability of water for personal and public use cannot be taken for granted. According to the World Health Organization (WHO), in "10 Facts about Water Scarcity" (March 2009, http://www.who.int/features/factfiles/water/en/index.html), one-third of the world's population lacks enough water to meet daily needs, and the situation is getting worse.

Water is vital to human survival. People can survive for a month—possibly two—without food, but they would die in about a week without water. Human survival is maintained, in part, because water is the most common substance on Earth. It covers three-fourths of Earth's surface and makes up about 65% of the adult human body, including 90% of its blood and 75% of its brain. Water is the main ingredient in most of the fruits, vegetables, and meats that people eat. For example, the U.S. Department of Agriculture notes in the fact sheet "Meat Preparation: Water in Meat and Poultry" (August 2007, http://www.fsis.usda.gov/fact_sheets/Water_in_Meats/index.asp) that water makes up 66% of chicken and 71% of beef brisket. The high water content of foods is one reason that a tremendous amount of water is needed to grow crops and sustain animals used for food. In *Minimum Water Quantity Needed for Domestic Use in Emergencies* (July 1, 2005, http://www.searo.who.int/LinkFiles/List_of_Guidelines_for_Health_Emergency_Minimum_water_quantity.pdf), the WHO reports that 60 liters (15.9 gallons) of water per person per day or 21,900 liters (5,785.4 gallons) per person per year are needed to produce enough food to provide an adequate diet for a human being for one year.

Water is essential to human existence, but it can also cause severe damage and destruction. It is terror to the swimmer caught in a rip current. It contributes to rusting in cars and rotting in wood. Water in the form of hailstones can destroy crops, and in the winter ice coats roads, making driving dangerous. Too much rain can cause flooding, which has the potential for destroying homes and killing people. Too little rain can cause droughts, which have the potential to result in the dehydration and eventual death of living things. Water can carry pathogens, which cause disease; in developing countries waterborne diseases are commonplace and often deadly.

WATER'S CHEMICAL COMPOSITION

Water is a molecule consisting of two hydrogen (H) atoms and one oxygen (O) atom. (See Figure 1.1.) The atoms in a molecule of water share electrons, forming strong chemical bonds that hold water molecules together. Because of the way these electrons are shared, the oxygen portion of the water molecule carries a slight positive charge, whereas the hydrogen portions carry a slight negative charge. These partial charges make water an excellent solvent; it dissolves substances by surrounding their charged particles. For example, sodium chloride (NaCl; salt) is dissolved in water when the negative "ends" of water molecules surround positively charged sodium ions and the positive "ends" of water molecules surround negatively charged chloride ions, separating sodium and chloride with water.

THREE STATES OF WATER

Water exists naturally in three states: a liquid (its most common form), a solid (ice), and a gas (water vapor). It is the only substance on Earth in which all three of its natural states occur within the normal range of climatic conditions, sometimes at the same time. Familiar examples of water in its three natural states are rain, snow or hail, and steam.

Compared with other liquids, water has some unusual properties. For example, most liquids contract (shrink) as they freeze. That is, their molecules move closer together.

FIGURE 1.1

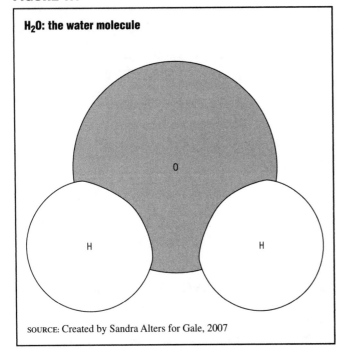

H₂0: the water molecule

SOURCE: Created by Sandra Alters for Gale, 2007

Water contracts only until it reaches 39.2° Fahrenheit (F; 4° Celsius [C]). Then it expands (its molecules move farther apart from one another) until it reaches its freezing point of 32°F (0°C). This expansion can exert a tremendous force on surrounding objects, enough to crack an unprotected automobile engine, burst a basement water pipe, or even shatter a boulder. Expansion makes ice less dense than water, which is why ice floats. This phenomenon causes ice to form on rivers and lakes from the top down, and aquatic life survives beneath the ice.

When ice is warmed to a temperature higher than 32°F, it melts, becoming liquid. As a liquid, its molecules are more loosely bound together than in the "locked" crystalline lattice of ice, and they can move around each other rather freely. The molecules' ability to slip and slide around gives water and other liquids their fluid properties.

In the gaseous or vapor state, water molecules move rapidly about and have little attraction for one another, creating the diffuse appearance of steam or mist, or the haze of a humid day. (Humidity is the measure of the amount of water vapor in the air.) Evaporation is the general term used to describe the process by which water in its liquid form is changed to its gaseous state. Evaporation can occur under a wide variety of conditions. Examples include water vaporizing off of wet pavement following rainfall, boiling in a pot on the stove and producing steam, or evaporating from clothes hanging on a line to dry.

WATER: THE EARTH MOVER

Scientists believe Earth formed about 4.5 billion years ago. Within its primitive atmosphere were the basic elements needed to form water. As Earth cooled from a mass of molten rock, water formed in the atmosphere and then fell to the ground in a rain that lasted for millions of years, forming the oceans.

The flow of water flattens mountains and cuts canyons deep into the surface of Earth. It hollows out underground caverns and leaves behind various types of formations. Water creates soil by breaking down rocks and organic material and depositing it elsewhere. Water in the form of ice crafted the face of Earth as glaciers advanced and receded many thousands of years ago. The slow, relentless processes of water freezing, melting, flowing, and evaporating will likely make Earth's appearance as different a million years from the present as it was a million years ago.

HYDROLOGIC CYCLE

The U.S. Geological Survey (USGS) explains in *Where Is Earth's Water Located?* (March 4, 2009, http://ga.water .usgs.gov/edu/earthwherewater.html) that Earth is a vast reservoir, containing an estimated 332.5 million cubic miles (1,386 million cubic km) of water. It is everywhere: in the atmosphere, on Earth's surface, and in the ground. The relative distribution of the world's water supply is shown in Figure 1.2. About 97% of water on Earth is saltwater in the oceans, and about 3% is freshwater. Of the freshwater, 68.7% consists of ice caps and glaciers, 30.1% is groundwater (water found within the ground), and 0.3% is surface water (water at the surface, such as lakes and rivers). Only 0.9% of water is found in the atmosphere, mainly in the form of invisible water vapor.

Of all this water, what can humans use for their daily water needs? The 97% of water found in the oceans cannot be used unless the salt is removed. The desalination process is quite costly, although recent technologies have made this process more economically feasible (see Chapter 8). Any community, business, or industry that considers desalination as a method of obtaining freshwater must determine whether the cost of desalination is lower than the cost of other water supply alternatives. Bernie Woodall reports in "Biggest Desalination Plant in W. Hemisphere Gets OK" (Reuters, August 22, 2008) that in 2008 there were approximately 22,000 desalination plants in 120 countries worldwide.

Most of the desalination facilities currently in operation around the world are in the Middle East. The article "Ashkelon Desalination Plant, Seawater Reverse Osmosis (SWRO) Plant, Israel, Israel" (2009, http://www.water-technology.net/projects/israel/) explains that in 2005 Israel began operating the Ashkelon Desalination Plant, the world's largest desalination plant. Located along the country's southern Mediterranean coast, it provides 100 million cubic meters (26.4 billion gallons [99.9 billion L]) of desalinated water per year, about 13% of the total household water in Israel. In the United States, Florida and

FIGURE 1.2

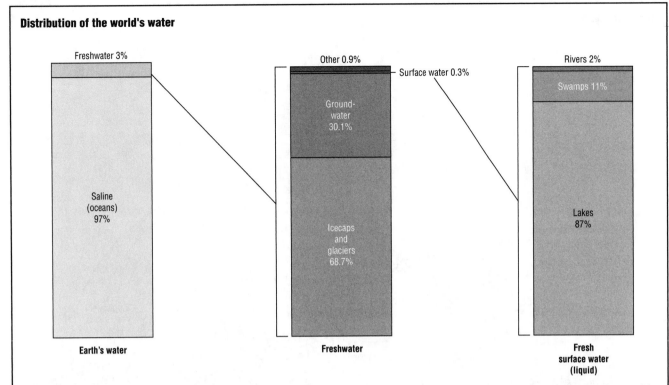

Distribution of the world's water

SOURCE: Peter Gleick (data) and Howard Perlman (rendering), "Distribution of Earth's Water," in *Where is Earth's Water Located?* U.S. Department of the Interior, U.S. Geological Survey, August 28, 2006, http://ga.water.usgs.gov/edu/earthwherewater.html (accessed March 8, 2009)

California have desalination plants. California officials announced in 2008 that the largest desalination plant in the Western Hemisphere was approved for construction in Carlsbad, California. Woodall indicates that the plant will produce 50 million gallons (189.3 million L) of fresh water per day, which will supply about 10% of the water needs of San Diego County. The plant will begin operation in 2011.

Regardless, most of the water people use every day comes from rivers, which is only 2% of all surface water, and surface water makes up only 0.3% of all the water on Earth. (See Figure 1.2.) Most of the freshwater available for use (30.1% of all freshwater) is stored in the ground. The rest of the freshwater on Earth is not available for human use because it is frozen in icecaps and glaciers.

As shown in Figure 1.3, Earth's water is continually being cycled between the ground and the air. This exchange is caused by the heat of the sun and the force of gravity. Water evaporates from the surface of Earth (e.g., from moist ground, the leaves of vegetation, and bodies of water). It then rises into the atmosphere as water vapor. The water vapor condenses to a liquid from its gaseous form and falls as precipitation, in the form of rain, mist, sleet, hail, or snow.

The precipitation, in turn, replenishes Earth's surface and underground waters, which eventually join the ponds, lakes, rivers, and oceans. The evaporation of water from the land and oceans and the transpiration from plants (evaporation of water from the leaves) put the water (as vapor) back into the air. In this way water travels from the ground to the atmosphere and back to the ground continuously. The exchange of water between the ground and the air is called the hydrologic cycle or water cycle. (See Figure 1.3.) The term *hydrologic* is derived from two Greek words: *hydro*, which means "water," and *loge*, which means "knowledge of."

The hydrologic cycle is a natural, constantly running distillation and pumping system. As a cycle, this flow has no beginning and no end. Within the hydrologic cycle water is neither lost nor gained; it simply changes form as it moves through the cycle. The molecules of water in the world's oceans, lakes, rivers, ponds, streams, and atmosphere today are the same molecules that formed 4.5 billion years ago.

Although constantly in motion, water is transferred between phases of the hydrologic cycle at different rates, depending on where it is located. For instance, a water molecule exists as water vapor in the atmosphere an average of eight days, but when it enters the ocean it may remain there for the next 2,500 years.

The hydrologic cycle shapes and sustains life on Earth. It is largely responsible for determining climate and types of vegetation. Because it is an open system, outside actions may affect any phase of the cycle, and they may have both immediate and long-term consequences.

FIGURE 1.3

The water cycle

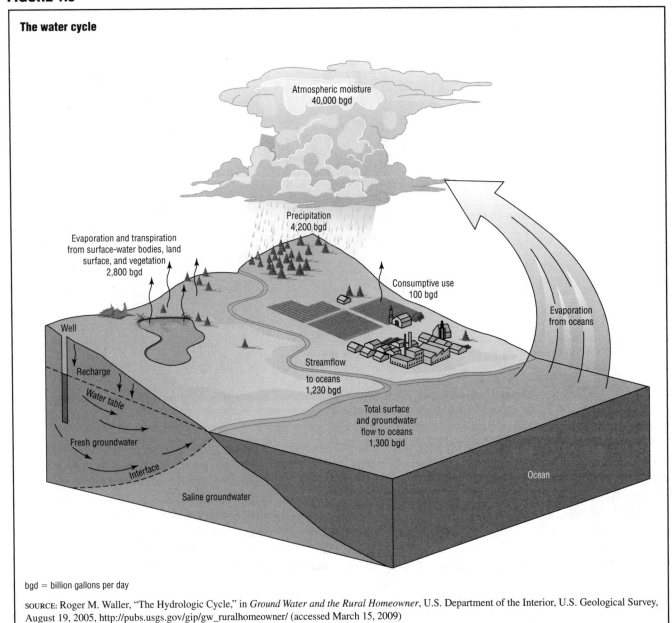

Atmospheric moisture
40,000 bgd

Precipitation
4,200 bgd

Evaporation and transpiration
from surface-water bodies, land
surface, and vegetation
2,800 bgd

Consumptive use
100 bgd

Evaporation
from oceans

Well

Recharge

Water table

Streamflow
to oceans
1,230 bgd

Fresh groundwater

Total surface
and groundwater
flow to oceans
1,300 bgd

Interface

Ocean

Saline groundwater

bgd = billion gallons per day

SOURCE: Roger M. Waller, "The Hydrologic Cycle," in *Ground Water and the Rural Homeowner*, U.S. Department of the Interior, U.S. Geological Survey, August 19, 2005, http://pubs.usgs.gov/gip/gw_ruralhomeowner/ (accessed March 15, 2009)

Soil Moisture

Even though it represents only a small percentage of Earth's water supply, soil moisture is extremely important. It supplies water to plants, which are a vital link in the food chain. Some plants grow directly in water or in marshy ground, but most live on dry land. This is possible because the land is truly dry in just a few places, and often only temporarily.

Dust is generally considered dry, but the dust kicked up by a car on a dry dirt road may contain up to 15% water by weight. Vegetation, however, cannot grow and flourish on that road because the dry soil holds its small percentage of moisture so strongly that plant roots cannot extract it. Other than some desert plants that store water in their own tissues during infrequent wet periods, most plants can grow

only where there is a regular supply of extractable water in the soil. Some plants grow in certain climates only during the rainy season. Thus, Earth's vegetation continually withdraws moisture from the ground in large amounts, and frequent renewals of soil moisture, either by precipitation or irrigation, are needed.

Atmospheric Moisture

Rain, snow, sleet, and hail are all forms of precipitation. This moisture in the air comes from the evaporation of water from the ground and from bodies of water such as lakes, rivers, and, especially, the oceans. Plants also release moisture into the air through their leaves. This process is called transpiration. The plant moisture is first taken up by the roots from the soil, moves up the plant in the sap, and then emerges from the plant through thousands of tiny holes on the underside of each leaf. According to the USGS, in "The Water Cycle: Evapotranspiration" (November 7, 2008, http://ga.water.usgs.gov/edu/watercycleevapotranspiration .html), an acre of corn transpires 3,000 to 4,000 gallons (11,400 to 15,100 L) of water every day and a large tree may release over 100 gallons (379 L) per day.

Transpiration from plants is one of the important sources of water vapor in the air and usually produces more moisture than evaporation from the ground, lakes, and streams. The most important source of water vapor in the air, however, is evaporation from the oceans, especially those parts of the ocean that are located in the warmest parts of the planet. Heat is required to change water from a liquid to a vapor. Thus, the higher the temperature, the faster the water evaporates from the oceans. However, the winds in the upper atmosphere carry this moisture far from the oceans. For example, someone who lives in the central part of the United States may receive rain that consists of water particles evaporated from the ocean near the equator or the Gulf of Mexico.

Ice Caps and Glaciers

Over two-thirds (68.7%) of all freshwater in the world is stored as ice. (See Figure 1.2.) In "Earthshots: Satellite Images of Environmental Change" (May 1, 2007, http:// earthshots.usgs.gov/Filchner/Filchner), the USGS states that most of the world's ice is held by the Antarctic ice cap—about 90% of all existing ice. However, this ice sheet has lost significant mass in recent years due to changing climate conditions.

Ice is also held in glaciers. A glacier is any large mass of snow or ice that persists on land for many years and moves under its own weight. Glaciers are formed in locations where, over a number of years, more snow falls than melts. As this snow accumulates, it compresses and changes into dense, solid ice—a glacier.

Robert M. Krimmel notes in *Glaciers of the Contermi-nous United States* (March 7, 2002, http://pubs.usgs.gov/ pp/p1386j/us/westus-lores.pdf), the most recent report of its kind as of mid-2009, that even though most people associate glaciers with remote, frozen regions such as Antarctica, there are more than 1,600 glaciers in the lower 48 U.S. states, most of them quite small. They cover about 229.2 square miles (593.7 square km) in parts of California, Colorado, Idaho, Montana, Nevada, Oregon, Utah, Washington, and Wyoming. Alaska has uncounted numbers of glaciers that cover many thousands of square miles.

Permafrost

Permafrost is permanently frozen ground, which accounts for approximately one-fifth of Earth's entire land surface. It exists in Antarctica but is more extensive in the Northern Hemisphere. In the land surrounding the Arctic Ocean, its maximum thickness has been measured in thousands of

FIGURE 1.4

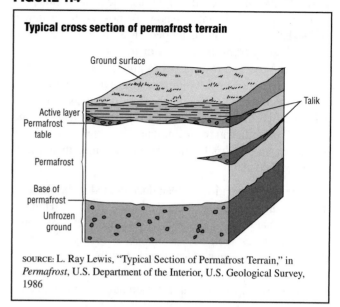

Typical cross section of permafrost terrain

SOURCE: L. Ray Lewis, "Typical Section of Permafrost Terrain," in *Permafrost*, U.S. Department of the Interior, U.S. Geological Survey, 1986

feet—about 5,000 feet (1,524 m) in Siberia and 2,000 feet (610 m) in Alaska. Even though the surface permafrost (called the active layer, see Figure 1.4) thaws quickly in the summer and refreezes in winter, it would take thousands of years of thawing conditions to melt the thick, frozen layer beneath. The deepest part of permafrost was formed during the Great Ice Age, which occurred about 3 million years ago. Talik, which is shown in Figure 1.4, are patches of ground within permafrost that never freeze because of a local irregularity in conditions.

In North America the discovery of gold in Alaska and the Yukon in the early 1900s sparked an increased interest in the nature of the vast areas of permafrost. After World War II (1939–1945), increasing numbers of nonnative people migrated to areas of frozen ground, and the construction of roads, railroads, and buildings and the clearing of land led to the disruption and thawing of previously undisturbed permafrost. This caused unstable ground, landslides, mud-flows, and, consequently, dangerous living conditions. In addition, Larry C. Smith et al. report in "Disappearing Arctic Lakes" (*Science*, vol. 308, no. 5727, June 3, 2005) that warming in the Arctic, which has sped up since the 1980s, is causing the loss of permafrost in Arctic regions. In the press release "Permafrost Threatened by Rapid Retreat of Arctic Sea Ice, NCAR Study Finds" (June 10, 2008, http://www.ucar.edu/news/releases/2008/permafrost.jsp), the University Corporation for Atmospheric Research notes that research results also show that an accelerated thawing of sea ice near Arctic permafrost land masses leads to an accelerated warming of the land and thawing of the permafrost.

Snowmelt

Except for the disruption of day-to-day life caused by winter snowstorms in certain areas of the United States, most Americans are largely unaware of the importance of snow. Unlike many other countries, the United States is economically dependent on snow. Almost all the water in the arid West that can be tapped on a large-volume basis comes directly from spring snowmelt. The amount of water in a given year's snowpack varies greatly from one year to another. The snowpack volume is of crucial importance to regional economics. Too much snow can cause flooding and extensive damage to crops, livestock, businesses, and homes. Too little can mean shortages in water for drinking, irrigation, and hydroelectric power, affecting their availability and cost.

The latter scenario has been documented in the West by many studies, including Tim P. Barnett et al.'s "Human-Induced Changes in the Hydrology of the Western United States" (*Science*, vol. 319, no. 5866, February 22, 2008). Barnett et al. note that characteristics of the water cycle in the West have changed over the last half-century, with the amount of rain increasing in the mountains and the amount of snow decreasing. The shrinkage of the snowpack reduces the supply of water to western states; the researchers warn of water shortages as a result, along with other "critical impacts." Barnett et al. also examine possible causes of the changes and determine that much of the change is due to global warming.

FRESHWATER

Despite the enormous amount of water that surrounds us, only about 3% of it is freshwater and, therefore, suitable for use by land-based animals, plants, and humans. (See Figure 1.2.) The availability of freshwater depends on many factors: climate, location, rainfall, and local activity. The USGS reports in *Where Is Earth's Water Located?* that the world's freshwater lakes contain 21,830 cubic miles (90,991 cubic km) of water, and the world's rivers contain 509 cubic miles (2,122 cubic km) of freshwater. Together, lakes and rivers make up about 0.015% of the total water on Earth. Groundwater totals about 5.6 million cubic miles (23.3 million cubic km), or 1.7% of the total water supply.

VARIATIONS IN PRECIPITATION

The amount of precipitation that falls around the world can range from less than 0.1 of an inch (2.5 mm) per year in the deserts to hundreds of inches per year in the tropics. In "Global Measured Extremes of Temperature and Precipitation" (August 20, 2008, http://www.ncdc.noaa.gov/oa/climate/globalextremes.html), the National Climatic Data Center reports that the lowest average annual precipitation occurs in Arica, Chile, with 0.03 inches (0.76 mm). The world's wettest spot is Lloro, Colombia, with an estimated average annual rainfall of 523.6 inches (1,330 cm).

Variations in precipitation occur not only in various regions of the globe but also seasonally and annually. For example, southern Florida has a rainy season (May to October) followed by a dry season (November to April). Most of the 45 to 60 inches (114.3 to 152.4 cm) of annual rain that normally falls in this area occurs in the rainy season. In exceptionally dry years, droughts occur because the area receives little or no precipitation in the rainy season; in exceptionally wet years, flooding may occur.

Natural phenomena known as El Niño and La Niña influence weather and precipitation. El Niño is a naturally occurring disruption of the ocean-atmosphere system in the tropical Pacific Ocean, which has important consequences for weather around the globe. It is characterized by an unusually warm current of water that appears every three to five years in the eastern Pacific Ocean. Unusually warm sea surface temperature results in a decline in primary productivity (microscopic plants and animals) that in turn brings sharp declines in commercial fisheries and bird populations that are dependent on fish. Unusual weather conditions occur around the globe as jet streams, storm tracks, and monsoons are shifted. Some other consequences are increased rainfall across the southern United States and Peru, which has caused destructive flooding in the past, and drought in Australia and Indonesia. El Niño brings warmer than normal temperatures to the north-central states and cooler than normal temperatures to the southeastern and southwestern states.

La Niña global climate impacts tend to be the opposite of El Niño because La Niña is characterized by unusually cold ocean temperatures in the equatorial Pacific. In the United States winter temperatures are warmer than normal in the Southeast and cooler than normal in the Northwest. La Niña events occur after some, but not all, El Niño events. Generally, La Niña occurs half as frequently as El Niño.

HUMAN INFLUENCES ON WATER

As human populations continually modify the environment to suit their needs and desires, the natural processes, including the hydrologic cycle, are significantly disrupted. People are finding out that Earth, even with its remarkable recuperative powers, has limits beyond which it cannot sustain a livable environment.

There are two ways by which humans change the basic quality and natural distribution of water: by introducing materials and organisms into a body of water (including the water in the atmosphere)—commonly known as pollution—and by intervening in any phase of the hydrologic cycle in such a way that the cycle is altered. Dams, irrigation, and hydroelectric plants are examples of alterations.

Water Pollution

For centuries, the world's lakes, rivers, and oceans have been the dumping sites for many of the undesirable by-products of civilization. People have dumped indiscriminately, believing that bodies of water had an inexhaustible capacity to disperse and neutralize any amount of waste. What was not dissolved or dispersed settled to the bottom, where it could not be seen.

Dumping waste into the oceans and waterways led to few apparent problems as long as waste products were few and consisted mainly of naturally occurring materials. However, as the world's population grew and technology began introducing huge numbers of new products and processes, this natural disposal system began breaking down under an overload of natural and synthetic contaminants. Fish and marine animals died; dead zones, where no life could survive, developed in harbors and oceans; drinking water became contaminated; and beaches became littered with garbage.

Water that has been physically or chemically changed and that adversely affects the health of humans and other organisms is said to be polluted. There are many sources and types of water pollution. Every day, industrial by-products and household wastes such as toxic chemicals, metals, plastics, medical refuse, radioactive waste, and sludge (the solid material left after water is extracted from raw sewage) are deposited into the nation's rivers, lakes, harbors, and oceans. Septic tanks, landfills, and mining operations often produce hazardous substances that seep into the soil and then into underground aquifers (areas within subsurface rock where water is stored). Table 1.1 lists the most common sources of water pollution. (The term *riparian*, which is used in Table 1.1, refers to the banks of a body of water, such as a riverbank.) Figure 1.5 shows how pollutants, including warmed water from cooling towers of power plants, can be introduced into water and have extensive effects.

Water pollution is acknowledged by both scientists and the WHO as a global problem and one that results in the serious health issue of waterborne disease. Concern over water pollution helped launch the environmental movement of the 1970s. The 1972 Federal Water Pollution Control Act, commonly known as the Clean Water Act, was the first major piece of environmental legislation enacted by Congress. Since then, many laws and regulations designed to protect, preserve, and clean up the national waters have been passed. Even though substantial progress has been made, many problems remain to be solved.

Point and Nonpoint Sources of Pollution

There are two types of water pollution sources: point and nonpoint sources. Point sources are specific sites, such as sewage treatment plants, factories, and ships, that discharge pollutants into bodies of water at single points via pipes, sewers, or ditches. Nonpoint sources are not specific sites; pollutants enter bodies of water over large areas rather than at single points. Nonpoint sources of water pollution include agricultural runoff, mining activities, and soil erosion.

The Water Pollution Control Act and its amendments, such as the Clean Water Act, established the National Pollutant Discharge Elimination System, which controls water pollution by regulating point sources. This system uses water quality standards and discharge permits as a means of regulation. Water quality standards establish the upper limit for the amount of a pollutant that will not cause an adverse effect on humans or other living things. Cities, companies, and other entities that want to discharge into water apply for permission

TABLE 1.1

Sources of water pollution

Category	Examples
Agriculture	Crop production, feedlots (including concentrated animal feeding operations), grazing, manure runoff
Atmospheric deposition	Airborne pollution from many diverse sources (such as factory and automobile emissions and pesticide applications) that settles to land or water
Construction	Residential development, bridge and road construction, land development
Habitat alterations (not directly related to hydromodification)	Riparian and in-stream habitat modification and loss, filling and draining of wetlands, removal of riparian vegetation, streambank erosion
Hydromodification	Pond construction, channelization, dam construction, dredging, flow alterations from water diversions, flow regulation, hydropower generation, streambank destabilization and modification, upstream impoundments
Industrial	Factories, industrial and commercial areas, cooling water intake structures, mill tailings
Land application/waste sites/tanks	Salt storage piles, land application of biosolids, land disposal, landfills, leaking underground storage tanks
Legacy/historical pollutants	Brownfield sites, contaminated sediments, in-place contaminants
Municipal discharges/sewage	Septic systems, sewage treatment plants, domestic sewage lagoons, sanitary sewer overflows, municipal dry and wet weather discharges, unpermitted discharges of domestic wastes, combined sewer overflows, septage disposal
Natural/wildlife	Flooding, drought-related impacts, waterfowl
Recreation and tourism	Golf courses, marinas, turf management, boat maintenance
Resource extraction	Abandoned mining, acid mine drainage, coal mining, dredge mining, mountaintop mining, petroleum/natural gas activities, surface mining
Silviculture (forestry)	Forest management, forest fire suppression, forest roads, reforestation, woodlot site clearance
Spills/dumping	Accidental releases/spills, pipeline breaks
Unknown	Source of impairment is unknown
Unspecified nonpoint source	Source of impairment is identified as nonpoint, but no further information available
Urban-related runoff/stormwater	Discharges from municipal separate storm sewers, parking lot and impervious surfaces runoff, highway and road runoff, storm sewers, urban runoff, permitted stormwater discharges

SOURCE: "Table 2. Major Pollutant Source Categories Used in This Report," in *National Water Quality Inventory: Report to Congress, 2004 Reporting Cycle*, U.S. Environmental Protection Agency, Office of Water, January 2009, http://www.epa.gov/owow/305b/2004report/2004_305Breport.pdf (accessed March 8, 2009)

FIGURE 1.5

Linkages between sources of pollutants and infectious agents, and freshwater, estuaries, and the coastal ocean

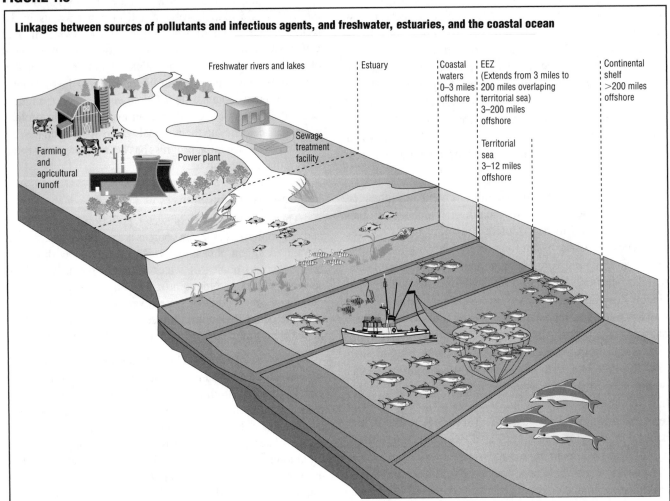

SOURCE: "Figure 1-6. Linkages between the Stressors in Freshwater Systems, Estuaries, and the Coastal Ocean," in *National Coastal Condition Report III*, U.S. Environmental Protection Agency, Office of Water and Office of Research and Development, December 2008, http://www.epa.gov/owow/oceans/ nccr3/pdf/nccr3_entire.pdf (accessed March 11, 2009).

and, if approved, receive a permit. The permit specifies the amount and type of pollutants that may be discharged and not cause a violation of the water quality standard. Dischargers are required to monitor what they release and report the results. When limits are exceeded, fines and other penalties are imposed, including requirements for additional treatment and cleanup.

Nonpoint sources of pollution are harder to control. Agriculture results in a great deal of nonpoint source pollution. For example, when water runs off fertilized land, it carries fertilizer with it into bodies of water. Fertilizer promotes the growth of plants and algae in the water. A high concentration of plant and algal growth results in the water becoming cloudy with their growth and, therefore, light cannot easily penetrate. When the reduced levels of light and the concentration of nutrients can no longer support high plant and algal growth, these organisms die, fall to the bottom, and decay. As bacteria feed on the dead plant material, they use oxygen, which results in less dissolved oxygen for fish. Fish that need higher levels of oxygen die out, whereas other

species that can survive in low oxygen levels multiply. The dead fish decay as well—a process that lowers the dissolved oxygen even more. At this point, the water is said to be eutrophic and may become slimy and smelly.

Human Activities That Contribute to Water Pollution and Degrade Water Quality

Many human activities promote water pollution. For example, modern technological developments allow massive quantities of water to be pumped out of the ground for use as drinking water and irrigation of crops. When large amounts of water are removed from the ground (and from the water cycle), underground aquifers can become depleted much more quickly than they can naturally replenish themselves. In some areas this has led to the subsidence, or sinking, of the ground above major aquifers. Removing too much water from an aquifer in coastal areas can result in saltwater intrusion into the aquifer, rendering the water too brackish (salty) to drink. The natural filtering process that occurs as water travels through rocks and sand is also impaired when aquifer levels become depleted, leaving the aquifer more vulnerable to contamination.

Building dams also interferes with the hydrologic cycle and may promote water pollution. The huge dams built in the United States just before and after World War II have substantially changed the natural flow of rivers. By reducing the amount of water available downstream and slowing stream flow, a dam not only affects a river but also the river's entire ecological system. For example, wetlands have the ability to clean water by trapping and filtering pollutants. This water-cleansing process can be reduced or stopped if dams cause wetlands to dry up.

Deforestation and overgrazing worldwide have destroyed thousands of acres of vegetation that play a vital role

in controlling erosion. Erosion is the process by which a material is worn away by a stream of water or air, usually because of the abrasive particles in the water or air. Erosion results in soil runoff into rivers and streams, causing turbidity (cloudiness or discoloration), siltation (depositing of soil on the bottoms of rivers and streams), and disruption of stream flow. The removal of vegetation on the land also reduces the amount of water released into the atmosphere by transpiration. In some areas less water in the atmosphere can mean less rainfall, causing fertile regions to become deserts.

Along with agricultural activities, industrial, urban, and residential development can also lead to soil runoff. As Figure 1.6 shows, timber harvesting leads to compacted soil, less ground cover, and disturbed ground. Some agricultural and industrial practices also lead to these results,

FIGURE 1.6

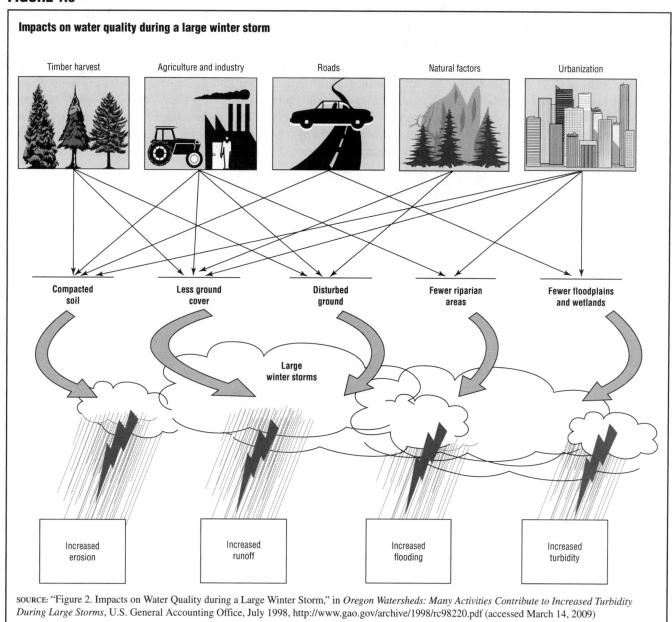

SOURCE: "Figure 2. Impacts on Water Quality during a Large Winter Storm," in *Oregon Watersheds: Many Activities Contribute to Increased Turbidity During Large Storms*, U.S. General Accounting Office, July 1998, http://www.gao.gov/archive/1998/rc98220.pdf (accessed March 14, 2009)

along with fewer riparian areas. Building roads results in compacted soil and fewer floodplains and wetlands. Urbanization (the building of cities with paved surfaces covering the land) leads to all these results. Under these conditions, storms often lead to increased turbidity, flooding, runoff, and erosion.

WORLDWIDE WATER CRISIS

Despite conservation (the careful use and protection of water resources) and reclamation (the treatment of wastewater so that it can be reused) efforts to lessen the effects of human activities on water quality, the world still faces a severe scarcity of sanitary water. According to the article "Experts Warn of Severe Water Shortages by 2080" (Associated Press, November 18, 2008), the United Nations (UN) Intergovernmental Panel on Climate Change predicts that 3.2 billion people could be living with a shortage of clean water for drinking, cleaning, and bathing by 2080. The panel notes that the region hit the hardest will be Asia, particularly India and China, both of which have high populations.

The scarcity of clean water throughout the world also has significant implications for public health. The UN Educational, Scientific, and Cultural Organization finds in "Meeting Basic Needs" (2006, http://www.unesco.org/water/wwap/facts_figures/basic_needs.shtml) that water contami-

nated with bacteria, parasites, and other microbes causes about 6,000 deaths every day.

Water shortages also affect international politics. Alexandra Hudson reports in "Selfish Use of Rivers Seen Threatening Political Stability" (Reuters, March 19, 2009) that 60% of the world's fresh water comes from rivers shared by at least two countries. Conflicts arise when one country tries to dam up, siphon off, or pollute the shared water. According to Meredith A. Giordano and Aaron T. Wolf, in *Atlas of International Freshwater Agreements* (2002, http://www.transboundarywaters.orst.edu/publications/atlas/), since 1820 there have been more than 400 agreements related to water as a limited and consumable resource. Giordano and Wolf note that while cooperation about water resources between and among countries during the past 50 years has outnumbered conflicts by more than 2 to 1, problems still occur. For example, between 1948 and 2002 they count 37 incidents of violent conflict over water, 30 of which were between Israel and one of its neighbors. Peter H. Gleick of the Pacific Institute for Studies in Development, Environment, and Security identifies in "Water Conflict Chronology" (November 2008, http://worldwater.org/conflictchronology.pdf) several more instances between 2003 and 2008, including conflicts in China, Colombia, Ethiopia, India, Iraq, Israel, Kenya, Lebanon, Mexico, Pakistan, Somalia, Sri Lanka, Sudan, Tibet, and Yemen.

CHAPTER 2
WATER USE

Water is used in every society. Individuals use water for drinking, cooking, cleaning, and recreation. Industry uses it to make chemicals, manufacture goods, and clean factories and equipment. Cities use water to fight fires, clean streets, and fill public swimming pools and fountains. Farmers give water to their livestock, irrigate their crops, and clean their barns. Hydroelectric power stations use water to drive generators, and thermonuclear power stations use it for cooling. No plant or animal can survive without water. Water is vital to life, yet, as Chapter 1 describes, it is a finite (limited) resource. There is no more water in the 21st century than was on Earth 4.5 billion years ago.

FRESHWATER AVAILABILITY

Most human and land-based animal and plant activities that use water require freshwater. In the vast majority of cases, saltwater cannot be used without treating it to remove the salt. The U.S. Geological Survey (USGS) notes in *Where Is Earth's Water Located?* (March 4, 2009, http://ga.water.usgs.gov/edu/earthwherewater.html) that the world's total water supply is about 332.5 million cubic miles (1,386 million cubic km), but freshwater makes up only about 3% of this water. (See Figure 1.2 in Chapter 1.) If this water were distributed equally over the planet relative to population density and animal and plant needs, it would be more than enough to sustain all life. This, however, is not the case.

Freshwater supplies vary not only from region to region on Earth but also from year to year within regions. Within the continental United States some parts of the country may not have adequate supplies, whereas other parts may be experiencing floods. Worldwide, the National Climatic Data Center reports in *Climate of 2008—In Historical Perspective: Annual Report* (January 14, 2009, http://www.ncdc.noaa.gov/oa/climate/research/2008/ann/ann08.html) that Brazil, Ethiopia, Panama, the Philippines, Venezuela, and Vietnam experienced widespread flooding during November 2008,

whereas a severe drought existed in parts of Texas and the U.S. Southeast.

The first human settlements were based on the availability of water. Where water was plentiful, large numbers of people flourished; where water was scarce, small groups of people eked out a living. Villages and cities thrived in areas of constant water supply. In more arid regions nomads wandered in search of water. Great nations grew up along the Nile River in Egypt, the Tigris and the Euphrates rivers in the Middle East, the Indus River in India, and the Yellow River in China.

Modern societies, which have more control over the water supply than did ancient societies, have developed technologies that bring water to arid regions and divert water from areas likely to flood. Modern, elaborate irrigation systems have made it possible for cities to exist in places where two centuries ago only the hardiest plants and animals could survive. For example, without these water systems Los Angeles, California, would be a semiarid desert.

HOW WATER IS SUPPLIED

Freshwater that is potable (safe to drink) is the most crucial resource for the maintenance of human societies. Freshwater, however, is limited in total supply, unevenly distributed, and often of unacceptable quality, particularly in areas where the supply is limited.

Most people in the United States obtain water through water utility companies, also called water purification and distribution plants. Utility companies are those that serve the public, such as an electric company, sewage treatment plant, or water purification and distribution plant. Utility companies may be owned by cities, towns, or private entities.

Water utility companies withdraw water from either surface or groundwater sources to supply their customers. The customers pay the utility companies for the water they use.

FIGURE 2.1

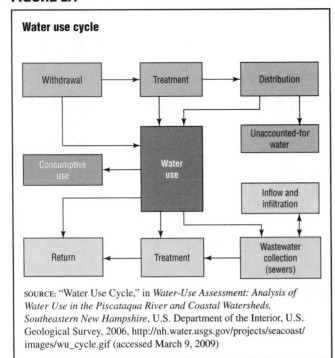

Water use cycle

SOURCE: "Water Use Cycle," in *Water-Use Assessment: Analysis of Water Use in the Piscataqua River and Coastal Watersheds, Southeastern New Hampshire*, U.S. Department of the Interior, U.S. Geological Survey, 2006, http://nh.water.usgs.gov/projects/seacoast/images/wu_cycle.gif (accessed March 9, 2009)

Water may also be self-supplied, that is, withdrawn directly from wells, lakes, or rivers by those users who have the equipment, technology, and water rights necessary to withdraw and process water for their individual and family use.

As described in Chapter 1, water cycles naturally within the environment. (See Figure 1.3 in Chapter 1.) Water withdrawn from surface or groundwater sources by humans eventually returns to the water cycle, but sometimes it is returned in a condition different from which it was withdrawn. The water's condition can greatly affect the ability to reuse the water. For example, water used for irrigation may end up as agricultural runoff containing pesticides and fertilizers, making it unfit for other uses such as drinking. Water used to flush a toilet mixes with body wastes, making it unfit for other uses as well.

Figure 2.1 shows a flowchart of water use activities. The phrase *water use* means human activities that use and transfer both surface and groundwater. Water use begins when water is withdrawn from surface or groundwater. It may be withdrawn and used directly, such as when a person has a well serving the home, or it may be withdrawn, treated, and distributed by a water utility company. After use, water that is not consumed is called wastewater, and it is returned to a river or to a wastewater treatment plant where, after treatment, it is discharged into a river. Consumed water is that which evaporates during water use or is used in a way that makes it unavailable for other uses, such as water incorporated into a product being manufactured. Unaccounted-for water includes public water use (firefighting, street washing,

water treatment plant back flushing of filters, and municipal parks and swimming pools), leakage (conveyance loss), and meter errors.

TYPES OF WATER USE IN THE UNITED STATES

Water use in the United States is monitored and reported by the USGS, which classifies water use as in-stream or off-stream. In-stream use means that water is used at its source—usually a river or stream—and the vast majority of that water is returned immediately to the source. Little or no water is consumed. Examples are a hydroelectric plant where water flows through turbines, which drive generators, and old mills where flowing water turns a wheel, which moves grinding stones. In the hydroelectric plant, the flowing water immediately returns to the river from which it came. In the old mill, the water never leaves the river. Off-stream use means that the water is withdrawn from a surface or groundwater source and conveyed to the place where it is used.

Off-Stream Use

Table 2.1 shows total off-stream water use by source, type, and state for 2000. Nationwide, off-stream water use was 408 billion gallons per day (Bgal/d; 1.5 trillion L per day). In *Estimated Use of Water in the United States in 2000* (2004, http://pubs.usgs.gov/circ/2004/circ1268/pdf/circular1268.pdf), the most recent report available as of mid-2009, Susan S. Hutson et al. of the USGS note that this was slightly more than the 402 Bgal/d (1.5 trillion L per day) used in 1995. Of the water involved in off-stream use, 345 Bgal/d (1.3 trillion L per day) was freshwater in 2000.

At 51.2 Bgal/d (193.8 billion L per day), California, with the largest state population, used more water than any other state in 2000. (See Table 2.1.) Texas, with the second-largest state population, was the second-largest water user at 29.6 Bgal/d (112 billion L per day). Florida, the state with the fourth-largest population, was the third-largest water user at 20.1 Bgal/d (76.1 billion L per day).

In many cases off-stream use results in substantial consumptive use of water. Consumptive use is of two types: quantitative or qualitative. Quantitative consumption means that part of the water withdrawn has evaporated, been transpired (given off) by plants, been incorporated into products or crops, been consumed by humans or livestock, or otherwise removed from the immediate water environment so that the quantity returned to the source is substantially less than the quantity of water withdrawn. An example of consumptive use is spray irrigation. According to the USGS, in "Irrigation Techniques" (November 7, 2008, http://ga.water.usgs.gov/edu/irmethods.html), about 60% of the water used to irrigate crops with spray irrigation is returned to the source. The other 40% of the water evaporates, is incorporated into plant structure, or is transpired by plants.

TABLE 2.1

Total water use by source and state, 2000

[Figures may not sum to totals because of independent rounding]

State	Population (in thousands)	Withdrawals (in million gallons per day)									Withdrawals (in thousand acre-feet per year)		
		By source and type						Total			Total		
		Groundwater			Surface water								
		Fresh	Saline	Total	Fresh	Saline	Total	Fresh	Saline	Total	Fresh	Saline	Total
Alabama	4,450	440	0	440	9,550	0	9,550	9,990	0	9,990	11,200	0	11,200
Alaska	627	50.2	90.4	141	111	53.4	164	161	144	305	181	161	342
Arizona	5,130	3,420	8.17	3,430	3,300	0	3,300	6,720	8.17	6,730	7,530	9.16	7,540
Arkansas	2,670	6,920	.08	6,920	3,950	0	3,950	10,900	.08	10,900	12,200	.09	12,200
California	33,900	15,200	152	15,400	23,200	12,600	35,800	38,400	12,800	51,200	43,100	14,300	57,400
Colorado	4,300	2,320	0	2,320	10,300	0	10,300	12,600	0	12,600	14,200	0	14,200
Connecticut	3,410	143	0	143	565	3,440	4,010	708	3,440	4,150	794	3,860	4,650
Delaware	784	115	0	115	466	741	1,210	582	741	1,320	652	831	1,480
District of Columbia	572	0	0	0	9.87	0	9.87	9.87	0	9.87	11.1	0	11.1
Florida	16,000	5,020	0	5,020	3,110	12,000	15,100	8,140	12,000	20,100	9,120	13,400	22,500
Georgia	8,190	1,450	0	1,450	4,960	91.7	5,060	6,410	91.7	6,500	7,190	103	7,290
Hawaii	1,210	433	.85	434	208	0	208	640	.85	641	718	.95	719
Idaho	1,290	4,140	0	4,140	15,300	0	15,300	19,500	0	19,500	21,800	0	21,800
Illinois	12,400	813	0	813	12,900	0	12,900	13,700	0	13,700	15,400	0	15,400
Indiana	6,080	656	0	656	9,460	0	9,460	10,100	0	10,100	11,300	0	11,300
Iowa	2,930	679	0	679	2,680	0	2,680	3,360	0	3,360	3,770	0	3,770
Kansas	2,690	3,790	0	3,790	2,820	0	2,820	6,610	0	6,610	7,410	0	7,410
Kentucky	4,040	189	0	189	3,970	0	3,970	4,160	0	4,160	4,660	0	4,660
Louisiana	4,470	1,630	0	1,630	8,730	0	8,730	10,400	0	10,400	11,600	0	11,600
Maine	1,270	80.8	0	80.8	423	295	718	504	295	799	565	330	895
Maryland	5,300	225	0	225	1,200	6,490	7,690	1,430	6,490	7,910	1,600	7,270	8,870
Massachusetts	6,350	269	0	269	783	3,610	4,390	1,050	3,610	4,660	1,180	4,050	5,220
Michigan	9,940	734	0	734	9,260	0	9,260	10,000	0	10,000	11,200	0	11,200
Minnesota	4,920	720	0	720	3,150	0	3,150	3,870	0	3,870	4,340	0	4,340
Mississippi	2,840	2,180	0	2,180	632	148	781	2,810	148	2,960	3,150	166	3,320
Missouri	5,600	1,780	0	1,780	6,450	0	6,450	8,230	0	8,230	9,220	0	9,220
Montana	902	188	0	188	8,100	0	8,100	8,290	0	8,290	9,300	0	9,300
Nebraska	1,710	7,860	4.55	7,860	4,390	0	4,390	12,200	4.55	12,300	13,700	5.10	13,700
Nevada	2,000	757	0	757	2,050	0	2,050	2,810	0	2,810	3,140	0	3,140
New Hampshire	1,240	85.2	0	85.2	362	761	1,120	447	761	1,210	501	854	1,350
New Jersey	8,410	584	0	584	1,590	3,390	4,980	2,170	3,390	5,560	2,430	3,800	6,230
New Mexico	1,820	1,540	0	1,540	1,710	0	1,710	3,260	0	3,260	3,650	0	3,650
New York	19,000	893	0	893	6,190	5,010	11,200	7,080	5,010	12,100	7,940	5,610	13,600
North Carolina	8,050	580	0	580	9,150	1,620	10,800	9,730	1,620	11,400	10,900	1,810	12,700
North Dakota	642	123	0	123	1,020	0	1,020	1,140	0	1,140	1,280	0	1,280
Ohio	11,400	878	0	878	10,300	0	10,300	11,100	0	11,100	12,500	0	12,500
Oklahoma	3,450	771	256	1,030	990	0	990	1,760	256	2,020	1,970	287	2,260
Oregon	3,420	993	0	993	5,940	0	5,940	6,930	0	6,930	7,770	0	7,770
Pennsylvania	12,300	666	0	666	9,290	0	9,290	9,950	0	9,950	11,200	0	11,200
Rhode Island	1,050	28.6	0	28.6	110	290	400	138	290	429	155	326	481
South Carolina	4,010	330	0	330	6,840	0	6,840	7,170	0	7,170	8,040	0	8,040
South Dakota	755	222	0	222	306	0	306	528	0	528	592	0	592
Tennessee	5,690	417	0	417	10,400	0	10,400	10,800	0	10,800	12,100	0	12,100
Texas	20,900	8,470	504	8,970	16,300	4,350	20,700	24,800	4,850	29,600	27,800	5,440	33,200
Utah	2,230	1,020	26.5	1,050	3,740	177	3,920	4,760	203	4,970	5,340	228	5,570
Vermont	609	43.2	0	43.2	404	0	404	447	0	447	501	0	501
Virginia	7,080	314	0	314	4,880	3,640	8,520	5,200	3,640	8,830	5,830	4,080	9,900
Washington	5,890	1,470	0	1,470	3,800	39.9	3,840	5,270	39.9	5,310	5,910	44.7	5,960
West Virginia	1,810	90.9	0	90.9	5,060	0	5,060	5,150	0	5,150	5,770	0	5,770
Wisconsin	5,360	813	0	813	6,780	0	6,780	7,590	0	7,590	8,510	0	8,510
Wyoming	494	541	222	763	4,400	0	4,400	4,940	222	5,170	5,540	248	5,790
Puerto Rico	3,810	137	0	137	483	2,190	2,670	620	2,190	2,810	695	2,460	3,150
U.S. Virgin Islands	109	1.03	0	1.03	10.6	136	147	11.6	136	148	13.0	153	166
Total	**285,000**	**83,300**	**1,260**	**84,500**	**262,000**	**61,000**	**323,000**	**345,000**	**62,300**	**408,000**	**387,000**	**69,800**	**457,000**

SOURCE: Susan S. Hutson et al., "Table 1. Total Water Withdrawals by Source and State, 2000," in *Estimated Use of Water in the United States in 2000*, U.S. Department of the Interior, U.S. Geological Survey, 2004, http://pubs.usgs.gov/circ/2004//circ1268/pdf/circular1268.pdf and revision data February 7, 2005, http://pubs.usgs.gov/circ/2004//circ1268/control/revisions.html (accessed March 14, 2009)

Qualitative consumption occurs when the quality of the water is substantially altered so that it is no longer acceptable by downstream users, but the quantity remains substantially unchanged. An example would be discharge of industrial wastewater into a body of water that renders the water unfit for drinking. Many water withdrawals result in both quantitative and qualitative consumption.

Off-stream use is further divided into eight categories:

- Public supply
- Domestic
- Irrigation
- Livestock
- Aquaculture
- Industrial
- Mining
- Thermoelectric power

Table 2.2 shows the total amount of water withdrawn for each category by state. The two activities that use the most freshwater are irrigation (137 Bgal/d [518.6 billion L per day] nationally in 2000) and thermoelectric power (136 Bgal/d [514.8 billion L per day] nationally in 2000). Thermoelectric power is the generation of electricity by means of steam-driven turbine generators. No other category of use comes close to using the amount of freshwater that is used for irrigation and thermoelectric power.

PUBLIC-SUPPLY WATER USE. Public-supply water use is water withdrawn by public and private water suppliers (utility companies) and delivered for domestic, commercial, industrial, and thermoelectric power uses. It may be used for public services such as filling public pools, watering vegetation in parks, supplying public buildings, firefighting, and street washing. In 2000 water utility companies supplied 43.3 Bgal/d (163.9 billion L per day). (See Table 2.2.) The rest of the water shown in Table 2.2 under the various other categories was self-supplied. That is, the water was withdrawn from surface or groundwater sources by the users, not by water utility companies.

According to Hutson et al., public suppliers serviced about 242 million people in 2000 (about 85% of the total U.S. population of 285 million at that time). (See Table 2.3.) This figure represents an 8% increase over the number of people supplied with water by public suppliers in 1995. Of the 43.3 Bgal/d (163.9 billion L per day) of water that public suppliers withdrew, 27.3 Bgal/d (103.3 billion L per day; 63%) came from surface sources and 16 Bgal/d (60.6 billion L per day; 37%) from groundwater sources. California, Texas, New York, Florida, Illinois, Pennsylvania, and Oklahoma accounted for a majority of U.S. public-supply withdrawals in 2000.

DOMESTIC USE. Domestic water use includes water for typical household purposes, such as drinking; food preparation; bathing; washing clothes, dishes, and cars; flushing toilets; and watering lawns and gardens. Even though people need to take in about 2 quarts (1.9 L) of water a day from what they eat or drink to replace water loss, water needs for household use (indoor and outdoor) add to the amount of water people require each day.

The USGS notes in "Water Q&A: Water Use at Home" (January 29, 2009, http://ga.water.usgs.gov/edu/qahome.html) that each person in the United States uses about 80 to 100 gallons (303 to 379 liters) of water per day. According to the USGS, the activity that uses the most water is flushing the toilet, and the second highest use activity is showering and bathing. That is why low-flow toilets and shower heads are so important in water conservation.

In 1992 Congress passed the Energy Policy and Conservation Act. This legislation established uniform national standards for the manufacture of water-efficient plumbing fixtures, such as low-flow toilets and showers. The purpose was to promote water conservation by residential and commercial users. Since that time many water suppliers have sponsored programs offering rebates on water bills and other incentives to encourage the use of these devices to reduce water use.

AQUACULTURE. Aquaculture is the practice of raising animals that live in water—such as finfish and shellfish—for food, restoration, conservation, or sport. According to Table 2.4, aquaculture use accounted for 3.7 Bgal/d (14 billion L per day) of water use nationally in 2000. Surface water was the source for 2.6 Bgal/d (9.8 billion L per day; 71%) of this total. Idaho alone accounted for nearly 2 Bgal/d (7.6 billion L per day; 53%) of the aquaculture water use reported.

IRRIGATION. The term *irrigation* usually brings to mind arid or semiarid deserts transformed into lush green fields of crops by the turn of a handle, bringing life and prosperity where before there had been only sagebrush and cactus. To some extent this is true. Many parts of the American West and Midwest do not average enough yearly rainfall to sustain the crops that are grown there; the cultivation of those crops is made possible only with the water supplied by irrigation. Irrigation is also used to supplement rainfall in areas with adequate water supplies to increase the number of plantings per year, improve yield, and reduce the risk of crop failure during drought years.

According to Hutson et al., irrigation accounted for 137 Bgal/d (518.6 billion L per day) of freshwater withdrawals for all off-stream categories in 2000. (See Table 2.2.) Approximately 80 Bgal/d (302.8 billion L per day; 58%) of withdrawals were from surface-water sources, and the remaining 56.9 Bgal/d (215.4 billion L per day; 42%) were from groundwater sources. (See Table 2.5.) The quantity of freshwater used for irrigation varies greatly from region to region. Irrigation is by far the largest water use category in the West. California alone used 30.5 Bgal/d (115.5 billion L per day; 22%) of all irrigation water in 2000.

Hutson et al. note that irrigation has the highest consumptive use of any of the eight categories of off-stream

TABLE 2.2

Total water use by usage category and state, 2000

[Figures may not sum to totals because of independent rounding. All values are in million gallons per day.]

State	Public supply Fresh	Domestic Fresh	Irrigation Fresh	Live-stock Fresh	Aqua-culture Fresh	Industrial Fresh	Industrial Saline	Mining Fresh	Mining Saline	Thermoelectric power Fresh	Thermoelectric power Saline	Total Fresh	Total Saline	Total
Alabama	834	78.9	43.1	—	10.4	833	0	—	—	8,190	0	9,990	0	9,990
Alaska	80.0	11.2	1.01	—	—	8.12	3.86	27.4	140	33.6	0	161	144	305
Arizona	1,080	28.9	5,400	—	—	19.8	0	85.7	8.17	100	0	6,720	8.17	6,730
Arkansas	421	28.5	7,910	—	198	134	.08	2.78	0	2,180	0	10,900	.08	10,900
California	6,120	286	30,500	409	537	188	13.6	23.7	153	352	12,600	38,400	12,800	51,200
Colorado	899	66.8	11,400	—	—	120	0	—	—	138	0	12,600	0	12,600
Connecticut	424	56.2	30.4	—	—	10.7	0	—	—	187	3,440	708	3,440	4,150
Delaware	94.9	13.3	43.5	3.92	.07	59.4	3.25	—	—	366	738	582	741	1,320
District of Columbia	0	0	.18	—	—	0	0	—	—	9.69	0	9.87	0	9.87
Florida	2,440	199	4,290	32.5	8.02	291	1.18	217	0	658	12,000	8,140	12,000	20,100
Georgia	1,250	110	1,140	19.4	15.4	622	30	9.80	0	3,250	61.7	6,410	91.7	6,500
Hawaii	250	12.0	364	—	—	14.5	.85	—	—	0	0	640	.85	641
Idaho	244	85.2	17,100	34.9	1,970	55.5	0	—	—	0	0	19,500	0	19,500
Illinois	1,760	135	154	37.6	—	391	0	—	—	11,300	0	13,700	0	13,700
Indiana	670	122	101	41.9	—	2,400	0	82.5	0	6,700	0	10,100	0	10,100
Iowa	383	33.2	21.5	109	—	237	0	32.8	0	2,540	0	3,360	0	3,360
Kansas	416	21.6	3,710	111	5.60	53.3	0	31.4	0	2,260	0	6,610	0	6,610
Kentucky	525	27.5	29.3	—	—	317	0	—	—	3,260	0	4,160	0	4,160
Louisiana	753	41.2	1,020	7.34	243	2,680	0	—	—	5,610	0	10,400	0	10,400
Maine	102	35.7	5.84	—	—	247	0	—	—	113	295	504	295	799
Maryland	824	77.1	42.4	10.4	19.6	65.8	227	8.31	.02	379	6,260	1,430	6,490	7,910
Massachusetts	739	42.2	126	11.3	—	36.8	0	—	—	108	3,610	1,050	3,610	4,660
Michigan	1,140	239	201	11.3	—	698	0	—	—	7,710	0	10,000	0	10,000
Minnesota	500	80.8	227	52.8	—	154	0	588	0	2,270	0	3,870	0	3,870
Mississippi	359	69.3	1,410	—	371	242	0	—	—	362	148	2,810	148	2,960
Missouri	872	53.6	1,430	72.4	83.3	62.7	0	16.9	0	5,640	0	8,230	0	8,230
Montana	149	18.6	7,950	—	—	61.3	0	—	—	110	0	8,290	0	8,290
Nebraska	330	48.4	8,790	93.4	—	38.1	0	128	4.55	2,820	0	12,200	4.55	12,300
Nevada	629	22.4	2,110	—	—	10.3	0	—	—	36.7	0	2,810	0	2,810
New Hampshire	97.1	41.0	4.75	—	16.3	44.9	0	6.8	0	236	761	447	761	1,210
New Jersey	1,050	79.7	140	1.68	6.46	132	0	110	0	650	3,390	2,170	3,390	5,560
New Mexico	296	31.4	2,860	—	—	10.5	0	—	—	56.4	0	3,260	0	3,260
New York	2,570	142	35.5	—	—	297	0	—	—	4,040	5,010	7,080	5,010	12,100
North Carolina	945	189	287	121	7.88	293	0	36.4	0	7,850	1,620	9,730	1,620	11,400
North Dakota	63.6	11.9	145	—	—	17.6	0	—	—	902	0	1,140	0	1,140
Ohio	1,470	134	31.7	25.3	1.36	807	0	88.5	0	8,590	0	11,100	0	11,100
Oklahoma	675	25.5	718	151	16.4	25.9	0	2.48	256	146	0	1,760	256	2,020
Oregon	566	76.2	6,080	—	—	195	0	—	—	15.3	0	6,930	0	6,930
Pennsylvania	1,460	132	13.9	—	—	1,190	0	182	0	6,980	0	9,950	0	9,950
Rhode Island	119	8.99	3.45	—	—	4.28	0	—	—	2.40	290	138	290	429
South Carolina	566	63.5	267	—	—	565	0	—	—	5,710	0	7,170	0	7,170
South Dakota	93.3	9.53	373	42.0	—	5.12	0	—	—	5.24	0	528	0	528
Tennessee	890	32.6	22.4	—	—	842	0	—	—	9,040	0	10,800	0	10,800
Texas	4,230	131	8,630	308	—	1,450	907	220	504	9,820	3,440	24,800	4,850	29,600
Utah	638	16.1	3,860	—	116	42.7	5.08	26.3	198	62.2	0	4,760	203	4,970
Vermont	60.1	21.0	3.78	—	—	6.91	0	—	—	355	0	447	0	447
Virginia	720	133	26.4	—	—	470	53.3	—	—	3,850	3,580	5,200	3,640	8,830
Washington	1,020	125	3,040	—	—	577	39.9	—	—	519	0	5,270	39.9	5,310
West Virginia	190	40.4	.04	—	—	968	0	—	—	3,950	0	5,150	0	5,150
Wisconsin	623	96.3	196	66.3	70.2	447	0	—	—	6,090	0	7,590	0	7,590
Wyoming	107	6.57	4,500	—	—	5.78	0	79.5	222	243	0	4,940	222	5,170
Puerto Rico	513	.88	94.5	—	—	11.2	0	—	—	0	2,190	620	2,190	2,810
U.S. Virgin Islands	6.09	1.69	.50	—	—	3.34	0	—	—	0	136	11.6	136	148
Total	**43,300**	**3,590**	**137,000**	**1,760**	**3,700**	**18,500**	**1,280**	**2,010**	**1,490**	**136,000**	**59,500**	**345,000**	**62,300**	**408,000**

SOURCE: Susan S. Hutson et al., "Table 2. Total Water Withdrawals by Water-Use Category, 2000," in *Estimated Use of Water in the United States in 2000*, U.S. Department of the Interior, U.S. Geological Survey, 2004, http://pubs.usgs.gov/circ/2004//circ1268/pdf/circular1268.pdf and revision data February 7, 2005, http://pubs.usgs.gov/circ/2004//circ1268/control/revisions.html (accessed March 14, 2009)

water use. In many irrigated areas about 75% to 85% of the irrigation water is lost to evaporation, transpiration, or retained in the crops. The remaining 15% to 25% either slowly makes its way through the soil to recharge (replenish) groundwater, a process called irrigation return flow, or is returned to nearby surface water through a drainage system.

The average quantities of water applied range from several inches to more than 20 inches (50.8 cm) per year, depending on local conditions.

Significant changes in water quality can be caused by irrigation. The water lost in evapotranspiration (evaporation

TABLE 2.3

Public supply water use by source and state, 2000

[Figures may not sum to totals because of independent rounding]

State	Population (in thousands)			Withdrawals (in million gallons per day)			Withdrawals (in thousand acre-feet per year)		
		Served by public supply		By source			By source		
	Total	Population	Population (in percent)	Ground-water	Surface water	Total	Ground-water	Surface water	Total
Alabama	4,450	3,580	80	281	553	834	315	620	935
Alaska	627	421	67	29.3	50.7	80.0	32.9	56.9	89.7
Arizona	5,130	4,870	95	469	613	1,080	526	688	1,210
Arkansas	2,670	2,320	87	132	289	421	148	324	472
California	33,900	30,100	89	2,800	3,320	6,120	3,140	3,730	6,860
Colorado	4,300	3,750	87	53.7	846	899	60.2	948	1,010
Connecticut	3,410	2,660	78	66.0	358	424	74.0	402	476
Delaware	784	617	79	45.0	49.8	94.9	50.5	55.9	106
District of Columbia	572	572	100	0	0	0	0	0	0
Florida	16,000	14,000	88	2,200	237	2,440	2,470	266	2,730
Georgia	8,190	6,730	82	278	968	1,250	311	1,090	1,400
Hawaii	1,210	1,140	94	243	7.60	250	272	8.52	281
Idaho	1,290	928	72	219	25.3	244	245	28.3	274
Illinois	12,400	10,900	88	353	1,410	1,760	396	1,580	1,970
Indiana	6,080	4,480	74	345	326	670	386	365	751
Iowa	2,930	2,410	83	303	79.8	383	340	89.5	429
Kansas	2,690	2,500	93	172	244	416	193	273	466
Kentucky	4,040	3,490	86	71.0	455	525	79.5	510	589
Louisiana	4,470	3,950	88	349	404	753	392	453	844
Maine	1,270	726	57	29.6	72.5	102	33.2	81.3	115
Maryland	5,300	4,360	82	84.6	740	824	94.8	829	924
Massachusetts	6,350	5,880	93	197	542	739	220	608	828
Michigan	9,940	7,170	72	247	896	1,140	277	1,000	1,280
Minnesota	4,920	3,770	77	329	171	500	369	192	561
Mississippi	2,840	2,190	77	319	40.4	359	357	45.3	402
Missouri	5,600	4,770	85	278	594	872	311	666	978
Montana	902	664	74	56.1	92.4	149	62.9	104	167
Nebraska	1,710	1,390	81	266	63.8	330	299	71.6	370
Nevada	2,000	1,870	94	151	478	629	169	536	705
New Hampshire	1,240	756	61	33.0	64.1	97.1	37.0	71.9	109
New Jersey	8,410	7,460	89	400	650	1,050	449	729	1,180
New Mexico	1,820	1,460	80	262	33.8	296	294	37.9	332
New York	19,000	17,100	90	583	1,980	2,570	653	2,220	2,880
North Carolina	8,050	5,350	66	166	779	945	186	873	1,060
North Dakota	642	493	77	32.4	31.2	63.6	36.3	35.0	71.3
Ohio	11,400	9,570	84	500	966	1,470	560	1,080	1,640
Oklahoma	3,450	3,150	91	113	562	675	127	631	757
Oregon	3,420	2,730	80	118	447	566	133	501	634
Pennsylvania	12,300	10,100	82	212	1,250	1,460	237	1,400	1,640
Rhode Island	1,050	922	88	16.9	102	119	19.0	115	134
South Carolina	4,010	3,160	79	105	462	566	117	517	635
South Dakota	755	625	83	54.2	39.1	93.3	60.7	43.9	105
Tennessee	5,690	5,240	92	321	569	890	360	638	997
Texas	20,900	19,700	94	1,260	2,970	4,230	1,420	3,330	4,740
Utah	2,230	2,180	97	364	274	638	408	307	715
Vermont	609	362	59	19.5	40.6	60.1	21.8	45.6	67.4
Virginia	7,080	5,310	75	70.7	650	720	79.3	728	808
Washington	5,890	4,900	83	464	552	1,020	520	619	1,140
West Virginia	1,810	1,300	72	41.6	149	190	46.6	167	213
Wisconsin	5,360	3,620	67	330	293	623	370	329	699
Wyoming	494	406	82	57.2	49.4	107	64.1	55.3	119
Puerto Rico	3,810	3,800	100	88.5	425	513	99.2	476	576
U.S. Virgin Islands	109	53.4	49	.52	5.57	6.09	.58	6.24	6.83
Total	**285,000**	**242,000**	**85**	**16,000**	**27,300**	**43,300**	**17,900**	**30,600**	**48,500**

SOURCE: Susan S. Hutson et al., "Table 5. Public-Supply Water Withdrawals, 2000," in *Estimated Use of Water in the United States in 2000*, U.S. Department of the Interior, U.S. Geological Survey, 2004, http://pubs.usgs.gov/circ/2004//circ1268/pdf/circular1268.pdf and revision data February 7, 2005, http://pubs.usgs.gov/circ/2004//circ1268/control/revisions.html (accessed March 14, 2009)

from the surface of plants and the soil) is relatively pure because nonwater chemicals are left behind, precipitating as salts and accumulating in the soil. The salts accumulate as irrigation continues. The accumulation of salts in the soil can cause the concentration of salts in the irrigation return flows to be higher than in the original irrigation water. Excessive salts in the soil can also interfere with crop growth, sometimes resulting in soil that is unsuitable for crop growth. To stop

TABLE 2.4

Water use for aquaculture by source and state, 2000

[Figures may not sum to totals because of independent rounding]

State	Withdrawals (in million gallons per day)			Withdrawals (in thousand acre-feet per year)		
	By source			By source		
	Groundwater	Surface water	Total	Groundwater	Surface water	Total
Alabama	8.93	1.44	10.4	10.0	1.61	11.6
Alaska	—	—	—	—	—	—
Arizona	—	—	—	—	—	—
Arkansas	187	10.4	198	210	11.6	222
California	158	380	537	177	426	603
Colorado	—	—	—	—	—	—
Connecticut	—	—	—	—	—	—
Delaware	.07	0	.07	.08	0	.08
District of Columbia	—	—	—	—	—	—
Florida	7.81	.21	8.02	8.76	.24	8.99
Georgia	7.70	7.72	15.4	8.63	8.65	17.3
Hawaii	—	—	—	—	—	—
Idaho	51.5	1,920	1,970	57.7	2,150	2,210
Illinois	—	—	—	—	—	—
Indiana	—	—	—	—	—	—
Iowa	—	—	—	—	—	—
Kansas	3.33	2.27	5.60	3.73	2.54	6.28
Kentucky	—	—	—	—	—	—
Louisiana	128	115	243	144	129	273
Maine	—	—	—	—	—	—
Maryland	4.81	14.8	19.6	5.39	16.6	22.0
Massachusetts	—	—	—	—	—	—
Michigan	—	—	—	—	—	—
Minnesota	—	—	—	—	—	—
Mississippi	321	49.8	371	360	55.9	416
Missouri	2.01	81.3	83.3	2.25	91.2	93.4
Montana	—	—	—	—	—	—
Nebraska	—	—	—	—	—	—
Nevada	—	—	—	—	—	—
New Hampshire	3.12	13.1	16.3	3.50	14.7	18.2
New Jersey	6.46	0	6.46	7.24	0	7.24
New Mexico	—	—	—	—	—	—
New York	—	—	—	—	—	—
North Carolina	7.88	0	7.88	8.83	0	8.83
North Dakota	—	—	—	—	—	—
Ohio	1.36	0	1.36	1.52	0	1.52
Oklahoma	.29	16.1	16.4	.33	18.1	18.4
Oregon	—	—	—	—	—	—
Pennsylvania	—	—	—	—	—	—
Rhode Island	—	—	—	—	—	—
South Carolina	—	—	—	—	—	—
South Dakota	—	—	—	—	—	—
Tennessee	—	—	—	—	—	—
Texas	—	—	—	—	—	—
Utah	116	0	116	130	0	130
Vermont	—	—	—	—	—	—
Virginia	—	—	—	—	—	—
Washington	—	—	—	—	—	—
West Virginia	—	—	—	—	—	—
Wisconsin	39.8	30.4	70.2	44.6	34.1	78.7
Wyoming	—	—	—	—	—	—
Puerto Rico	—	—	—	—	—	—
U.S. Virgin Islands	—	—	—	—	—	—
Total	**1,060**	**2,640**	**3,700**	**1,180**	**2,960**	**4,150**

SOURCE: Susan S. Hutson et al., "Table 9. Aquaculture Water Withdrawals, 2000," in *Estimated Use of Water in the United States in 2000*, U.S. Department of the Interior, U.S. Geological Survey, 2004, http://pubs.usgs.gov/circ/2004//circ1268/pdf/circular1268.pdf and revision data February 7, 2005, http://pubs.usgs.gov/circ/2004//circ1268/control/revisions.html (accessed March 14, 2009)

excessive buildup of salts in the soil, extra irrigation water is often used to flush the salts from the soil and transport them into the groundwater. In locations where these dissolved salts reach high concentrations, the recharge of the groundwater from irrigation return flow can reduce the quality of surface and groundwater to which the groundwater discharges.

LIVESTOCK. Livestock water use includes drinking water for livestock, dairy and feedlot operations, and other on-farm needs. Hutson et al. indicate that 1.8 Bgal/d (6.8 billion L per day) of water was used for these purposes in 2000. (See Table 2.2.) Total withdrawals for livestock increased slightly between 1995

TABLE 2.5

Acres of land being irrigated by type of irrigation, source, and state, 2000

[Figures may not sum to totals because of independent rounding]

State	Irrigated land (in thousand acres) By type of irrigation				Withdrawals (in million gallons per day) By source		
	Sprinkler	Micro-irrigation	Surface	Total	Groundwater	Surface water	Total
Alabama	68.7	1.30	0	70.0	14.5	28.7	43.1
Alaska	2.43	0	.07	2.50	.99	.02	1.01
Arizona	183	14.0	779	976	2,750	2,660	5,400
Arkansas	631	0	3,880	4,510	6,510	1,410	7,910
California	1,660	3,010	5,470	10,100	11,600	18,900	30,500
Colorado	1,190	1.16	2,220	3,400	2,160	9,260	11,400
Connecticut	20.6	.39	0	21.0	17.0	13.4	30.4
Delaware	81.1	.71	0	81.8	35.6	7.89	43.5
District of Columbia	.32	0	0	.32	0	.18	.18
Florida	515	704	839	2,060	2,180	2,110	4,290
Georgia	1,470	73.8	0	1,540	750	392	1,140
Hawaii	16.7	105	0	122	171	193	364
Idaho	2,440	4.70	1,300	3,750	3,720	13,300	17,100
Illinois	365	0	0	365	150	4.25	154
Indiana	250	0	0	250	55.5	45.4	101
Iowa	84.5	0	0	84.5	20.4	1.08	21.5
Kansas	2,660	2.14	647	3,310	3,430	288	3,710
Kentucky	66.6	0	0	66.6	1.14	28.2	29.3
Louisiana	110	0	830	940	791	232	1,020
Maine	35.0	.95	.03	36.0	.61	5.23	5.84
Maryland	57.3	3.32	0	60.6	29.8	12.6	42.4
Massachusetts	26.6	2.35	0	29.0	19.7	106	126
Michigan	401	8.67	4.87	415	128	73.2	201
Minnesota	546	0	26.9	573	190	36.6	227
Mississippi	455	0	966	1,420	1,310	99.1	1,410
Missouri	532	1.43	792	1,330	1,380	48.1	1,430
Montana	506	0	1,220	1,720	83.0	7,870	7,950
Nebraska	4,110	0	3,710	7,820	7,420	1,370	8,790
Nevada	192	0	456	647	567	1,540	2,110
New Hampshire	6.08	0		6.08	.50	4.25	4.75
New Jersey	109	15.7	3.70	128	22.8	117	140
New Mexico	461	7.17	530	998	1,230	1,630	2,860
New York	70.0	8.73	1.84	80.6	23.3	12.1	35.5
North Carolina	193	3.70	0	196	65.8	221	287
North Dakota	200	0	26.7	227	72.2	73.2	145
Ohio	61.0	0	0	61.0	13.9	17.8	31.7
Oklahoma	392	1.50	113	507	566	151	718
Oregon	1,160	4.02	1,000	2,170	792	5,290	6,080
Pennsylvania	28.9	7.17	0	36.0	1.38	12.5	13.9
Rhode Island	4.48	.29	.05	4.82	.46	2.99	3.45
South Carolina	166	3.66	17.5	187	106	162	267
South Dakota	276	0	78.3	354	137	236	373
Tennessee	51.2	5.35	3.96	60.5	7.33	15.1	22.4
Texas	4,010	89.4	2,390	6,490	6,500	2,130	8,630
Utah	526	1.68	880	1,410	469	3,390	3,860
Vermont	4.95	0	0	4.95	.33	3.45	3.78
Virginia	64.3	13.9	0	78.2	3.57	22.8	26.4
Washington	1,270	49.9	252	1,570	747	2,290	3,040
West Virginia	2.21	0	.98	3.19	.02	.02	.04
Wisconsin	355	0	0	355	195	1.57	196
Wyoming	190	4.73	964	1,160	413	4,090	4,500
Puerto Rico	15.5	33.0	5.35	53.8	36.9	57.5	94.5
U.S. Virgin Islands	.20	0	0	.20	.29	.21	.50
Total	**28,300**	**4,180**	**29,400**	**61,900**	**56,900**	**80,000**	**137,000**

SOURCE: Adapted from Susan S. Hutson et al., "Table 7. Irrigation Water Withdrawals, 2000," in *Estimated Use of Water in the United States in 2000*, U.S. Department of the Interior, U.S. Geological Survey, 2004, http://pubs.usgs.gov/circ/2004//circ1268/pdf/circular1268.pdf and revision data February 7, 2005, http://pubs.usgs.gov/circ/2004//circ1268/control/revisions.html (accessed March 14, 2009)

and 2000 for the 22 states that reported data for both years. However, withdrawals actually increased only in 8 of the 22 reporting states. Combined, California, Texas, and Oklahoma accounted for 868 million gallons per day (Mgal/d; 3.3 billion L per day; 49%) of the U.S. total livestock water use in 2000, and 496.2 Mgal/d (1.9 billion L per day; 66%) of the surface water used. (See Table 2.6.)

TABLE 2.6

Water use for livestock by source and state, 2000

[Figures may not sum to totals because of independent rounding]

| State | Withdrawals (in million gallons per day) | | | Withdrawals (in thousand acre-feet per year) | | |
| | By source | | | By source | | |
	Groundwater	Surface water	Total	Groundwater	Surface water	Total
Alabama	—	—	—	—	—	—
Alaska	—	—	—	—	—	—
Arizona	—	—	—	—	—	—
Arkansas	—	—	—	—	—	—
California	182	227	409	204	255	458
Colorado	—	—	—	—	—	—
Connecticut	—	—	—	—	—	—
Delaware	3.70	.22	3.92	4.15	.25	4.39
District of Columbia	—	—	—	—	—	—
Florida	31.0	1.51	32.5	34.7	1.69	36.4
Georgia	1.66	17.7	19.4	1.86	19.9	21.7
Hawaii	—	—	—	—	—	—
Idaho	27.7	7.20	34.9	31.0	8.07	39.1
Illinois	37.6	0	37.6	42.1	0	42.1
Indiana	27.3	14.6	41.9	30.6	16.4	47.0
Iowa	81.8	27.1	109	91.8	30.4	122
Kansas	87.2	23.5	111	97.7	26.3	124
Kentucky	—	—	—	—	—	—
Louisiana	4.03	3.31	7.34	4.52	3.71	8.23
Maine	—	—	—	—	—	—
Maryland	7.18	3.18	10.4	8.05	3.56	11.6
Massachusetts	—	—	—	—	—	—
Michigan	10.2	1.15	11.3	11.4	1.29	12.7
Minnesota	52.8	0	52.8	59.2	0	59.2
Mississippi	—	—	—	—	—	—
Missouri	18.3	54.1	72.4	20.5	60.6	81.1
Montana	—	—	—	—	—	—
Nebraska	76.0	17.4	93.4	85.2	19.5	105
Nevada	—	—	—	—	—	—
New Hampshire	—	—	—	—	—	—
New Jersey	1.68	0	1.68	1.88	0	1.88
New Mexico	—	—	—	—	—	—
New York	—	—	—	—	—	—
North Carolina	89.1	32.3	121	99.9	36.2	136
North Dakota	—	—	—	—	—	—
Ohio	8.20	17.1	25.3	9.19	19.2	28.4
Oklahoma	53.6	97.2	151	60.0	109	169
Oregon	—	—	—	—	—	—
Pennsylvania	—	—	—	—	—	—
Rhode Island	—	—	—	—	—	—
South Carolina	—	—	—	—	—	—
South Dakota	16.9	25.2	42.0	18.9	28.2	47.1
Tennessee	—	—	—	—	—	—
Texas	137	172	308	153	192	346
Utah	—	—	—	—	—	—
Vermont	—	—	—	—	—	—
Virginia	—	—	—	—	—	—
Washington	—	—	—	—	—	—
West Virginia	—	—	—	—	—	—
Wisconsin	60.3	6.02	66.3	67.6	6.75	74.4
Wyoming	—	—	—	—	—	—
Puerto Rico	—	—	—	—	—	—
U.S. Virgin Islands	—	—	—	—	—	—
Total	**1,010**	**747**	**1,760**	**1,140**	**838**	**1,980**

SOURCE: Susan S. Hutson et al., "Table 8. Livestock Water Withdrawals, 2000," in *Estimated Use of Water in the United States in 2000*, U.S. Department of the Interior, U.S. Geological Survey, 2004, http://pubs.usgs.gov/circ/2004//circ1268/pdf/circular1268.pdf and revision data February 7, 2005, http://pubs.usgs.gov/circ/2004//circ1268/control/revisions.html (accessed March 14, 2009)

INDUSTRIAL. Even those industries that do not use water directly in their products may use substantial quantities of water during operations. Water for industrial use is commonly divided into four categories: cooling water, process water, boiler feed water, and sanitary and service water (for personal use by employees, for cleaning plants and equipment, and for the operation of valves and other equipment). Industries that use the most water include steel, chemical and allied products, paper and related products, and petroleum refining.

According to Hutson et al., water supplied for industrial use in 2000 totaled 19.7 Bgal/d (74.6 billion L per day), 11% less than in 1995. (See Table 2.2.) Approximately 16.2 Bgal/d (61.3 billion L per day; 82%) was withdrawn from surface water. (See Table 2.7.) Louisiana, Indiana, and Texas together consumed 7.4 Bgal/d (28 billion L per day; 38%) of the nation's industrial water withdrawals.

Most manufacturers use processed water at some point in the course of making a product. Water is the solvent (the

TABLE 2.7

Industrial water use by source, type, and state, 2000

[Figures may not sum to totals because of independent rounding]

State	Withdrawals (in million gallons per day)									Withdrawals (in thousand acre-feet per year)		
	By source and type						Total			By type		
	Groundwater			Surface water								
	Fresh	Saline	Total	Fresh	Saline	Total	Fresh	Saline	Total	Fresh	Saline	Total
Alabama	56.0	0	56.0	777	0	777	833	0	833	934	0	934
Alaska	4.32	0	4.32	3.80	3.86	7.66	8.12	3.86	12.0	9.10	4.33	13.4
Arizona	19.8	0	19.8	0	0	0	19.8	0	19.8	22.2	0	22.2
Arkansas	67.0	.08	67.1	66.8	0	66.8	134	.08	134	150	.09	150
California	183	0	183	5.65	13.6	19.3	188	13.6	202	211	15.3	226
Colorado	23.6	0	23.6	96.4	0	96.4	120	0	120	135	0	135
Connecticut	4.13	0	4.13	6.61	0	6.61	10.7	0	10.7	12.0	0	12.0
Delaware	17.0	0	17.0	42.5	3.25	45.7	59.4	3.25	62.7	66.6	3.64	70.3
District of Columbia	0	0	0	0	0	0	0	0	0	0	0	0
Florida	216	0	216	74.7	1.18	75.9	291	1.18	292	326	1.32	328
Georgia	290	0	290	333	30	363	622	30.0	652	698	33.6	731
Hawaii	14.5	.85	15.4	0	0	0	14.5	.85	15.4	16.2	0.95	17.2
Idaho	35.8	0	35.8	19.7	0	19.7	55.5	0	55.5	62.2	0	62.2
Illinois	132	0	132	259	0	259	391	0	391	438	0	438
Indiana	99.7	0	99.7	2,300	0	2,300	2,400	0	2,400	2,690	0	2,690
Iowa	226	0	226	11.7	0	11.7	237	0	237	266	0	266
Kansas	46.6	0	46.6	6.74	0	6.74	53.3	0	53.3	59.8	0	59.8
Kentucky	95.2	0	95.2	222	0	222	317	0	317	356	0	356
Louisiana	285	0	285	2,400	0	2,400	2,680	0	2,680	3,010	0	3,010
Maine	9.90	0	9.90	237	0	237	247	0	247	277	0	277
Maryland	15.9	0	15.9	49.9	227	277	65.8	227	292	73.8	254	328
Massachusetts	10.7	0	10.7	26.2	0	26.2	36.8	0	36.8	41.3	0	41.3
Michigan	110	0	110	589	0	589	698	0	698	782	0	782
Minnesota	56.3	0	56.3	97.8	0	97.8	154	0	154	173	0	173
Mississippi	118	0	118	124	0	124	242	0	242	271	0	271
Missouri	29.2	0	29.2	33.5	0	33.5	62.7	0	62.7	70.3	0	70.3
Montana	31.9	0	31.9	29.3	0	29.3	61.3	0	61.3	68.7	0	68.7
Nebraska	35.5	0	35.5	2.60	0	2.60	38.1	0	38.1	42.7	0	42.7
Nevada	5.29	0	5.29	5.00	0	5.00	10.3	0	10.3	11.5	0	11.5
New Hampshire	6.95	0	6.95	37.9	0	37.9	44.9	0	44.9	50.3	0	50.3
New Jersey	65.3	0	65.3	66.2	0	66.2	132	0	132	147	0	147
New Mexico	8.80	0	8.80	1.67	0	1.67	10.5	0	10.5	11.7	0	11.7
New York	145	0	145	152	0	152	297	0	297	333	0	333
North Carolina	25.6	0	25.6	267	0	267	293	0	293	329	0	329
North Dakota	6.88	0	6.88	10.7	0	10.7	17.6	0	17.6	19.7	0	19.7
Ohio	162	0	162	645	0	645	807	0	807	905	0	905
Oklahoma	6.83	0	6.83	19.1	0	19.1	25.9	0	25.9	29.1	0	29.1
Oregon	12.1	0	12.1	183	0	183	195	0	195	218	0	218
Pennsylvania	155	0	155	1,030	0	1,030	1,190	0	1,190	1,330	0	1,330
Rhode Island	2.19	0	2.19	2.09	0	2.09	4.28	0	4.28	4.80	0	4.80
South Carolina	50.9	0	50.9	514	0	514	565	0	565	633	0	633
South Dakota	3.16	0	3.16	1.96	0	1.96	5.12	0	5.12	5.74	0	5.74
Tennessee	56.3	0	56.3	785	0	785	842	0	842	944	0	944
Texas	244	.50	244	1,200	906	2,110	1,450	907	2,350	1,620	1,020	2,640
Utah	34.3	5.08	39.4	8.38	0	8.38	42.7	5.08	47.8	47.8	5.69	53.5
Vermont	2.05	0	2.05	4.86	0	4.86	6.91	0	6.91	7.75	0	7.75
Virginia	104	0	104	365	53.3	419	470	53.3	523	526	59.7	586
Washington	138	0	138	439	39.9	479	577	39.9	617	647	44.7	692
West Virginia	9.70	0	9.70	958	0	958	968	0	968	1,090	0	1,090
Wisconsin	83.0	0	83.0	364	0	364	447	0	447	501	0	501
Wyoming	4.31	0	4.31	1.47	0	1.47	5.78	0	5.78	6.48	0	6.48
Puerto Rico	11.2	0	11.2	0	0	0	11.2	0	11.2	12.5	0	12.5
U.S. Virgin Islands	.22	0	.22	3.12	0	3.12	3.34	0	3.34	3.74	0	3.74
Total	**3,570**	**6.51**	**3,580**	**14,900**	**1,280**	**16,200**	**18,500**	**1,280**	**19,700**	**20,700**	**1,440**	**22,100**

SOURCE: Susan S. Hutson et al., "Table 10. Industrial Self-Supplied Water Withdrawals, 2000," in *Estimated Use of Water in the United States in 2000*, U.S. Department of the Interior, U.S. Geological Survey, 2004, http://pubs.usgs.gov/circ/2004//circ1268/pdf/circular1268.pdf and revision data February 7, 2005, http://pubs.usgs.gov/circ/2004//circ1268/control/revisions.html (accessed March 14, 2009)

substance in which other substances are dissolved) in many chemical processes. In some manufacturing plants the item being manufactured is in contact with water at almost every step in its conversion from raw materials to finished product. For example, in the production of pulp and paper, water is used for removing bark from pulpwood, moving the ground wood and pulp from one process to another, cooking the wood chips for removal of lignin (the woody pulp of plant cells), and washing the pulp. Another example is the food industry, which uses huge quantities of water for cleaning and cooking vegetables and meat, canning and cooling canned products, and cleaning equipment and facilities.

The need for large quantities of easily accessible water has led to industrial development around or near coastlines, rivers, and lakes. The Great Lakes region and the Ohio River valley are examples. This development has often caused serious deterioration of water quality in the area because, after it is used, water may be returned to its source carrying pollutants.

MINING. Mining is the extraction of naturally occurring materials, including petroleum, from Earth's crust. Water is used for washing and milling (processing). All water for mining operations is self-supplied and may come from a freshwater or saline (saltwater) source. Hutson et al. classify water as saline if it contains more than 1,000 milligrams per liter or more of dissolved solids (salts).

Hutson et al. estimate that 3.5 Bgal/d (13.2 billion L per day) of water was withdrawn for mining in 2000. (See Table 2.2.) Most water used for mining purposes was in the Texas Gulf area, followed by the Great Lakes region. Texas, Minnesota, and Wyoming together accounted for 1.6 Bgal/d (6.1 billion L per day; 46%) of the mining withdrawals reported.

Acid mine drainage is a by-product of mining activity. It is the drainage that results from the activity of removing and processing large amounts of rock to recover desired ores of heavy metals, minerals, and coal. Thousands of miles of streams are severely affected by drainage and runoff from abandoned coal mines, which are the single-largest source of adverse water-quality impacts to both surface and groundwater in the United States.

THERMOELECTRIC POWER. Thermoelectric power plants are those that use turbines or similar devices to convert pressurized steam into electricity. Hydroelectric power plants use moving water to produce electricity, and nuclear power plants use water to cool nuclear reactors. Only the thermoelectric plants remove water for off-stream use. The water used in hydroelectric plants and nuclear power plants is in-stream use, so it is not included here.

Water used for thermoelectric power generation accounted for almost half (48%) of all withdrawals for off-stream use in 2000. (See Table 2.8.) Hutson et al. note that the largest total withdrawals were in Texas. States in

TABLE 2.8

Total water use by usage category, 2000

Category	Percent
Public supply	11
Irrigation	34
Aquaculture	<1
Mining	<1
Domestic	<1
Livestock	<1
Industrial	5
Thermoelectric power	48

SOURCE: Adapted from Susan S. Hutson et al., "Figure 1. Total Water Withdrawals by Category, 2000," in *Estimated Use of Water in the United States in 2000*, U.S. Department of the Interior, U.S. Geological Survey, 2004, http://pubs.usgs.gov/circ/2004//circ1268/pdf/circular1268.pdf and revision data February 7, 2005, http://pubs.usgs.gov/circ/2004//circ1268/control/revisions.html (accessed March 14, 2009)

the eastern portion of the country accounted for about 83% of the total thermoelectric water use. Figure 2.2 shows the geographic distribution of total, total freshwater, and total saline water withdrawals for thermoelectric power. These maps also visually show that California, Texas, and states in the eastern United States use the most off-stream water to produce electricity. In contrast, the Pacific Northwest uses hydroelectric power generation (an in-stream use) to supply a substantial part of the regional demand for electricity.

WASTE DISPOSAL. Water has been used to dilute and disperse waste since the earliest human settlements. If the wastewater is properly treated, the water environment can dilute, disperse, and assimilate waste products without harm to water quality or aquatic communities. The first step in the process is to identify the total maximum daily load of individual pollutants that particular water bodies can receive and not violate state water quality standards. The next step is to design, construct, and operate wastewater treatment facilities that provide the necessary level of treatment before discharging wastewater.

As of mid-2009, the USGS had reported wastewater releases and return flow only once, in *Estimated Use of Water in the United States in 1995* (1998, http://water.usgs.gov/watuse/pdf1995/html/) by Wayne B. Solley, Robert R. Pierce, and Howard A. Perlman of the USGS. This report focuses on facilities that collect, treat, and dispose of water through sewer systems and wastewater treatment plants, generally to surface waters. Over 16,400 publicly owned treatment facilities released 41 Bgal/d (155.2 billion L per day) of treated wastewater nationwide in 1995. The annual average was 1 million to 2 million gallons (3.8 million to 7.6 million L) of treated water per facility per day. Illinois (4.9 Bgal/d; 18.2 billion L per day) and Ohio (4.7 Bgal/d; 17.8 billion L per day) reported the largest releases of treated wastewater.

FIGURE 2.2

Water use (fresh and saline) for thermoelectric power by state, 2000

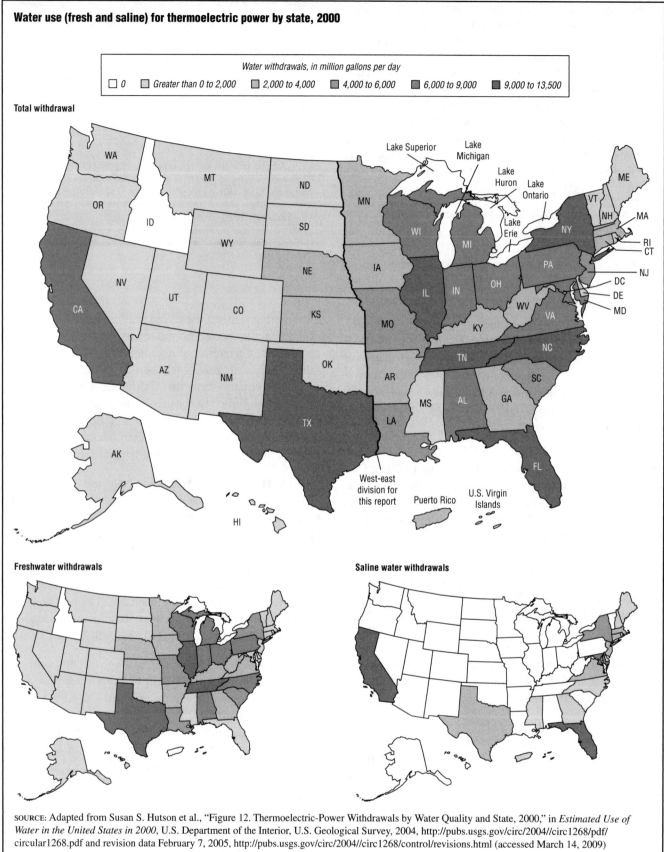

SOURCE: Adapted from Susan S. Hutson et al., "Figure 12. Thermoelectric-Power Withdrawals by Water Quality and State, 2000," in *Estimated Use of Water in the United States in 2000*, U.S. Department of the Interior, U.S. Geological Survey, 2004, http://pubs.usgs.gov/circ/2004//circ1268/pdf/circular1268.pdf and revision data February 7, 2005, http://pubs.usgs.gov/circ/2004//circ1268/control/revisions.html (accessed March 14, 2009)

Not all treated wastewater is return flow. Because of the increasing demand for water and the cost of treating drinking water, more emphasis is being placed on water conservation and water reclamation (reuse). Reclaimed water is wastewater that has been treated for uses such as irrigation of golf courses or public parks instead of being discharged back to source waters. Florida (271 Mgal/d; 1 billion L per day), California (216 Mgal/d; 817.6 million L per day), and Arizona (209 Mgal/d; 791.2 million L per day) reported large uses of reclaimed wastewater in 1995.

RIGHT TO WATER USE

The off-stream water-use categories described earlier are generally recognized as representing the most essential human uses of water. Sometimes there is not enough water available at a given location to meet all the demands for it. In these situations, who owns the water?

Water rights are held in trust by the states (held by the state for the benefit of the state's residents) and may be assigned to individuals and corporations according to statutes (laws) regulating water use. A state may also challenge water use to ensure public access to water that lies within or along its boundaries. State laws, regulations, and procedures establish how an individual, company, or other organization obtains and protects water rights. When water rights are disputed, particularly in the West, the question is often resolved through a judicial determination known as adjudication. According to the U.S. Fish and Wildlife Service, in "403 FW 2, Authorities and Definitions" (USFWS; April 29, 1993, http://www.fws.gov/policy/403fw2.html), adjudications may determine "all rights to use water in a particular stream system or watershed to establish the priority, point of diversion, place and nature of use, and the quantity of water used among the various claimants." When the water involved crosses state boundaries, states enter into agreements for water sharing. When an agreement cannot be reached between states, the matter is usually settled in the federal courts, or in some cases by an act of Congress.

Riparian Rights

The right of private landowners to use the water next to their property in streams, lakes, ponds, and other bodies of water is known as a riparian right, and this right underlies the laws regulating water in most states in the eastern part of the country. Even though local statutes are often written to pertain specifically to the bodies of water they regulate, the riparian system generally assigns each landowner an equal right to reasonable use of the water. Defining reasonable use can lead to disputes among neighboring landowners, but it typically allows common agricultural and private uses that do not involve holding water in storage.

Doctrine of Prior Appropriation

The relative scarcity of water in the West has led to a unique set of laws regulating water use, based on what is known as the doctrine of prior appropriation. Covering both surface and groundwater, the appropriation doctrine determines water rights by applying two standards: the timing of water claims and the nature of the water use. Rather than assigning rights based on landownership, the doctrine of appropriation considers both when and why water is used. The earliest water user is considered to hold a claim to the water, and the extent of those rights is judged by whether or not that use is considered beneficial. To determine beneficial use, two areas are considered: the purpose of the use and its efficiency (i.e., that the use is not wasteful). Individual states define the scope of beneficial uses within their boundaries.

A notable difference from the riparian system is that under the doctrine of appropriation water rights may be forfeited if the rights holder fails to use the water in a manner approved by the state or discontinues beneficial use for a designated length of time.

Another feature of the appropriation system is that rights are not shared equally among all users of a body of water. The USFWS explains in "403 FW 2, Authorities and Definitions" that "priority determines the order of rank of the rights to use water in a system.... [The] person first using water for a beneficial purpose has a right superior to those commencing their use later." Therefore, when water shortages occur, all rights holders are not affected equally as they are under the riparian system. Prior claims take precedence. However, because water shortages in the West can affect community water needs, priority may be awarded to some vital uses regardless of the date of first claim.

Conflicts over Federal Water Rights

Sometimes conflicts over water rights arise that involve the federal government, and since the 1990s the federal government has been involved in several long court battles to determine the precedence of water claims in the West. For example, in *Tulare Lake Basin Water Storage District v. United States* (49 Fed. Cl. 313 [2001]), Judge John P. Wiese (1934–) found that even though the federal government had a right to withhold water from farmers for irrigation to preserve salmon and smelt in California, by doing so the government had deprived farmers in the San Joaquin Valley of their rightful use of water. In December 2004 the administration of George W. Bush (1946–) agreed to pay $16.7 million to compensate the farmers for their loss. The case was considered to have negative implications for environmental projects in the West, where the high costs associated with preservation efforts might make them untenable. Previously, the protection of endangered species was considered a higher priority than individual rights to water access.

In another case involving the federal government, *Trout Unlimited v. U.S. Department of Agriculture* (D.C. No. 96-WY-2686-WD), a conservation organization challenged the approval by the U.S. Forest Service of access to the Long

Draw Reservoir in Colorado that did not establish bypass flow regulations for water projects. A bypass flow is the minimum amount of water needed to flow freely around a dam or diversion to sustain the area's aquatic life. On April 30, 2004, a federal judge determined that the Forest Service had not only the authority but also a responsibility to consider the protection of wildlife when issuing permits for water projects on federal lands.

A more recent water rights dispute has made its way to the U.S. Supreme Court. In June 2007 the South Carolina attorney general Henry D. McMaster (1947–) petitioned the court to stop North Carolina from pumping up to 10 million gallons (37.9 million L) of water per day from the Catawba River, which arises in the Appalachian Mountains in North Carolina and flows into South Carolina. Its waters eventually reach the Atlantic Ocean. Meg Kinnard reports in "Amid Drought, South Carolina Sues North Carolina over Water from Shared River" (Associated Press, June 7, 2007) that the river provides drinking water for 1.3 million people and electricity for 1 million via hydroelectric plants along its course. The case regards a permit issued by the North Carolina Environment Management Commission to allow two North Carolina cities to withdraw water from the Catawba but return the treated wastewater to a river closer to their communities than the Catawba. The Supreme Court officially agreed to hear the case in January 2009; however, as of mid-2009, no ruling had been rendered.

Georgia, Florida, and Alabama—states just southeast of the Carolinas—have also been in a conflict over water rights, but this fight has been ongoing for nearly 20 years and was exacerbated during a 3-year drought from 2006 to 2009. WaterWebster.org explains in "Florida, Alabama, Georgia Water Sharing" (2009, http://www.waterwebster .com/FloridaAlabamaGeorgia.htm) that the dispute began in 1990, when the U.S. Army Corps of Engineers proposed diverting massive amounts of water from Lake Lanier, located northeast of Atlanta, Georgia (the population of which has doubled to 5 million since 1980), for drinking water and recreational purposes for Atlanta-area residents. Alabama, to the west of Georgia, and Florida, located south of Georgia, contested this diversion. The two states receive water from Lake Lanier via the Chattahoochee, Flint, and Apalachicola rivers, and use the water for a variety of purposes, including drinking water and farming. In addition, the water flow helps maintain the proper salinity for oyster beds in the Apalachicola Bay in Florida. If the water flow into the bay were to be reduced, the salinity would rise and threaten the oysters and other endangered species. After 19 years of water-sharing talks, plans, lawsuits, and interim agreements that did not resolve the issue, the case went to the Supreme Court, but in January 2009 the high court refused to hear Georgia's appeal of a lower court ruling. In May 2009 seven lawsuits on the legality of the Army Corps of Engineers water supply allocations were consolidated into one to be decided by the U.S. District judge Paul A. Magnuson (1937–). No quick decision was expected by the senior judge. Also in May 2009, Florida Governor Charlie Crist requested that Interior Secretary Paul Salazar become involved in talks between the states. Salazar offered to help with the discussions, but stated he would not force any of the parties to negotiate.

PROTECTION OF AQUATIC LIFE

Since the enactment of the Clean Water Act in 1972, with its emphasis on maintaining the physical, chemical, and biological characteristics of the nation's waters, there has been an increasing awareness of the need to protect and maintain the insects, plants, and animals that make up the ecosystem of surface-water bodies. Because life on Earth began in the ancient seas, aquatic life has been an integral part of overall water resources. This fact has frequently been ignored as human civilizations evolved, resulting in widespread change in and annihilation of aquatic systems.

In the United States, allocating water to maintain aquatic systems was rarely recognized as a legitimate use until the last two decades of the 20th century. Before that time dam construction frequently disrupted whole ecological systems by reducing the water available to aquatic life in large stretches of rivers and streams below dams, which interfered with the life cycles of migrating fish and other organisms and flooding habitats. In some river systems, such as the Colorado River, the entire flow was allocated and appropriated, resulting in drastic changes to the lush waterscape observed decades before at the delta of the Sea of Cortez, where the Colorado River deposited its rich silt. Rivers and streams have been lined with impermeable surfaces such as concrete, or channelized to conserve water, control flooding, or provide passage for boats.

These practices are slowly changing. Permits issued for dam construction or reissued for dam operation are beginning to contain a provision for maintenance of minimum flow below the dam at a level sufficient to protect the natural system. In several cases this has required reduction in the water allocated to other users. Many states have programs to restore natural systems by removing abandoned or obsolete dams and other waterway obstructions and by constructing fish ladders, structures that help fish move to waters on the other side of an obstruction, such as a dam. Water allocation decisions in areas where water is a scarce resource are increasingly designating a portion for aquatic life protection. Proposals to divert or use water are more closely scrutinized to avoid adverse impacts to aquatic life. Recognizing aquatic life protection as a legitimate water use will have a profound effect on future water allocation decisions.

Except for a few rare instances, water is owned by the states, not the federal government. Therefore, the USFWS has adopted a policy of obtaining water rights. The objective is to obtain water supplies of adequate quantity and quality and the legal rights to use that water from the states for development, use, and management of USFWS lands and facilities and for other congressionally authorized objectives, such as protection of endangered species and maintenance of in-stream flows.

The following are some examples since 2000 of the evolving recognition of aquatic life protection as a legitimate water use:

- In May 2004 President Bush issued an executive order that created a federal Great Lakes Interagency Task Force that would work to improve the deteriorating health of the Great Lakes. This task force and other regional groups convened in December 2004 and developed the Great Lakes Regional Collaboration Strategy to Restore and Protect the Great Lakes (December 2005, http://www.glrc.us/documents/strat egy/GLRC_Strategy.pdf). This strategy includes plans to stop the overflow of untreated sewage into the lakes, reduce agricultural runoff, protect wetlands, and control foreign species such as zebra mussels that are disrupting the aquatic food chain. As of mid-2009, three significant strategy plans had been developed: the Lake Erie Protection and Restoration Plan (2008, http://lakeerie .ohio.gov/Portals/0/Reports/2008LEPRplan.pdf), the MI–Great Lakes Plan (January 2009, http://www.michi gan.gov/documents/deq/MI-GLPlan_262388_7.pdf), and a draft of the Wisconsin Great Lakes Strategy (2006, http://www.dnr.state.wi.us/org/water/greatlakes/ wistrategy/wigreatlakesstrategydraft3.pdf).

- In "Region 9: Progress Report 2002" (July 18, 2007, http://www.epa.gov/region09/annualreport/02/water .html), the U.S. Environmental Protection Agency (EPA) discusses the success of the salmon recovery project in Northern California's Butte Creek. The project, which was undertaken by the CALFED Bay–Delta Program, has resulted in an average spring salmon spawning of about 6,000 fish—up from about 1,000 fish per spring from the 1960s through the 1990s. The removal of four small dams that had blocked salmon passage was funded by the local Western Canal Water District and Southern California's Metropolitan Water District.

- According to the Connecticut River Coordinator's Office, in "Fish Passage Accomplishments" (May 8, 2009, http://www.fws.gov/r5crc/Habitat/fish_passage .htm), removal of the New England Box Company dam on the Ashuelot River in Winchester, New Hampshire, in 2002 restored approximately 15 miles (24 km) of the river to free-flowing for the first time in 100 years. The project was part of a river restoration plan intended to help bring back thousands of American shad, blueback herring, and Atlantic salmon to the river. As one of New Hampshire's major tributaries to the Connecticut River, the Ashuelot is historically important for migratory fish.

TRENDS IN WATER USE SINCE 1950

After continual increases in U.S. total water withdrawals since the USGS began reporting in 1950, water use peaked in 1980, declined through 1990, and has remained relatively stable since then. (See Table 2.9.) From 1995 to 2000, a period that experienced a 7% increase in the U.S. population, total off-stream water use increased by only 2%. Water use for public supply increased by 8%, irrigation by 2%, and thermoelectric power use by 3%.

Hutson et al. state that the general increase in water use from 1950 to 1980 and the decrease from 1980 to 2000 can be attributed to several factors, including:

- Expansion of irrigation systems and increases in energy development from 1950 to 1980.

- The development and increasing use of two irrigation methods—center-pivot irrigation systems and drip irrigation (the application of water directly to the roots of plants)—that are more efficient in delivering water to crops than the traditional sprayer arms that project the water into the air, where much is lost to wind and evaporation.

- Higher energy prices in the 1970s and a decrease in groundwater levels in some areas increased the cost of irrigation water.

- A downturn in the farm economy in the 1980s, which reduced demands for irrigation water.

- New industrial technologies requiring less water, improved efficiency, increased water recycling, higher energy prices, and changes in the law to reduce pollution.

- Active conservation programs and increased awareness by the general public of the need to conserve water.

WATER USE—THE FUTURE

The usefulness and availability of water can fluctuate dramatically in natural systems. Both the quality and quantity of water resources need to be protected for the nation's present and future generations. Furthermore, even though current water use can be determined, total water needs for most uses are changing. Water use is dependent on prices, technology, customs, and regulations. As such, water use data are good indicators of where and how the nation consumes water, but they are not necessarily good predictors of future water use trends.

Although the United States is not running out of water, the era of free and easily developed water supplies has ended for much of the country; in some areas water use is approaching or has exceeded the available supply.

TABLE 2.9

Water use trends, selected years 1950–2000

[In billion gallons per day (thousand million gallons per day); rounded to two significant figures for 1950–80, and to three significant figures for 1985–2000; percentage change is calculated from unrounded number]

	1950[a]	1955[b]	1960[c]	1965[d]	1970[d]	1975[c]	1980[c]	1985[c]	1990[c]	1995[c]	2000[c]	Percentage change 1995–2000
Population, in millions	150.7	164.0	179.3	193.8	205.9	216.4	229.6	242.4	252.3	267.1	285.3	+7
Offstream use:												
Total withdrawals	**180**	**240**	**270**	**310**	**370**	**420**	**440**	**399**	**408**	**402**	**408**	**+2**
Public supply	14	17	21	24	27	29	34	36.5	38.5	40.2	43.2	+8
Rural domestic and livestock:												
Self-supplied domestic	2.1	2.1	2.0	2.3	2.6	2.8	3.4	3.32	3.39	3.39	3.59	+6
Livestock and aquaculture	1.5	1.5	1.6	1.7	1.9	2.1	2.2	4.47[e]	4.50	5.49	[f]	—
Irrigation	89	110	110	120	130	140	150	137	137	134	137	+2
Industrial:												
Thermoelectric-power use	40	72	100	130	170	200	210	187	195	190	195	+3
Other industrial use	37	39	38	46	47	45	45	30.5	29.9	29.1	[g]	—
Source of water:												
Ground:												
Fresh	34	47	50	60	68	82	83	73.2	79.4	76.4	83.3	+9
Saline	[h]	.6	.4	.5	1.0	1.0	.9	.65	1.22	1.11	1.26	+14
Surface:												
Fresh	140	180	190	210	250	260	290	265	259	264	262	−1
Saline	10	18	31	43	53	69	71	59.6	68.2	59.7	61.0	+2

[a]48 states and District of Columbia, and Hawaii.
[b]48 states and District of Columbia.
[c]50 states and District of Columbia, Puerto Rico, and U.S. Virgin Islands.
[d]50 states and District of Columbia, and Puerto Rico.
[e]From 1985 to present this category includes water use for fish farms.
[f]Data not available for all states; partial total was 5.46.
[g]Commercial use not available; industrial and mining use totaled 23.2.
[h]Data not available.

SOURCE: Susan S. Hutson et al., "Table 14. Trends in Estimated Water Use in the United States, 1950–2000," in *Estimated Use of Water in the United States in 2000*, U.S. Department of the Interior, U.S. Geological Survey, 2004, http://pubs.usgs.gov/circ/2004//circ1268/pdf/circular1268.pdf and revision data February 7, 2005, http://pubs.usgs.gov/circ/2004//circ1268/control/revisions.html (accessed March 14, 2009)

Projections of freshwater usage by use-category are presented by Thomas C. Brown of the Forest Service in *Past and Future Freshwater Use in the United States* (September 1999, http://www.fs.fed.us/rm/pubs/rmrs_gtr039.pdf), which was the most recent report available as of mid-2009. According to Brown, freshwater usage in the United States will reach 364 Bgal/d (1.4 trillion L per day) by 2040. This figure represents a 7% increase over the 1995 usage rate of 340 Bgal/d (1.3 trillion L per day).

Brown's projections anticipate increased freshwater usage for livestock and domestic and public water services. (See Figure 2.3.) Water usage for thermoelectric generation will rise slightly. The dark bars in Figure 2.3 indicate past withdrawals and the light bars indicate future withdrawals (projected as of 1999). The dots show levels of related factors, with dark dots showing past levels and light dots future levels. The related factor and its scale is on the right.

Freshwater usage for livestock and domestic and public water services is projected to increase at about the same rate as the U.S. population. Water usage for thermoelectric generation will rise only slightly, even though the kilowatt

hours generated will increase much more substantially. In 1995 freshwater withdrawals for thermoelectric use were 132 Bgal/d (499.7 billion L per day); in 2040 the withdrawals are estimated at 143 Bgal/d (541.3 billion L per day). Even though water withdrawals per day are projected to be higher in 2040 than they were in 1995, the increased kilowatt hours produced will result in a decreasing water withdrawal per kilowatt hour of electricity that will be produced.

The quantity of water used by industry and for commercial applications is anticipated to remain stable through 2040. (See Figure 2.3.) The Bureau of Economic Analysis reports in the press release "State Personal Income 2008" (March 24, 2009, http://www.bea.gov/newsreleases/regional/spi/2009/pdf/spi0309.pdf) that even though personal income growth slowed to 3.9% in 2008, down from 6% in 2007, annual growth in per capita income still continued. Additionally, as the U.S. population increases along with per capita personal income, an increase in water withdrawals by industry and commercial applications is expected. However, Brown reports that a more efficient use of water in industrial

FIGURE 2.3

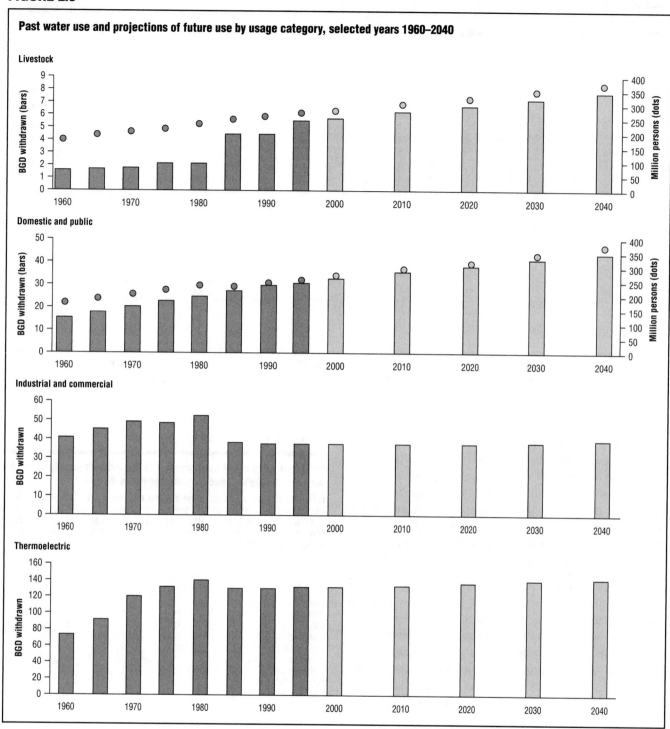

Past water use and projections of future use by usage category, selected years 1960–2040

and commercial processes and greater levels of water recycling are expected to offset economic and population growth, resulting in industrial and commercial withdrawals remaining stable for the next couple decades.

Through 2040 the amount of irrigated acreage is expected to increase modestly, from 57.9 million acres (23.4 million ha) in 1995 to 62.4 million acres (25.3 million ha) in 2040. (See Figure 2.3.) Water withdrawals, however, are expected to decline modestly, from 134

Bgal/d (507.2 billion L per day) in 1995 to 130 Bgal/d (492.1 billion L per day) in 2040.

Through 2040 the amount of irrigated acreage is expected to increase modestly, from 57.9 million acres (23.4 million ha) in 1995 to 62.4 million acres (25.3 million ha) in 2040. (See Figure 2.3.) Water withdrawals, however, are expected to decline modestly, from 134 Bgal/d (507.2 billion L per day) in 1995 to 130 Bgal/d (492.1 billion L per day) in 2040.

FIGURE 2.3

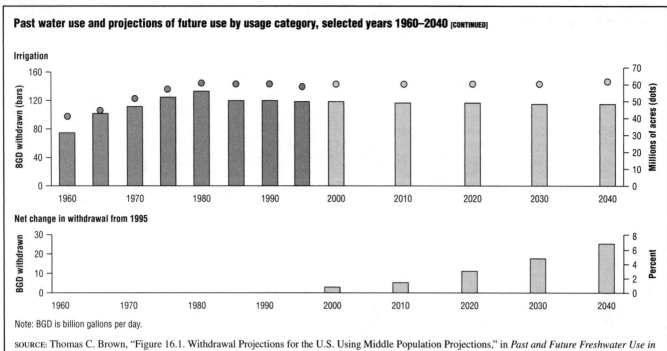

Past water use and projections of future use by usage category, selected years 1960–2040 [CONTINUED]

Note: BGD is billion gallons per day.

SOURCE: Thomas C. Brown, "Figure 16.1. Withdrawal Projections for the U.S. Using Middle Population Projections," in *Past and Future Freshwater Use in the United States: A Technical Document Supporting the 2000 USDA Forest Service RPA Assessment*, U.S. Department of Agriculture, Forest Service, Rocky Mountain Research Station, September 1999, http://www.fs.fed.us/rm/pubs/rmrs_gtr039.pdf (accessed March 16, 2009)

Per capita freshwater withdrawals are projected to decline through 2040, although the overall change will be an increase of about 7% due to increased population. (See Figure 2.3.) Several factors are expected to contribute to the lower per capita freshwater usage rates. According to Brown, the two most prominent factors are improved efficiencies projected for the municipal, industrial, and thermoelectric generating sectors, and reduced irrigation withdrawals.

Increasing awareness among the traditional users of water and the general public of the finite nature of clean water supplies, particularly freshwater, has resulted in growing conservation efforts and innovative approaches to water conservation and reclamation. Water conservation is the careful use and protection of water resources. Water reclamation, also called water recycling, is the treatment of wastewater so that it can be reused for certain purposes, such as landscape irrigation.

This increased awareness is shown on a "worry scale" in Table 2.10. This table shows that in 2009, 49% of Americans worried a great deal about having enough fresh water for their household needs. Even though this figure has remained somewhat stable since 2002, it is up from 35% of Americans who worried about sufficient water supplies in 2001. Also, since 2002 only 9% or less of the population did not worry about having a sufficient supply of fresh water.

Water Conservation

Water conservation and reclamation efforts take place all over the United States. The following are a few exam-

TABLE 2.10

Public concern about maintenance of the nation's supply of fresh water for household needs, selected years 2000–09

I'M GOING TO READ YOU A LIST OF ENVIRONMENTAL PROBLEMS. AS I READ EACH ONE, PLEASE TELL ME IF YOU PERSONALLY WORRY ABOUT THIS PROBLEM A GREAT DEAL, A FAIR AMOUNT, ONLY A LITTLE, OR NOT AT ALL. FIRST, HOW MUCH DO YOU PERSONALLY WORRY ABOUT MAINTENANCE OF THE NATION'S SUPPLY OF FRESH WATER FOR HOUSEHOLD NEEDS?

	Great deal %	Fair amount %	Only a little %	Not at all %	No opinion %
2009 Mar 5–8	49	31	14	5	*
2008 Mar 6–9	48	31	15	5	*
2007 Mar 11–14	51	27	16	5	*
2006 Mar 13–16	49	27	14	9	1
2004 Mar 8–11	47	25	20	8	*
2003 Mar 3–5	49	28	15	8	*
2002 Mar 4–7	50	28	17	5	*
2001 Mar 5–7	35	34	19	10	2
2000 Apr 3–9	42	31	14	12	1

*Less than 0.5%

SOURCE: "I'm Going to Read You a List of Environmental Problems. As I Read Each One, Please Tell Me If You Personally Worry about This Problem a Great Deal, a Fair Amount, Only a Little, or Not at All. First, How Much Do You Personally Worry about—Maintenance of the Nation's Supply of Fresh Water for Household Needs?" in *Gallup's Pulse of Democracy: The Environment*, The Gallup Organization, 2009, http://www.gallup.com/poll/1615/Environment.aspx#1 (accessed March 23, 2009). Copyright © 2009 by The Gallup Organization. Reproduced by permission of The Gallup Organization.

ples to show the types of activities that have been undertaken and their outcomes.

In "Conservation Ordinance" (2009, http://www.saws.org/conservation/ordinance/), the San Antonio Water System indicates that the city of San Antonio, Texas, passed a conservation ordinance that went into effect in 2006. Even though the city had a conservation program that had been in place since 1993, the conservation ordinance was expected to save an additional 1.3 billion gallons (4.9 billion L) of water each year. The ordinance included the restricted use of power washers, conditions of use of irrigation systems, promotion of xeriscape landscaping (which reduces or eliminates the need for irrigation by using drought-resistant plants and other methods), and the development of a water advisory council.

According to the Las Vegas Valley Water District, in "Turf Installation" (2007, http://www.lvvwd.com/html/ws_drought_restrictions_turf.html), the city of Las Vegas, Nevada, has focused on reducing water use for irrigation. As of January 1, 2004, owners of new homes in Las Vegas were restricted in their planting of grass in their side and backyards and were not allowed to plant grass in their front yards. Owners of existing lawns were offered "cash for grass" to rip out the turf. Even though this program has been innovative and effective in reducing the amount of water used in irrigation, Heather Cooley et al. note in *Hidden Oasis: Water Conservation and Efficiency in Las Vegas* (November 2007, http://www.pacinst.org/reports/las_vegas/hidden_oasis.pdf) that it is criticized by the Pacific Institute as not doing enough to promote indoor water conservation. In "Cash for Grass Program Taking Steps to Entice More Businesses" (*Las Vegas Sun*, June 17, 2008), Phoebe Sweet reports that Las Vegas stepped up its "cash for grass" program in 2007 by offering homeowners and businesses an unprecedented $2 per square foot of lawn they removed from their premises for up to 1,500 square feet (139.4 square m), and $1.50 per square foot after that. In 2007, 5,400 homeowners removed 6.5 million square feet (603,900 square m) of grass, and 468 businesses removed 12 million square feet (1.1 million square m) of grass. From the inception of the program in 2003 through mid-2008, 107 million square feet (9.9 million square m) of turf was removed.

Water Reclamation

The water department in Tampa, Florida, has been working to maximize the yield from its water supply. The Reclaimed Water Project features the use of high-quality reclaimed water from the Howard F. Curran Wastewater Treatment Facility to satisfy the demands of high-volume irrigation users in South Tampa. Water is made available through a water system that is separate from the drinking water supply to prevent any possibility of cross contamination. The project began as a grassroots effort by Westshore residents concerned about future water supplies. Important conditions of the project were voluntary participation in it; only citizens who want reclaimed water participate in the project, and user fees make the project self-supporting.

The city of Tampa indicates in "Reclaimed Water—Frequently Asked Questions" (August 3, 2008, http://www.tampagov.net/dept_Water/programs_and_services/Reclaimed_Water/) that in the first four months of the project sign-up, over 4,200 homeowners and businesses enrolled. Construction of Phase I began in 2002 and as of November 2008 the final boundaries of the system had not yet been determined. The first users began drawing water from the system in July 2004. Recommended uses for reclaimed water are crop irrigation, lawn and landscape watering, washing cars, and general cleaning. In 2007 Tampa was able to reduce the reclaimed water fee, making this option even more economically viable for Tampa-area residents.

The San Diego County Water Authority (2009, http://www.sdcwa.org/manage/recycled-facilities.phtml) operates the San Pasqual water reclamation plant, which is located in the San Pasqual Valley near Escondido, California. The purpose of the plant, which can treat up to 1 Mgal/d (3.8 million L per day) of water, is to supply reclaimed water to the community. The wastewater received at the treatment facility is treated to the primary level when solids are removed. The screened primary effluent is then fed into as many as 24 aquatic treatment ponds, where the wastewater is biologically stabilized. The ponds are stocked with water hyacinth, mosquito fish, crayfish, and other organisms to create an aquatic ecosystem that removes pollutants from wastewater. Water hyacinths grow quickly in the ponds. About 50% of the plants are harvested weekly from the ponds, dried for composting, and sold for reuse as a soil amendment. After the water passes through the aquatic treatment ponds, it is clarified, filtered, and disinfected for use in irrigation and research.

Rainwater and Gray Water Harvesting

In "Tucson Passes Nation's First Rainwater Harvesting Ordinance for Commercial Properties" (*Land Letter,* October 16, 2008), April Reese reports that in 2008 the city of Tucson, Arizona, was the first municipality to create an ordinance requiring builders of commercial properties to use reclaimed rainwater for at least 50% of the property's irrigation needs. Lawmakers and builders expect that the ordinance can be satisfied by water reclamation measures such as using water-penetrable paving materials, sloping parking areas to divert water to planted areas, and collecting rainwater on rooftops to feed drip irrigation systems. Reese notes that other municipalities, such as Santa Fe and Albuquerque, New Mexico, have similar residential rainwater harvesting ordinances for new construction. According to the EPA, in the press release "U.S. EPA Honors Five Arizona Environmental Heroes" (April 16, 2009, http://yosemite.epa.gov/opa/admpress.nsf/0/DF60FDEA7405CE3B8525759A006C60FE), Tucson has tackled the residential situation with a gray water ordinance, which requires all new residential construction to be plumbed to allow for future installation of a gray water system. In gray water systems, all water from sinks (except those with garbage disposals), showers, bathtubs, and washing machines are treated and then used for irrigation.

Water Pressure: Population Growth in the West and South

Table 2.11 shows cumulative estimates of population change for states and regions of the United States from 2000 to 2008. During this period the West was the fastest-growing portion of the country by percentage. However, the South was the region of the country that gained the most people. Thus, both the West and the South vie for first and second place as the fastest-growing regions of the United States. Population growth in these areas is expected to put enormous pressure on natural resources, including water, and to force continued changes in water consumption practices and prices.

Percentage-wise, Nevada (30.1%) was the state that grew the most between 2000 and 2008, followed by Arizona (26.7%), Utah (22.5%), Georgia (18.3%), Idaho (17.8%), Texas (16.7%), Colorado (14.8%), Florida (14.7%), and North Carolina (14.6%). (See Table 2.11.) The state that grew the most in numbers of new residents was Texas (3.5 million), followed by California (2.9 million), Florida (2.3 million), Georgia (1.5 million), Arizona (1.4 million), North Carolina (1.2 million), Virginia (690,000), Washington (655,000), Colorado (637,000), and Nevada (602,000). Louisiana lost population during this period, with much of that decline attributed to Hurricane Katrina and its aftermath. North Dakota had a small decline in population, which the North Dakota State Data Center attributes in "Data Trends" (March 4, 2009, http://www.ndsu.edu/sdc/data/populationtrends .htm) to the emigration of young families from rural areas, leaving an older population that is past its reproductive years.

WHERE WATER IS POWER—INTERNATIONAL WATER WARS?

As usable water becomes rarer because of increasing population and the pollution of water supplies, it is expected to become a commodity such as iron or oil. Peter Allison states in "World Overview: Water Wars—The Global Viewpoint" (2006, http://www.itt.com/waterbook/ world.asp) that "over 20 countries depend on the flow of water from other nations for much of their supply. And more than 300 of the world's river basins are shared by two or more countries." All are potential objects of world political power struggles over this critical resource.

Africa, the Middle East, and South Asia are three areas of the world that are particularly short of water. Other dry areas include the southwest of North America, limited areas in South America, and large parts of Australia.

The rivers in the Middle East are the lifeblood of an arid region. Freshwater has never come easily to this area. Rainfall occurs only in winter and drains quickly through the parched land. Most Middle Eastern countries are joined by common aquifers. The United Nations cautions that future wars in the Middle East may be fought over water.

Since April 2001 tensions between Israel and Lebanon have been escalating over the Lebanese construction of a pumping station along the Hasbani River. The Hasbani flows into the Sea of Galilee, which is Israel's primary freshwater reservoir. In 2001 Israel was undergoing a water crisis, and the sea was at its lowest level ever. Tensions periodically arise as droughts tighten supply in the area, but since mid-2005 the tensions between Israel and Lebanon regarding Lebanon's pumping of water from the Hasbani River have been handled diplomatically, with the assistance of the European Union and the United Nations.

The oil-rich Middle Eastern nation of Kuwait has little water, but it has the money to secure it. To use seawater, Kuwait has constructed six large-scale, oil-powered desalination plants. According to the Saudi Arabia Market Information Resource, in "Desalination" (April 20, 2009, http://www.saudinf.com/main/a541.htm), in 2009 Saudi Arabia's 27 plants produced 70% of the kingdom's freshwater needs.

Water quality and water shortages are just two of the problems facing the world in the years to come. The September 11, 2001, terrorist attacks in the United States increased concerns about bioterrorism. In June 2002 Congress passed the Public Health Security and Bioterrorism Act. Title IV (Drinking Water Security and Safety) of the act mandates that every community water system that serves a population of between 3,300 and 50,000 people must:

- Conduct a vulnerability assessment.

- Certify and submit a copy of the assessment to the EPA administrator.

- Prepare or revise an emergency response plan that incorporates the results of the vulnerability assessment.

- Certify to the EPA administrator, within six months of completing the vulnerability assessment, that the system has completed or updated its emergency response plan.

TABLE 2.11

Estimates of population change by region, state, and Puerto Rico, 2000–08

Geographic area	Population estimates		Change, 2000 to 2008		National ranking of regions and states			
					Population estimates		Change, 2000 to 2008	
	July 1, 2008	April 1, 2000 estimates base	Number	Percent	July 1, 2008	April 1, 2000 estimates base	Number	Percent
United States	304,059,724	281,424,602	22,635,122	8.0	(X)	(X)	(X)	(X)
Northeast	54,924,779	53,594,797	1,329,982	2.5	4	4	4	4
Midwest	66,561,448	64,395,207	2,166,241	3.4	3	2	3	3
South	111,718,549	100,235,848	11,482,701	11.5	1	1	1	2
West	70,854,948	63,198,750	7,656,198	12.1	2	3	2	1
Alabama	4,661,900	4,447,355	214,545	4.8	23	23	25	32
Alaska	686,293	626,931	59,362	9.5	47	48	42	15
Arizona	6,500,180	5,130,607	1,369,573	26.7	14	20	5	2
Arkansas	2,855,390	2,673,386	182,004	6.8	32	33	27	21
California	36,756,666	33,871,650	2,885,016	8.5	1	1	2	18
Colorado	4,939,456	4,302,015	637,441	14.8	22	24	9	7
Connecticut	3,501,252	3,405,604	95,648	2.8	29	29	33	40
Delaware	873,092	783,595	89,497	11.4	45	45	35	11
District of Columbia	591,833	572,053	19,780	3.5	50	50	46	36
Florida	18,328,340	15,982,813	2,345,527	14.7	4	4	3	8
Georgia	9,685,744	8,186,812	1,498,932	18.3	9	10	4	4
Hawaii	1,288,198	1,211,538	76,660	6.3	42	42	37	25
Idaho	1,523,816	1,293,955	229,861	17.8	39	39	23	5
Illinois	12,901,563	12,419,660	481,903	3.9	5	5	14	35
Indiana	6,376,792	6,080,522	296,270	4.9	16	14	20	31
Iowa	3,002,555	2,926,381	76,174	2.6	30	30	38	42
Kansas	2,802,134	2,688,816	113,318	4.2	33	32	32	34
Kentucky	4,269,245	4,042,284	226,961	5.6	26	25	24	28
Louisiana	4,410,796	4,468,968	-58,172	-1.3	25	22	51	51
Maine	1,316,456	1,274,922	41,534	3.3	40	40	44	38
Maryland	5,633,597	5,296,516	337,081	6.4	19	19	17	24
Massachusetts	6,497,967	6,349,113	148,854	2.3	15	13	30	43
Michigan	10,003,422	9,938,492	64,930	0.7	8	8	41	47
Minnesota	5,220,393	4,919,492	300,901	6.1	21	21	19	26
Mississippi	2,938,618	2,844,666	93,952	3.3	31	31	34	37
Missouri	5,911,605	5,596,678	314,927	5.6	18	17	18	27
Montana	967,440	902,190	65,250	7.2	44	44	40	20
Nebraska	1,783,432	1,711,266	72,166	4.2	38	38	39	33
Nevada	2,600,167	1,998,257	601,910	30.1	35	35	10	1
New Hampshire	1,315,809	1,235,785	80,024	6.5	41	41	36	23
New Jersey	8,682,661	8,414,360	268,301	3.2	11	9	21	39
New Mexico	1,984,356	1,819,041	165,315	9.1	36	36	29	17
New York	19,490,297	18,976,816	513,481	2.7	3	3	12	41
North Carolina	9,222,414	8,046,500	1,175,914	14.6	10	11	6	9
North Dakota	641,481	642,195	-714	-0.1	48	47	50	50
Ohio	11,485,910	11,353,160	132,750	1.2	7	7	31	46
Oklahoma	3,642,361	3,450,640	191,721	5.6	28	27	26	29
Oregon	3,790,060	3,421,437	368,623	10.8	27	28	16	13
Pennsylvania	12,448,279	12,281,052	167,227	1.4	6	6	28	45
Rhode Island	1,050,788	1,048,319	2,469	0.2	43	43	49	49
South Carolina	4,479,800	4,011,809	467,991	11.7	24	26	15	10
South Dakota	804,194	754,837	49,357	6.5	46	46	43	22
Tennessee	6,214,888	5,689,270	525,618	9.2	17	16	11	16
Texas	24,326,974	20,851,811	3,475,163	16.7	2	2	1	6
Utah	2,736,424	2,233,204	503,220	22.5	34	34	13	3
Vermont	621,270	608,826	12,444	2.0	49	49	47	44
Virginia	7,769,089	7,079,025	690,064	9.7	12	12	7	14
Washington	6,549,224	5,894,143	655,081	11.1	13	15	8	12
West Virginia	1,814,468	1,808,345	6,123	0.3	37	37	48	48
Wisconsin	5,627,967	5,363,708	264,259	4.9	20	18	22	30
Wyoming	532,668	493,782	38,886	7.9	51	51	45	19
Puerto Rico	3,954,037	3,808,603	145,434	3.8	(X)	(X)	(X)	(X)

Note: The April 1, 2000, population estimates base reflects changes to the Census 2000 population from the count question resolution program and geographic program revisions. (X) = Not applicable.

SOURCE: "Table 2. Cumulative Estimates of Resident Population Change for the United States, Regions, States and Puerto Rico and Region and State Rankings: April 1, 2000 to July 1, 2008," U.S. Census Bureau, Population Division, December 22, 2008, http://www.census.gov/popest/states/NST-pop-chg.html (accessed March 11, 2009)

CHAPTER 3
SURFACE WATER: RIVERS, STREAMS, AND LAKES

Most of Earth's water, about 97%, is the saltwater of the oceans. (See Figure 1.2 in Chapter 1.) By comparison, freshwater accounts for only 3% of Earth's water, and surface water is only 0.3% of that 3%. Furthermore, rivers and lakes account for 2% and 87%, respectively, of surface water. Thus, rivers contain only 0.002% and lakes only 0.013% of Earth's water. Nonetheless, this tiny fraction of the total water supply has shaped the course of human development. Throughout human history societies have depended on these surface-water resources for food, drinking water, transportation, commerce, power, and recreation.

In 2000 out of a total of 345 billion gallons per day (Bgal/d; 1.3 trillion L per day) of the total freshwater consumption in the United States, water from streams, rivers, and lakes accounted for 262 Bgal/d (991.8 billion L per day; 76%). (See Table 2.1 in Chapter 2.) The remaining 83.3 Bgal/d (315.3 billion L per day; 24%) came from groundwater. Public utilities (public and private water suppliers) used 27.3 Bgal/d (103.3 billion L per day; 63%) of surface water for their operations. (See Table 2.3 in Chapter 2.) Industries consumed 14.9 Bgal/d (56.4 billion L per day; 76%) of surface freshwater for their requirements. (See Table 2.7 in Chapter 2.) Meanwhile, crop irrigation used 80 Bgal/d (302.8 billion L per day; 58%) of surface water to water crops. (See Table 2.5 in Chapter 2.)

The withdrawal of surface water varies greatly throughout the United States. Table 2.1 shows that in 2000 California, Texas, and Florida used the most water per day, whereas North Dakota and South Dakota used the least.

CHARACTERISTICS OF RIVERS AND LAKES
Rivers and Streams

The great rivers of the world have influenced human history. Settlements on rivers have thrived since earliest recorded history, with most of the world's great civilizations growing up along rivers. Flowing rivers provided water to drink, fish and shellfish to eat, dispersion and removal of wastes, and transport for goods. The bountiful supply of freshwater in flowing rivers is one of the primary reasons for the rapid growth of settlement, industry, and agriculture in the United States during both colonial and modern times.

Unlike lakes, rivers and streams consist of flowing water. Perennial rivers and streams flow continuously, although the volume may vary with runoff conditions. Intermittent, or ephemeral, rivers and streams stop flowing for some period, usually because of dry conditions. Both large and small rivers and streams are an important part of the hydrologic cycle. (See Figure 1.3 in Chapter 1.)

Rivers receive water from rain and melting snow, from underground springs and aquifers, and from lakes. A large river is usually fed by tributaries (smaller rivers and streams) and so increases in size as it travels from its source, or origin. Its final destination may be an ocean, a lake, or sometimes open land, where the water simply evaporates. This phenomenon usually happens only with small rivers or streams.

As water flows down a river, it carries with it grains of soil, sand, and, where there is a strong current, small stones and other debris. These objects are important in two ways. First, as they are pulled along by the river's current, they grind against the bottom and sides of the riverbank and slowly cut the riverbed deeper and deeper into the earth, thereby changing the contour of the land. (The Grand Canyon is an example of how a river can carve the land.) Second, when the river reaches its destination (an ocean or lake), the flow is slowed and then stopped where the bodies of water meet, and the soil that has been carried along is deposited. These deposits are called sediment. Finely grained sediment is called silt.

Over long periods, sediment deposited at the mouths of rivers forms triangular-shaped areas called deltas. During flood conditions some of the sediment of the delta floodwaters is deposited on the low-lying land (floodplain) surrounding the river. Enriched with this sediment, the delta floodplain often provides a rich base for agriculture. The ancient civilizations of Egypt, for example, depended on the land surrounding the delta of the Nile River to grow their food supply. On the contrary, deposited sediment can become a nuisance by filling lakes and harbors and smothering aquatic life. Many ports and harbors in the United States must be dredged regularly to remove deposits that would otherwise obstruct navigation.

The U.S. Geological Survey (USGS) reports in "Lengths of the Major Rivers" (November 7, 2008, http://ga.water.usgs.gov/edu/riversofworld.html) that the two longest rivers in the world are the Nile (4,132 miles [6,650 km]) and the Amazon (4,000 miles [6,437 km]). The Mississippi-Missouri river system is the third longest in the world. Taken separately, the Missouri (2,540 miles; 4,088 km) is the longest in the United States and the Mississippi (2,340 miles; 3,766 km) the second longest. (See Table 3.1.)

The Mississippi River has an enormous watershed, the land from which it receives runoff water from rainfall or snowmelt. According to the National Park Service, in "Mississippi River Facts" (February 23, 2009, http://www.nps.gov/miss/riverfacts.htm), this watershed is approximately 1.8 million square miles (4.8 million square km),

or about 40% of the total land area of the lower 48 states. The Mississippi River is considered the largest river in the United States by the measure of the average volume at its mouth. (See Table 3.1.) The "Mighty Mississippi," as it is often called, discharges its water into the Gulf of Mexico at an average rate of 593,000 cubic feet per second (16,792 cubic m per second).

Lakes

Unlike rivers, lakes are depressions in the earth that hold water for extended periods. Reservoirs are human-made lakes created when a dam is built on a river. They are generally used to store water for uses such as drinking, irrigation, or producing electricity. Often, reservoir areas are used for recreation as well. Some ponds are made for livestock watering, fire control, storm water management, duck and fish habitat, and recreation.

The source of the water in lakes, reservoirs, and ponds may be rivers, streams, groundwater, rainfall, melting snow runoff, or a combination of these. Any of these sources may carry contaminants. Because water exits from these water bodies at a slow rate, pollutants can become trapped and build up.

Many of the world's lake beds were formed during the Ice Age, when advancing and retreating glaciers gouged holes in the soft bedrock and spread dirt and debris in uneven patterns. Some lakes fill the craters of extinct volcanoes, and others have formed in the shallow basins of ocean bottoms uplifted by geological activity to become part of Earth's solid surface.

As soon as a lake or pond is formed, it is destined to die. "Death" occurs over a long time, particularly in the case of large lakes. Soil and debris carried by in-flowing rivers and streams slowly build up the basin floor. At the same time, water is removed by out-flowing rivers and streams, whose channels become ever wider and deeper, allowing them to carry more water away. Even lakes that have no river inlets or outlets eventually fill with soil eroded from the surrounding land.

FRESHWATER VERSUS SALTWATER. According to the U.S. Environmental Protection Agency (EPA), in *The Hydrologic (Water) Cycle* (2009, http://www.epa.gov/OGWDW/kids/wsb/pdfs/9121.pdf), the large freshwater lakes of the world contain about 30,000 cubic miles (125,045 cubic km) of water and cover a combined surface area of about 330,000 square miles (854,696 square km). In "NatureWorks: Lakes" (2007, http://www.nhptv.org/Natureworks/nwep7c.htm), New Hampshire Public Television indicates that by surface area Lake Superior, which is located on the U.S.-Canadian border, is the largest freshwater lake in the world. Lake Baikal in Asiatic Russia, however, is the deepest freshwater lake in the world, and Oregon's Crater Lake is the deepest in the United States.

TABLE 3.1

Largest rivers in the United States in length and average discharge volume at mouth

River	Location at mouth	Average discharge at mouth (cfs)	Length[a] (ml.)
Mississippi	LA	593,000	2,340
St. Lawrence	Canada	348,000	1,900
Ohio	IL, KY	281,000	1,310
Columbia	WA	265,000	1,240
Yukon	AK	225,000	1,980
Missouri	MO	76,200	2,540
Tennessee	KY	68,000	886
Mobile	AL	67,200	774
Kuskoswim	AK	67,000	724
Copper	AK	59,000	286
Atchafalaya	LA	58,000	140[b]
Snake	WA	56,900	1,040
Stikine	AK	56,000	379
Red	LA	56,000	1,290
Susitna	AK	51,000	313
Tanana	AK	41,000	659
Arkansas	AR	41,000	1,460
Susquehanna	MD	38,200	447
Willamette	OR	37,400	309
Nushagak	AK	36,000	285

Note: cfs is cubic feet per second.
[a]Including headwaters and sections in Canada.
[b]Below Mississippi diversion, without headwaters.

SOURCE: Adapted from J.C. Kammerer, "Largest Rivers in the United States in Discharge, Drainage Area, or Length," in *Water Fact Sheet: Largest Rivers in the United States*, U.S. Department of the Interior, U.S, Geological Survey, May 1990, http://pubs.usgs.gov/of/1987/ofr87-242/pdf/ofr87242.pdf (accessed March 9, 2009)

Harvey A. Bootsma and Robert E. Hecky report in "A Comparative Introduction to the Biology and Limnology of the African Great Lakes" (*Journal of Great Lakes Research*, vol. 29, no. 2, 2003) that the large lakes of Africa (Victoria, Tanganyika, and Malawi) contain about 32% of the volume of all freshwater lakes on Earth (7,062 cubic miles [29,436 cubic km] of 21,832 cubic miles [91,000 cubic km]). The North American Great Lakes (Superior, Michigan, Huron, Erie, and Ontario) hold slightly less, or about 25% of the volume of the freshwater lakes (5,472 cubic miles [22,808 cubic km]). Lake Baikal holds slightly more water (5,662 cubic miles [23,600 cubic km]) than the North American Great Lakes, holding about 26% of the volume of Earth's freshwater lakes. Together, these nine lakes hold 83% of the volume of all freshwater lakes.

The USGS notes in *Where Is Earth's Water Located?* (March 4, 2009, http://ga.water.usgs.gov/edu/earthwhere water.html) that the saline (saltwater) lakes of the world contain almost as much water as the freshwater lakes (20,490 cubic miles [85,406 cubic km]). In "Ponds, Lakes, and Oceans" (*Environmental Organic Chemistry*, 2003), René P. Schwarzenbach, Philip M. Gschwend, and Dieter M. Imboden indicate that of that volume, however, 92% is in the Caspian Sea (18,761 cubic miles [78,199 cubic km]), which borders Russia and Iran. Most of the remainder is in lakes in Asia. North America's shallow Great Salt Lake is comparatively insignificant; it varies in depth and volume with climatic conditions, so exact comparisons are difficult.

NEED FOR POLLUTION CONTROL

People have always congregated on the shores of lakes and rivers. Benefiting from the many advantages of nearby water sources, they established permanent homes, then towns, cities, and industries. One of these advantages has been that lakes and rivers were convenient places to dispose of waste. As industrial societies developed, the amount of waste became enormous. Frequently, the wastes contained synthetic and toxic materials that could not be assimilated by the waters' ecosystems. Millions of tons of sewage, pesticides, chemicals, and garbage were dumped into waterways worldwide until there were few that were not contaminated to some extent. Some were (and some still are) contaminated to the point of ecological death—meaning that they were unable to sustain a balanced aquatic-life system.

Worry about water pollution has declined among the American public in the past 20 years. The Gallup Organization has surveyed Americans since 1989 regarding how much they worry about the pollution of rivers, lakes, and reservoirs. Table 3.2 shows the results of that polling from 1989 through 2009. In 1989 nearly three-quarters (72%) of respondents worried a great deal about the pollution of rivers, lakes, and reservoirs, and by 2009 about half (52%) worried a great deal. The results are similar when

TABLE 3.2

Public concern about pollution of rivers, lakes, and reservoirs, selected years 1989–2009

I'M GOING TO READ YOU A LIST OF ENVIRONMENTAL PROBLEMS. AS I READ EACH ONE, PLEASE TELL ME IF YOU PERSONALLY WORRY ABOUT THIS PROBLEM A GREAT DEAL, A FAIR AMOUNT, ONLY A LITTLE, OR NOT AT ALL. FIRST, HOW MUCH DO YOU PERSONALLY WORRY ABOUT POLLUTION OF RIVERS, LAKES, AND RESERVOIRS?

	Great deal	Fair amount	Only a little	Not at all	No opinion
	%	%	%	%	%
2009 Mar 5–8	52	31	13	4	*
2008 Mar 6–9	50	34	12	4	—
2007 Mar 11–14	53	31	13	3	—
2006 Mar 13–16	51	33	11	5	*
2004 Mar 8–11	48	31	16	5	*
2003 Mar 3–5	51	31	13	5	—
2002 Mar 4–7	53	32	12	3	*
2001 Mar 5–7	58	29	10	3	*
2000 Apr 3–9	66	24	8	2	*
1999 Apr 13–14	61	30	7	2	*
1999 Mar 12–14	55	30	12	3	*
1991 Apr 11–14	67	21	8	3	1
1990 Apr 5–8	64	23	9	4	—
1989 May 4–7	72	19	5	3	1

*Less than 0.5%

SOURCE: "I'm Going to Read You a List of Environmental Problems. As I Read Each One, Please Tell Me If You Personally Worry about This Problem a Great Deal, a Fair Amount, Only a Little, or Not at All. First, How Much Do You Personally Worry about—Pollution of Rivers, Lakes, and Reservoirs?" in *Gallup's Pulse of Democracy: The Environment*, The Gallup Organization, 2009, http://www.gallup.com/poll/1615/Environment.aspx#1 (accessed March 23, 2009). Copyright © 2009 by The Gallup Organization. Reproduced by permission of The Gallup Organization.

Americans were asked by Gallup pollsters how much they worried about the contamination of soil and water by toxic waste. (See Table 3.3.) When queried about this topic, 69% of respondents in 1989 said they worried a great deal, whereas 52% responded the same way in 2009.

Clean Water Act

In October 2002 President George W. Bush (1946–) proclaimed the beginning of the Year of Clean Water in commemoration of the 30th anniversary of the signing of the Federal Water Pollution Control Act, which is better known as the Clean Water Act (CWA).

The CWA was enacted by Congress in 1972 in response to growing public concern over the nation's polluted waters. The Federal Water Pollution Control Act was originally enacted in 1948, but it was amended many times and then reorganized and expanded in 1972. It continues to be amended almost every year.

The original 1948 legislation was intended to eliminate or reduce the pollution of interstate waters and improve the sanitary condition of surface and underground waters. However, on June 22, 1969, the Cuyahoga River in Cleveland, Ohio, burst into flames, the result of oil and debris that had accumulated on the river's surface. Clearly, the legislation was not achieving its desired goal.

TABLE 3.3

Public concern about contamination of soil and water by toxic waste, selected years 1989–2009

I'M GOING TO READ YOU A LIST OF ENVIRONMENTAL PROBLEMS. AS I READ EACH ONE, PLEASE TELL ME IF YOU PERSONALLY WORRY ABOUT THIS PROBLEM A GREAT DEAL, A FAIR AMOUNT, ONLY A LITTLE, OR NOT AT ALL. FIRST, HOW MUCH DO YOU PERSONALLY WORRY ABOUT CONTAMINATION OF SOIL AND WATER BY TOXIC WASTE?

	Great deal %	Fair amount %	Only a little %	Not at all %	No opinion %
2009 Mar 5–8	52	28	14	5	*
2008 Mar 6–9	50	30	14	6	*
2007 Mar 11–14	52	28	13	7	*
2006 Mar 13–16	52	29	13	6	*
2004 Mar 8–11	48	26	21	5	*
2003 Mar 3–5	51	28	16	5	*
2002 Mar 4–7	53	29	15	3	*
2001 Mar 5–7	58	27	12	3	*
2000 Apr 3–9	64	25	7	4	*
1999 Apr 13–14	63	27	7	3	*
1999 Mar 12–14	55	29	11	5	*
1991 Apr 11–14	62	21	11	5	1
1990 Apr 5–8	63	22	10	5	*
1989 May 4–7	69	21	6	3	*

*Less than 0.5%

SOURCE: "I'm Going to Read You a List of Environmental Problems. As I Read Each One, Please Tell Me If You Personally Worry about This Problem a Great Deal, a Fair Amount, Only a Little, or Not at All. First, How Much Do You Personally Worry about—Contamination of Soil and Water by Toxic Waste?" in *Gallup's Pulse of Democracy: The Environment*, The Gallup Organization, 2009, http://www.gallup.com/poll/1615/Environment.aspx#1 (accessed March 23, 2009). Copyright © 2009 by The Gallup Organization. Reproduced by permission of The Gallup Organization.

The objective of the CWA was to "restore and maintain the chemical, physical, and biological integrity" of the nation's waters. Primary authority for the enforcement of this law lies with the EPA.

The CWA requires that, where attainable, water quality be such to allow for the "protection and propagation of a balanced population of shellfish, fish and wildlife, and to allow recreational activities, in and on the water." This requirement is referred to as the act's "fishable/swimmable" goal. Many people credit the CWA with reversing, in a single generation, what had been a decline in the health of the nation's water since the mid-19th century.

Assessing and Monitoring the Quality of Water

Under section 305(b) of the CWA, the states are required to submit assessments of their water quality to the EPA every two years. The EPA is required to compile and summarize this information in the biennial report *National Water Quality Inventory Report to Congress*. The purpose of the biennial reports is to inform both Congress and the public about water quality in the United States. The *National Water Quality Inventory* reports characterize water quality, identify water quality problems of national significance, and describe programs implemented to restore and protect the nation's water.

In *Water Quality: Key EPA and State Decisions Limited by Inconsistent and Incomplete Data* (March 2000, http://www.gao.gov/new.items/rc00054.pdf), the U.S. General Accounting Office (GAO; now the U.S. Government Accountability Office) states that "the *National Water Quality Inventory* does not accurately portray water quality conditions nationwide." The GAO notes that states collectively assessed only a small percentage of waters and that monitoring assessments and the interpretation of assessment results varied across states. Thus, the GAO indicates that "the information in the *Inventory* cannot be meaningfully compared across states." In addition, the data collected by the states were often insufficient to enable them to pinpoint and clean up their water quality problems.

As a result, the EPA, states, tribes, and other federal agencies began collaborating on a new process to monitor the nation's waterways. Following the publication of *2000 National Water Quality Inventory* (August 2002, http://www.epa.gov/305b/2000report/), the EPA entered a transition period in the gathering and analysis of water quality data in nationally consistent, statistically valid assessment reports. Its new reporting schedule is discussed in "Schedule for Statistically Valid Surveys of the Nation's Waters" (December 5, 2005, http://www.epa.gov/owow/monitoring/guide.pdf).

As of mid-2009, the reports available that were developed under the new process were:

- *National Coastal Condition Report II (2005)* (December 2004, http://www.epa.gov/owow/oceans/nccr/2005/downloads.html) and *National Coastal Condition Report III* (December 2008, http://www.epa.gov/owow/oceans/nccr3/pdf/nccr3_entire.pdf)

- *National Estuary Program Coastal Condition Report* (June 2007, http://www.epa.gov/owow/oceans/nepccr/pdf/nepccr_natchap.pdf)

- *National Water Quality Inventory: Report to Congress, 2004 Reporting Cycle* (January 2009, http://www.epa.gov/owow/305b/2004report/report2004pt1.pdf)

- *The Wadeable Streams Assessment: A Collaborative Survey of the Nation's Streams* (December 2006, http://www.epa.gov/owow/streamsurvey/pdf/WSA_Assessment_May2007.pdf)

In "An Introduction to Water Quality Monitoring" (March 21, 2007, http://www.epa.gov/owow/monitoring/monintr.html), the EPA reports that the five major purposes for water quality assessment and monitoring are to:

- Characterize waters and identify changes or trends in water quality over time;

- Identify specific existing or emerging water quality problems;

- Gather information to design specific pollution prevention or remediation programs;

- Determine whether program goals—such as compliance with pollution regulations or implementation of effective pollution control actions—are being met; and

- Respond to emergencies, such as spills and floods.

Agriculture Takes up the Challenge

According to the U.S. Department of Agriculture (USDA), in *2007 Census of Agriculture* (February 2009, http://www.agcensus.usda.gov/Publications/2007/Full_Report/usv1.pdf), 922.1 million acres (373.2 million ha) in the United States were used for agricultural production in 2007. Cropland accounted for 44.1% of the agricultural acreage (406 million acres [164.5 million ha]), and permanent pasture and range land made up 44.3% (409 million acres [165.4 million ha]). The rest included woodlands and land used for buildings.

Agricultural land use is recognized in many jurisdictions and localities throughout the United States as the most desirable land use for economic, environmental, and social reasons. At the same time, the public and the agricultural community recognize that agricultural practices are a source of nonpoint pollution nationwide. (Nonpoint source pollutants enter bodies of water over large areas rather than at single points. Nonpoint sources of water pollution include agricultural runoff and soil erosion.) This situation presents a challenge to water quality management efforts.

The agricultural community shares in the growing national concern over water quality degradation. There has been a steady increase in the use of best management practices and implementation of farm water quality plans to protect wetlands and water bodies. The success of this effort can be seen in the decrease in soil erosion of U.S. cropland between 1982 and 2003. (See Figure 3.1.) In 1982 a total of 3.1 billion tons (2.8 billion t) of cropland eroded from the nation's agricultural areas. By 2003 this figure had dropped to 1.8 billion tons (1.6 billion t), a 42% decrease. The USDA, with state and local agencies, is providing technical assistance and financial incentives through many programs to help farmers balance good stewardship of natural resources with market demands. Technical assistance through these programs has had success in getting farmers to voluntarily adopt more environmentally sensitive practices.

ASSESSING THE WATER QUALITY OF WADEABLE STREAMS

What Are Wadeable Streams?

Wadeable streams are exactly what their name suggests: flowing bodies of water in which people can walk throughout. Researchers can perform tests and take samples of water in wadeable streams without a boat. The EPA notes in *Wadeable Streams Assessment* that approximately 90% of stream and river miles in the United States are wadeable streams. Thus, an assessment of the

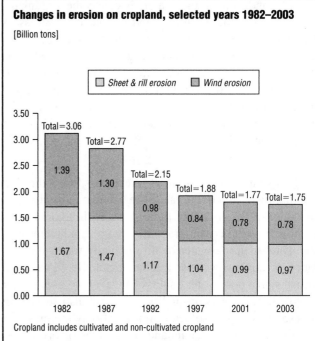

FIGURE 3.1

Changes in erosion on cropland, selected years 1982–2003

[Billion tons]

Cropland includes cultivated and non-cultivated cropland

SOURCE: "Erosion on Cropland by Year," in *National Resources Inventory 2003 Annual NRI*, U.S. Department of Agriculture, Natural Resources Conservation Service, May 2006, http://www.nrcs.usda.gov/technical/NRI/2003/nri03eros-mrb.html (accessed March 11, 2009). Surveys were done in cooperation with Iowa State University's Center for Survey Statistics and Methodology.

water quality of the nation's wadeable streams is an excellent indicator of the water quality of much of the flowing freshwater in the country.

Wadeable Streams Assessment covers streams within the lower 48 states. Wadeable stream assessments in Alaska, Hawaii, Puerto Rico, and Guam are not included in the 2006 report, but will be included in future reports. The EPA reports on the water quality of wadeable streams nationally and by dividing the nation into three regions: the West, the Plains and Lowlands, and the Eastern Highlands. The West includes mountainous and dry regions; the Plains and Lowlands include low-elevation areas of the East and Southeast and the plains areas (vast grassland regions); and the Eastern Highlands are the mountainous regions east of the Mississippi River. The sampling areas were selected using techniques that provided a random sample having the full range of variation of the wadeable streams of the United States.

Indicators of the Biological Health of Freshwater Streams

To determine the biological health of freshwater streams, EPA researchers examine the biological condition of the aquatic macroinvertebrates living there. Aquatic macroinvertebrates are animals without backbones that live in water and can be seen with the naked eye, such as certain fly larvae, worms, and beetles. The number and types of the aquatic macroinvertebrates living in a stream reflect the biological condition of the water, because the organisms are exposed to the pollutants and various other stressors in the water. Certain species of macroinvertebrates can survive only in freshwater of good quality, whereas others can survive in good-, fair-, or poor-quality water. Fish live on the macroinvertebrates in a stream, so the presence of certain species of fish reflects not only the conditions in which certain fish species survive but also the presence of certain types of aquatic macroinvertebrates on which they typically feed.

In a simplified example, if researchers find a thriving community of mayfly larvae, riffle beetles, and trout, then the water quality is likely to be good. If these organisms are absent and crayfish, dragonfly nymph, and clams predominate, then the water quality is likely fair. An abundance of aquatic worms, leeches, black fly larvae, and catfish signal poor water quality. However, organisms that survive in fair- or poor-quality water can also survive in good-quality water, so determining not only the presence but also the relative abundance of species of organisms inhabiting the stream sample area is important.

Factors Responsible for Diminished Water Quality

For the 2006 *Wadeable Streams Assessment*, EPA researchers also measured factors responsible for diminished water quality, which are called aquatic indicators of stress, stressor indicators, or, simply, stressors. Some stressors are naturally occurring, and some are the result of human activity. The EPA explains that "most physical stressors are created when we modify the physical habitat of a stream or its watershed, such as through extensive urban or agricultural development, excessive upland or bank erosion, or loss of streamside trees and vegetation. Examples of chemical stressors include toxic compounds (e.g., heavy metals, pesticides), excess nutrients (e.g., nitrogen and phosphorus), or acidity from acidic deposition or mine drainage. Biological stressors are characteristics of the biota that can influence biological integrity, such as the proliferation of non-native or invasive species (either in the streams and rivers, or in the riparian areas adjacent to these waterbodies)."

Water of good quality has low levels of pollutants and other stressors, and a high level of dissolved oxygen. Fair water quality has a higher level of pollutants and other stressors than good-quality water, and a lower level of dissolved oxygen. Poor water quality has even higher levels of pollutants and other stressors, and even lower levels of dissolved oxygen.

The USDA reports in the press release "Agriculture Secretary Vilsack Announces $84.8 Million for Vital Watershed Projects" (April 16, 2009, http://www.usda.gov/wps/portal/!ut/p/_s.7_0_A/7_0_1OB?contentidonly=true&contentid=2009/04/0110.xml) that as part of the Obama administration's American Recovery and Reinvestment Act of 2009, $84.8 million was committed to state and local governments in 2009 to help improve water quality. Rural watersheds were targeted, which emphasized the importance of the physical habitats of streams and their watersheds in water quality.

WATER QUALITY OF THE NATION'S STREAMS

An overall look at the water quality of U.S. rivers and streams in 2004 is shown in Figure 3.2. This report assesses not only wadeable streams but also deeper rivers and streams. Figure 3.2 is from the EPA report *National Water Quality Inventory: Report to Congress, 2004 Reporting Cycle*. This report shows that in 2004, 53% of assessed river and stream miles were in good condition and 44% were impaired.

Wadeable Streams Assessment rates the condition of wadeable streams by section of the country in 2004. According to this report, wadeable streams in the West had the best water quality, with 45.1% in good condition, whereas 29% of the wadeable streams in the Plains and Lowlands and 18.2% of those in the Eastern Highlands were in good condition. Overall, this report rates only 28.2% of the wadeable streams in the coterminous (lower 48) states of the United States as in good condition.

The EPA notes that the water quality of the wadeable streams in the Eastern Highlands was of the greatest concern. Not only were a mere 18.2% in good condition but also over half (51.8%) were in poor condition. This compares to 40% in poor condition in the Plains and Lowlands and 27.4% in poor condition in the West. Overall, 41.9% of the nation's wadeable streams were in poor condition.

Macroinvertebrate Index of Biotic Condition

The Macroinvertebrate Index of Biotic Condition is a statistical measure that provides a total score based on six characteristics of the macroinvertebrates found in a particular water sample. This total score is one indicator of water quality. Researchers determine which species of macroinvertebrates are present in a particular water sample; the proportion of each; the level of diversity of species within the sample (a high-quality water has a high level of diversity); and the feeding habits, habitats, and pollution tolerance of the species present. Each of these characteristics is an indicator of water quality, and together they provide a snapshot of the macroinvertebrate "naturalness" in the portion of the stream tested. The researchers then use this total score, factor in the stream length represented by the study site, and use the data from all the study sites to compile the Macroinvertebrate Index ratings for the stream miles of a region and for the nation.

FIGURE 3.2

Water quality in rivers and streams, 2004

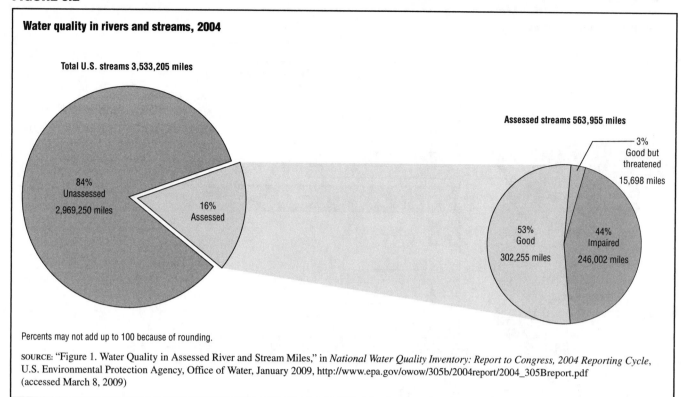

Percents may not add up to 100 because of rounding.

SOURCE: "Figure 1. Water Quality in Assessed River and Stream Miles," in *National Water Quality Inventory: Report to Congress, 2004 Reporting Cycle*, U.S. Environmental Protection Agency, Office of Water, January 2009, http://www.epa.gov/owow/305b/2004report/2004_305Breport.pdf (accessed March 8, 2009)

Figure 3.3 shows the Macroinvertebrate Index of Biotic Condition for the coterminous states as well as for the Eastern Highlands, the Plains and Lowlands, and the West in 2004. Nationally, of the total miles of wadeable streams, 28.2% was in good condition in terms of macroinvertebrate life, 24.9% was in fair condition, and 41.9% was in poor condition. The Eastern Highlands had the most stream length in poor condition: 51.8%. The West had the most stream length in good condition: 45.1%.

Chemical Stressors

Four chemical stressors were assessed for the 2006 *Wadeable Streams Assessment*: phosphorus, nitrogen, salinity, and acidification. The levels of these stressors in the samples were compared with data from a set of "least disturbed" reference sites in each region to develop regional thresholds for all indicators.

PHOSPHORUS AND NITROGEN. Phosphorus and nitrogen are plant nutrients. When phosphorus and nitrogen enter bodies of water—usually as runoff from fertilized land, leaking septic systems, or sewage discharges—they promote aquatic plant and algal growth. Plant and algal growth can become excessive, a process called eutrophication. This excessive growth can result in waters clogged with plants and algae, which can look unsightly, slow water flow, and interfere with swimming and fishing. Mats of algae can grow on the surface of the water, blocking light to the plants below. When these plants die, bacteria degrade them, using oxygen in the process and

diminishing the concentration of oxygen in the water available for aquatic macroinvertebrates and fish. With lowered dissolved oxygen in the water, many fish and invertebrates die, worsening the situation.

Phosphorus is a common component of fertilizers and was routinely found in laundry detergents until the industry removed phosphates from its products in 1994. However, phosphates are still found in dishwashing detergents and in some cleaners. These phosphates wash down the drain during or after use and enter either septic systems or sewage treatment plants. From there, the phosphates can end up in bodies of water as they leach into the ground from septic systems or are discharged into streams with treated wastewater from sewage treatment plants. Agricultural runoff containing phosphate fertilizers is also a common source of added phosphates in bodies of water. In *Wadeable Streams Assessment*, the EPA indicates that "high phosphorus concentrations in streams may be associated with poor agricultural practices, urban runoff, or point-source discharges (e.g., effluents from sewage treatment plants)."

Figure 3.4 shows the percent of stream miles with low, medium, and high levels of phosphorus compared to regional references in 2004. "Low" means the concentrations were most similar to the reference (most natural) condition. "Medium" and "high" had statistical bases, but they can be thought of as above the regional reference (medium) and much above the regional reference (high). Nationally, nearly one-third (30.9%) of all stream miles

FIGURE 3.3

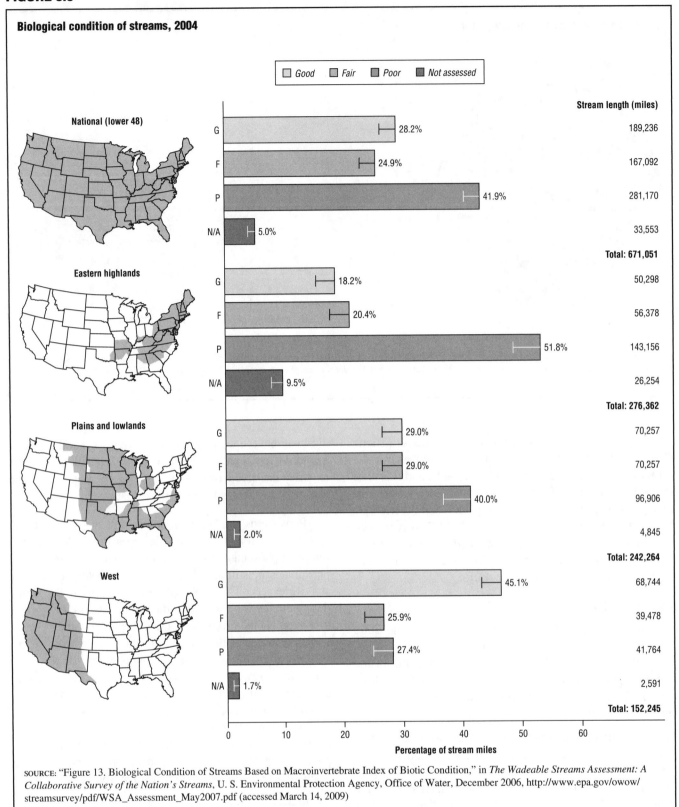

Biological condition of streams, 2004

☐ *Good* ☐ *Fair* ☐ *Poor* ■ *Not assessed*

	Stream length (miles)
National (lower 48)	
G 28.2%	189,236
F 24.9%	167,092
P 41.9%	281,170
N/A 5.0%	33,553
	Total: 671,051
Eastern highlands	
G 18.2%	50,298
F 20.4%	56,378
P 51.8%	143,156
N/A 9.5%	26,254
	Total: 276,362
Plains and lowlands	
G 29.0%	70,257
F 29.0%	70,257
P 40.0%	96,906
N/A 2.0%	4,845
	Total: 242,264
West	
G 45.1%	68,744
F 25.9%	39,478
P 27.4%	41,764
N/A 1.7%	2,591
	Total: 152,245

Percentage of stream miles

SOURCE: "Figure 13. Biological Condition of Streams Based on Macroinvertebrate Index of Biotic Condition," in *The Wadeable Streams Assessment: A Collaborative Survey of the Nation's Streams*, U. S. Environmental Protection Agency, Office of Water, December 2006, http://www.epa.gov/owow/streamsurvey/pdf/WSA_Assessment_May2007.pdf (accessed March 14, 2009)

had high levels of total phosphorus. However, nearly half (48.8%) of all stream miles had low levels of this chemical stressor.

Regionally, the highest percentage of stream miles with high levels of phosphorus was in the Eastern High-lands, where 42.6% of all stream miles had high levels of the chemical. (See Figure 3.4.) The Plains and Lowlands had 24.9% of its stream miles high in phosphorus, whereas the West had the least number of stream miles with high levels of this chemical stressor: 18.5%.

FIGURE 3.4

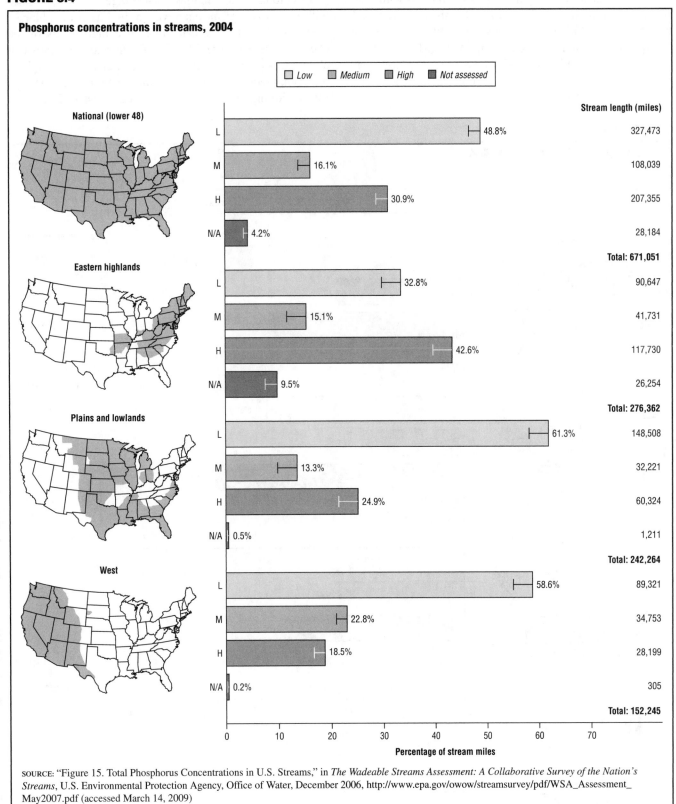

Phosphorus concentrations in streams, 2004

☐ Low ▨ Medium ▨ High ■ Not assessed

		Stream length (miles)
National (lower 48)		
L	48.8%	327,473
M	16.1%	108,039
H	30.9%	207,355
N/A	4.2%	28,184
		Total: 671,051
Eastern highlands		
L	32.8%	90,647
M	15.1%	41,731
H	42.6%	117,730
N/A	9.5%	26,254
		Total: 276,362
Plains and lowlands		
L	61.3%	148,508
M	13.3%	32,221
H	24.9%	60,324
N/A	0.5%	1,211
		Total: 242,264
West		
L	58.6%	89,321
M	22.8%	34,753
H	18.5%	28,199
N/A	0.2%	305
		Total: 152,245

Percentage of stream miles

SOURCE: "Figure 15. Total Phosphorus Concentrations in U.S. Streams," in *The Wadeable Streams Assessment: A Collaborative Survey of the Nation's Streams*, U.S. Environmental Protection Agency, Office of Water, December 2006, http://www.epa.gov/owow/streamsurvey/pdf/WSA_Assessment_May2007.pdf (accessed March 14, 2009)

Nitrogen is another plant nutrient, as noted previously. It finds its way into streams primarily from agricultural runoff (it is found in fertilizer), wastewater and animal waste (it is a waste product from the digestion of protein), and atmospheric deposition (it is released into the air when fossil fuels, such as gasoline and coal, are burned). Nitrogen is particularly important as a contributor to the rapid, excessive growth of algae along coastal waters and in estuaries, where freshwater meets the saltwater of the ocean.

Figure 3.5 shows the percent of stream miles with low, medium, and high levels of nitrogen compared to regional references in 2004. The statistics are similar to those for phosphorus. Nationally, nearly one-third (31.8%) of all stream miles had high levels of total nitrogen. However, close to half (43.3%) of all stream miles had low levels of this chemical stressor.

Regionally, the highest percentage of stream miles with high levels of nitrogen was in the Eastern Highlands, where 42.4% of all stream miles had high levels of the chemical. (See Figure 3.5.) The Plains and Lowlands had about one-quarter (27.1%) of their stream miles high in nitrogen, whereas the West had the least number of stream miles with high levels of this chemical stressor: 20.5%.

FIGURE 3.5

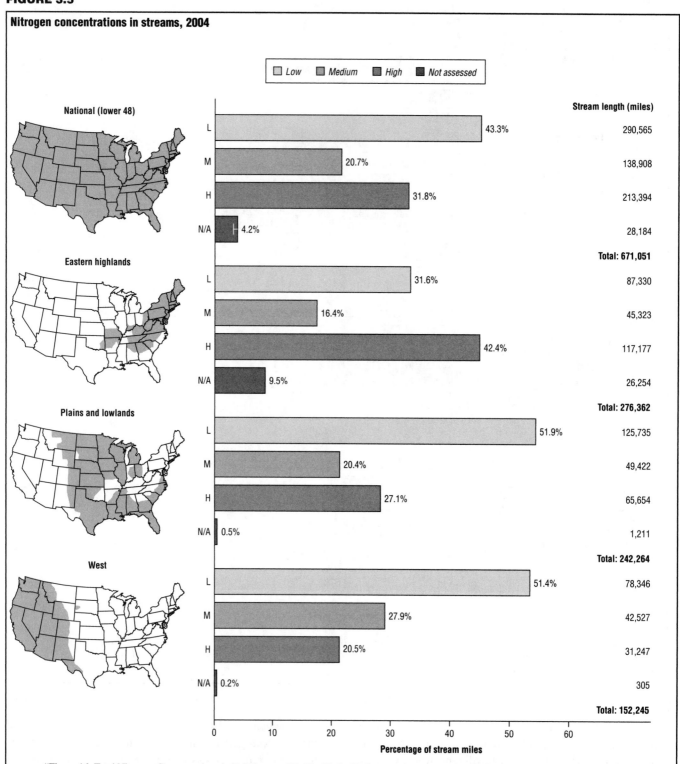

Nitrogen concentrations in streams, 2004

SOURCE: "Figure 16. Total Nitrogen Concentrations in U.S. Streams," in *The Wadeable Streams Assessment: A Collaborative Survey of the Nation's Streams*, U.S. Environmental Protection Agency, Office of Water, December 2006, http://www.epa.gov/owow/streamsurvey/pdf/WSA_Assessment_May2007.pdf (accessed March 11, 2009)

SALINITY. Excessive salinity in freshwater streams generally occurs because water is lost from the stream, not because excessive salts enter the stream. This happens when the evaporation rate of stream water is high. Already high salinity from evaporation can be made higher by repeated water withdrawals for irrigation or other purposes.

Figure 3.6 shows the percent of stream miles with low, medium, and high levels of salinity compared to

FIGURE 3.6

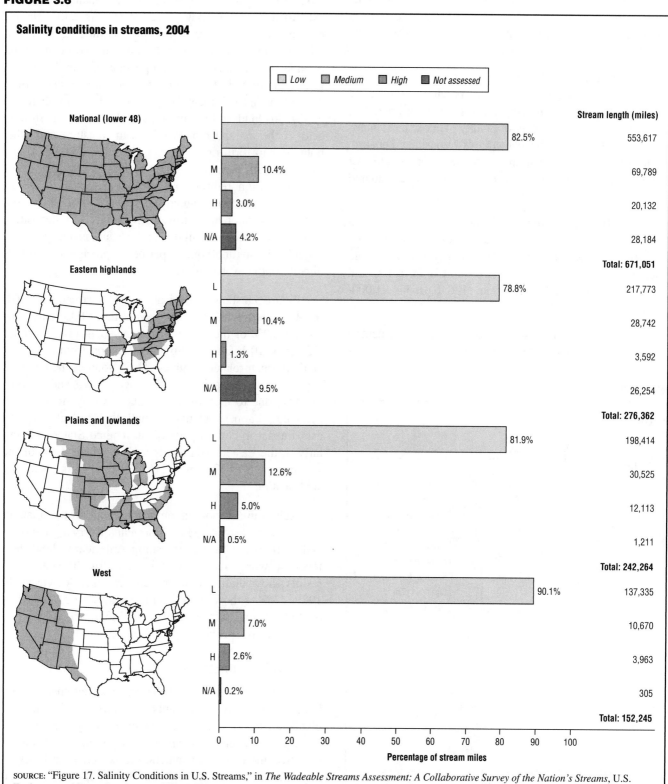

Salinity conditions in streams, 2004

SOURCE: "Figure 17. Salinity Conditions in U.S. Streams," in *The Wadeable Streams Assessment: A Collaborative Survey of the Nation's Streams*, U.S. Environmental Protection Agency, Office of Water, December 2006, http://www.epa.gov/owow/streamsurvey/pdf/WSA_Assessment_May2007.pdf (accessed March 11, 2009)

regional references in 2004. Nationally, 3% of all stream miles had high salinity conditions, whereas 82.5% had low salinity conditions.

Regionally, the highest percentage of stream miles with high salinity conditions was in the Plains and Lowlands, where 5% of all stream miles had high levels of salts. (See Figure 3.6.) The West had only 2.6% of its stream miles experiencing high salinity, and the Eastern Highlands had the least number of stream miles with high levels of this chemical stressor: 1.3%.

ACIDIFICATION. Stream acidification means that the water has become more acidic than is natural. Figure 3.7 shows that the pH of a healthy lake (or stream) is about 6.5. The pH scale shows levels of acidity. This scale is numbered from 0 to 14, with a pH value of 7 considered neutral. Values higher than seven are considered more alkaline or basic; values that are lower than seven are considered acidic. Pure, distilled water has a pH level of seven.

The pH scale is a logarithmic measure. This means that every pH drop of 1 is a 10-fold increase in acid content. Therefore, a decrease from pH 6 to pH 5 is a 10-fold increase in acidity; a drop from pH 6 to pH 4 is a 100-fold increase in acidity; and a drop from pH 6 to pH 3 is a 1,000-fold increase.

"Clean" rainfall has a pH of 5.6. It is not neutral because it is not pure water; it accumulates naturally occur-

ring sulfur oxides and nitrogen oxides as it passes through the atmosphere. In comparison, acid rain (or acid deposition) has a pH of about 4.2 to 4.4. The introduction of large volumes of acid deposition can eventually increase the acidity of a body of water by as much as a 100-fold.

One of the main components of acid deposition is sulfur dioxide from the burning of fossil fuels, mainly from auto exhaust and coal-burning power plants. As sulfur dioxide reaches the atmosphere, it becomes sulfuric acid when it joins with hydrogen atoms in the air. Nitric oxide and nitric dioxide are the other major components of acid deposition. Like sulfur dioxide, these nitrogen oxides are produced from the burning of fossil fuels. They rise into the atmosphere and oxidize in clouds to form nitric acid. Nitric acid and sulfuric acid in the air and clouds mix with moisture and other pollutants to form dry (aerosols, particles, and gases) and wet (fog, hail, rain, sleet, snow, and dew) acid deposition. Wet deposition returns to Earth as precipitation, which enters the water body directly, percolates through the soil, or becomes runoff to nearby water bodies. Dry deposition builds up over time on all dry surfaces and is transported to water bodies in runoff during periods of precipitation or falls directly onto a water surface.

Figure 3.8 shows acidification in U.S. streams in 2004. In *Wadeable Streams Assessment*, the EPA states that "about 2.2% of the nation's stream length (14,763 miles [23,759 km]) is impacted by acidification from anthropogenic [human-related] sources. These sources include acid deposition (0.7%), acid mine drainage (0.4%), and episodic [acidity] due to high-runoff events (1%). Although these percentages appear relatively small, they reflect a significant impact in certain parts of the United States, particularly in the Eastern Highlands region, where 3.4% of the stream length (9,396 miles [15,121 km]) is impacted by acidification."

Acid rain is not an environmental problem about which a high percentage of Americans worry a great deal. Gallup pollsters have been asking Americans about their level of worry regarding acid rain for 20 years, and results show that Americans' concern has decreased. In 1989, 41% of those polled said that they worried a great deal about acid rain; in 2008, only 23% worried a great deal about this problem. (See Table 3.4.)

Physical Habitat Stressors

Freshwater streams are the physical habitats (natural homes) for a variety of plants and animals. The physical characteristics of a stream can be changed by human activities, and those changes can be stressors for the organisms that live there. EPA researchers assessed four types of physical characteristics of wadeable streams: streambed sediments, in-stream fish habitat, riparian vegetative cover, and riparian disturbance.

FIGURE 3.7

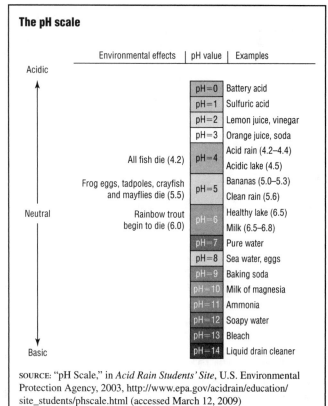

The pH scale

	Environmental effects	pH value	Examples
Acidic		pH=0	Battery acid
		pH=1	Sulfuric acid
		pH=2	Lemon juice, vinegar
		pH=3	Orange juice, soda
	All fish die (4.2)	pH=4	Acid rain (4.2–4.4) / Acidic lake (4.5)
	Frog eggs, tadpoles, crayfish and mayflies die (5.5)	pH=5	Bananas (5.0–5.3) / Clean rain (5.6)
Neutral	Rainbow trout begin to die (6.0)	pH=6	Healthy lake (6.5) / Milk (6.5–6.8)
		pH=7	Pure water
		pH=8	Sea water, eggs
		pH=9	Baking soda
		pH=10	Milk of magnesia
		pH=11	Ammonia
		pH=12	Soapy water
		pH=13	Bleach
Basic		pH=14	Liquid drain cleaner

SOURCE: "pH Scale," in *Acid Rain Students' Site*, U.S. Environmental Protection Agency, 2003, http://www.epa.gov/acidrain/education/site_students/phscale.html (accessed March 12, 2009)

FIGURE 3.8

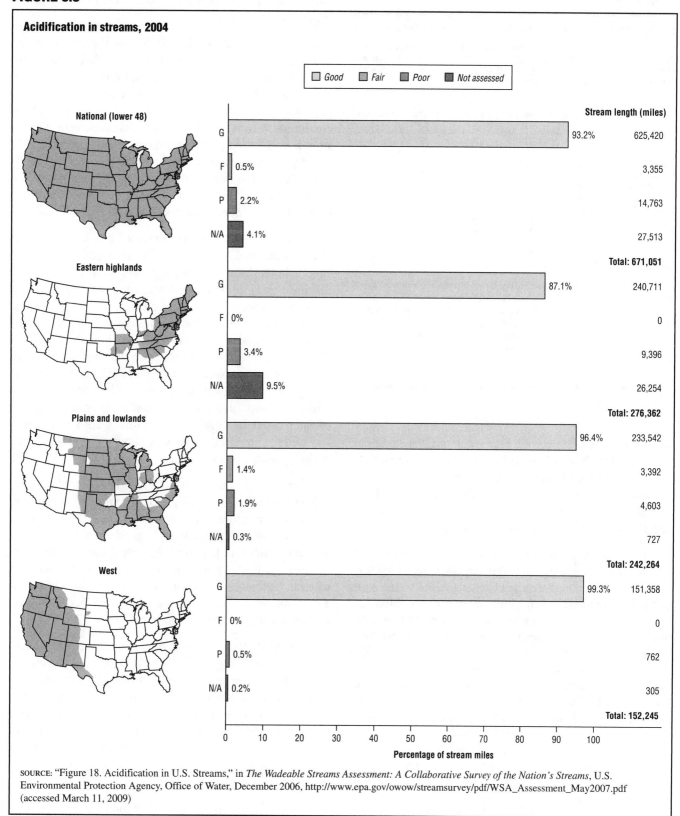

Acidification in streams, 2004

☐ *Good*   ☐ *Fair*   ■ *Poor*   ■ *Not assessed*

SOURCE: "Figure 18. Acidification in U.S. Streams," in *The Wadeable Streams Assessment: A Collaborative Survey of the Nation's Streams*, U.S. Environmental Protection Agency, Office of Water, December 2006, http://www.epa.gov/owow/streamsurvey/pdf/WSA_Assessment_May2007.pdf (accessed March 11, 2009)

STREAMBED SEDIMENTS. Water and sediments drain into streams as the result of a number of human-related activities, including agriculture, road building, construction, and the grazing of farm animals. The drainage of water and sediments into a stream can affect its size and shape. In addition, the size of the sediment particles can affect the streambed. If sediment particles are large, the stream may not be able to move them downstream, so they eventually accumulate in the streambed, changing habitats. If the particles are small but excessive, the stream may not

TABLE 3.4

Public concern about acid rain, selected years 1989–2008

I'M GOING TO READ YOU A LIST OF ENVIRONMENTAL PROBLEMS. AS I READ EACH ONE, PLEASE TELL ME IF YOU PERSONALLY WORRY ABOUT THIS PROBLEM A GREAT DEAL, A FAIR AMOUNT, ONLY A LITTLE, OR NOT AT ALL. FIRST, HOW MUCH DO YOU PERSONALLY WORRY ABOUT ACID RAIN?

	Great deal %	Fair amount %	Only a little %	Not at all %	No opinion %
2008 Mar 6–9	23	27	26	23	1
2007 Mar 11–14	25	25	28	20	1
2006 Mar 13–16	24	28	24	23	1
2004 Mar 8–11	20	26	27	26	1
2003 Mar 3–5	24	26	27	21	2
2002 Mar 4–7	25	23	31	19	2
2001 Mar 5–7	28	28	26	16	2
2000 Apr 3–9	34	31	19	15	1
1999 Apr 13–14	29	35	23	11	2
1991 Apr 11–14	34	30	20	14	3
1990 Apr 5–8	34	30	18	14	4
1989 May 4–7	41	27	19	11	3

SOURCE: "I'm Going to Read You a List of Environmental Problems. As I Read Each One, Please Tell Me If You Personally Worry about This Problem a Great Deal, a Fair Amount, Only a Little, or Not at All. First, How Much Do You Personally Worry about—Acid Rain?" in *Gallup's Pulse of Democracy: The Environment*, The Gallup Organization, 2009, http://www.gallup.com/poll/1615/Environment.aspx#1 (accessed March 23, 2009). Copyright © 2009 by The Gallup Organization. Reproduced by permission of The Gallup Organization.

be able to move them as well. Fine sediments that are left in the streambed can begin filling in the habitat spaces between stones and boulders on the stream bottom. Suspended fine sediments can block sunlight to aquatic plants and abrade the gills of fish. All these occurrences can negatively affect macroinvertebrates and fish.

The EPA notes in *Wadeable Streams Assessment* that "25% of the nation's stream length (167,092 miles [268,909 km]) has streambed sediment characteristics in poor condition compared to regional reference condition.... Streambed sediment characteristics are rated fair in 20% of the nation's stream length (132,197 miles [212,750 km]) and good in 50% of stream length (336,197 miles [541,057 km]) compared to reference condition. The two regions with the greatest percentage of stream length in poor condition for streambed sediment characteristics are the Eastern Highlands (28%, or 77,381 miles [124,533 km]) and the Plains and Lowlands (26.4%, or 63,958 miles [102,930 km]) regions, whereas the West region has the lowest percentage of stream length (17.4%, or 26,522 miles [42,683 km]) in poor condition for this indicator." (See Figure 3.9.)

IN-STREAM FISH HABITAT. Streams and rivers that have diverse and complex habitats support a diversity of fish and macroinvertebrates. Such habitats include undercut banks with exposed tree roots, brush and large pieces of wood within the stream, and boulders within the stream and at the stream bank. Cover from overhanging vegetation also affects stream habitats. When humans use streams, they often change these complex habitats to simpler ones,

which often results in a reduction in the diversity of the organisms living there.

Figure 3.10 shows that 19.5% of the stream miles across the nation had poor in-stream habitat conditions in 2004. About one-fourth (24.9%) had fair conditions, and about half (51.5%) had good conditions. The highest percentage of stream miles with poor in-stream habitat conditions was in the Plains and Lowlands, with 37% of stream miles rated poor. The West was next, with 12.3% of stream miles rated poor, and the Eastern Highlands had only 8.2% of stream miles rated poor. Regardless, the West had the greatest number of stream miles with in-stream habitats rated good: 66.4%.

RIPARIAN VEGETATIVE COVER. The term *riparian* refers to the banks of a body of water, such as a river or stream. In *Wadeable Streams Assessment*, the EPA explains that the term *riparian vegetative cover* refers to the amount and type of vegetation growing on or next to stream banks; it is an indicator of the health of a stream. Complex, multi-layered riparian vegetation helps maintain the health of the stream by reducing runoff from the surrounding land, preventing stream bank erosion, supplying shade, and providing food and habitats in the form of leaf litter and large wood. As with in-stream habitats, riparian coverage is often changed, or simplified, by humans. EPA researchers assessed the ground layer, woody shrubs, and canopy trees of the riparian cover of streams.

Figure 3.11 shows that in 2004, 19.3% of the wadeable stream miles nationally were in poor condition "due to severely simplified riparian vegetation," 28.3% were in fair condition, and 47.6% were in good condition. Regionally, the Plains and Lowlands had the greatest percentage of stream miles in poor condition (26%) with respect to riparian coverage. The Eastern Highlands followed with 17.6% in poor condition, and the West had the least number of stream miles in poor condition: 12.2%.

RIPARIAN DISTURBANCE. As mentioned earlier, human activities can change or disturb the riparian vegetative cover. The closer potentially disturbing human activities take place to the stream bank, the more likely they are to cause riparian disturbance. To determine riparian human disturbance, EPA researchers tallied 11 forms of human activities and disturbances along sections of streams and weighted them according to how close they were to the streams.

Figure 3.12 shows that in 2004, nationally one-fourth (25.5%) of stream length had high riparian disturbance when compared to reference sites. Nearly half (46.8%) had fair riparian disturbance, and one-fourth (23.6%) had low riparian disturbance. The EPA notes in *Wadeable Streams Assessment* that "one of the striking findings [was] the widespread distribution of intermediate levels of riparian disturbance," both nationally and regionally.

FIGURE 3.9

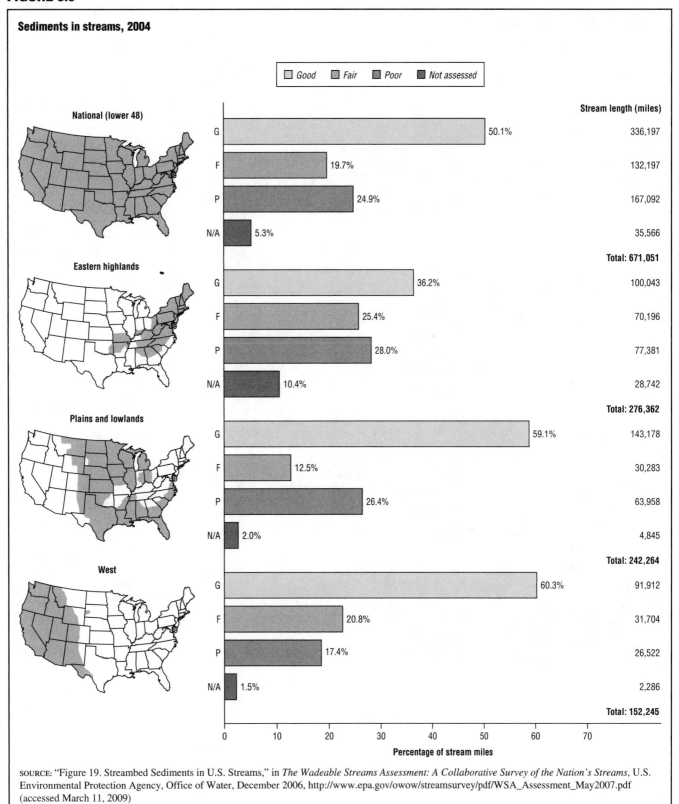

Sediments in streams, 2004

Legend: ☐ Good ▨ Fair ▨ Poor ■ Not assessed

National (lower 48)

Stream length (miles)

G	50.1%	336,197
F	19.7%	132,197
P	24.9%	167,092
N/A	5.3%	35,566

Total: 671,051

Eastern highlands

G	36.2%	100,043
F	25.4%	70,196
P	28.0%	77,381
N/A	10.4%	28,742

Total: 276,362

Plains and lowlands

G	59.1%	143,178
F	12.5%	30,283
P	26.4%	63,958
N/A	2.0%	4,845

Total: 242,264

West

G	60.3%	91,912
F	20.8%	31,704
P	17.4%	26,522
N/A	1.5%	2,286

Total: 152,245

Percentage of stream miles

SOURCE: "Figure 19. Streambed Sediments in U.S. Streams," in *The Wadeable Streams Assessment: A Collaborative Survey of the Nation's Streams*, U.S. Environmental Protection Agency, Office of Water, December 2006, http://www.epa.gov/owow/streamsurvey/pdf/WSA_Assessment_May2007.pdf (accessed March 11, 2009)

Furthermore, the EPA states, "It is worth noting that for the nation and the three regions, the amount of stream length with good riparian vegetative cover was significantly greater than the amount of stream length with low levels of human disturbance in the riparian zone. This finding warrants additional investigation, but suggests that land managers and property owners are protecting and maintaining healthy riparian vegetation buffers, even along streams where disturbance from roads, agriculture, and grazing is widespread."

FIGURE 3.10

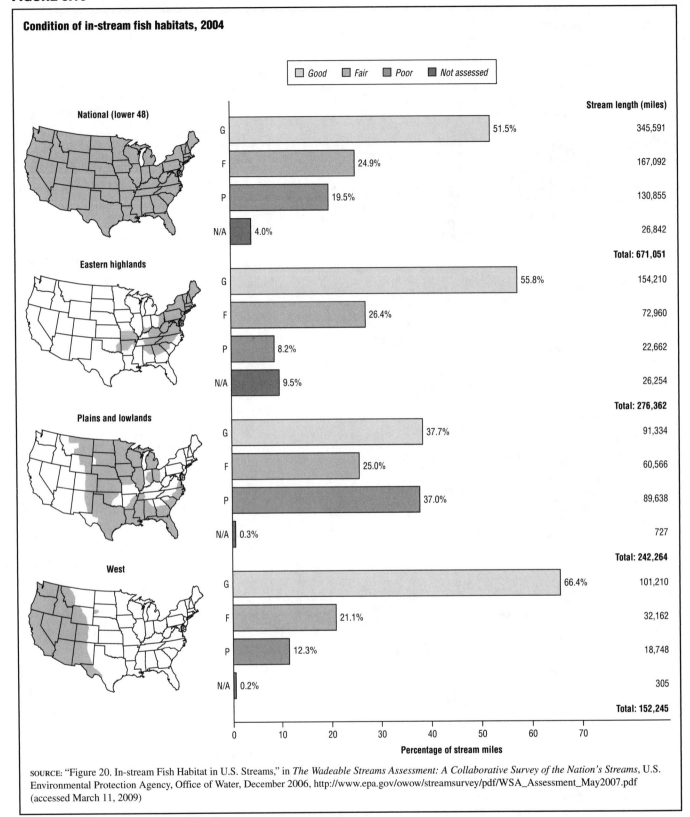

Condition of in-stream fish habitats, 2004

Good   Fair   Poor   Not assessed

SOURCE: "Figure 20. In-stream Fish Habitat in U.S. Streams," in *The Wadeable Streams Assessment: A Collaborative Survey of the Nation's Streams*, U.S. Environmental Protection Agency, Office of Water, December 2006, http://www.epa.gov/owow/streamsurvey/pdf/WSA_Assessment_May2007.pdf (accessed March 11, 2009)

Relative Extent and Relative Risk of Stressors

Figure 3.13 is a summary of the stressors described previously in this chapter and shows what percentage of stream length nationally each stressor affects and

what its relationship is to the other stressors. Each stressor is ranked according to the proportion of stream length that was in poor condition nationally and regionally.

FIGURE 3.11

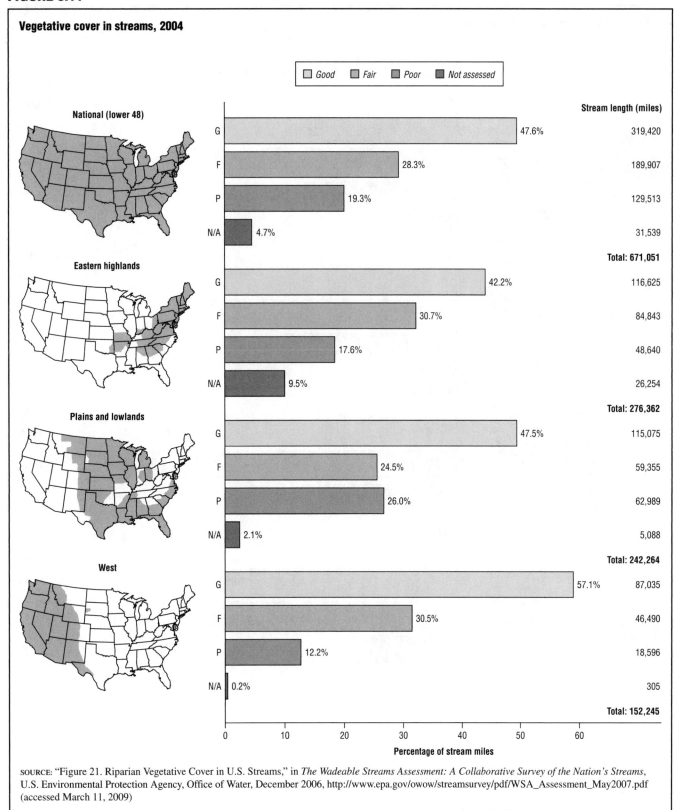

Vegetative cover in streams, 2004

Legend: ☐ Good ☐ Fair ■ Poor ■ Not assessed

National (lower 48)

Stream length (miles)

G	47.6%	319,420
F	28.3%	189,907
P	19.3%	129,513
N/A	4.7%	31,539

Total: 671,051

Eastern highlands

G	42.2%	116,625
F	30.7%	84,843
P	17.6%	48,640
N/A	9.5%	26,254

Total: 276,362

Plains and lowlands

G	47.5%	115,075
F	24.5%	59,355
P	26.0%	62,989
N/A	2.1%	5,088

Total: 242,264

West

G	57.1%	87,035
F	30.5%	46,490
P	12.2%	18,596
N/A	0.2%	305

Total: 152,245

Percentage of stream miles

SOURCE: "Figure 21. Riparian Vegetative Cover in U.S. Streams," in *The Wadeable Streams Assessment: A Collaborative Survey of the Nation's Streams*, U.S. Environmental Protection Agency, Office of Water, December 2006, http://www.epa.gov/owow/streamsurvey/pdf/WSA_Assessment_May2007.pdf (accessed March 11, 2009)

Nationally, excessive nitrogen levels affected the greatest percentage of stream miles at 31.8%. Phosphorus, the other plant nutrient assessed, was a close second, affecting 30.9% of stream miles nationally. Excess salinity and acidification affected the least percentage of stream miles, 2.9% and 2.2%, respectively.

FIGURE 3.12

Extent of streambank (riparian) disturbance, 2004

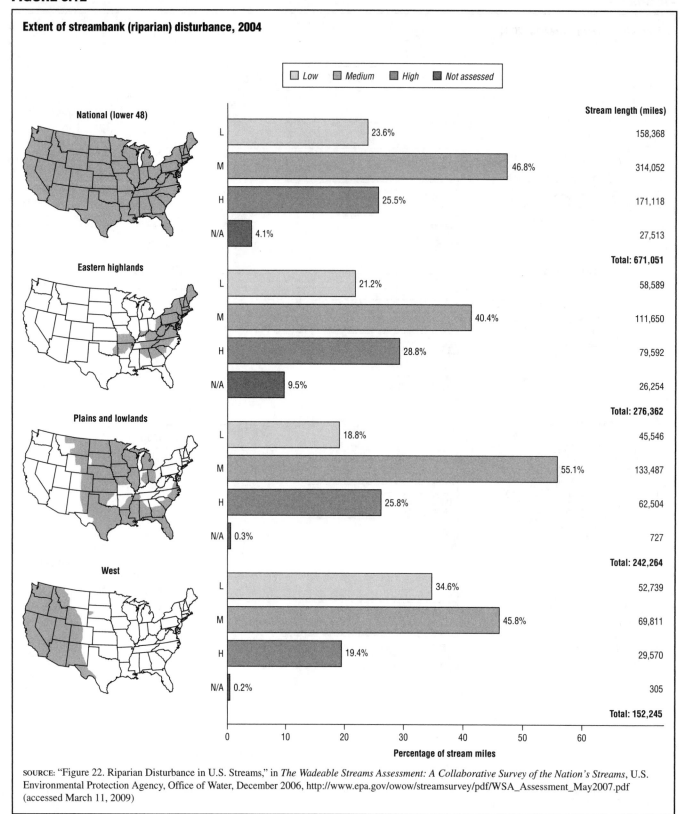

SOURCE: "Figure 22. Riparian Disturbance in U.S. Streams," in *The Wadeable Streams Assessment: A Collaborative Survey of the Nation's Streams*, U.S. Environmental Protection Agency, Office of Water, December 2006, http://www.epa.gov/owow/streamsurvey/pdf/WSA_Assessment_May2007.pdf (accessed March 11, 2009)

Regionally, nitrogen and phosphorus levels affected the greatest percentage of stream miles in the Eastern Highlands, whereas poor in-stream fish habitat was problematic for the greatest percentage of stream miles in the Plains and Lowlands. In the West, nitrogen and riparian disturbance affected the greatest percentage of stream miles. Excess salinity and acidification affected the least percentage of stream miles in each region.

FIGURE 3.13

Proportion of stream length ranked in poorest category for each stressor, 2004

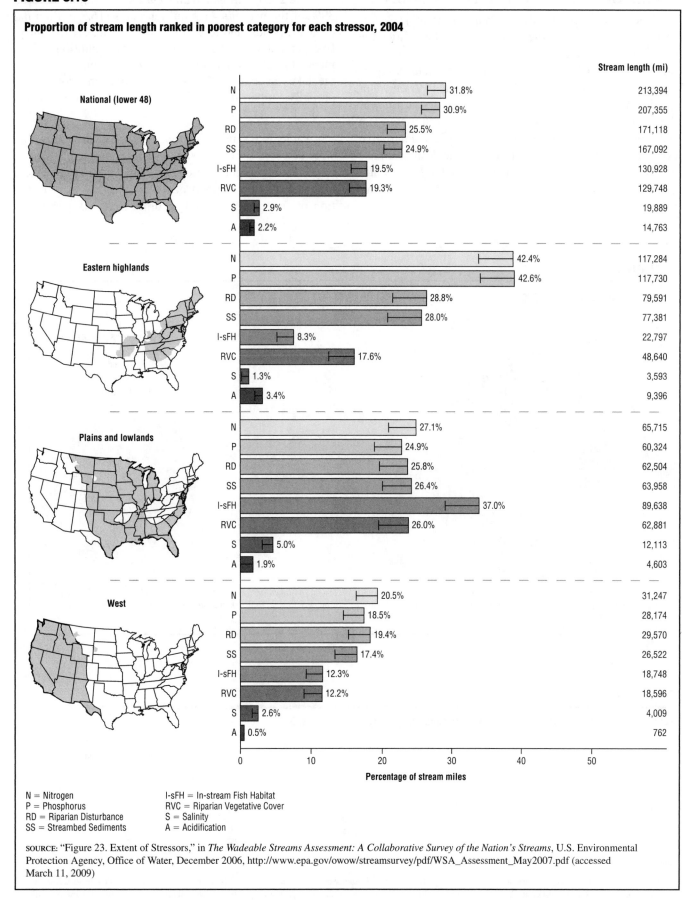

N = Nitrogen
P = Phosphorus
RD = Riparian Disturbance
SS = Streambed Sediments

I-sFH = In-stream Fish Habitat
RVC = Riparian Vegetative Cover
S = Salinity
A = Acidification

SOURCE: "Figure 23. Extent of Stressors," in *The Wadeable Streams Assessment: A Collaborative Survey of the Nation's Streams*, U.S. Environmental Protection Agency, Office of Water, December 2006, http://www.epa.gov/owow/streamsurvey/pdf/WSA_Assessment_May2007.pdf (accessed March 11, 2009)

WATER QUALITY OF THE NATION'S LAKES

The EPA's *National Water Quality Inventory: Report to Congress, 2004 Reporting Cycle* is stylized after the older EPA water quality reports, which were set up quite differently from *Wadeable Streams Assessment*, a report typical of the new reports published by the EPA on water quality. In *National Water Quality Inventory*, a use was designated for surface water bodies in each state. The state then established water quality numeric and narrative criteria to protect each use. More than one designated use was frequently assigned to a water body. Most water bodies were designated for recreation, drinking water use, and protection of aquatic life.

The 2004 *National Water Quality Inventory* assessed 39% of the nation's 41.7 million acres (16.9 million ha) of lakes, ponds, and reservoirs. (See Figure 3.14.) Thirty-five percent were found to be in good condition, which means that they fully supported their designated uses. Of the lakes assessed, 64% were impaired and could only partially support their designated uses. An additional 1% of the lake acres were threatened.

Table 3.5 shows the top-five designated uses that were assessed for the 2004 *National Water Quality Inventory*. Twenty-eight percent of total lake acres were assessed for their support of the protection and propagation of fish, shellfish, and wildlife. Sixty-six percent of

FIGURE 3.14

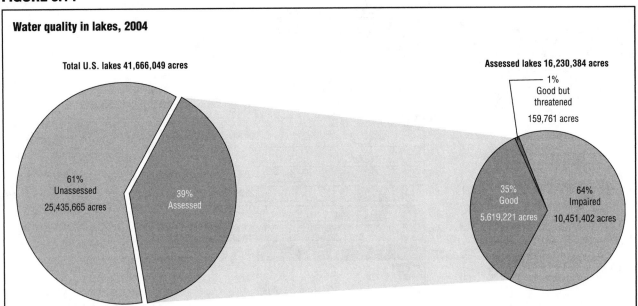

Water quality in lakes, 2004

SOURCE: "Figure 4. Water Quality in Assessed Lakes Acres," in *National Water Quality Inventory: Report to Congress, 2004 Reporting Cycle*, U.S. Environmental Protection Agency, Office of Water, January 2009, http://www.epa.gov/owow/305b/2004report/2004_305Breport.pdf (accessed March 8, 2009)

TABLE 3.5

Percentage of lake, reservoir, and pond waters supporting designated uses, 2004

Designated use	Acres assessed	Percentage of total U.S. lake acres	Percentage of waters assessed		
			Good	Threatened	Impaired
Fish, shellfish, and wildlife protection/propagation	11,770,370	28%	66%	4%	30%
Aquatic life harvesting	9,390,396	23%	26%	1%	73%
Recreation	8,069,018	19%	70%	4%	26%
Public water supply	6,427,687	15%	78%	1%	20%
Industrial	2,848,335	7%	82%	<1%	17%

Note: Waterbodies can have multiple designated uses, resulting in an overlap of acres assessed.

SOURCE: "Table 4. Individual Use Support in Assessed Lake, Reservoir, and Pond Acres," in *National Water Quality Inventory: Report to Congress, 2004 Reporting Cycle*, U.S. Environmental Protection Agency, Office of Water, January 2009, http://www.epa.gov/owow/305b/2004report/2004_305Breport.pdf (accessed March 8, 2009)

the lake, reservoir, and pond waters assessed for this designated use were rated as good, which means that they supported this use. Thirty percent were impaired, meaning that they could only partially support this use. Four percent were good but threatened, meaning that they currently supported this use but the water quality was deteriorating.

The aquatic life harvesting use refers primarily to fishing in which the fish caught are eaten. Twenty-three percent of lake acres were assessed; the finding was that 73% of the waters assessed did not support this designated use. (See Table 3.5.) This is in sharp contrast to 70% of assessed lake waters (19% of total acres assessed) supporting recreation, 78% of assessed lake waters (15% of total acres assessed) supporting use as a public water supply, and 82% of assessed lake waters (7% of total acres assessed) supporting industrial uses.

Leading Pollutants/Stressors in Lakes, Ponds, and Reservoirs

A lake's water quality reflects the condition and management of its watershed. In 2004 elevated levels of mercury were identified as the most common stressor, contributing to approximately 55% of the impaired water quality in lakes. (See Figure 3.15.) This finding was caused mostly by the widespread detection of mercury in fish tissue. Because it is difficult to measure mercury in water, and because mercury readily accumulates in tissue (bioaccumulates), most states measure mercury contamination using fish tissue samples. Mercury generally enters the water from the air, often released from the smokestacks of power-generating facilities, waste incinerators, and other sources.

Polychlorinated biphenyls (PCBs) were the second most common stressor in the lake waters that were assessed. (See Figure 3.15.) PCBs are toxic chemicals used in various industrial processes and can enter water supplies via municipal waste disposal and industrial spills and leaks. Like mercury, PCBs accumulate in fish tissues, so water containing PCBs would not support aquatic life harvesting.

Plant nutrients (phosphorus and nitrogen) were identified as the third most common stressor, affecting about 17% of the impaired lake acres that were assessed. The remaining stressors in order from high to low of their percent of impaired lake acres affected were metals, oxygen depletion, nuisance exotic species (such as zebra mussels), sediment, pathogens (disease-causing organisms), and turbidity (cloudiness of the water).

Sources of Pollutants/Stressors in Lakes

Atmospheric deposition was a significant source of pollution for lakes, affecting about 19% of impaired lake acres in 2004. (See Figure 3.16.) The substances that enter bodies of water from the air (by atmospheric dep-

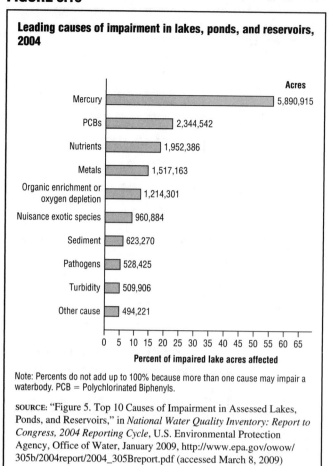

FIGURE 3.15

Leading causes of impairment in lakes, ponds, and reservoirs, 2004

Note: Percents do not add up to 100% because more than one cause may impair a waterbody. PCB = Polychlorinated Biphenyls.

SOURCE: "Figure 5. Top 10 Causes of Impairment in Assessed Lakes, Ponds, and Reservoirs," in *National Water Quality Inventory: Report to Congress, 2004 Reporting Cycle*, U.S. Environmental Protection Agency, Office of Water, January 2009, http://www.epa.gov/owow/305b/2004report/2004_305Breport.pdf (accessed March 8, 2009)

osition) are primarily mercury, PCBs, and other metals that are emitted from power plants.

After the category "unknown," agriculture was the second most significant source of lake pollution, affecting about 16% of impaired lake acres. (See Figure 3.16.) Pasture grazing and both irrigated and nonirrigated crop production were the leading sources of agricultural impairments to lake water quality. Pasture grazing is a pollution risk because the animals that graze leave large quantities of manure (feces) on the land. The manure poses a runoff risk during rain or with irrigation as does fertilizer used in crop production. Wildlife also poses a pollution risk by contaminating water with feces.

Hydrologic modifications (hydromodification) resulting from regulation of the flow of water, dredging, and construction of dams degraded approximately 12% of the impaired lake, pond, and reservoir acres. Urban runoff and municipal sewage sources affected 11% of the impaired acres.

GREAT LAKES

The Great Lakes Environmental Research Laboratory reports in "About Our Great Lakes: Great Lakes Basin

FIGURE 3.16

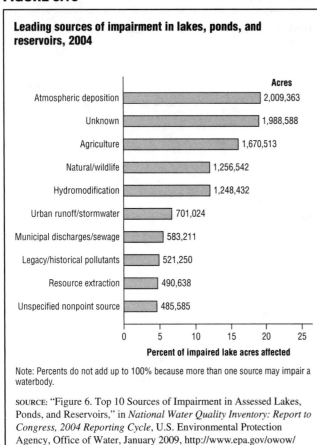

Leading sources of impairment in lakes, ponds, and reservoirs, 2004

Note: Percents do not add up to 100% because more than one source may impair a waterbody.

SOURCE: "Figure 6. Top 10 Sources of Impairment in Assessed Lakes, Ponds, and Reservoirs," in *National Water Quality Inventory: Report to Congress, 2004 Reporting Cycle*, U.S. Environmental Protection Agency, Office of Water, January 2009, http://www.epa.gov/owow/305b/2004report/2004_305Breport.pdf (accessed March 8, 2009)

FIGURE 3.17

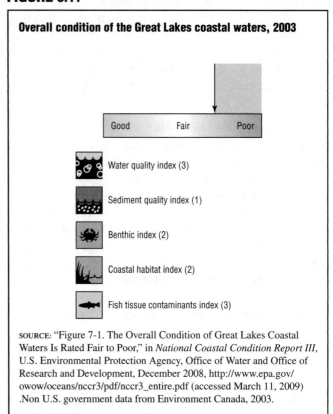

Overall condition of the Great Lakes coastal waters, 2003

SOURCE: "Figure 7-1. The Overall Condition of Great Lakes Coastal Waters Is Rated Fair to Poor," in *National Coastal Condition Report III*, U.S. Environmental Protection Agency, Office of Water and Office of Research and Development, December 2008, http://www.epa.gov/owow/oceans/nccr3/pdf/nccr3_entire.pdf (accessed March 11, 2009). Non U.S. government data from Environment Canada, 2003.

Facts" (June 18, 2004, http://www.glerl.noaa.gov/pr/ourlakes/facts.html) that the Great Lakes basin, which is shared with Canada, is home to 35 million people. The lakes provide drinking water for about 40 million people. The five lakes are the largest surface area of freshwater in the world, at 95,000 square miles (246,000 square km). The water in the Great Lakes accounts for 90% of all the freshwater in the United States. The total shoreline of the Great Lakes in the United States and Canada, a "fourth seacoast," is 10,210 miles (16,431 km) long and equal to about one-quarter of Earth's circumference. International shipping on the Great Lakes annually transports 200 million tons (181.4 million t) of cargo, and sport fishing contributes $4 billion to the economy.

The prosperity of the Great Lakes region, however, has taxed its ecological health. Urban and industrial discharges, agricultural and forestry activity, development of recreation facilities, poor waste disposal practices, invasive species, and habitat degradation have all contributed to ecosystem decline. Figure 3.17 shows that the overall condition of the Great Lakes in 2003 was rated fair to poor. Despite these problems, the most serious of which are the sediment quality index followed by the benthic and coastal habitat indices, the watershed still contains many ecologically rich areas. In "About Our Great

Lakes: Ecology" (June 2, 2004, http://www.glerl.noaa.gov/pr/ourlakes/ecology.html), the Great Lakes Environmental Research Laboratory indicates that approximately 3,500 species of plants and animals inhabit the Great Lakes basin.

Great Lakes Water Quality Agreement

In 1972 the United States and Canada entered into the Great Lakes Water Quality Agreement, which is a worldwide model for cooperative environmental protection and natural resource management. The agreement imposes reporting requirements on both of its member countries, and in an attempt to meet these requirements a conference series was established. The conferences, which are held every two years, are called the State of the Lakes Ecosystem Conference (SOLEC). The first such conference was convened in 1994 and the most recent as of mid-2009 was in late 2008.

The SOLEC meetings are designed as a venue for scientists and policy makers to share information about the state of the Great Lakes ecosystem. The focus is on assessing and sharing information about the results of Great Lakes programs and studies. In the year following each conference, the United States and Canada prepare a report that presents the findings accumulated at the SOLEC.

The report published after SOLEC 2006, *State of the Great Lakes 2007* (2007, http://www.epa.gov/glnpo/solec/sogl2007/SOGL2007.pdf), presents the following mixed news about the chemical, physical, and biological integrity of the waters of the Great Lakes basin ecosystem. Some of the positive features identified include:

- Levels of most contaminants in herring gull eggs and predator fish continue to decrease.

- Phosphorus targets have been met in Lake Ontario, Lake Huron, Lake Michigan, and Lake Superior.

- The Great Lakes are a good source for treated drinking water.

- Sustainable forestry programs throughout the Great Lakes basin are helping environmentally friendly management practices.

- Lake trout stocks in Lake Superior have remained self-sustaining, and some natural reproduction of lake trout is occurring in Lake Ontario and in Lake Huron.

- Mayfly (*Hexagenia*) populations have partially recovered in western Lake Erie.

Some of the negative features identified include:

- Concentrations of the flame retardant PBDEs [polybrominated diphenylethers] are increasing in herring gull eggs.

- Nuisance growth of the green alga *Cladophora* has reappeared along the shoreline in many places.

- Phosphorus levels are still above guidelines in Lake Erie.

- Non-native species (aquatic and terrestrial) are pervasive throughout the Great Lakes basin, and they continue to exert impacts on native species and communities.

- Populations of *Diporeia*, the dominant, native, bottom-dwelling invertebrate, continue to decline in Lake Michigan, Lake Huron, and Lake Ontario, and they may be extinct in Lake Erie.

- Groundwater withdrawals for municipal water supplies and irrigation, and the increased proportion of impervious surfaces in urban areas, have negatively impacted groundwater.

- Long range atmospheric transport is a continuing source of PCBs and other contaminants to the Great Lakes basin, and can be expected to be significant for decades.

- Land use changes in favor of urbanization along the shoreline continue to threaten natural habitats in the Great Lakes and St. Lawrence River ecosystems.

- Some species of amphibians and wetland-dependent birds are showing declines in population numbers, in part due to wetland habitat conditions.

FISH ADVISORIES

When fish or shellfish in particular locations contain harmful levels of pollutants, the state issues advisories to recreational fishermen against eating the fish. Commercial fishing is usually banned. Since 1993 the EPA has compiled these advisories annually and made them available to the public. Fish advisories are advice to limit or avoid eating certain fish.

Figure 3.18 shows the number of advisories against eating fish reported by the states to the EPA in 2006. These advisories are specific as to location, species, and pollutant. Some advisories caution against eating any fish from a particular location, whereas others caution against eating a particular species of fish only because it is more likely to bioaccumulate the chemical of concern. Advisories from the EPA and the U.S. Food and Drug Administration in 2006 included warnings that women who are pregnant or nursing and young children should avoid eating certain kinds of fish. Consuming mercury can damage the developing nervous systems of babies and children.

In 2006, 50 states, the District of Columbia, American Samoa, Guam, the Virgin Islands, and Puerto Rico reported 3,852 fish consumption advisories. (See Figure 3.18.) Most advisories are caused by pollutants that accumulate in fish tissues, such as mercury, PCBs, chlordane, dioxins, and dichloro-diphenyl-trichloroethane (DDT). These pollutants are called bioaccumulative because when ingested by certain species of fish and waterfowl they are not metabolized and excreted from the organism. Instead, they are stored in the fatty tissues and remain there. As more chemical is ingested, more accumulates in the organism. The use of PCBs, chlordane, and DDT has been banned for more than 20 years, yet these compounds persist in the sediments and are taken in through the food chain. Mercury is emitted by coal-burning power plants and falls from the atmosphere into bodies of water.

Recreational Water-Associated Outbreaks

In "Surveillance for Waterborne Disease and Outbreaks Associated with Recreational Water Use and Other Aquatic Facility-Associated Health Events—United States, 2005–2006" (*Morbidity and Mortality Weekly Report*, vol. 57, SS-9, September 12, 2008), Jonathan S. Yoder et al. list the incidence of disease outbreaks caused by recreational water contact. During this 2-year period, 31 states reported 78 outbreaks involving 4,412 people. Of the 78 recreational waterborne disease outbreaks reported, 48 involved gastroenteritis. Figure 3.19 shows the number of waterborne disease outbreaks due to recreational water use annually from 1978 to 2006, with a breakdown by illness.

As part of the Beaches Environmental Assessment and Coastal Health (BEACH) Act of 2000, Congress directed the EPA to develop a new set of guidelines for recreational water based on new water quality indicators. Beginning in 2003 the EPA was required to conduct a series of epidemiologic studies at recreational freshwater and marine beaches. These studies were to be used to help in the development of the new guidelines for recreational water.

FIGURE 3.18

Number of fish consumption advisories by state, 2006

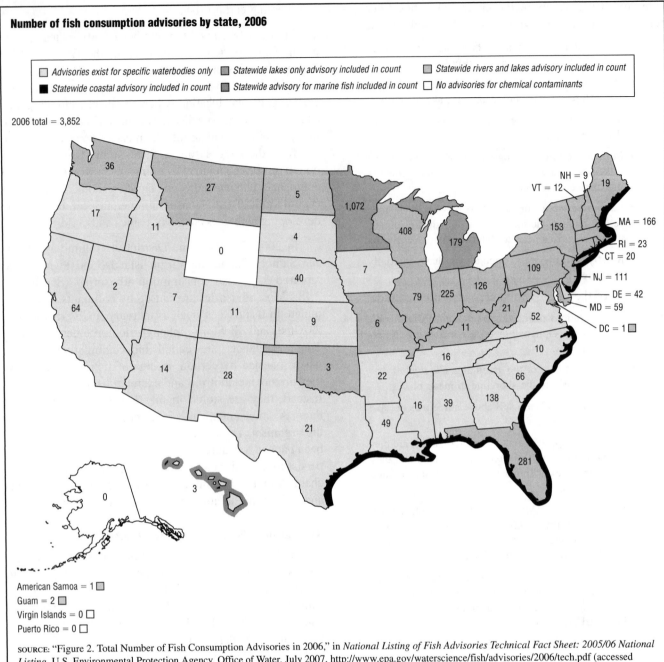

SOURCE: "Figure 2. Total Number of Fish Consumption Advisories in 2006," in *National Listing of Fish Advisories Technical Fact Sheet: 2005/06 National Listing*, U.S. Environmental Protection Agency, Office of Water, July 2007, http://www.epa.gov/waterscience/fish/advisories/2006/tech.pdf (accessed March 10, 2009)

The EPA summarizes in *Implementing the BEACH Act of 2000: Report to Congress* (October 2006, http://www.epa.gov/waterscience/beaches/report/full-rtc.pdf) the following achievements:

1. States have significantly improved their assessment and monitoring of beaches; the number of monitored beaches has increased from about 1,000 in 1997 to more than 3,500 out of approximately 6,000 beaches, as identified to EPA by the states for the 2004 swimming season.

2. EPA has strengthened water quality standards throughout all the coastal recreation waters in the United States; the number of coastal and Great Lakes states with up-to-date water quality criteria has increased from 11 in 2000 to 35 in 2004.

3. EPA has improved public access to data on beach advisories and closings by improving its electronic system for beach data collection and delivery systems; the system is known as "eBeaches." The public can view the beach information at http://oaspub.epa.gov/beacon/beacon_national_page.main.

4. EPA is working to improve pollution control efforts that reduce potential adverse health effects

FIGURE 3.19

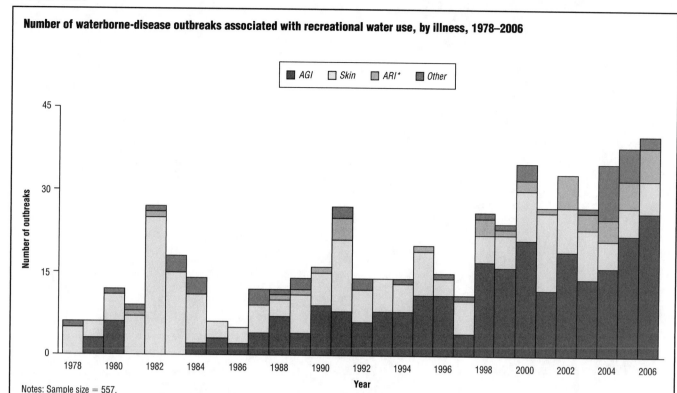

Number of waterborne-disease outbreaks associated with recreational water use, by illness, 1978–2006

Notes: Sample size = 557.

AGI: acute gastrointestinal illness; Skin: illness, condition, or symptom related to skin; ARI: acute respiratory illness; Other: includes keratitis, conjunctivitis, otitis, bronchitis, meningitis, meningoencephalitis, hepatitis, leptospirosis, and combined illnesses.

*All outbreaks of legionellosis (i.e., Legionnaires' disease and Pontiac fever) are classified as ARI.

SOURCE: Jonathan S. Yoder et al., "Figure 8. Number of Recreational Water-Associated Outbreaks (n=557), by Year and Illness—United States, 1978–2006," in "Surveillance for Waterborne Disease and Outbreaks Associated with Recreational Water Use and Other Aquatic Facility-Associated Health Events—United States, 2005–2006," *Morbidity and Mortality Weekly Report, Surveillance Summaries*, vol. 57, no. SS-9, September 12, 2008, http://www.cdc.gov/mmwr/PDF/ss/ss5709.pdf (accessed March 10, 2009).

at beaches. EPA's Strategic Plan and recent National Water Program Guidance describe these actions to coordinate assessment of problems affecting beaches and to reduce pollution. . . .

5. EPA is conducting research to develop new or revised water quality criteria and more rapid methods for assessing water quality at beaches so that results can be made available in hours rather than days. Quicker tests will allow beach managers to make faster decisions about the safety of beach waters and thus help reduce the risk of illness among beachgoers.

The BEACH Act also required the EPA to publish a list of the nation's coastal and Great Lakes beaches and identify whether there is a monitoring program for each beach. In 2008 the EPA published its first updated list of beaches and their monitoring status as of the summer of 2007. The full list of beaches for each state with coastal or Great Lakes beaches is listed in *National List of Beaches* (September 2008, http://www.epa.gov/waterscience/beaches/list/list-of-beaches.pdf). The list includes 6,247 beaches, 3,655 of which were monitored in 2007.

CHAPTER 4
GROUNDWATER

A VAST HIDDEN RESOURCE

Water lies beneath almost every part of Earth's surface—mountains, plains, and deserts—but underground water is not always easy to find, and, once found, it may not be readily accessible. Groundwater may lie close to the surface, as in a marsh, or it may occur many hundreds of feet below the surface, as in some dry areas of the nation's West.

People have known about the presence of groundwater since ancient times, but it is only recently that geologists have learned how to gauge the quantity of groundwater and have begun to estimate its vast potential for use. The U.S. Geological Survey (USGS) states in *Groundwater* (February 9, 2009, http://pubs.usgs.gov/gip/gw/index.html) that even though an estimated 1 million cubic miles (4.2 million cubic km) of Earth's groundwater is located within half a mile (0.8 km) of the surface (there are 1.1 trillion gallons [4.2 trillion L] in a cubic mile), only a small amount of this reservoir of underground water can be tapped and made available for human use through wells and springs. Furthermore, in *Where Is Earth's Water Located?* (March 4, 2009, http://ga.water.usgs.gov/edu/earthwherewater.html), the USGS notes that the total amount of fresh groundwater on Earth at all depths is estimated at about 2.5 million cubic miles (10.5 million cubic km).

HOW GROUNDWATER OCCURS

Groundwater is not in underground lakes, nor is it water flowing in underground rivers. It is simply water that fills pores or cracks in subsurface rocks. When rain falls or snow melts on the surface of the ground, some water may run off into lower land areas or lakes and streams. What is left may be absorbed by the soil, seep into deeper layers of soil and rock, or evaporate into the atmosphere.

Below the topsoil—the rich upper layer of soil in which plants have most of their roots—is an area called the unsaturated zone. In times of adequate rainfall the

small spaces between rocks and grains of soil in the unsaturated zone contain at least some water, whereas the larger spaces contain mostly air. After a major rain, however, all the open spaces may fill with water temporarily. During a drought, the area may become drained and almost completely dry, although a certain amount of water is held in the soil and rocks by molecular attraction.

Lying beneath the unsaturated zone is the saturated zone. The water table is the level at which the unsaturated zone and the saturated zone meet. Water drains through the unsaturated zone to the saturated zone. The saturated zone is full of water—all the spaces between soil and rocks, and within the rocks themselves, contain water. Water from streams, lakes, wetlands, and other water bodies may seep into the saturated zone. Streams are commonly a significant source of recharge to groundwater downstream from mountain fronts and steep hillsides in arid and semiarid areas, and in areas underlaid by limestone and other porous rock.

The water table is not fixed, but may rise or fall, depending on water availability. In areas where the climate is fairly consistent, the level of the water table may vary little; in areas subject to extreme flooding and drought, it may rise and fall substantially.

Groundwater Flow

Water is always in motion. Groundwater generally moves from recharge areas, where water enters the ground, to discharge areas, where it exits from the ground into a wetland, river, lake, or ocean. Transpiration by plants whose roots extend to a point near the water table is another form of discharge. The path of groundwater movement may be short and simple or incredibly complex, depending on the geology of the area through which the water passes. The complexity of the path also determines the length of time a molecule of water remains in the ground between recharge and discharge points. (See Figure 4.1.)

FIGURE 4.1

Direction and rate of groundwater movement

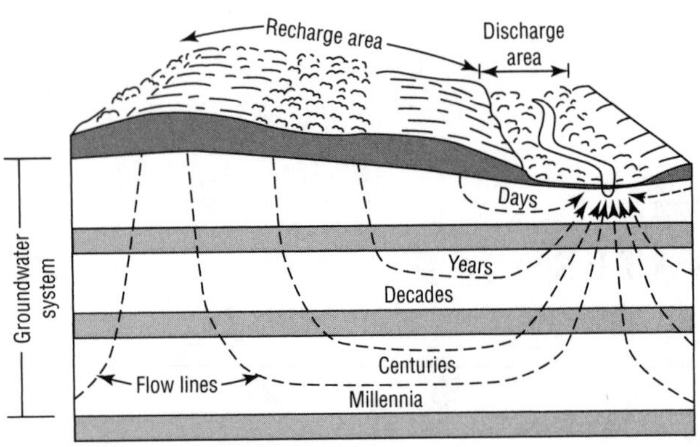

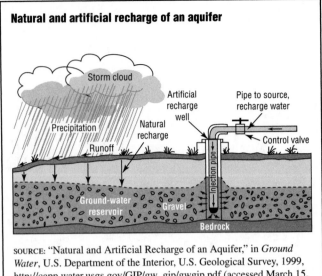

SOURCE: Roger M. Waller, "Direction and Rate of Ground-Water Movement," in *Ground Water and the Rural Homeowner*, U.S. Department of the Interior, U.S. Geological Survey, August 19, 2005, http://pubs.usgs.gov/gip/gw_ruralhomeowner/ (accessed March 15, 2009)

FIGURE 4.2

Natural and artificial recharge of an aquifer

SOURCE: "Natural and Artificial Recharge of an Aquifer," in *Ground Water*, U.S. Department of the Interior, U.S. Geological Survey, 1999, http://capp.water.usgs.gov/GIP/gw_gip/gwgip.pdf (accessed March 15, 2009)

The velocities of groundwater flow are generally low and are orders of magnitude less than the velocities of stream flow. Groundwater movement normally occurs as slow seepage through the spaces between particles of unconsolidated material or through networks of fractures and openings in consolidated rocks. A velocity of 1 foot (30.5 cm) per day or more is a high rate of movement in groundwater. Groundwater velocities can be as low as 1 foot per decade or 1 foot per century. By contrast, stream flows are generally measured in feet per second. A velocity of 1 foot (30.5 cm) per second is about 16 miles (25.7 km) per day. The low velocities of groundwater flow can have important implications, particularly in relation to the movement of contaminants.

The age of water (time since recharge) varies in different parts of groundwater flow systems. Groundwater gets steadily older along a particular flow path from an area of recharge to an area of discharge. In shallow, local-scale flow systems, groundwater age at areas of discharge can vary from less than a day to a few hundred years. (See Figure 4.1.) In deep, regional flow systems with long flow paths, groundwater age may reach thousands or tens of thousands of years.

AQUIFERS

An aquifer is a saturated zone that contains enough water to yield significant amounts of water when a well is dug. The zone is actually a path of porous or permeable material through which substantial quantities of water flow relatively easily. The term *aquifer* comes from the Latin *aqua* (water) and *ferre* (to bear or carry). An aquifer can be a layer of gravel or sand, a layer of sandstone or cavernous limestone, a rubble zone between lava flows, or even a

large body of massive rock, such as fractured granite. An aquifer may lie above, below, or in between confining beds that are layers of hard, nonporous material (e.g., clay or solid granite).

There are two types of aquifers: unconfined and confined. In an unconfined or water table aquifer, precipitation filters down from the land's surface until it hits an impervious layer of rock or clay. The water then accumulates and forms a zone of saturation. Because runoff water can easily seep down to the water table, an unconfined aquifer is susceptible to contamination.

In a confined or artesian aquifer, the confining beds act somewhat like underground boundaries, making it difficult for water to enter or leave the aquifer, so that the water is forced to continue its slow movement to its discharge point. Water from precipitation enters the aquifer through a recharge area, where the soil allows the water to percolate down to the level of the aquifer. The ability of an aquifer to recharge is dependent on various factors, such as the ease with which water is able to move down through the geological formations (permeability) and the size of the spaces between the rock particles (porosity). Figure 4.2 illustrates natural and artificial aquifer recharge.

Usually, the permeability and porosity of rocks decreases as their depth below the surface increases. How much water can be removed from an aquifer depends on the type of rock. For example, dense granite will supply almost no water to a well even if the water is near the surface. Porous sandstone, however, possibly thousands of feet below the surface, can yield hundreds of gallons of water per minute. Porous rocks that are capable of supplying freshwater have been found at depths of more than 6,000 feet (1,829 m) below the surface. Saline (salty) water has been discovered in aquifers that lie more than 30,000 feet (9,144 m) underground.

Aquifers vary from a few feet thick to tens or hundreds of feet thick. They can be located just below Earth's surface or thousands of feet beneath it. An aquifer can cover a few acres of land or many thousands of square miles. Furthermore, any one aquifer may be a part of a large system of aquifers that feed into each other.

Figure 4.3 shows 30 of the principal aquifers in the United States. Thomas E. Reilly et al. of the USGS state in *Ground-Water Availability in the United States* (2008, http://pubs.usgs.gov/circ/1323/pdf/Circular1323_book_508.pdf)

FIGURE 4.3

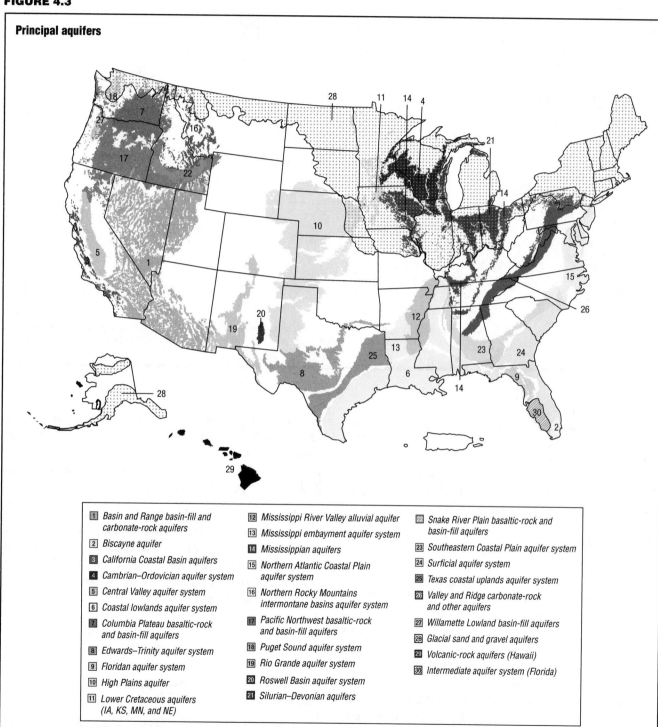

Principal aquifers

1. Basin and Range basin-fill and carbonate-rock aquifers
2. Biscayne aquifer
3. California Coastal Basin aquifers
4. Cambrian–Ordovician aquifer system
5. Central Valley aquifer system
6. Coastal lowlands aquifer system
7. Columbia Plateau basaltic-rock and basin-fill aquifers
8. Edwards–Trinity aquifer system
9. Floridan aquifer system
10. High Plains aquifer
11. Lower Cretaceous aquifers (IA, KS, MN, and NE)
12. Mississippi River Valley alluvial aquifer
13. Mississippi embayment aquifer system
14. Mississippian aquifers
15. Northern Atlantic Coastal Plain aquifer system
16. Northern Rocky Mountains intermontane basins aquifer system
17. Pacific Northwest basaltic-rock and basin-fill aquifers
18. Puget Sound aquifer system
19. Rio Grande aquifer system
20. Roswell Basin aquifer system
21. Silurian–Devonian aquifers
22. Snake River Plain basaltic-rock and basin-fill aquifers
23. Southeastern Coastal Plain aquifer system
24. Surficial aquifer system
25. Texas coastal uplands aquifer system
26. Valley and Ridge carbonate-rock and other aquifers
27. Willamette Lowland basin-fill aquifers
28. Glacial sand and gravel aquifers
29. Volcanic-rock aquifers (Hawaii)
30. Intermediate aquifer system (Florida)

SOURCE: Thomas E. Reilly et al., "Figure 23. Thirty Principal Aquifers That Collectively Account for about 94 Percent of the Nation's Total Ground-Water Withdrawals for Public Supply, Irrigation, and Self-Supplied Industrial Uses Combined," in *Ground-Water Availability in the United States*, U.S. Department of the Interior, U.S. Geological Survey, 2008, http://pubs.usgs.gov/circ/1323/pdf/Circular1323_book_508.pdf (accessed March 15, 2009)

TABLE 4.1

Water use estimates for principal aquifers, 2000

Regional principal aquifer	Total water use	Irrigation	Public supply	Self-supplied industrial
	Million gallons per day			
High Plains aquifer	17,488	17,000	389	99
Central Valley aquifer system	9,808	8,910	839	59
Mississippi River Valley alluvial aquifer	9,290	9,150	70	70
Basin and Range basin-fill and carbonate-rock aquifers	5,695	4,550	1,080	65
Glacial sand and gravel aquifers	4,075	1,170	2,273	632
Floridan aquifer system	3,645	1,930	1,330	385
California Coastal Basin aquifers	3,446	1,760	1,580	106
Snake River Plain basaltic-rock and basin-fill aquifers	3,075	2,900	151	24
Coastal lowlands aquifer system	2,368	933	1,010	425
Pacific Northwest basaltic-rock and basin-fill aquifers	1,340	1,206	121	13
Rio Grande aquifer system	1,119	867	240	12
Columbia Plateau basaltic-rock and basin-fill aquifers	1,077	810	223	44
Northern Atlantic Coastal Plain aquifer system	1,035	70	793	172
Mississippi embayment aquifer system	946	195	576	175
Cambrian–Ordovician aquifer system	933	92	590	251
Southeastern Coastal Plain aquifer system	860	382	340	138
Biscayne aquifer	812	114	698	0
Edwards–Trinity aquifer system	740	282	411	47
Surficial aquifer system (southeastern United States)	650	364	263	23
Volcanic-rock aquifers (Hawaii)	429	171	243	15
Willamette Lowland basin-fill aquifers	420	245	99	76
Roswell Basin aquifer system	386	364	21	1
Texas coastal uplands aquifer system	381	188	148	45
Northern Rocky Mountains intermontane basins aquifer system	377	264	78	35
Valley and Ridge carbonate-rock and other aquifers	363	7	226	130
Intermediate aquifer system (Florida)	354	292	61	1
Lower Cretaceous aquifers (Iowa, Kansas, Minnesota, and Nebraska only)	317	259	53	5
Mississippian aquifers	285	6	211	68
Puget Sound aquifer system	260	45	192	23
Silurian–Devonian aquifers	246	27	164	55

SOURCE: Thomas E. Reilly et al., "Table 1. The 30 Regional Principal Aquifers with the Greatest Amount of Ground-Water Use," in *Ground-Water Availability in the United States*, U.S. Department of the Interior, U.S. Geological Survey, 2008, http://pubs.usgs.gov/circ/1323/pdf/Circular1323_book_508.pdf (accessed March 15, 2009)

that these aquifers supply approximately 94% of the United States' total groundwater. Table 4.1 lists the principal aquifers in order of total water use, from highest to lowest, and the amounts used for irrigation, public supply, and self-supplied industrial uses. The High Plains (Ogallala) Aquifer is listed first because it is the largest.

The Ogallala Aquifer

The Ogallala or High Plains Aquifer is one of the world's largest aquifers and is the largest in North America. According to Peter B. McMahon et al. of the USGS, in *Water-Quality Assessment of the High Plains Aquifer, 1999–2004* (2007, http://pubs.usgs.gov/pp/1749/downloads/pdf/P1749front.pdf), the aquifer stretches from southern South Dakota to the Texas panhandle and covers 174,000 square miles (450,658 square km). (See Figure 4.4.) The Ogallala supplies most of the water for irrigation and drinking to the Great Plains states and yields more than one-fourth of the nation's water for irrigation.

Kevin F. Dennehy of the USGS reports in *High Plains Aquifer, USA: Groundwater Development and Sustain-*

ability (2002, http://co.water.usgs.gov/nawqa/hpgw/journals/DENNEHY1.html) that the Ogallala Aquifer is being pumped far in excess of recharge in many places and that its water quality is deteriorating. Thus, the future sustainability of the aquifer is tenuous.

In 1999 the Texas oil tycoon T. Boone Pickens (1928–) formed Mesa Water, Inc., to market water from part of the Ogallala Aquifer to large Texas cities for municipal use. About 100 landowners and 200,000 acres (80,937 ha) of land in the Texas panhandle were affected by Pickens's plan. The project sparked controversy in Texas, where the 100-year-old rule of capture was still in effect. The rule of capture, which was at one time standard doctrine in much of the United States, states that the owner of land that is located above an underground water source can pump out unlimited amounts of water regardless of the impact on surrounding property owners.

Concerned that the already rapidly draining water source would become depleted even further, residents of the surrounding panhandle area protested, arguing that their essential source of water should not be pumped

FIGURE 4.4

High Plains aquifer system

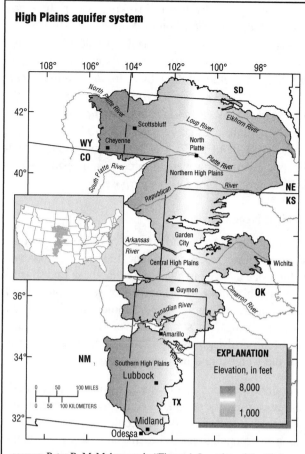

SOURCE: Peter B. McMahon et al., "Figure 1. Location of the High Plains Aquifer," in *Water Quality Assessment of the High Plains Aquifer, 1999–2004*, U.S. Department of the Interior, U.S. Geological Survey, 2007, http://pubs.usgs.gov/pp/1749/downloads/pdf/P1749front.pdf (accessed March 11, 2009)

hundreds of miles away. Many Texans began campaigning for tighter government regulations on water rights. However, comprehensive water legislation that would have modified the rule of capture failed to reach a vote in the Texas state senate in May 2005. The following month the article "Private Water Group Preparing to Pump the Ogallala Aquifer and Sell Groundwater to Far-Away Texas Cities" (*Western Water Law and Policy Reporter*, June 2005) announced that Mesa Water would begin building a system of wells and pipelines to sell the water to major urban centers throughout Texas.

According to Betsy Blaney, in "Texas Water Marketers See Future Demand with Growing Population, Declining Water Supply" (Associated Press, June 15, 2007), in the years that followed, no city or agency signed up for Pickens's water, even though drought conditions had persisted and water use was high. In "Water Pipeline Plan Suspended Indefinitely" (Associated Press, September 15, 2008), Blaney notes that Pickens and Mesa Water suspended plans to build the system of wells and pipelines in September 2008. This decision came

after the U.S. Department of Justice blocked changes to Texas law that had allowed Pickens to create the Panhandle fresh water district in November 2007.

SPRINGS

A spring is a natural discharge of water at Earth's surface from a saturated zone that has been filled to overflowing. Springs are classified either according to the amount of water they produce or according to the temperature of the water (hot, warm, or cold). Giant Springs in Great Falls, Montana, is the largest freshwater spring in the United States and is the source of the Missouri and Roe rivers. According to Montana State Parks (http://fwp.mt.gov/lands/site_282690.aspx), the spring removes 156 million gallons (590.5 million L) per day from underground reserves.

Thermal springs have water that is warm or, in some places, hot. They are fed by groundwater that is heated by contact with hot rocks deep below the surface. In some areas water can descend slowly to deep levels, getting warmer the farther down it goes. If it rises faster than it descended, it does not have time to cool off before it emerges on the surface. Well-known thermal springs are the Warm Springs in Georgia and the Hot Springs in Arkansas. Geysers are thermal springs that erupt periodically. Old Faithful in Yellowstone National Park is perhaps the most famous and spectacular geyser in the world. It erupts at intervals of 30 to 90 minutes. The park maintains a Webcam (http://www.nps.gov/yell/photosmultimedia/yellowstonelive.htm) so that virtual visitors can see Old Faithful erupt even if they cannot see it in person.

NATURAL CHARACTERISTICS OF GROUNDWATER

As groundwater travels its course from recharge to discharge area, it undergoes chemical and physical changes as it mixes with other groundwater and reacts with the minerals in the sand or rocks through which it flows. These interactions can greatly affect water quality and its suitability or unsuitability for a particular use.

Minerals

Water is a natural solvent capable of dissolving many other substances. Spring waters may contain dissolved minerals and gases that give them subtle flavors. Without minerals and gases, water tastes flat. The most common dissolved mineral substances are calcium, magnesium, sodium, potassium, chloride, sulfate, and bicarbonate. However, water is considered undesirable for drinking if it contains more than 1,000 milligrams per liter (mg/L) of dissolved minerals. In areas where less-mineralized water is not available, water with a few thousand mg/L of dissolved minerals is used routinely, although it is classified as saline.

Some well and spring waters contain such high levels of dissolved minerals that they cannot be tolerated by humans, plants, or animals. In high concentrations, certain minerals can be especially harmful. A large quantity of sodium in drinking water is unhealthy for people with heart disease. Boron, a mineral that is good for some plants in small amounts, is toxic to other plants in only slightly elevated concentrations. Such highly mineralized groundwater usually lies deep below the surface and has limited uses.

Water Hardness

Water that contains a lot of calcium and magnesium is said to be hard. The hardness of water can be expressed in terms of the amount of calcium carbonate (the principal constituent of limestone) or equivalent minerals that remain when the water is evaporated. Water is considered soft when it contains 0 to 60 mg/L of hardness constituents, moderately hard from 61 to 120 mg/L, hard between 121 and 180 mg/L, and very hard if over 181 mg/L.

Very hard water is not desirable for many domestic uses and leaves a scaly deposit on the insides of pipes, boilers, and tanks. Hard water can be made soft at a fairly reasonable cost, although it is not always desirable to remove all the minerals from drinking water because some are beneficial to health. Extremely soft water can corrode metals but is suitable for doing laundry, dishwashing, and bathing. Whenever possible, most communities seek a balance between hard and soft water in their municipal water systems.

CURRENT GROUNDWATER USE

Human Needs

The nation's use of groundwater grew dramatically in the last several decades of the 20th century. Susan S. Hutson et al. of the USGS report in *Estimated Use of Water in the United States in 2000* (2004, http://pubs.usgs.gov/circ/2004/circ1268/pdf/circular1268.pdf), the most recent report available as of mid-2009, that the rate of withdrawal was 34 billion gallons per day (Bgal/d; 128.7 billion L per day) of fresh groundwater in 1950. It increased to 83 Bgal/d (314.2 billion L per day) in 1980 and decreased some over the next several years before reaching a new high of 83.3 Bgal/d (315.3 billion L per day) in 2000.

In "Ground Water Use in the United States" (November 7, 2008, http://ga.water.usgs.gov/edu/wugw.html), the USGS estimates that in 2000 approximately 26% of the freshwater used in the United States was groundwater. (The rest was surface water.) Over two-thirds (68%) of all groundwater was used for irrigation. One-fifth (19%) was used for public uses such as drinking, bathing, and cooking. The remaining 13% was used for industry, mining, domestic use (self-supplied water via wells), livestock watering, thermoelectric power plants, and commercial purposes.

Figure 4.5 shows the estimated percent of the population using groundwater as drinking water. In many states—including Florida, Idaho, Minnesota, Mississippi, Nebraska, and New Mexico—drinking water is obtained almost exclusively from groundwater sources. According John S. Zogorski et al. of the USGS, in *The Quality of Our Nation's Waters: Volatile Organic Compounds in the Nation's Ground Water and Drinking-Water Supply Wells* (2006, http://pubs.usgs.gov/circ/circ1292/pdf/circular1292.pdf), in 2000 about 50% of U.S. residents used groundwater as their drinking water source. Rural residents rely heavily on groundwater for this purpose.

Ecological Needs

Historically, surface and groundwater have been managed as separate resources. Since the 1970s, however, there has been a growing awareness that these two sources are inseparably linked. Groundwater seeps into rivers, streams, lakes, and other water bodies and breaks the surface as springs. In some parts of the United States, especially in arid regions, aquifers contribute a large portion of the water found in rivers and streams.

Groundwater recharge of surface water is particularly important during dry periods. Reductions in surface water can have adverse effects on the ecology of a watershed, stressing fish populations and their food supply, wetlands, and the plants and animals living along the banks of rivers and streams. Groundwater depletion in some areas has resulted in the death of aquatic and semiaquatic species that depended on groundwater flow to surface-water streams.

Overpumping

Pumping groundwater from a well always causes a decline in groundwater levels at and near the well, and it always causes a diversion of groundwater that was moving slowly to its natural, possibly distant, area of discharge. Pumping a single well typically has only a local effect on the groundwater flow system. Pumping many wells (sometimes hundreds or thousands of wells) in large areas can have significant regional effects on groundwater systems.

If a groundwater system is not overused, the rate of groundwater recharge and discharge balance one another. However, when the rate of withdrawal exceeds the rate at which the groundwater source is recharged, the result is the lowering of groundwater to levels that may impair the resource.

Overpumping groundwater can have many different effects, including:

- Neighboring wells can dry up, requiring the construction of new, deeper wells or significant changes to existing wells.

FIGURE 4.5

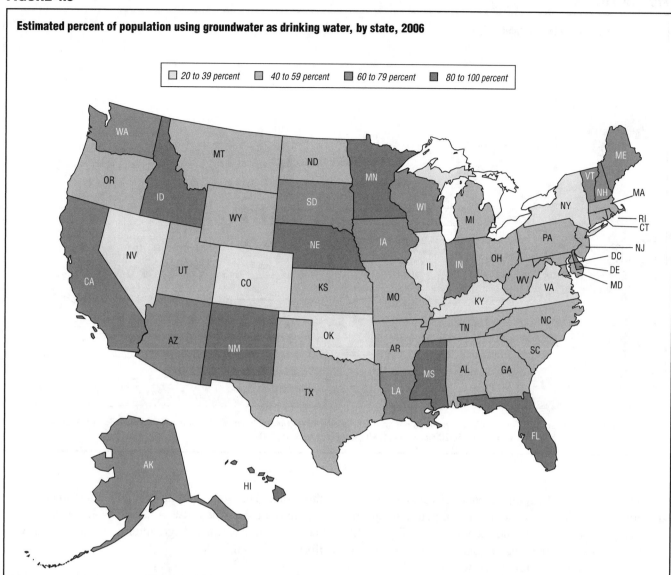

Estimated percent of population using groundwater as drinking water, by state, 2006

□ 20 to 39 percent   ■ 40 to 59 percent   ■ 60 to 79 percent   ■ 80 to 100 percent

SOURCE: John S. Zogorski et al., "Estimated Use of Ground Water for Drinking Water," in *The Quality of Our Nation's Waters: Volatile Organic Compounds in the Nation's Ground Water and Drinking-Water Supply Wells*, U.S. Department of the Interior, U.S. Geological Survey, 2006, http://pubs.usgs.gov/circ/circ1292/pdf/circular1292.pdf (accessed March 10, 2009)

- Aquifer materials can compact, causing the land above the aquifer to sink and leaving gaping holes in the land that cause damage to buildings, roads, canals, pipelines, and other infrastructure.

- Aquifer capacity may be permanently lost because of compaction of aquifer materials, resulting in higher pumping costs and a decrease in well yields.

- Changes in the volume and direction of groundwater flow can induce the flow of saltwater and water of lower quality into a well.

- Wetlands can dry up and cause adverse effects on ecological systems that are dependent on groundwater discharge.

According to the USGS, large withdrawals of groundwater have altered the flow systems and geological and chemical conditions of some of the major aquifers in the United States. Declining groundwater levels can change the location and size of recharge areas and reduce discharge rates. Some aquifers in the West have suffered major losses in aquifer storage because of overpumping.

VULNERABLE RESOURCE— GROUNDWATER QUALITY

Until the mid-20th century people believed that soil provided a barrier or protective filter that neutralized the downward migration of contaminants from the land surface and prevented water resources from becoming contaminated. However, the discovery of pesticides and contaminants in groundwater demonstrated that human activities do influence groundwater quality and that soil may not be as effective a filter as once thought.

FIGURE 4.6

Sources of groundwater contamination

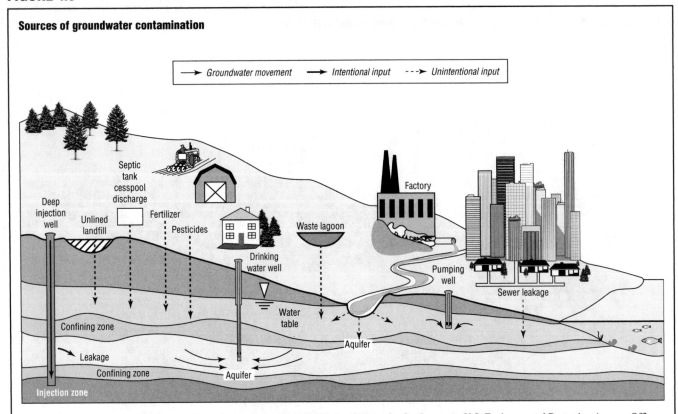

SOURCE: "Figure 6-2. Sources of Ground Water Contamination," in *2000 National Water Quality Inventory*, U.S. Environmental Protection Agency, Office of Water, August 2002, http://www.epa.gov/305b/2000report/chp6.pdf (accessed March 16, 2009)

The potential for a contaminant to affect groundwater quality is dependent on its ability to migrate through the overlying soils to the groundwater resource. Figure 4.6 shows sources of groundwater contamination. Contamination can occur as a relatively well-defined localized plume coming from a specific source. It can also occur as a generalized deterioration over a large area due to diffuse nonpoint sources such as fertilizer and pesticide applications.

Once groundwater contamination was recognized, researchers needed to determine which waters were contaminated, the severity of contamination, and what should be done about the contamination. Many government and private organizations began working to find the answers, but it was not an easy task.

According to the EPA's *Ground Water Report to Congress: Summaries of State Ground Water Conditions* (October 1999, http://www.gwpc.org/e-library/documents/state _fact_sheets/introduction.pdf) and *2000 National Water Quality Inventory* (August 2002, http://www.epa.gov/305b/ 2000report/), the quality of most of the available groundwater in the United States is believed to be good. (The *National Water Quality Inventory: Report to Congress, 2004 Reporting Cycle* [January 2009, http://www.epa.gov/ owow/305b/2004report/report2004pt1.pdf] does not address

this issue.) The worst groundwater contamination is generally in the areas where use is heaviest—towns and cities, industrial complexes, and agricultural regions, such as California's Central Valley.

Recognizing the need to protect valuable and vulnerable groundwater sources, the states have begun to implement comprehensive groundwater protection programs. In addition, in October 2006 the EPA finalized the Ground Water Rule (http://www.epa.gov/safewater/dis infection/gwr/basicinformation.html), which requires states to conduct sanitary surveys of water provided by public utilities from underground sources, take corrective action if contamination is found, and ensure that disinfection of drinking water is effective.

FACTORS AFFECTING GROUNDWATER CONTAMINATION

All pollutants do not cause the same rate of contamination for the same amount of pollutant. Groundwater is affected by many of the following factors:

- The distance between the land surface where pollution occurs and the depth of the water table. The greater the distance, the greater the chance that the pollutant will biodegrade or react with soil minerals.

- The mineral composition of the soil and rocks in the unsaturated zone. Heavy soil and organic materials decrease the potential for contamination.

- The presence or absence of biodegrading microbes in the soil.

- The amount of rainfall. Less rainfall results in less water entering the saturated zone and, therefore, lower quantities of contaminants.

- The evapotranspiration rate. (This is the rate at which water is discharged into the atmosphere as a result of evaporation from the soil, surface water, and plants.) High rates reduce the amount of contaminated water reaching the saturated zone.

GROUNDWATER CONTAMINATION

Reilly et al. describe various problems with determining not only the amount of groundwater that is available but also its availability in terms of recoverability and purity. For example, groundwater is a "hidden" resource, so it cannot be directly measured as can a lake. In addition, groundwater systems differ from one another; their sources of recharge differ, and the time required for the effects of withdraws to be seen differ. Characterizing such differing and changeable systems is difficult.

Major Types of Groundwater Contaminants

The EPA indicates in *National Water Quality Inventory: 1998 Report to Congress* (June 2000, http://www.epa.gov/305b/98report/) that 31 of the 37 reporting states identified the types of contaminants they found in groundwater. The states said that nitrates, metals, volatile and semivolatile organic compounds, and pesticides were the pollutants found most often. In *2000 National Water Quality Inventory*, the EPA discusses the major sources of groundwater pollution in these states. (The *National Water Quality Inventory: Report to Congress, 2004 Reporting Cycle* does not address this issue.)

In *Factors Affecting Occurrence and Distribution of Selected Contaminants in Ground Water from Selected Areas in the Piedmont Aquifer System, Eastern United States, 1993–2003* (2006, http://pubs.usgs.gov/sir/2006/5104/pdf/sir2006-5104.pdf), Bruce D. Lindsey et al. of the USGS discuss the Piedmont Aquifer System (PAS), which is a fingerlike area extending from Pennsylvania and New Jersey in the north to Georgia and Alabama in the south. It is a major aquifer in the eastern United States that follows the eastern foothills of the Appalachian Mountains. Lindsey et al. sampled wells and springs in the PAS as part of the USGS's National Water Quality Assessment Program.

In general, Lindsey et al. provide a positive report concerning groundwater contaminants in this aquifer. In the press release "Ground Water Meets Most Federal Standards in Major Eastern U.S. Aquifer" (December 20, 2006, http://www.usgs.gov/newsroom/article.asp?ID=1593), the USGS states:

> Many chemicals were detected in ground water from selected areas of the Piedmont Aquifer System (PAS), but concentrations of those chemicals were below drinking-water standards in most cases.... The findings in the PAS, based on samples from 255 wells and 19 springs, do not generally imply present human-health risk; however, they are an early warning that land-use activities have an effect on regional water quality. For example, concentrations of nitrate were significantly higher in ground water underlying agricultural land use than in ground water underlying undeveloped or urban land. Herbicides were detected more frequently in agricultural wells, whereas insecticides, VOCs [volatile organic compounds], chloroform, and MTBE [methyl tertiary butyl ether] were more frequently detected in urban wells.

> Findings also show that rock settings can have a great effect on ground-water quality, particularly for radon, a natural product from the radioactive decay of uranium.

A list of drinking water contaminants, their sources, and their health effects is shown in Table 4.2. Some of the more common groundwater contaminants are described in the following sections.

ARSENIC. Arsenic is a naturally occurring element in rocks and soils and is the 20th most common element in Earth's crust. The presence of arsenic in groundwater is largely the result of minerals dissolving from naturally weathered rocks and soils. Arsenic research shows that humans need arsenic as a trace element in their diet to survive. However, too much arsenic can be harmful. According to Paolo Boffetta and Fredrik Nyberg of the Karolinska Institute in Stockholm, Sweden, in "Contribution of Environmental Factors to Cancer Risk" (*British Medical Bulletin*, vol. 68, no. 1, December 2003), prolonged exposure to arsenic can contribute to skin, bladder, and other types of cancers.

In "Arsenic in Drinking Water: Basic Information" (March 26, 2007, http://www.epa.gov/ogwdw000/arsenic/basicinformation.html), the EPA notes that the nation's groundwater typically contains 1 to 10 parts per billion (ppb) of arsenic, which is within the range of the EPA standard. (One ppb is equal to approximately 1 teaspoon of powdered arsenic in two Olympic-sized swimming pools.) High arsenic levels—those above the 10 ppb high end of the EPA standard—do occur in some areas throughout the nation due to geology, geochemistry, and climate. Elevated arsenic concentrations are more often found in the western United States than in other parts of the country, but pockets of elevated levels can be found anywhere. Public water systems must comply with the EPA standard and lower their arsenic levels if they are too high.

TABLE 4.2

Drinking water contaminants, their sources, and potential health effects, 2003

Type	Contaminant	MCL or TT[a] (mg/L)[b]	Potential health effects from exposure above the MCL	Common sources of contaminant in drinking water	Public health goal
OC	Acrylamide	TT[h]	Nervous system or blood problems; increased risk of cancer	Added to water during sewage/wastewater treatment	zero
OC	Alachlor	0.002	Eye, liver, kidney or spleen problems; anemia; increased risk of cancer	Runoff from herbicide used on row crops	zero
R	Alpha particles	15 picocuries per liter (pCi/L)	Increased risk of cancer	Erosion of natural deposits of certain minerals that are radioactive and may emit a form of radiation known as alpha radiation	zero
IOC	Antimony	0.006	Increase in blood cholesterol; decrease in blood sugar	Discharge from petroleum refineries; fire retardants; ceramics; electronics; solder	0.006
IOC	Arsenic	0.010 as of 1/23/06	Skin damage or problems with circulatory systems, and may have increased risk of getting cancer	Erosion of natural deposits; runoff from orchards, runoff from glass & electronics production wastes	C
IOC	Asbestos (fibers >10 micrometers)	7 million fibers per liter (MFL)	Increased risk of developing benign intestinal polyps	Decay of asbestos cement in water mains; erosion of natural deposits	7 MFL
OC	Atrazine	0.003	Cardiovascular system or reproductive problems	Runoff from herbicide used on row crops	0.003
IOC	Barium	2	Increase in blood pressure	Discharge of drilling wastes; discharge from metal refineries; erosion of natural deposits	2
OC	Benzene	0.005	Anemia; decrease in blood platelets; increased risk of cancer	Discharge from factories; leaching from gas storage tanks and landfills	zero
OC	Benzo(a)pyrene (PAHs)	0.0002	Reproductive difficulties; increased risk of cancer	Leaching from linings of water storage tanks and distribution lines	zero
IOC	Beryllium	0.004	Intestinal lesions	Discharge from metal refineries and coal-burning factories; discharge from electrical, aerospace, and defense industries	0.004
R	Beta particles and photon emitters	4 millirems per year	Increased risk of cancer	Decay of natural and man-made deposits of certain minerals that are radioactive and may emit forms of radiation known as photons and beta radiation	zero
DBP	Bromate	0.010	Increased risk of cancer	By-product of drinking water disinfection	zero
IOC	Cadmium	0.005	Kidney damage	Corrosion of galvanized pipes; erosion of natural deposits; discharge from metal refineries; runoff from waste batteries and paints	0.005
OC	Carbofuran	0.04	Problems with blood, nervous system, or reproductive system	Leaching of soil fumigant used on rice and alfalfa	0.04
OC	Carbon tetrachloride	0.005	Liver problems; increased risk of cancer	Discharge from chemical plants and other industrial activities	zero
D	Chloramines (as Cl$_2$)	MRDL=4.0[a]	Eye/nose irritation; stomach discomfort, anemia	Water additive used to control microbes	MRDLG=4[a]
OC	Chlordane	0.002	Liver or nervous system problems; increased risk of cancer	Residue of banned termiticide	zero
D	Chlorine (as Cl$_2$)	MRDL=4.0[a]	Eye/nose irritation; stomach discomfort	Water additive used to control microbes	MRDLG=4[a]
D	Chlorine dioxide (as ClO$_2$)	MRDL=0.8[a]	Anemia; infants & young children: nervous system effects	Water additive used to control microbes	MRDLG=0.8[a]
DBP	Chlorite	1.0	Anemia; infants & young children: nervous system effects	By-product of drinking water disinfection	0.8
OC	Chlorobenzene	0.1	Liver or kidney problems	Discharge from chemical and agricultural chemical factories	0.1
IOC	Chromium (total)	0.1	Allergic dermatitis	Discharge from steel and pulp mills; erosion of natural deposits	0.1
IOC	Copper	TT[g]; action level=1.3	Short-term exposure: gastrointestinal distress. Long-term exposure: liver or kidney damage. People with Wilson's Disease should consult their personal doctor if the amount of copper in their water exceeds the action level	Corrosion of household plumbing systems; erosion of natural deposits	1.3
M	Cryptosporidium	TT[c]	Gastrointestinal illness (e.g., diarrhea, vomiting, cramps)	Human and animal fecal waste	zero
IOC	Cyanide (as free cyanide)	0.2	Nerve damage or thyroid problems	Discharge from steel/metal factories; discharge from plastic and fertilizer factories	
OC	2,4-D	0.07	Kidney, liver, or adrenal gland problems	Runoff from herbicide used on row crops	
OC	Dalapon	0.2	Minor kidney changes	Runoff from herbicide used on rights of way	

NITRATES. Many scientists and geologists consider nitrates to be the most widespread groundwater contaminant. Nitrates are simply another form of nitrogen, a plant nutrient. Nitrogen and nitrates, as discussed in Chapter 3, enter bodies of water usually as runoff from fertilized land, leaking septic systems, or sewage discharges. Generally, a level of 3 ppb or more in groundwater is considered indicative of human impact.

Nitrate contamination occurs most frequently in shallow groundwater (less than 100 feet [30.5 m] below the surface) and in aquifers that allow the rapid movement of

Type	Contaminant	MCL or TT[a] (mg/L)[b]	Potential health effects from exposure above the MCL	Common sources of contaminant in drinking water	Public health goal
OC	1,2-Dibromo-3-chloropropane (DBCP)	0.0002	Reproductive difficulties; increased risk of cancer	Runoff/leaching from soil fumigant used on soybeans, cotton, pineapples, and orchards	zero
OC	o-Dichlorobenzene	0.6	Liver, kidney, or circulatory system problems	Discharge from industrial chemical factories	0.6
OC	p-Dichlorobenzene	0.075	Anemia; liver, kidney or spleen damage; changes in blood	Discharge from industrial chemical factories	0.075
OC	1,2-Dichloroethane	0.005	Increased risk of cancer	Discharge from industrial chemical factories	zero
OC	1,1-Dichloroethylene	0.007	Liver problems	Discharge from industrial chemical factories	0.007
OC	cis-1,2-Dichloroethylene	0.07	Liver problems	Discharge from industrial chemical factories	0.07
OC	trans-1,2-Dichloroethylene	0.1	Liver problems	Discharge from industrial chemical factories	0.1
OC	Dichloromethane	0.005	Liver problems; increased risk of cancer	Discharge from drug and chemical factories	zero
OC	1,2-Dichloropropane	0.005	Increased risk of cancer	Discharge from industrial chemical factories	zero
OC	Di(2-ethylhexyl) adipate	0.4	Weight loss, liver problems, or possible reproductive difficulties	Discharge from chemical factories	0.4
OC	Di(2-ethylhexyl) phthalate	0.006	Reproductive difficulties; liver problems; increased risk of cancer	Discharge from rubber and chemical factories	zero
OC	Dinoseb	0.007	Reproductive difficulties	Runoff from herbicide used on soybeans and vegetables	0.007
OC	Dioxin (2,3,7,8-TCDD)	0.00000003	Reproductive difficulties; increased risk of cancer	Emissions from waste incineration and other combustion; discharge from chemical factories	zero
OC	Diquat	0.02	Cataracts	Runoff from herbicide use	0.02
OC	Endothall	0.1	Stomach and intestinal problems	Runoff from herbicide use	0.1
OC	Endrin	0.002	Liver problems	Residue of banned insecticide	0.002
OC	Epichlorohydrin	TT[h]	Increased cancer risk, and over a long period of time, stomach problems	Discharge from industrial chemical factories; an impurity of some water treatment chemicals	zero
OC	Ethylbenzene	0.7	Liver or kidneys problems	Discharge from petroleum refineries	0.7
OC	Ethylene dibromide	0.00005	Problems with liver, stomach, reproductive system, or kidneys; increased risk of cancer	Discharge from petroleum refineries	zero
IOC	Fluoride	4.0	Bone disease (pain and tenderness of the bones); children may get mottled teeth	Water additive which promotes strong teeth; erosion of natural deposits; discharge from fertilizer and aluminum factories	4.0
M	Giardia lamblia	TT[c]	Gastrointestinal illness (e.g., diarrhea, vomiting, cramps)	Human and animal fecal waste	zero
OC	Glyphosate	0.7	Kidney problems; reproductive difficulties	Runoff from herbicide use	0.7
DBP	Haloacetic acids (HAA5)	0.060	Increased risk of cancer	By-product of drinking water disinfection	n/a[f]
OC	Heptachlor	0.0004	Liver damage; increased risk of cancer	Residue of banned termiticide	zero
OC	Heptachlor epoxide	0.0002	Liver damage; increased risk of cancer	Breakdown of heptachlor	zero
M	Heterotrophic plate count (HPC)	TT[c]	HPC has no health effects; it is an analytic method used to measure the variety of bacteria that are common in water. The lower the concentration of bacteria in drinking water, the better maintained the water system is.	HPC measures a range of bacteria that are naturally present in the environment	n/a
OC	Hexachlorobenzene	0.001	Liver or kidney problems; reproductive difficulties; increased risk of cancer	Discharge from metal refineries and agricultural chemical factories	zero
OC	Hexachlorocyclopentadien[e]	0.05	Kidney or stomach problems	Discharge from chemical factories	0.05
IOC	Lead	TT[g]; action level=0.015	Infants and children: delays in physical or mental development; children could show slight deficits in attention span and learning abilities; adults: kidney problems; high blood pressure	Corrosion of household plumbing systems; erosion of natural deposits	zero
M	Legionella	TT[c]	Legionnaire's Disease, a type of pneumonia	Found naturally in water; multiplies in heating systems	zero
OC	Lindane	0.0002	Liver or kidney problems	Runoff/leaching from insecticide used on cattle, lumber, gardens	0.0002
IOC	Mercury (inorganic)	0.002	Kidney damage	Erosion of natural deposits; discharge from refineries and factories; runoff from landfills and croplands	0.002
OC	Methoxychlor	0.04	Reproductive difficulties	Runoff/leaching from insecticide used on fruits, vegetables, alfalfa, livestock	0.04

TABLE 4.2

Drinking water contaminants, their sources, and potential health effects, 2003 [CONTINUED]

Type	Contaminant	MCL or TT[a] (mg/L)[b]	Potential health effects from exposure above the MCL	Common sources of contaminant in drinking water	Public health goal
IOC	Nitrate (measured as nitrogen)	10	Infants below the age of six months who drink water containing nitrate in excess of the MCL could become seriously ill and, if untreated, may die. Symptoms include shortness of breath and blue-baby syndrome.	Runoff from fertilizer use; leaching from septic tanks, sewage; erosion of natural deposits	10
IOC	Nitrite (measured as nitrogen)	1	Infants below the age of six months who drink water containing nitrite in excess of the MCL could become seriously ill and, if untreated, may die. Symptoms include shortness of breath and blue-baby syndrome.	Runoff from fertilizer use; leaching from septic tanks, sewage; erosion of natural deposits	1
OC	Oxamyl (vydate)	0.2	Slight nervous system effects	Runoff/leaching from insecticide used on apples, potatoes, and tomatoes	0.2
OC	Pentachlorophenol	0.001	Liver or kidney problems; increased cancer risk	Discharge from wood preserving factories	zero
OC	Picloram	0.5	Liver problems	Herbicide runoff	0.5
OC	Polychlorinated biphenyls (PCBs)	0.0005	Skin changes; thymus gland problems; immune deficiencies; reproductive or nervous system difficulties; increased risk of cancer	Runoff from landfills; discharge of waste chemicals	zero
R	Radium 226 and radium 228 (combined)	5 pCi/L	Increased risk of cancer	Erosion of natural deposits	zero
IOC	Selenium	0.05	Hair or fingernail loss; numbness in fingers or toes; circulatory problems	Discharge from petroleum refineries; erosion of natural deposits; discharge from mines	0.05
OC	Simazine	0.004	Problems with blood	Herbicide runoff	0.004
OC	Styrene	0.1	Liver, kidney, or circulatory system problems	Discharge from rubber and plastic factories; leaching from landfills	0.1
OC	Tetrachloroethylene	0.005	Liver problems; increased risk of cancer	Discharge from factories and dry cleaners	zero
IOC	Thallium	0.002	Hair loss; changes in blood; kidney, intestine, or liver problems	Leaching from ore-processing sites; discharge from electronics, glass, and drug factories	0.0005
OC	Toluene	1	Nervous system, kidney, or liver problems	Discharge from petroleum factories	1
M	Total coliforms (including fecal coliform and E. coli)	5.0%[d]	Not a health threat in itself; it is used to indicate whether other potentially harmful bacteria may be present[e]	Coliforms are naturally present in the environment as well as feces; fecal coliforms and E. coli only come from human and animal fecal waste.	zero
DBP	Total trihalomethanes (TTHMs)	0.10 0.080 after 12/31/03	Liver, kidney, or central nervous system problems; increased risk of cancer	By-product of drinking water disinfection	n/a[f]
OC	Toxaphene	0.003	Kidney, liver, or thyroid problems; increased risk of cancer	Runoff/leaching from insecticide used on cotton and cattle	zero
OC	2,4,5-TP (silvex)	0.05	Liver problems	Residue of banned herbicide	0.05
OC	1,2,4-Trichlorobenzene	0.07	Changes in adrenal glands	Discharge from textile finishing factories	0.07
OC	1,1,1-Trichloroethane	0.2	Liver, nervous system, or circulatory problems	Discharge from metal degreasing sites and other factories	0.20
OC	1,1,2-Trichloroethane	0.005	Liver, kidney, or immune system problems	Discharge from industrial chemical factories	0.003
OC	Trichloroethylene	0.005	Liver problems; increased risk of cancer	Discharge from metal degreasing sites and other factories	zero
M	Turbidity	TT[c]	Turbidity is a measure of the cloudiness of water. It is used to indicate water quality and filtration effectiveness (e.g., whether disease-causing organisms are present). Higher turbidity levels are often associated with higher levels of disease-causing micro-organisms such as viruses, parasites, and some bacteria. These organisms can cause symptoms such as nausea, cramps, diarrhea, and associated headaches.	Soil runoff	n/a
R	Uranium	30 ug/L as of 12/08/03	Increased risk of cancer, kidney toxicity	Erosion of natural deposits	zero
OC	Vinyl chloride	0.002	Increased risk of cancer	Leaching from PVC pipes; discharge from plastic factories	zero

water. Regional differences in nitrate levels are related to soil drainage properties, other geologic characteristics, and agricultural practices. Nitrates in groundwater are generally highest in areas with well-drained soils and intensive cultivation of row crops, particularly corn, cotton, and vegetables. Low nitrate concentrations are found

TABLE 4.2

Drinking water contaminants, their sources, and potential health effects, 2003 [CONTINUED]

Type	Contaminant	MCL or TT[a] (mg/L)[b]	Potential health effects from exposure above the MCL	Common sources of contaminant in drinking water	Public health goal
M	Viruses (enteric)	TT[c]	Gastrointestinal illness (e.g., diarrhea, vomiting, cramps)	Human and animal fecal waste	zero
OC	Xylenes (total)	10	Nervous system damage	Discharge from petroleum factories; discharge from chemical factories	10

Type Legend:
D=Disinfectant
DBP=Disinfection by product
OC=Inorganic chemical
M=Microorganism
OC=Organic chemical
R=Radionuclides
Notes:
[a]Definitions
- Maximum Contaminant Level Goal (MCLG)—The level of a contaminant in drinking water below which there is no known or expected risk to health. MCLGs allow for a margin of safety and are non-enforceable public health goals.
- Maximum Contaminant Level (MCL)—The highest level of a contaminant that is allowed in drinking water. MCLs are set as close to MCLGs as feasible using the best available treatment technology and taking cost into consideration. MCLs are enforceable standards.
- Maximum Residual Disinfectant Level Goal (MRDLG)—The level of a drinking water disinfectant below which there is no known or expected risk to health. MRDLGs do not reflect the benefits of the use of disinfectants to control microbial contaminants.
- Maximum Residual Disinfectant Level (MRDL)—The highest level of a disinfectant allowed in drinking water. There is convincing evidence that addition of a disinfectant is necessary for control of microbial contaminants.
- Treatment Technique (TT)—A required process intended to reduce the level of a contaminant in drinking water.
[b]Units are in milligrams per liter (mg/L) unless otherwise noted. Milligrams per liter are equivalent to parts per million (ppm).
[c]EPA's surface water treatment rules require systems using surface water or groundwater under the direct influence of surface water to (1) disinfect their water, and (2) filter their water or meet criteria for avoiding filtration so that the following contaminants are controlled at the following levels:
- Cryptosporidium (as of 1/1/02 for systems serving >10,000 and 1/14/05 for systems serving <10,000) 99% removal.
- Giardia lamblia: 99.9% removal/inactivation.
- Viruses: 99.99% removal/inactivation.
- Legionella: No limit, but EPA believes that if Giardia and viruses are removed/inactivated, Legionella will also be controlled.
- Turbidity: At no time can turbidity (cloudiness of water) go above 5 nephelolometric turbidity units (NTU); systems that filter must ensure that the turbidity go no higher than 1 NTU (0.5 NTU for conventional or direct filtration) in at least 95% of the daily samples in any month. As of January 1, 2002, for systems servicing >10,000, and January 14, 2005, for systems servicing <10,000, turbidity may never exceed 1 NTU, and must not exceed 0.3 NTU in 95% of daily samples in any month.
- HPC: No more than 500 bacterial colonies per milliliter.
- Long Term 1 Enhanced Surface Water Treatment (Effective Date: January 14, 2005); Surface water systems or (GWUDI) systems serving fewer than 10,000 people must comply with the applicable Long Term 1 Enhanced Surface Water Treatment Rule provisions (e.g. turbidity standards, individual filter monitoring, Cryptosporidium removal requirements, updated watershed control requirements for unfiltered systems).
- Filter Backwash Recycling: The Filter Backwash Recycling Rule requires systems that recycle to return specific recycle flows through all processes of the system's existing conventional or direct filtration system or at an alternate location approved by the state.
[d]No more than 5.0% samples total coliform-positive in a month. (For water systems that collect fewer than 40 routine samples per month, no more than one sample can be total coliform-positive per month.) Every sample that has total coliform must be analyzed for either fecal coliforms or E. coli if two consecutive TC-positive samples, and one is also positive for E. coli fecal coliforms, system has an acute MCL violation.
[e]Fecal coliform and E. coli are bacteria whose presence indicates that the water may be contaminated with human or animal wastes. Disease-causing microbes (pathogens) in these wastes can cause diarrhea, cramps, nausea, headaches, or other symptoms. These pathogens may pose a special health risk for infants, young children, and people with severely compromised immune systems.
[f]Although there is no collective MCLG for this contaminant group, there are individual MCLGs for some of the individual contaminants
- Haloacetic acids: dichloroacetic acid (zero); trichloroacetic acid (0.3 mg/L)
- Trihalomethanes: bromodichloromethane (zero); bromoform (zero); dibromochloromethane (0.06 mg/L)
[g]Lead and copper are regulated by a Treatment Technique that requires systems to control the corrosiveness of their water. If more than 10% of tap water samples exceed the action level, water systems must take additional steps. For copper, the action level is 1.3 mg/L, and for lead is 0.015 mg/L.
[h]Each water system must certify, in writing, to the state (using third-party or manufacturers certification) that when it uses acrylamide and/or epichlorohydrin to treat water, the combination (or product) of dose and monomer level does not exceed the levels specified, as follows: Acrylamide=0.05% dosed at 1 mg/L (or equivalent); Epichlorohydrin=0.01% dosed at 20 mg/L (or equivalent).

SOURCE: "EPA National Primary Drinking Water Standards," U.S. Environmental Protection Agency, Office of Water, June 2003, http://www.epa.gov/safewater/consumer/pdf/mcl.pdf (accessed March 16, 2009)

in areas of poorly drained soil and where pasture and woodland are intermixed with cropland. The primary sources of nitrates are fertilizers used in agriculture and, in some areas, feedlot operations.

Nitrates are important because they affect both human and ecological health. They can cause a public health risk to infants and young livestock. In some areas of the country substantial amounts of nitrates in surface water are contributed by groundwater sources. In "Consumer Fact Sheet on Nitrates/Nitrites" (November 28, 2006, http://www.epa.gov/OGWDW/contaminants/dw_contamfs/nitrates.html),

the EPA notes that the standard for nitrates is between 1 and 10 parts per million (ppm). Public water suppliers must reduce the level of nitrates in the water they provide should it exceed this level.

PESTICIDES. Robert J. Gilliom et al. of the USGS report in *The Quality of Our Nation's Water: Pesticides in the Nation's Streams and Ground Water, 1992–2001* (February 15, 2007, http://pubs.usgs.gov/circ/2005/1291/pdf/circ1291.pdf) that pesticides are found less frequently in groundwater than in surface water. Nonetheless, pesticides and their broken-down products are frequently found in shallow groundwater, especially in residential and agricultural areas. However, the pesticides are rarely found in concentrations exceeding water quality benchmarks for human health.

Kate Barrett and Ki Mae Heussner report in "States Battle Pesticides in Groundwater" (ABC News, September 9, 2008) that even though there has not been much concern about pesticides in groundwater in recent years, Oregon issued a report in 2008 that revealed that seven pesticides were contaminating groundwater there. Because the EPA does not have standards for safe water levels of many pesticides, Oregon was unable to immediately address its water quality issue.

VOLATILE ORGANIC COMPOUNDS. Volatile organic compounds (VOCs) contain the element carbon and tend to evaporate more quickly than water. Examples of substances that contain a variety of VOCs are gasoline, diesel fuel, paint, glue, spot removers, and cleaning solutions. VOCs are used extensively in industry to manufacture products such as cars, electronics, computers, adhesives, dyes, and plastics; they are also used in dry cleaning and refrigeration.

VOCs can cause cancer, have adverse effects on various body organs and systems, and affect the brain, ears, eyes, skin, and throat. Groundwater contamination can occur from landfills, hazardous waste facilities, and septic systems into which VOCs have been discarded, or from sources such as leaking underground storage tanks. They can be released into the environment from industry, enter the atmosphere, and fall to the ground as atmospheric deposition. Some VOCs do not degrade quickly and can remain in groundwater for years and even decades. VOCs are of concern not only because they contaminate groundwater but also because their presence in groundwater signals that soil and other conditions favor VOCs reaching the groundwater.

According to Zogorski et al., the most frequently detected groups of VOCs in aquifers are the trihalomethanes and organic solvents. Trihalomethanes are used as solvents and in refrigeration. Organic solvents are substances containing carbon that dissolve other substances. They include chloroform and alcohol but do not include water.

Zogorski et al. note that VOCs are detected frequently in domestic and public wells, but that only 1% to 2% of the samples taken from these wells had VOC concentrations of potential human-health concern.

Sources of Groundwater Contaminants

In 2000 the EPA requested that states identify the major sources that potentially threaten groundwater in each state. The EPA notes in *2000 National Water Quality Inventory* that 52 states, tribes, and territories reported the major sources of the pollution of their groundwater.

Thirty-nine states rated underground storage tanks as the most serious threat to their groundwater quality. (See Figure 4.7.) Septic systems, landfills, industrial facilities, agriculture, and pesticides were also important contamination sources. (The *National Water Quality Inventory: Report to Congress, 2004 Reporting Cycle* does not address this issue.)

LEAKING UNDERGROUND STORAGE TANKS. Leaking underground storage tanks (LUSTs) have been identified by the EPA as the leading source of groundwater contamination since the mid-1990s and were cited as such in *2000 National Water Quality Inventory* and as a source of VOC groundwater contamination by Zogorski et al.

In general, most underground storage tanks (USTs) are found at commercial and industrial facilities in the more heavily developed urban and suburban areas. USTs are used to store gasoline, hazardous and toxic chemicals, and diluted wastes. Gasoline leaking from UST systems at service stations is one of the most common causes of groundwater contamination. The primary causes of leakage in USTs are faulty installation and corrosion of tanks and pipelines.

At one time, USTs were made of steel, which eventually rusted and disintegrated, releasing their contents into the soil. This led to the discovery that a contaminant in the ground is likely to become a contaminant of groundwater. The Sierra Club reports in the press release "Leaking Underground Storage Tanks Continue to Contaminate Groundwater" (April 19, 2005, http://www.sierraclub.org/pressroom/releases/pr2005-04-19.asp) that 1 gallon (3.8 L) of gasoline can contaminate 1 million gallons (3.8 million L) of water. The fuel additive MTBE, which is a VOC, is particularly troublesome because it migrates quickly through soils into groundwater, and small amounts can render groundwater undrinkable. Figure 4.8 shows how groundwater can be contaminated by LUSTs.

In 1986 Subtitle I of the Solid Waste Disposal Act created the Underground Storage Tank Program under the management of the EPA. In 1988 the EPA issued "comprehensive and stringent" rules that required devices to detect leaks, modification of tanks to prevent corrosion, regular monitoring, and immediate cleanup of leaks and spills. By December 1998 existing tanks had to be upgraded to meet those standards, replaced with new tanks, or closed. Existing tanks were to be replaced with expensive tanks made of durable, noncorrosive materials.

In August 2005 President George W. Bush (1946–) signed the Energy Policy Act, which contained amendments to Subtitle I of the Solid Waste Disposal Act. These amendments were titled the Underground Storage Tank Compliance Act of 2005, required major changes to the UST Program, and were aimed at preventing releases from USTs. The new legislation also expanded eligible

FIGURE 4.7

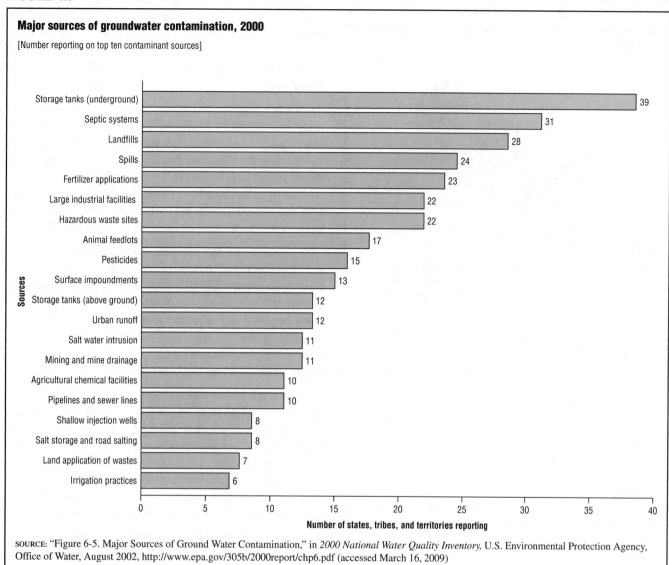

Major sources of groundwater contamination, 2000

[Number reporting on top ten contaminant sources]

SOURCE: "Figure 6-5. Major Sources of Ground Water Contamination," in *2000 National Water Quality Inventory,* U.S. Environmental Protection Agency, Office of Water, August 2002, http://www.epa.gov/305b/2000report/chp6.pdf (accessed March 16, 2009)

uses of the LUST Trust Fund and included provisions regarding inspections, containment, financial responsibility, and cleanup.

Figure 4.9 shows the number of LUSTs that were cleaned up between 2000 and 2007. In *FY 2008 Annual Report on the Underground Storage Tank Program* (March 2009, http://www.epa.gov/OUST/pubs/OUST_FY08 _Annual_Report-_Final_3-19-09.pdf), the EPA states that at the end of fiscal year 2008 over 377,000 UST cleanups had been completed since the beginning of the UST Program, which accounted for nearly 80% of the total LUSTs. Thus, a backlog of almost 103,000 LUSTs remained. As Figure 4.9 shows, the pace of cleanups from 2000 to 2007 has declined. At the 2007 pace, and if no new LUSTs are reported, the backlog will not be cleaned up until approximately 2015.

LANDFILLS AND SURFACE IMPOUNDMENTS. In 2000 septic systems and landfills were the second and third largest sources of groundwater contamination, respectively. (See Figure 4.7.) Landfills are areas set aside for the disposal of garbage, trash, and other municipal wastes. Early environmental regulation, aimed at reducing air and surface-water pollution, called for the disposing of solid wastes—including industrial wastes—underground and gave little consideration to the potential for groundwater contamination. Landfills were generally situated on land considered to have no other use. Many of the disposal sites were nothing more than large holes in the ground, abandoned gravel pits, old strip mines, marshlands, and sinkholes.

The leachate (the liquid that percolates through the waste materials) from landfills contains contaminants that can easily pollute groundwater when disposal areas are not properly lined. Landfills built and operated before the passage of the 1976 Resource Conservation and Recovery Act (RCRA; also known as the Solid Waste Disposal Act) are believed to represent the greatest risk.

FIGURE 4.8

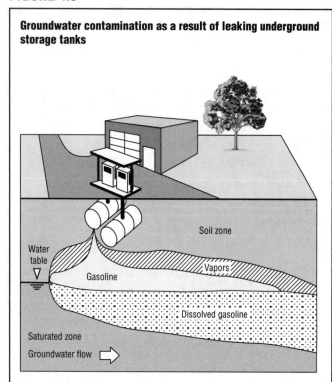

Groundwater contamination as a result of leaking underground storage tanks

SOURCE: "Figure 6-3. Ground Water Contamination As a Result of Leaking Underground Storage Tanks," in *2000 National Water Quality Inventory*, U.S. Environmental Protection Agency, Office of Water, August 2002, http://www.epa.gov/305b/2000report/chp6.pdf (accessed March 16, 2009)

FIGURE 4.9

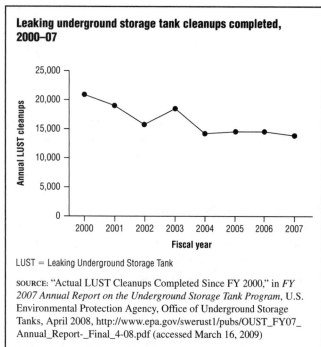

Leaking underground storage tank cleanups completed, 2000–07

LUST = Leaking Underground Storage Tank

SOURCE: "Actual LUST Cleanups Completed Since FY 2000," in *FY 2007 Annual Report on the Underground Storage Tank Program*, U.S. Environmental Protection Agency, Office of Underground Storage Tanks, April 2008, http://www.epa.gov/swerust1/pubs/OUST_FY07_Annual_Report-_Final_4-08.pdf (accessed March 16, 2009)

The RCRA was enacted to protect human health and the environment by establishing a regulatory framework to investigate and address past, present, and future environ-mental contamination of groundwater and other media. The adoption of these new standards in 1976 forced many landfills to close, as they could not meet the RCRA's safety standards. However, the garbage already dumped in these landfills remained in place and is a threat to groundwater.

Surface impoundments are the industrial equivalent of landfills for liquids. They usually consist of human-made pits, lagoons, and ponds that receive treated or untreated wastes directly from the discharge point. They may also be used to store chemicals for later use, to wash or treat ores, or to treat water for further use. Most are small, less than 1 acre (0.4 ha), but some industrial and mining impoundments may be as large as 1,000 acres (404.7 ha).

Before the RCRA most impoundments were not lined with a synthetic or impermeable natural material, such as clay, to prevent liquids from leaching into the ground. This is particularly important because impoundments are often located over aquifers that are used as sources of drinking water and that may discharge into nearby surface water. Aquifers located under nonlined impoundments are vulnerable to contamination.

Since the passage of the RCRA, landfills and surface impoundments have been required to adhere to increasingly stringent regulations for site selection, construction, operation, and groundwater monitoring to avoid contaminating groundwater. The prevention of groundwater contamination is largely the responsibility of state and local governments. Examples of the more stringent requirements are landfill liners and groundwater monitoring.

Figure 4.10 shows the positioning of a lined landfill in the unsaturated zone. Groundwater monitoring is accomplished by sampling the water in an upgradient well to assess the quality of the groundwater before it passes the landfill site. Downgradient wells are used to assess the quality of groundwater at various levels after it flows past the landfill site.

HAZARDOUS WASTE SITES. In general, hazardous wastes are substances with the potential to harm human health and the environment. Hazardous waste is an unavoidable by-product of an industrial society, because many chemicals are used to manufacture goods. Hazardous waste generators can be large industries, such as automobile manufacturers, or small neighborhood businesses, such as the local cleaners. Even though the quantity of hazardous waste can be reduced through innovation and good management, it is impossible to eliminate all hazardous residue because of the demand for goods.

Contamination of groundwater with hazardous waste is frequently the result of historic indiscriminate waste disposal in landfills, impoundments, and dumps. Sites that handle hazardous waste or a mix of hazardous and nonhazardous waste are subject to strict controls.

FIGURE 4.10

Cross section of a minimal groundwater monitoring system

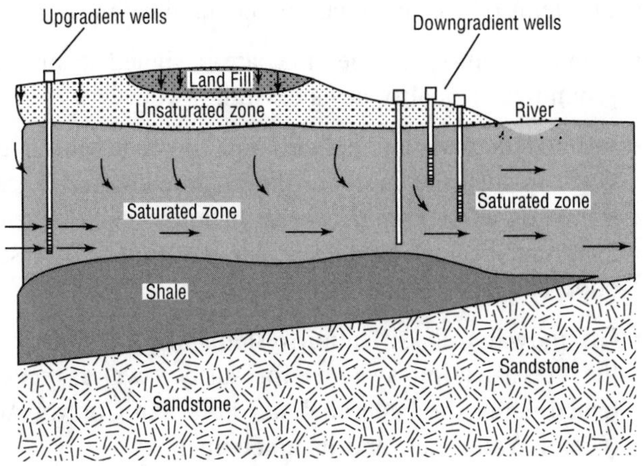

SOURCE: "Cross Section of a Minimal Groundwater Monitoring System," in *Hazardous Waste: Compliance with Groundwater Monitoring Requirements at Land Disposal Facilities*, U.S. General Accounting Office, February 1995, http://archive.gao.gov/f0902b/153695.pdf (accessed March 16, 2009)

When a waste site is found to be so badly contaminated with hazardous waste that it represents a serious threat to human health (e.g., groundwater used for drinking that has been contaminated with known carcinogens [cancer-causing agents]), it is placed on the National Priorities List, which was established by the Comprehensive Environmental Response, Compensation, and Liability Act of 1980 (commonly known as the Superfund). Sites placed on the Superfund list are eligible for federal intervention and cleanup assistance. The EPA reports in "NPL Site Totals by Status and Milestone" (April 20, 2009, http://www.epa.gov/superfund/sites/query/queryhtm/npltotal.htm) that as of April 2009, 1,264 sites were listed on the National Priorities List. Most were general sites such as industrial and municipal landfills and military bases.

INJECTION WELLS. An injection well is any bored, drilled, driven shaft, or dug hole that is deeper than it is wide that is used for the disposal of fluid waste underground. In "Classes of Wells" (February 12, 2008, http://www.epa.gov/safewater/uic/wells.html), the EPA identifies five classes of injection wells of the Underground Injection Control (UIC) Program:

- Class I wells are used to inject hazardous and nonhazardous waste beneath the lowest formation containing an underground source of drinking water (USDW).

- Class II wells are used to inject fluids associated with oil and natural gas recovery and storage of liquid hydrocarbons.

- Class III wells are used in connection with the solution mining of minerals that are not conventionally mined.

- Class IV wells are used to inject hazardous or radioactive waste into or above a USDW.

- Class V wells are injection wells not included in Classes I through IV.

Each well class can contaminate groundwater. Classes I through IV have specific regulations and are closely monitored. Class V wells are typically shallow wells used to place a variety of fluids underground.

The EPA reports that in 2008 there were 400,000 to 650,000 Class V injection wells in the United States. These wells are found in every state, especially in unsewered areas. There are many types of Class V wells, including large-capacity cesspools, motor vehicle waste disposal systems, storm water drainage wells, large-capacity septic systems, aquifer remediation wells, and many others. The waste entering these wells is not treated. Certain types of these wells have great potential to have high concentrations of contaminants that might endanger groundwater.

Class V injection wells are regulated by the UIC Program under the authority of the Safe Drinking Water Act (SDWA). Class V wells are "authorized by rule," which means that they do not require a permit if they comply with UIC Program requirements and do not endanger underground sources of drinking water. In December 1999 the EPA adopted regulations addressing Class V wells that were large-capacity cesspools and motor vehicle waste disposal wells. Under these regulations:

- New cesspools were prohibited as of April 2000.

- Existing cesspools had to be phased out by April 2005.

- New motor vehicle waste disposal wells were prohibited.

- Existing wells in regulated areas were to be phased out in groundwater protection areas identified in state source water assessment programs.

AGRICULTURE. As in surface-water contamination, agricultural practices play a major role in groundwater contamination. Agricultural practices that have the potential to contaminate groundwater include fertilizer and pesticide applications, animal feedlots, irrigation practices, agricultural chemical facilities, and drainage wells. Contamination can result from routine applications, spillage or misuse of pesticides and fertilizers during handling and storage, manure storage and spreading, improper storage of chemicals, irrigation practices, and irrigation return drains serving as direct conduits to groundwater. Fields with overapplied or misapplied fertilizer and pesticides can introduce nitrogen, pesticides, and other contaminants into groundwater. Animal feedlots often have impoundments from which wastes (bacteria, nitrates, and total and dissolved solids) may infiltrate groundwater.

Human-induced salinity in groundwater also occurs in agricultural regions where irrigation is used extensively. Irrigation water continually flushes nitrate-related compounds from fertilizers into shallow aquifers along with high levels of chloride, sodium, and several types of metals. This increases the salinity (dissolved solids) of the underlying aquifers. Overpumping can diminish the water in aquifers to the point where saltwater from nearby coastal areas will intrude into the aquifer. Salinas Valley, California, is an example of the occurrence of saltwater intrusion. Eleven states identified saltwater intrusion as a major source of groundwater contamination in their 2000 305(b) reports to the EPA. (See Figure 4.7.)

SEPTIC SYSTEMS. Septic systems were cited as the second most common source of groundwater contamination by 31 reporting states. (See Figure 4.7.) Septic systems are on-site waste disposal systems that are used where public sewerage is not available. Septic tanks are used to detain domestic wastes to allow the settling and digestion of solids before the distribution of liquid wastes into permeable leach beds for absorption into soil. Wastewater is digested in the leach beds by organisms in the soil and broken down over time.

According to the EPA, in "Septic Systems" (September 20, 2006, http://cfpub.epa.gov/owm/septic/faqs.cfm?program_id=70#359), the U.S. Census Bureau reports that approximately 26 million American homes use individual sewage disposal systems. The use of septic systems varies across the country from about 55% of the population in Vermont to around 10% in California. More than 60 million people nationwide live in homes with septic systems. Improperly constructed and poorly maintained septic systems may cause substantial and widespread contamination to groundwater of nitrogen and disease-causing microbes.

GROUNDWATER CLEANUP

Cleaning up the nation's groundwater is expensive. The costs associated with alternative water supplies, water treatment, and contaminant source removal or remediation are in the millions per site. In allocating limited resources, cleanup decisions are based on a cost-benefit analysis that considers factors such as the extent of the problem, the potential health effects, and the alternatives, if any. If the pollution is localized, it may be more practical to simply shut down the contaminated wells and find water elsewhere. Cleanup options range from capping a section of an aquifer with a layer of impermeable clay to prevent more pollution, to more complex (and expensive) methods, such as pumping out and treating the water and then returning it to the aquifer.

GROUNDWATER PROTECTION
The States' Role

The prevention of groundwater contamination is largely the responsibility of state and local governments. In 1991 the EPA established a national groundwater protection strategy to place greater emphasis on comprehensive state management of groundwater resources. The EPA

recognized that the wide range of land-use practices that can adversely affect groundwater quality are most effectively managed at the state and local levels. The states use three basic approaches to protect groundwater and address the problems of contaminants and contamination sources:

- Nondegradation policies that are designed to protect groundwater quality at its existing level.

- Limited degradation policies that involve setting up water quality standards to protect groundwater. These standards set maximum contamination levels for chemicals and bacteria and establish guidelines for taste, odor, and color of the water.

- Groundwater classification systems that are similar to the classification systems for surface waters established under the Federal Water Pollution Control Act (Clean Water Act) and its amendments.

These classification systems are used by state officials to determine which aquifers should receive higher or lower priorities for protection and cleanup. High-priority sites include recharge areas, which affect large quantities of water, or public water supplies, where pollution affects drinking water.

The most important benefit derived from comprehensive groundwater management approaches is the ability to establish coordinated priorities among the many groups involved in groundwater management. The following key components are common to successful state programs:

- Enacting legislation

- Publicly announcing protection regulations

- Establishing interagency coordination with surface-water and other programs

- Performing groundwater mapping and classification

- Monitoring groundwater quality

- Developing comprehensive data management systems

- Adopting and implementing prevention and remediation programs

The Federal Government's Role

Federal laws, regulations, and programs since the 1970s have reflected the growing recognition of the need to protect the nation's groundwater and use it wisely. The Clean Water Act in 1972 and the SDWA in 1974 began the federal role in groundwater protection. The passage of the RCRA in 1976 and the Comprehensive Environmental Response, Compensation, and Liability Act in 1980 cemented the federal government's current focus on groundwater remediation. Since the passage of these acts and subsequent amendments, the federal government has directed billions of dollars in private and public money and resources toward the cleanup of contaminated groundwater at Superfund sites, RCRA corrective action facilities, and LUSTs.

CHAPTER 5
DRINKING WATER—SAFETY ON TAP

HOW MUCH WATER DO AMERICANS USE?

In the American Water Works Association's benchmark study *Residential End Uses of Water Study* (1999, http://www.awwarf.org/research/topicsandprojects/exec Sum/241.aspx), Peter W. Mayer et al. report the results of their study on residential end uses of water in 1,188 single-family homes in 12 North American locations from 1996 to 1998. Mayer et al. reveal that, on average, Americans on community water supplies used about 100 gallons (378.5 L) of water per person per day. People with private wells used slightly less. About 69 gallons (261.2 liters) per day were used indoors and the rest was used outdoors. According to the University of North Carolina, Chapel Hill, in "Beverage Intake in the United States" (2009, http://www.cpc.unc.edu/projects/beverage), in 2001 only 46 ounces (1.4 L) were consumed each day as drinking water by an average American.

Residential water consumers use most water for purposes other than drinking, such as toilet flushing, bathing, cooking, and cleaning. In the United States significant amounts of water are used for kitchen and laundry appliances, such as garbage disposals, clothes washers, and automatic dishwashers; for automobile washing; and for lawn and garden watering. Additional community use includes firefighting, fountains, public swimming pools, and watering of public parks and landscaping.

DRINKING WATER SOURCES

The two primary sources of drinking water are surface freshwater and groundwater. In 2000, 27.3 billion gallons per day (Bgal/d; 103.3 billion L per day) of 43.3 Bgal/d (163.9 billion L per day) of public-supply water withdrawals were from surface-water sources (e.g., lakes, rivers, and reservoirs). (See Table 2.3 in Chapter 2.) The remaining 16 Bgal/d (60.6 billion L per day) were supplied with water that came from groundwater stored in aquifers

(see Chapter 4). Aquifers are underground geologic formations that consist of layers of sand and porous rock that are saturated with water. Aquifer water is obtained from wells and springs. The only other source of drinking water is desalinated seawater, which is used in only a few locations around the world and provides little of the total amount of drinking water worldwide.

PUBLIC AND PRIVATE WATER SUPPLIES
Public-Supply Water

As described in Chapter 2, public-supply water use is water withdrawn by public and private water suppliers (utility companies) and delivered for public uses: domestic, commercial, industrial, and thermoelectric power uses. It may be used for public services such as filling public pools, watering vegetation in parks, supplying public buildings, firefighting, and street washing. The U.S. Geological Survey (USGS) indicates that 43.3 Bgal/d (163.9 billion L per day) were supplied to users in 2000 by water utility companies (public supply). (See Table 2.2 in Chapter 2.) The rest of the water was self-supplied—that is, the water was withdrawn from surface or groundwater sources by the users, not by water utility companies.

According to the U.S. Environmental Protection Agency (EPA), in *Factoids: Drinking Water and Ground Water Statistics for 2008* (November 2008, http://www.epa.gov/OGWDW/databases/pdfs/data_factoids_2008.pdf), public-supply water systems (which can be publicly or privately owned) have at least 15 service connections or serve at least 25 people per day for 60 days of the year. There were 154,837 of these systems of varying size in the United States in 2008. (See Table 5.1.) The amount and type of treatment provided varies with source and quality. For example, some public systems using a groundwater source require no treatment, whereas others may need to disinfect the water or apply additional treatment.

TABLE 5.1

Types of public water systems, by water source and population served, 2008

Type	Groundwater	Surface water	Totals
CWS			
# systems	40,301	11,671	51,972
Pop. served	88,039,047	204,094,646	292,133,693
% of systems	78%	22%	100%
% of pop.	30%	70%	100%
NTNCWS			
# systems	18,041	688	18,729
Pop. served	5,462,056	788,360	6,250,416
% of systems	96%	4%	100%
% of pop.	87%	13%	100%
TNCWS			
# systems	82,126	2,010	84,136
Pop. served	11,036,800	2,534,900	13,571,700
% of systems	98%	2%	100%
% of pop.	81%	19%	100%
Total # systems	**140,468**	**14,369**	**154,837**

Groundwater systems = groundwater (GW), purchased groundwater (GWP)
Surface-water systems = surface water (SW), purchased surface water (SWP), groundwater under the direct influence of surface water (GU), purchased groundwater under the direct influence of surface water (GUP).
CWS = Community Water System: A public water system that supplies water to the same population year-round.
NTNCWS = Non-Transient Non-Community Water System: A public water system that regularly supplies water to at least 25 of the same people at least six months per year, but not year-round. Some examples are schools, factories, office buildings, and hospitals which have their own water systems.
TNCWS = Transient Non-Community Water System: A public water system that provides water in a place such as a gas station or campground where people do not remain for long periods of time and is open at least 60 days/year.

SOURCE: Adapted from "Water Source," in *Factoids: Drinking Water and Ground Water Statistics for 2008*, U.S. Environmental Protection Agency, Office of Water, November 2008, http://www.epa.gov/OGWDW/databases/pdfs/data_factoids_2008.pdf (accessed March 16, 2009)

There are three types of public water systems. Figure 5.1 shows a flowchart of drinking water systems, including public water systems. Table 5.1 displays their similarities and differences. Community water systems are those that supply water to the same population year round. Most people in the United States are served by community water systems. In 2008 there were 51,972 community water systems serving 292.1 million (94%) out of 311.9 million people in the United States. Of these systems, 40,301 (78%) accessed groundwater for their water supply. Nevertheless, they served only 88 million (30%) of the community water system population. In 2008, 204.1 million (70%) of that population was served by 11,671 (22%) community water systems that access surface water for their water supply.

Nontransient noncommunity water systems are the second type of public water system. They serve the public but not the same people year round. Examples of nontransient noncommunity systems are schools, factories, office buildings, hospitals, and other public accommodations. In 2008 there were 18,729 nontransient noncommunity water systems in the United States serving 6.3 million people, or 2% of the total U.S. population. (See Table 5.1.) Of these systems, 18,041 (96%) accessed groundwater for their water supply.

Transient noncommunity water systems are the third type of public water system. These are systems that provide water in places such as gas stations or campgrounds, where people do not remain for long periods of time. In 2008 there were 84,136 transient noncommunity water systems serving 13.6 million people, or 4% of the total U.S. population. (See Table 5.1.) Ninety-eight percent (82,126) of transient noncommunity water systems accessed groundwater for their water supply.

The EPA and state health and environment departments regulate public water supplies. Public suppliers are required to ensure that the water meets certain government-defined health standards under the Safe Drinking Water Act (SDWA) of 1974. This law mandates that all public suppliers test their water regularly to check for the existence of contaminants and treat their water supplies, if necessary, to take out or reduce certain pollutants to levels that will not harm human health.

The data in Table 5.1 show that more water systems have groundwater than surface water as a source, but more people drink from a surface-water system. Table 5.2 shows that 145,642 (94%) of public water systems were small or very small in 2008, each serving fewer than 3,300 people. The remaining systems (9,237, or 6%) were comparatively few in number but serviced many more people. The medium-sized systems each provide water to between 3,301 and 10,000 people. The large and very large systems provide water to more than 10,000 people each. Together, the medium, large, and very large public water services provided water for the vast majority of people who drank water from a public supply in the United States in 2008: 272.6 million people.

Private Water Systems

According to the EPA, in *Drinking Water from Household Wells* (January 2002, http://www.epa.gov/safewater/privatewells/pdfs/household_wells.pdf), 15% of Americans obtain their water from private wells, cisterns, and springs. System owners are solely responsible for the quality of the water provided from these sources.

Personal private water supplies, usually wells, are not regulated under the SDWA. Many states, however, have programs designed to help well owners protect their own water supplies. Usually, these state-run programs are not regulatory, but provide safety information. In addition, the EPA is a source of information. This type of information is vital because private wells are often shallower than those used by public suppliers. The more shallow the well, the greater the potential for contamination.

FIGURE 5.1

Types of drinking water systems

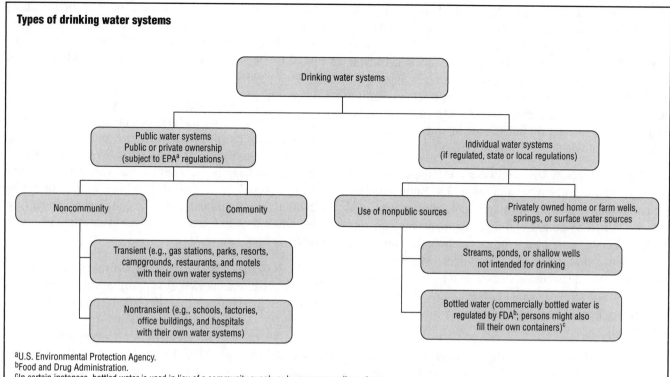

[a]U.S. Environmental Protection Agency.
[b]Food and Drug Administration.
[c]In certain instances, bottled water is used in lieu of a community supply or by noncommunity systems.

SOURCE: Jonathan Yoder et al., "Figure 1. Types of Drinking Water Systems—United States," in "Surveillance for Waterborne Disease and Outbreaks Associated with Drinking Water and Water Not Intended for Drinking—United States, 2005–2006," *Morbidity and Mortality Weekly Report, Surveillance Summaries*, vol. 57, no. SS-9, September 12, 2008, http://www.cdc.gov/mmwr/PDF/ss/ss5709.pdf (accessed March 10, 2009)

TABLE 5.2

Public water systems, by size and population served, 2008

	Very small 500 or less	Small 501–3,300	Medium 3,301–10,000	Large 10,001–100,000	Very large >100,000	Total
CWS						
# systems	29,160	13,858	4,838	3,728	404	51,988
Pop. served	4,857,104	19,868,795	28,134,557	106,310,834	133,128,786	292,300,076
% of systems	56%	27%	9%	7%	1%	100%
% of pop	2%	7%	10%	36%	46%	100%
NTNCWS						
# systems	15,954	2,641	130	16	1	18,742
Pop. served	2,234,688	2,701,807	702,369	412,160	203,000	6,254,024
% of systems	85%	14%	1%	0%	0%	100%
% of pop	36%	43%	11%	7%	3%	100%
TNCWS						
# systems	81,324	2,705	101	17	2	84,149
Pop. served	7,197,477	2,625,850	542,458	482,151	2,725,000	13,572,936
% of systems	97%	3%	0%	0%	0%	100%
% of pop	53%	19%	4%	4%	20%	100%
Total # systems	**126,438**	**19,204**	**5,069**	**3,761**	**407**	**154,879**

CWS = Community Water System: A public water system that supplies water to the same population year-round.
NTNCWS = Non-Transient Non-Community Water System: A public water system that regularly supplies water to at least 25 of the same people at least six months per year, but not year-round. Some examples are schools, factories, office buildings, and hospitals which have their own water systems.
TNCWS = Transient Non-Community Water System: A public water system that provides water in a place such as a gas station or campground where people do not remain for long periods of time and is open at least 60 days/year.

SOURCE: "System Size by Population Served," in *Factoids: Drinking Water and Ground Water Statistics for 2008*, U.S. Environmental Protection Agency, Office of Water, November 2008, http://www.epa.gov/OGWDW/databases/pdfs/data_factoids_2008.pdf (accessed March 16, 2009)

CONTAMINANTS IN DRINKING WATER

Water can dissolve many substances. Pure water rarely occurs in nature, because both surface and groundwater dissolve minerals and other substances in the soil and deposited from the atmosphere. At low levels dissolved contaminants generally are not harmful in drinking water. Removing all contaminants would be extremely expensive and might not provide greater protection of health. The concentration of harmful substances in water is the main determinant in whether the water is safe to drink.

Contaminants in drinking water are grouped into two broad categories: chemical and microbial. Both chemical and microbial contaminants may be naturally occurring or may be caused by human activity. Chemical contaminants include metals, pesticides, synthetic chemical compounds, suspended solids, and other substances. Microbial contaminants include bacteria, viruses, and microscopic parasites. A list of drinking water contaminants, their sources, and their potential health effects is shown in Table 4.2 in Chapter 4.

The health effects of drinking contaminated water can occur either over a short or long period. Short-term, or acute, reactions are those that occur within a few hours or days after drinking contaminated water. Acute reactions may be caused by a chemical or microbial contaminant. Long-term, or chronic, effects occur after water with relatively low doses of a pollutant has been consumed for several years or over a lifetime. Most chronic effects are caused by chemical contaminants.

The ability to detect contaminants improved considerably in the late 20th century. Scientists can now identify specific chemical pollutants in terms of 1 part contaminant in 1 billion parts of water. In some cases scientists can measure them in parts per trillion. One part per billion (ppb) is equal to 1 pound (0.5 kg) in 500,000 tons (454,000 t). Even though these measurements appear tiny, such small amounts can be significant in terms of health effects.

In 2002 the USGS implemented the Source Water-Quality Assessments (SWQAs) program to monitor contaminants in rivers and aquifers that are used as water sources for community water systems. Approximately 30 surface-water and 30 groundwater assessments will be conducted through 2013. Figure 5.2 shows the locations of the assessments that took place between 2002 and 2007. Additional sites will be added for future testing.

FIGURE 5.2

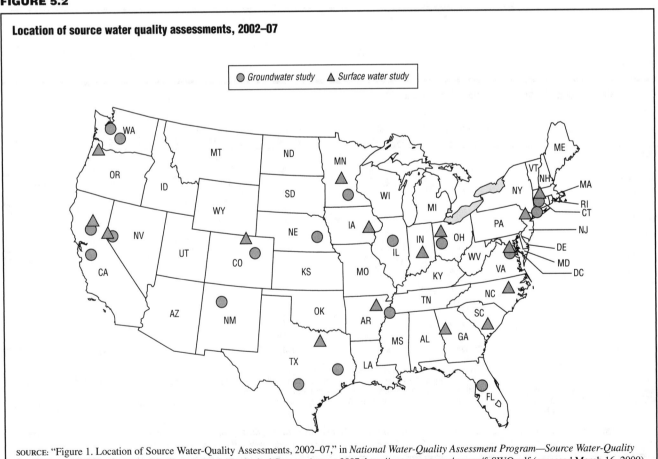

Location of source water quality assessments, 2002–07

SOURCE: "Figure 1. Location of Source Water-Quality Assessments, 2002–07," in *National Water-Quality Assessment Program—Source Water-Quality Assessments*, U.S. Department of the Interior, U.S. Geological Survey, August 2007, http://water.usgs.gov/nawqa/fsSWQ.pdf (accessed March 16, 2009)

Chemical Contaminants

All drinking water contains minerals dissolved from the earth. In small amounts some of these minerals are acceptable because they often enhance the quality of the water (e.g., giving it a pleasant taste). A few minerals in small amounts, such as zinc and selenium, contribute to good health. Other naturally occurring minerals are not desirable because they may cause a bad taste or odor (such as excessive amounts of iron, manganese, or sulfur) or because they may be harmful to health (such as boron).

A wide variety of contaminants may cause serious health risks in water supplies. Not all contaminants are found in all water supplies; furthermore, some water supplies have no undesirable contaminants and some supplies have no contaminants that have health significance. Contaminant presence is frequently the result of human activity and may have long-term consequences. Harmful levels of microorganisms generally make their presence known quickly by causing illness with fairly obvious symptoms, whereas the effects of some toxic chemicals may not be apparent for months or even years after exposure. Some chemical pollutants are known carcinogens (cancer-causing agents), and others are suspected of causing birth defects, miscarriages, and heart disease. In many cases the effects occur only after long-term exposure.

ARSENIC. Arsenic is a naturally occurring element in rocks and soils and is soluble in water. Arsenic has been recognized as a poison for centuries. However, research shows that humans need arsenic in their diet as a trace element. Paolo Boffetta and Fredrik Nyberg of the Karolinska Institute in Stockholm, Sweden, report in "Contribution of Environmental Factors to Cancer Risk" (*British Medical Bulletin*, vol. 68, no. 1, December 2003) that too much arsenic can contribute to skin, bladder, and lung cancers after prolonged exposure. Because of this risk, the current maximum contaminant level (MCL) for arsenic in drinking water is 10 ppb.

LEAD AND COPPER. Lead is a toxic metal that can cause serious health problems if ingested. Children are particularly at risk because their developing bodies absorb and retain more lead than adult bodies. Low-level exposures can result in a lowered intelligence quotient, impaired learning and language skills, loss of hearing, reduced attention spans, and poor school performance. High levels damage the brain and central nervous system and interfere with both learning and physical development. Pregnant women are also at risk. Lead can cause miscarriages, premature births, and impaired fetal development.

Unlike many water contaminants, lead has been extensively studied for its prevalence and effects on human health and for ways to eliminate it from the water supply. Lead is rarely found in either surface or groundwater sources for drinking. This contaminant usually enters the water supply after it leaves the treatment plant or the well.

The major sources of lead exposure are deteriorated lead paint in older houses and dust and soil that are contaminated by old paint and past emissions of leaded gasoline. Plumbing in older buildings has also contributed to overall blood lead levels. Until about 1930 many buildings in the United States had lead pipes in their interior plumbing and for the service connections that linked buildings to the public water supplies. In addition, lead solder was commonly used to connect pipes. There is little lead piping in use any more within buildings, but some lead service piping still exists in 100-year-old inner-city neighborhoods.

Copper pipes replaced lead in most buildings, but the practice of using lead solder to join the pipes continued. The corrosion of lead solder is believed to be the primary cause of most lead in residential water supplies in the 21st century. Low acidity, low calcium or magnesium levels in the water, and dissolved oxygen can all contribute to corrosion of lead solder. The common practice of grounding electrical equipment to water pipes also accelerates corrosion.

Most commonly, copper pipes are used to supply water from the street to a building, and to supply water to various parts of the building's interior. Even though copper is a dependable material, it can be corroded by acidic water.

In "Lead and Copper Rule" (October 17, 2007, http://www.epa.gov/safewater/lcrmr/index.html), the EPA notes that in June 1991 it established the Lead and Copper Rule (LCR) to help control lead and copper in drinking water. The rule requires community and nontransient noncommunity water systems to monitor drinking water at customer taps. If lead concentrations exceed 15 ppb or copper concentrations exceed 1.3 parts per million (ppm) in more than 10% of the customer taps sampled, then action must be taken to control corrosion and possibly replace lead service lines. If lead levels are exceeded, then the public must be informed about how to protect themselves against lead poisoning.

According to the EPA, in "Fact Sheet on the Revisions to the Regulations Controlling Lead in Drinking Water" (September 2007, http://www.epa.gov/safewater/lcrmr/fs_lcr_2007_final.html), final revisions to the LCR were enacted in 2007. These revisions focused on enhancing monitoring, treatment, customer awareness, and lead service line replacement. The changes also helped ensure that drinking water consumers receive meaningful, timely, and useful information to help them limit their exposure to lead in drinking water.

NITRATES. Nitrates are plant nutrients that enter both surface and groundwater primarily from fertilizer runoff, human sewage, and livestock manure, especially from feedlots. Nitrates in drinking water can be an immediate threat to children under six months of age. In some babies high levels of nitrates react with the red blood cells to reduce the blood's ability to transport oxygen.

According to the EPA, in "Consumer Factsheet on: Nitrates/Nitrites" (November 28, 2006, http://www.epa.gov/safewater/dwh/c-ioc/nitrates.html), the MCL for nitrates is set at 10 ppm. When nitrate levels exceed this limit, a water supplier must notify the public and provide additional treatment to reduce levels to meet the standards.

Microbial Contaminants

Microbes (bacteria, viruses, and protozoa) are found in untreated surface-water sources used for drinking water. Groundwater does not contain microbes unless they have been introduced through pollution of the aquifer. Unless the treatment system fails or contaminated water is introduced accidentally into the distribution system, treated drinking water is normally free of microorganisms or they are present in extremely low levels. When a water source or system is contaminated with human or animal fecal waste, some of the microorganisms may be pathogens (disease-causing organisms). The resulting illnesses can have symptoms that include headache, nausea, vomiting, diarrhea, abdominal pain, and dehydration. Although usually not life threatening, these illnesses can be debilitating and uncomfortable for victims. Extended illness or death may occur among young or elderly individuals or those who are immunocompromised (having weakened immune systems). Immunocompromised people include human immunodeficiency virus (HIV) and acquired immunodeficiency syndrome (AIDS) patients, those receiving treatment for certain kinds of cancer, organ-transplant recipients, and people on drugs that suppress their immune system.

Waterborne pathogens have been the cause of serious diseases throughout the world. In the United States in the early 1900s, cholera and typhoid fever were commonly associated with drinking water from public supplies. The practice of water treatment was begun to address this problem by reducing the number of pathogens present in water supply systems below an infective dose. The infective dose is the number of a particular microorganism required to induce disease and is different for different microbes. For example, one *Cryptosporidium* protozoan can induce disease, whereas 10,000 to 100,000 *Salmonella* bacteria are generally necessary for serious illness to occur.

HOW TURBIDITY AFFECTS MICROBIAL CONTAMINATION. Turbidity is a measure of the clarity of water. Turbidity is caused by suspended matter or impurities that make the water look cloudy. These impurities may include clay, silt, fine organic and inorganic matter, and plankton (minute floating aquatic plants and animals).

Figure 5.3 shows the types of activities in a watershed that cause turbidity in a water source. A watershed is the land area that drains water into a river system or other body of water. Figure 5.3 shows that water falls on the land as rain or snow, and that water runs along the ground and eventually seeps into the surface or groundwater. Human activities such as timber harvesting, road building, and residential development compact, pave, and clear the soil of much of its vegetation. During storms, rain runs over this land and erodes it, carrying with it impurities.

Turbidity is unappealing and may represent a health concern in drinking water. It interferes with the effectiveness of disinfection, which is the practice of killing pathogens in water by adding certain chemicals (e.g., chlorine or ozone) or exposing the water to ultraviolet light. Microorganisms can find shelter in the particulate matter, reducing their exposure to disinfectants and ultraviolet light. Even though turbidity is not a direct indicator of health risk, many studies show a strong relationship between the removal of turbidity and the removal of pathogens.

COLIFORM BACTERIA. Coliform bacteria are a group of closely related, mostly harmless bacteria that live in soil, water, and the intestines of animals. These bacteria are generally divided into two groups: total coliform and fecal coliform. The total coliform group includes all coliform bacteria. The fecal coliform group is a subgroup found in the intestines and fecal waste of warm-blooded animals. There are a few organisms in the fecal coliform group that can be harmful to humans, particularly to children and immunocompromised people.

The total coliform group is used as a first indicator to assess drinking water quality. This practice began in the early 1900s. It is based on the assumption that because coliform bacteria are always present in sewage from warm-blooded animals (including humans), and pathogens may be present in this same sewage, the presence of coliform bacteria may indicate the potential presence of pathogens. The most common problem caused by fecal pathogens is gastroenteritis, a general illness characterized by diarrhea, nausea, vomiting, and cramps. Even though gastroenteritis is typically not harmful to healthy adults, it can cause serious illness in children and immunocompromised individuals.

Testing the water for each of a wide variety of potential pathogens is difficult and expensive. Testing for total coliform, by comparison, is easy and inexpensive. For this reason, total coliform are used to indicate whether a water system is vulnerable to pathogens. The presence of total coliform in the water distribution system may indicate that the disinfection process is faulty, that a break or leak has occurred in the distribution piping, or that the distribution pipes need to be cleaned. No more than 5% of the drinking water samples collected monthly from a water supplier may be positive for total coliform. All samples that are positive for total coliform are analyzed for the presence of the fecal coliform group or *Escherichia coli* (*E. coli*), a specific member of the fecal coliform

FIGURE 5.3

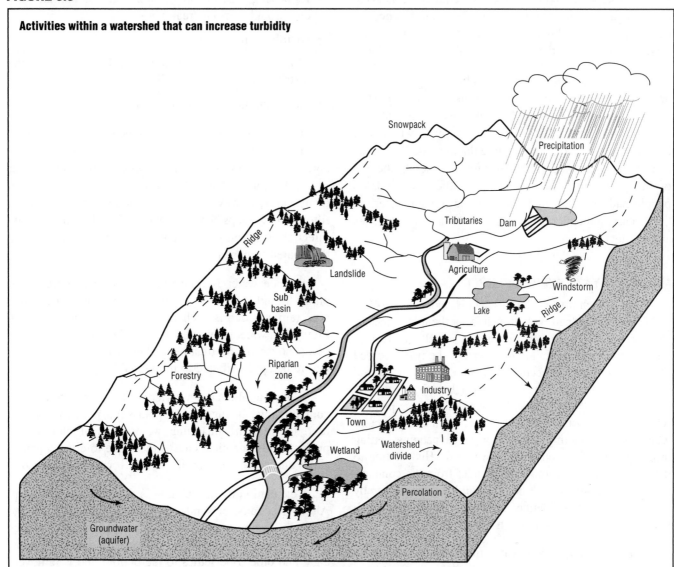

Activities within a watershed that can increase turbidity

SOURCE: "Figure 2.1. Activities within a Watershed That Can Increase Turbidity," in *Oregon Watersheds: Many Activities Contribute to Increased Turbidity during Large Storms*, U.S. General Accounting Office, July 1998, http://www.gao.gov/archive/1998/rc98220.pdf (accessed March 16, 2009)

group, both of which are more sensitive indicators of sewage pollution.

***GIARDIA LAMBLIA* AND *CRYPTOSPORIDIUM*. *Giardia lamblia* and *Cryptosporidium* are microscopic single-celled protozoa that can infect humans and other warm-blooded animals. They are frequently found in surface waters contaminated with animal or human fecal waste. Both organisms have a life stage called a cyst, in which the organism is dormant and protected by an outer shell that allows it to exist outside a host's body for a long time. If cysts are ingested, they can become active and cause an intestinal illness, the symptoms of which are nausea, vomiting, fever, and severe diarrhea. The symptoms last for several days, and a healthy human can generally rid his or her body of the organisms in one or two months. These two organisms are the most frequent cause of waterborne illness in the United States.

The EPA indicates in "Drinking Water Contaminants" (March 18, 2009, http://www.epa.gov/safewater/contaminants/index.html) that it requires water suppliers using surface water, or groundwater under the direct influence of surface water, to disinfect their water to control *Giardia* at the 99.9% inactivation and removal level. Groundwater is considered to be under the direct influence of surface water when the geologic formations (usually limestone or fractured bedrock) in which the aquifer lies do not provide adequate natural filtration.

A smaller parasite than *Giardia*, *Cryptosporidium* is 50 times more resistant to chlorine (the most commonly used drinking water disinfectant) than *Giardia*. Because of its high resistance to chemicals typically used to treat drinking water, it must be physically removed by filtration. The EPA notes that as of January 2002 water systems serving 10,000 or more people are required to provide filtration and achieve 99% removal or inactivation of *Cryptosporidium*. This requirement was applied to water systems serving less than 10,000 people in January 2005.

Cryptosporidium was responsible for what many people view as the nation's worst drinking water disaster. In April 1993 residents of Milwaukee were infected with *Cryptosporidium* in the city water supply, which had been turbid for several days. More than 800,000 residents were without drinkable tap water for a week. By the end of the disaster, 50 people had died and over 400,000 people had been infected. Besides the human suffering, the disease outbreak cost millions of dollars in lost wages and productivity.

MODERN WATER TREATMENT

Even though the Greek physician Hippocrates (c. 460–c. 377 BC) is credited with emphasizing the importance of clean water for good health as early as 400 BC (he recommended boiling and straining rainwater), the first recorded observation of the connection between drinking water and the spread of disease came from the English physician John Snow (1813–1858) in 1849. Snow noted that his patients who were getting their drinking water from one particular well were contracting cholera, whereas patients getting drinking water from other wells were not. His solution to the problem was to remove the handle from the contaminated well's pump so that no one could get water, thereby stopping a cholera epidemic. This event is generally credited as the beginning of modern water treatment.

The most significant water treatment event in the United States was the introduction of chlorine as a disinfectant in water supplies. Adding chlorine to water supplies began in the early 1900s. As towns and cities began implementing this practice, epidemics and incidences of typhoid, cholera, and dysentery were dramatically reduced. From this humble beginning evolved the complex drinking water treatment technology that is currently available.

The multiple-barrier approach is the basis for modern water treatment. This approach recognizes that contaminants reach drinking water through many pathways. Working together, water suppliers and health professionals try to erect as many barriers as possible to prevent contaminants from reaching consumers. These barriers include:

- Protecting the water source from contamination by eliminating or limiting waste discharges to the water source through a variety of protection programs

- Improved contaminant detection methods

- New and ongoing research into contaminants and their effects

- Removing contaminants or reducing contaminant levels through various treatments

- Disinfection

- Elimination of cross connections and breaks in the distribution lines

- Safe plumbing in residences and businesses

The water treatment process begins with choosing the highest quality surface or groundwater source available and ensuring its continued protection. Groundwater is usually pumped directly into the treatment plant. In many cases, however, because groundwater is naturally filtered as it seeps through layers of rock and soil, disinfection is the only treatment needed before the water is distributed to consumers.

Surface water is transported to the water treatment plant through aqueducts or pipes. A screen at the intake pipe removes debris such as tree branches and trash. In Figure 5.4, water is pumped from the Potomac River to the pump house of the treatment plant, filtered, and treated before being distributed to individual homes.

Water suppliers use a variety of treatments to remove contaminants. In Figure 5.4, potassium permanganate is used to treat the incoming water if algal blooms are present. This chemical causes the algae to cling together (floc) and settle more easily so that it can be removed.

Coagulation or flocculation is typically the next step. Alum, iron salts, or synthetic polymers are added to the water to combine smaller particles into larger particles (floc) to remove contaminants. In the sedimentation basins, algal and other floc settles to the bottom and is removed. The settled floc (sediment) is put through a sediment dewatering press to remove the excess water and is then trucked to farms.

The water is then sent to sand filtration beds to remove the remaining small particles, clarify the water, and enhance the effectiveness of disinfection. Chlorine, ozone, or ultraviolet light may be used as disinfectants. Orthophosphate is a rust inhibitor that helps preserve the pipes carrying the water. Fluoride helps prevent tooth decay in those who drink the water. Additional treatment may be required if the raw water shows signs of high levels of toxic chemicals.

At various points in the treatment process, the water is monitored, sampled, and tested using various physical, chemical, and microbial testing procedures. Water is stored in the clear well and then is gravity-fed to homes and businesses from a water tower. In other systems, water is stored in ground-level containers that require pumps to move the water. The water that ultimately flows from the tap should be clear, tasteless, and safe to drink.

FIGURE 5.4

Water treatment process

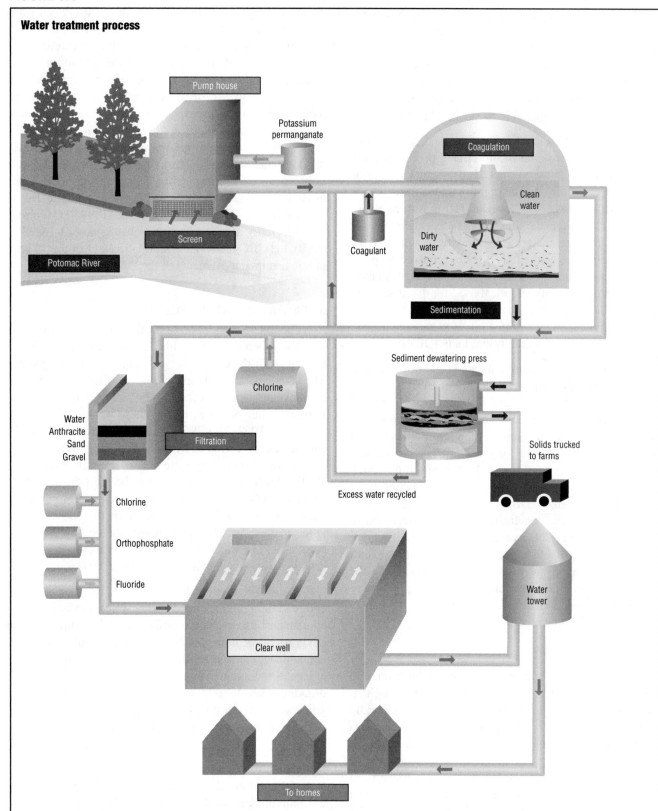

Pump house

Potassium permanganate

Coagulation

Clean water

Coagulant

Dirty water

Screen

Potomac River

Sedimentation

Sediment dewatering press

Chlorine

Solids trucked to farms

Water
Anthracite
Sand
Gravel

Filtration

Excess water recycled

Chlorine

Orthophosphate

Fluoride

Clear well

Water tower

To homes

SOURCE: Reprinted with permission of the City of Rockville from "The Water Treatment Process" in *How is Your Water Treated?* Rockville, Maryland, http://www.rockvillemd.gov/environment/drinking-water/treatment.html (accessed March 16, 2009). The City of Rockville makes no express or implied warranties or representations of any kind with respect to the reprinted material, and assumes no liability with respect to the reprinted material or any reliance or non-reliance thereon.

Chlorination

The most extensively used disinfectant in the United States is chlorine, which is used to kill infectious microorganisms and parasites in water. Disinfection with chlorine or other similar chemicals prevents waterborne-disease outbreaks (WBDOs). The practice of chlorination began in the early 1900s to eliminate the cholera and typhoid outbreaks that were widespread in the United States.

In the early 1970s some scientific researchers became concerned by the possible health effects of total trihalomethanes (THMs), a by-product of chlorination. Chlorine reacts with naturally occurring organic substances in water to form THMs. The level of THMs formed varies widely across water supplies and is dependent on the amount of organic material in drinking water and the amount of chlorine applied. THMs are removed by passing the water through activated carbon filters. Chlorine, however, is not the only chemical used for disinfection in water supplies and all have by-products. Collectively, by-products from chemical disinfection of water supplies are called chemical disinfection by-products (DBPs).

In "Occurrence, Genotoxicity, and Carcinogenicity of Regulated and Emerging Disinfection By-Products in Drinking Water: A Review and Roadmap for Research" (*Mutation Research*, vol. 636, nos. 1–3, September 12, 2007), Susan D. Richardson et al. review 30 years of research on DBPs. Eleven of the DBPs were regulated by the EPA at the time of the study. Seventy-four, which had moderate occurrence levels in drinking water, were considered "emerging" DBPs. Richardson et al.'s extensive report has many conclusions, which are too long to discuss in this chapter. However, the researchers find that much of the risk of bladder cancer from drinking water has to do with exposure to certain levels of THMs, the level of exposure during bathing or swimming (exposure through the skin or airways), and the presence of a particular susceptibility gene.

Fluoridation

Fluoride, which occurs naturally in combination with other minerals in rocks and soils, is nature's cavity fighter. Water fluoridation is the process of adjusting the naturally occurring level of fluoride in most water systems to a concentration (a range of 0.7 to 1.2 milligrams per L) sufficient to protect against tooth decay. The decision to add fluoride to drinking water is left to each community. If the community elects to use fluoride, the water must meet the EPA maximum concentration limit. The Centers for Disease Control and Prevention (CDC) maintains the Web site "Community Water Fluoridation" (http://www.cdc.gov/fluoridation/faqs.htm), which explains water fluoridation and its health effects.

In 1945 Grand Rapids, Michigan, became the first city in the world to add fluoride to its drinking water to prevent tooth decay. Since that time most community water systems in the United States have introduced water fluoridation. The fluoridation of drinking water proved so effective in reducing dental cavities that researchers also developed other methods to deliver fluoride to the public (such as toothpastes, rinses, and dietary supplements). The widespread use of these products has ensured that most people have been exposed to fluoride. The American Dental Association states in "Water Fluoridation" (2009, http://www.ada.org/public/manage/you/working_water.asp), "Thanks in large part to community water fluoridation, half of children ages 5 to 17 have never had a cavity in their permanent teeth." In "Ten Great Public Health Achievements—United States, 1900–1999" (*Morbidity and Mortality Weekly Report*, vol. 48, no. 12, April 2, 1999), the CDC recognizes fluoridation as 1 of the 10 great public health achievements of the 20th century.

SAFE DRINKING WATER ACT

The federal regulation of drinking water quality began in 1914, when the U.S. Public Health Service established standards for the bacteriological quality of drinking water. The standards applied only to systems that supplied water to interstate carriers such as trains, ships, and buses. The Public Health Service revised these standards in 1925, 1942, and 1962. The 1962 standards, which regulated 28 substances, were adopted by the health departments of all 50 states, even though they were not federally mandated. The Public Health Service continued to be the primary federal agency involved with drinking water until 1974, when the authority was transferred to the EPA via the SDWA, which is the main federal law that ensures the quality of Americans' drinking water. Table 5.3 shows a history of EPA drinking water regulations enacted since 1974.

The SDWA mandated that the EPA establish and enforce minimum national drinking water standards for any contaminant that presents a health risk and is known to, or is likely to, occur in public drinking water supplies. For each contaminant that was regulated, the EPA was required to set a legal limit on the amount of contaminant allowed in drinking water. In addition, the EPA was directed to develop guidance for water treatment and to establish testing, monitoring, and reporting requirements for water suppliers.

Congress intended that, after the EPA had set regulatory standards, each state would be granted primacy; that is, states would have the primary responsibility for enforcing the requirements of the SDWA. To be given primacy, a state must adopt drinking water standards and conduct monitoring and enforcement programs at least as stringent as those established by the EPA. Forty-nine states and all U.S. commonwealths and territories have received primacy (Wyoming and the District of Columbia do not have primacy). The EPA implements the drinking water program on Native American reservations.

TABLE 5.3

EPA drinking water regulations by year enacted, 1974–2006

Regulation	Year
Safe Drinking Water Act (SDWA)	1974
Interim Primary Drinking Water Standards	1975
National Primary Drinking Water Standards	1985
SDWA Amendments	1986
Surface Water Treatment Rule (SWTR)	1989
Total Coliform Rule	1989
Lead and Copper Regulations	1990
SDWA Amendments	1996
Information Collection Rule	1996
Interim Enhanced SWTR	1998
Disinfectants and Disinfection By-Products (D-DBPs) Regulation	1998
Contaminant Candidate List	1998
Unregulated Contaminant Monitoring Regulations	1999
Lead and Copper Rule—action levels	2000
Filter Backwash Recycling Rule	2001
Long Term 1 Enhanced SWTR	2002
Unregulated Contaminant Monitoring Regulations	2002
Drinking Water Contaminant Candidate List 2	2005
Long Term 2 Enhanced SWTR	2006
Stage 2 D-DBP Rule	2006
Ground Water Rule	2006

SOURCE: Jonathan Yoder et al., "Table 1. U.S. Environmental Protection Agency Regulations Regarding Drinking Water, by Year Enacted—United States, 1974–2006," in "Surveillance for Waterborne Disease and Outbreaks Associated with Drinking Water and Water Not Intended for Drinking— United States, 2005–2006," *Morbidity and Mortality Weekly Report, Surveillance Summaries*, vol. 57, no. SS-9, September 12, 2008, http://www.cdc.gov/mmwr/PDF/ss/ss5709.pdf (accessed March 10, 2009)

The EPA established the primary drinking water standards by setting MCLs for contaminants that are known to be detrimental to human health. The contaminants and their MCLs are shown in Table 4.2 in Chapter 4.

All public water systems in the United States are required to meet the primary standards. Only two contaminants regulated thus far, microorganisms and nitrates, pose an immediate health problem when the standards are exceeded. All other contaminants for which standards have been established must be controlled because ingesting water that exceeds these MCLs over a long period may cause long-term health problems, such as cancer, liver, or kidney disease or other harmful effects.

Secondary standards cover aspects of drinking water that have no health risks, such as odor, taste, staining properties, and color. Secondary standards are recommended but not required.

SDWA AMENDMENTS AND REGULATIONS

The EPA is continuing its work to protect drinking water from unsafe contaminant levels, to oversee the activities of the states that enforce federal or their own stricter standards, and to solicit public input as it develops new standards or other program requirements. Over the years the SDWA has been amended to require the EPA to:

- Set a maximum contaminant level goal (MCLG). An MCLG is the maximum amount of a contaminant that is not expected to cause any health problems over a lifetime of exposure. The EPA is mandated to set the MCL as close to the MCLG as technology and economics will permit.

- Specify the "best available technology" for treating each contaminant for which the EPA sets an MCL.

- Provide states with greater flexibility to implement the SDWA to meet their specific needs while arriving at the same level of public health protection.

- Set contaminant regulation priorities based on data about adverse public health effects of the contaminant, the occurrence of the contaminant in public water supplies, and the estimated reduction in health risk that can be expected from any new regulations.

- Provide a thorough analysis of the costs to water supplies and benefits to public health.

- Increase research to develop sound scientific data to provide a base for regulations.

- Ban the use of lead pipes and lead solder in new drinking water systems and in the repair of existing water systems.

- Establish a federal-state partnership for regulation enforcement.

COMPANION LEGISLATION TO THE SDWA

Water Efficiency Act

The Water Efficiency Act of 1992 established uniform national standards for the manufacture of water-efficient plumbing fixtures, such as low-flow toilets and showers. The purpose was to promote water conservation by residential and commercial users.

According to the U.S. General Accounting Office (now the U.S. Government Accountability Office), in *Water Infrastructure: Water-Efficient Plumbing Fixtures Reduce Water Consumption and Wastewater Flows* (August 2000, http://www.gao.gov/new.items/rc00232.pdf), preliminary results from studies by the American Water Works Association and the EPA indicate that by 2020 water consumption could be reduced by 3% to 9% in the areas studied. Wastewater flows to sewage treatment plants could be reduced 13% by 2016. For the 16 localities analyzed, the use of water-efficient plumbing fixtures could reduce the local water consumption enough to save local water utilities between $165.7 million and $231.2 million by 2020 because planned investments to expand drinking water treatment or storage capacity could be deferred or avoided.

In *Hidden Oasis: Water Conservation and Efficiency in Las Vegas* (November 2007, http://www.pacinst.org/ reports/las_vegas/hidden_oasis.pdf), Heather Cooley et al.

review the water conservation efforts and potential for the city of Las Vegas, Nevada. The researchers reveal that installing water-efficient fixtures, such as shower heads and toilets, and water-efficient appliances, such as front-loading washing machines, could reduce the current indoor water usage in Las Vegas by 40%.

Federal Water Pollution Control Act

The 1972 Federal Water Pollution Control Act (FWPCA) established the framework for regulating the discharge of pollutants to U.S. waters. This framework was strengthened by amendments in 1977 (the Clean Water Act) and in 1987 (the Water Quality Act). The FWPCA and its amendments established the National Pollution Discharge Elimination System to reduce the discharge of pollutants into water, including drinking water sources.

The FWPCA also requires the EPA and the states to identify water resources that need to be cleaned up to meet water quality standards and to establish stringent controls where needed to achieve the water quality standards. States are required to develop lists of contaminated waters, to identify the sources and amounts of pollutants causing water quality problems, and to develop individual control strategies for the sources of pollution.

COST OF CLEAN DRINKING WATER

From 1976 to 2004 the number of contaminants regulated under the SDWA roughly quadrupled. (See Figure 5.5.) As a result, new treatment technologies have been required. This has significantly increased the cost of water treatment in many locations. More than 90 contaminants are now regulated.

FIGURE 5.5

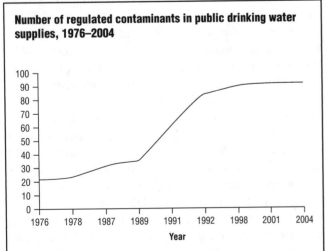

Number of regulated contaminants in public drinking water supplies, 1976–2004

SOURCE: "Number of Regulated Contaminants," in *Safe Drinking Water Act, Progress in Providing Safe Drinking Water*, U.S. Environmental Protection Agency, Office of Water, 2005

Besides treating water, public water supply systems must:

- Protect their water source
- Build, maintain, and repair the treatment plants and distribution systems
- Replace aging systems
- Recruit, pay, and train system operation staff
- Meet the expanding treatment requirements of the SDWA and its monitoring and reporting requirements
- Expand service areas
- Provide necessary administrative and support services to accomplish these tasks

Most of the money to support these services comes directly from users. The remainder of revenues comes from connection or inspection fees, fines, penalties, and other nonconsumption-based charges, as well as local or state grants or loans.

HOW CLEAN IS THE WATER?

Safe drinking water is a cornerstone of public health. Drinking water in the United States is generally safe. The vast majority of U.S. residents receive water from systems that have no reported violations of MCLs or flaws in treatment techniques, monitoring, or reporting.

However, in the 3,500-page *Victorian Water Treatment Enters the 21st Century* (1995), Brian Cohen and Eric Olson of the Natural Resources Defense Council document 250,000 violations of the SDWA that occurred between 1991 and 1992. The researchers find that 43% of the water systems (serving about 120 million people) had committed violations.

Even though substantial progress has been made in reducing SDWA violations since this study was issued, the EPA estimates in *Factoids* that 83.4 million people were supplied with water from community water systems that registered one or more violations for health-based SDWA standards in 2008. (See Table 5.4.) In 2007 there were 87.8 million people affected by systems registering violations; this represents a decrease of 5% from 2007 to 2008.

However, the number of systems experiencing violations declined by only 3%, from 21,544 in 2007 to 20,797 in 2008. (See Table 5.5.) Furthermore, the number of violations increased 40%, from 97,086 in 2007 to 136,373 in 2008. (See Table 5.6.)

Disease Caused by Contaminated Drinking Water

It is difficult to know the exact incidence of illness caused by contaminated drinking water. People may not know the source of their illnesses and may attribute them

TABLE 5.4

Community water system violations by population affected, 2003–08

Fiscal year	Total
2008	83,385,983
2007	87,843,223
2006	83,062,903
2005	90,890,243
2004	76,870,272
2003	80,765,799

SOURCE: Adapted from "CWS Violations Reported by FY, Population Affected," in *Factoids: Drinking Water and Ground Water Statistics for 2008*, U.S. Environmental Protection Agency, Office of Water, November 2008, http://www.epa.gov/OGWDW/databases/pdfs/data_factoids_2008.pdf (accessed March 16, 2009)

TABLE 5.5

Community water system violations by number of systems in violation, 2003–08

Fiscal year	Total
2008	20,797
2007	21,544
2006	21,618
2005	22,772
2004	21,055
2003	20,280

SOURCE: Adapted from "CWS Violations Reported by FY, Number of Systems in Violation," in *Factoids: Drinking Water and Ground Water Statistics for 2008*, U.S. Environmental Protection Agency, Office of Water, November 2008, http://www.epa.gov/OGWDW/databases/pdfs/data_factoids_2008.pdf (accessed March 16, 2009)

TABLE 5.6

Community water system violations by number of violations, 2003–08

Fiscal year	Total
2008	136,373
2007	97,086
2006	88,235
2005	139,981
2004	109,366
2003	78,334

SOURCE: Adapted from "CWS Violations Reported by FY, Number of Violations," in *Factoids: Drinking Water and Ground Water Statistics for 2008*, U.S. Environmental Protection Agency, Office of Water, November 2008, http://www.epa.gov/OGWDW/databases/pdfs/data_factoids_2008.pdf (accessed March 16, 2009)

to food poisoning, chronic illness, or infectious agents. Some researchers believe the actual number of drinking water disease cases is higher than the reported number, but the diseases are not reported because victims believe them to be "stomach upsets" and treat themselves.

Since 1971 the CDC and the EPA have maintained a surveillance system for collecting and reporting data on WBDOs. In "Surveillance for Waterborne Disease and Outbreaks Associated with Drinking Water and Water Not Intended for Drinking—United States, 2005–2006" (*Morbidity and Mortality Weekly Report*, vol. 57, no. SS-9, September 12, 2008), Jonathan Yoder et al. examine CDC data about outbreaks associated with water intended for drinking water and those associated with water used for recreation, such as beaches, hot tubs, and swimming pools.

During the 2005–06 period, 11 states reported a total of 20 WBDOs in water intended for drinking—8 in 2005 and 12 in 2006. (See Figure 5.6.) Yoder et al. report that those outbreaks caused an estimated 612 people to become ill and led to 4 deaths. As Figure 5.6 shows, New York had the highest number of outbreaks (six) for the 2005–06 period, Ohio had the second highest at three outbreaks, and Pennsylvania and Oregon each had two outbreaks.

Table 5.7 lists the eight WBDOs that were traced to contamination at or in the source water, treatment facility, or distribution system. They are listed by etiologic (disease-causing) agent and type of water system. Three of the outbreaks were associated with viruses, two with bacteria, one with more than one microbe (mixed agents), and two were unidentified. The highest percentage of outbreaks was associated with noncommunity water systems (62.5%), and these outbreaks affected the greatest percentage of people (87.6%).

Table 5.8 lists the eight WBDOs that were traced to contamination at or in the source water or treatment facility. They are listed by etiologic agent and water source. Approximately 87.5% of the disease outbreaks and 88.4% of the cases (people affected) were associated with groundwater. The remainder were associated with surface water.

Figure 5.7 shows that WBDOs occurred year round between 2005 and 2006 except for March and October. The number of outbreaks were relatively steady during the spring and into July, peaking in August. The number dropped over the fall, peaking again in December.

Figure 5.8 shows the number of WBDOs associated with drinking water in the United States from 1971 through 2006. The number of WBDOs declined from a peak of over 50 outbreaks in 1980 to 11 outbreaks in 2006. Since 1987 there have been fewer than 20 WBDOs each year, except for 1992 and 2000.

Figure 5.9 shows the distribution of outbreaks during the 2005–06 period by etiologic agents, water system, and water source. *Legionella* bacteria alone accounted for nearly one out of every two outbreaks (50%). (*Legionella* bacteria are commonly found in bodies of water, including air conditioning cooling towers, sink taps, and showerheads. Some species cause Legionnaires'

FIGURE 5.6

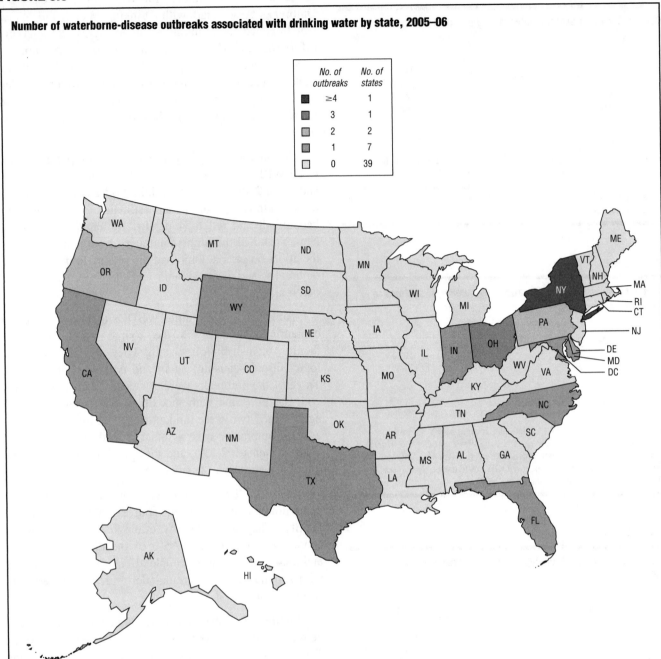

Number of waterborne-disease outbreaks associated with drinking water by state, 2005–06

	No. of outbreaks	No. of states
■	≥4	1
■	3	1
■	2	2
■	1	7
□	0	39

Notes: Sample size = 20; numbers are dependent on reporting and surveillance activities in individual states and do not necessarily indicate that more outbreaks occurred in a given state.

SOURCE: Jonathan Yoder et al., "Figure 2. Number of Waterborne-Disease Outbreaks Associated with Drinking Water—United States, 2005–2006," in "Surveillance for Waterborne Disease and Outbreaks Associated with Drinking Water and Water Not Intended for Drinking—United States, 2005–2006," *Morbidity and Mortality Weekly Report, Surveillance Summaries*, vol. 57, no. SS-9, September 12, 2008, http://www.cdc.gov/mmwr/PDF/ss/ss5709.pdf (accessed March 10, 2009)

disease, a pneumonia-like illness that often includes kidney, liver, and gastrointestinal symptoms as well.) All bacteria, including *Legionella*, were responsible for 60% of outbreaks. Parasites caused another 10% of outbreaks and viruses caused 15%. Most (87.5%) of the outbreaks were linked to groundwater sources. Noncommunity water systems had the highest proportion of outbreaks at 62.5%.

ARE AMERICANS CONCERNED ABOUT THEIR DRINKING WATER?

A Gallup poll conducted in 2007 indicated that water purity was one of the most important environmental concerns to Americans. Table 5.9 shows the results of this survey in which pollsters asked Americans which environmental concerns they worry about a "great deal." Their greatest concerns focus on various aspects of water

TABLE 5.7

Number of waterborne-disease outbreaks (WBDOs) associated with drinking water, by causative agent and type of water system, 2005–06

Etiologic agent	Type of water system[a]									
	Community		Noncommunity		Individual[b]		Mixed system		Total	
	WBDOs	Cases	WBDOs	Cases	WBDOs	Cases	WBDOs	Cases	WBDOs	Cases
Bacteria	1	32	1	60	0	0	0	0	2	92
Campylobacter spp.	1	32	0	0	0	0	0	0	1	32
Escherichia coli O157, C. jejuni, and Escherichia coli O145	0	0	1	60	0	0	0	0	1	60
Viruses	0	0	2	196	1	16	0	0	3	212
Hepatitis A	0	0	0	0	1	16	0	0	1	16
Norovirus G1	0	0	2	196	0	0	0	0	2	196
Mixed agents[c]	0	0	1	139	0	0	0	0	1	139
Norovirus G1, C. jejuni, and Norovirus G2	0	0	1	139	0	0	0	0	1	139
Unidentified	0	0	1	59	1	16	0	0	2	75
Unidentified[d]	0	0	1	59	1	16	0	0	2	75
Total	**1**	**32**	**5**	**454**	**2**	**32**	**0**	**0**	**8**	**518**
Percentage	(12.5)	(6.2)	(62.5)	(87.6)	(25.0)	(6.2)	(0.0)	(0.0)	(100.0)	(100.0)

Note: WBDOs with deficiencies 1–4 and 13 (i.e., surface water contamination, ground water contamination, water treatment deficiency, distribution system contamination, and untreated chemical contamination of source water) were used for analysis.
[a]Community and noncommunity water systems are public water systems that have ≥15 service connections or serve an average of ≥25 residents for ≥60 days/year. A community water system serves year-round residents of a community, subdivision, or mobile home park. A noncommunity water system serves an institution, industry, camp, park, hotel, or business and can be nontransient or transient. Nontransient systems serve ≥25 of the same persons for >6 months of the year but not year-round (e.g., factories and schools), whereas transient systems provide water to places in which persons do not remain for long periods of time (e.g., restaurants, highway rest stations, and parks). Individual water systems are small systems not owned or operated by a water utility that have <15 connections or serve <25 persons.
[b]Excludes commercially bottled water and water not intended for drinking, therefore, not comparable to Surveillance Summaries before 2003–2004.
[c]Multiple etiologic agent types (bacteria, parasite, virus, and/or chemical/toxin) identified.
[d]Norovirus suspected based on incubation period, symptoms, and duration of illness.

SOURCE: Jonathan Yoder et al., "Table 8. Number of Waterborne-Disease Outbreaks (WBDOs) Associated with Drinking Water (n = Eight), by Etiologic Agent and Type of Water System—United States, 2005–2006," in "Surveillance for Waterborne Disease and Outbreaks Associated with Drinking Water and Water Not Intended for Drinking—United States, 2005–2006," Morbidity and Mortality Weekly Report, Surveillance Summaries, vol. 57, no. SS-9, September 12, 2008, http://www.cdc.gov/mmwr/PDF/ss/ss5709.pdf (accessed March 10, 2009).

TABLE 5.8

Number of waterborne-disease outbreaks (WBDOs) associated with drinking water, by causative agent and type of water source, 2005–06

Etiologic agent	Water source									
	Groundwater		Surface water		Unknown		Mixed source		Total	
	WBDOs	Cases	WBDOs	Cases	WBDOs	Cases	WBDOs	Cases	WBDOs	Cases
Bacteria	1	32	1	60	0	0	0	0	2	92
Campylobacter spp.	1	32	0	0	0	0	0	0	1	32
Escherichia coli O157, C. jejuni and Escherichia coli O145	0	0	1	60	0	0	0	0	1	60
Viruses	3	212	0	0	0	0	0	0	3	212
Hepatitis A	1	16	0	0	0	0	0	0	1	16
Norovirus G1	2	196	0	0	0	0	0	0	2	196
Mixed agent type[a]	1	139	0	0	0	0	0	0	1	139
Norovirus G1, C. jejuni, and Norovirus G2	1	139	0	0	0	0	0	0	1	139
Unidentified	2	75	0	0	0	0	0	0	2	75
Unidentified[b]	2	75	0	0	0	0	0	0	2	75
Total	**7**	**458**	**1**	**60**	**0**	**0**	**0**	**0**	**8**	**518**
Percentage	(87.5)	(88.4)	(12.5)	(11.6)	(0.0)	(0.0)	(0.0)	(0.0)	(100.0)	(100.0)

Note: WBDOs with deficiencies 1–3 and 13 (i.e., surface water contamination, groundwater contamination, water treatment deficiency, and untreated chemical contamination of source water) were used for analysis.
[a]Multiple etiologic agent types (bacteria, parasite, virus, and/or chemical/toxin) identified.
[b]Norovirus suspected based on incubation period, symptoms, and duration of illness.

SOURCE: Jonathan Yoder et al., "Table 9. Number of Waterborne-Disease Outbreaks (WBDOs) Associated with Drinking Water (n = Eight), by Etiologic Agent and Water Source—United States, 2005–2006," in "Surveillance for Waterborne Disease and Outbreaks Associated with Drinking Water and Water Not Intended for Drinking—United States, 2005–2006," Morbidity and Mortality Weekly Report, Surveillance Summaries, vol. 57, no. SS-9, September 12, 2008, http://www.cdc.gov/mmwr/PDF/ss/ss5709.pdf (accessed March 10, 2009).

FIGURE 5.7

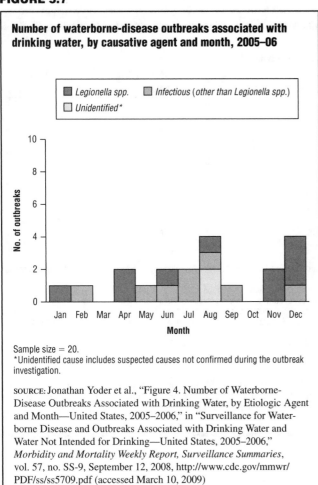

Number of waterborne-disease outbreaks associated with drinking water, by causative agent and month, 2005–06

Legend: ■ Legionella spp. ■ Infectious (other than Legionella spp.) □ Unidentified*

Sample size = 20.
*Unidentified cause includes suspected causes not confirmed during the outbreak investigation.

SOURCE: Jonathan Yoder et al., "Figure 4. Number of Waterborne-Disease Outbreaks Associated with Drinking Water, by Etiologic Agent and Month—United States, 2005–2006," in "Surveillance for Waterborne Disease and Outbreaks Associated with Drinking Water and Water Not Intended for Drinking—United States, 2005–2006," *Morbidity and Mortality Weekly Report, Surveillance Summaries*, vol. 57, no. SS-9, September 12, 2008, http://www.cdc.gov/mmwr/PDF/ss/ss5709.pdf (accessed March 10, 2009).

pollution. A majority (58%) had a great deal of concern about pollution of drinking water. Respondents also worried a great deal about the pollution of rivers, lakes, and reservoirs (53%); the contamination of the soil and water by toxic waste (52%); and maintenance of the nation's supply of freshwater for household needs (51%).

Table 5.10 compares respondents' levels of concern regarding the pollution of drinking water with their levels of concern since 1990. Even though a majority (59%) of Americans were concerned about this issue in 2009, the percentage of those who had a "great deal" of concern dropped from a high of 72% in 2000. The percentages of those who cared a "fair amount," "only a little," and "not at all" had risen since 1990.

BOTTLED WATER

Water is called bottled water only if it meets federal and state standards, is sealed in a sanitary container, and is sold for human consumption. The U.S. Food and Drug Administration (FDA) and state governmental agencies regulate bottled water as a packaged food product. In addition, members of the International Bottled Water Association (IBWA), who produce and distribute most of the bottled water sold in the United States, must adhere to association standards besides those imposed by the government and undergo annual unannounced plant inspections by an independent third-party organization.

Imported European bottled water must meet the same federal and state standards as bottled water produced by American companies. In addition, it must meet the strict standards set by the European Union. International bottler members who sell products in the United States must submit a certificate of inspection to the IBWA.

Growing Market

According to John G. Rodwan Jr., in "Confronting Challenges: U.S. and International Bottled Water Developments and Statistics for 2008" (*Bottled Water Reporter*, April–May 2009), Americans consumed 8.7 billion gallons (32.9 billion L) of bottled water during 2008, a 1% decrease from 2007. This figure translates into 28.5 gallons (107.9 L) per person in the United States, with bottled water ranking second only to carbonated soft drinks as the American beverage of choice.

Why Do Americans Like Bottled Water?

American consumers give a variety of reasons for their preference for bottled water. Some say they dislike the smell or taste of water from the tap or drawn from wells. Others cite the convenience of bottled water. In *Are Americans Financially Prepared for Disaster?* (October 18, 2005, http://www.gallup.com/poll/19264/Americans-Financially-Prepared-Disaster.aspx), Dennis Jacobe of the Gallup Organization reports that 71% of Americans keep bottled water on hand in case of emergency.

Besides convenience, taste, and emergency use, concerns over the safety of public water supply systems since the September 11, 2001, terrorist attacks on the United States are prompting more Americans to rely on bottled water for their drinking water needs. According to Carol Angrisani, in "Take Me to the Water" (*Supermarket News*, May 26, 2003), a number of retailers report that concerns about terrorism have fueled a surge in the consumption of bottled water in the United States. Angrisani states that between 1998 and 2003 sales of bottled water increased 150%.

Nonetheless, there has been a recent backlash against the use of bottled water. For example, Janet Larsen of the Earth Policy Institute notes in "Bottled Water Boycotts: Back-to-the Tap Movement Gains Momentum" (December 7, 2007, http://www.earth-policy.org/Updates/2007/Update68.htm) that in its 2007 meeting the U.S. Conference of Mayors discussed "the irony of purchasing bottled water for city employees and for city functions while at the same time touting the quality of municipal water." Larsen explains that many cities have banned the purchase of bottled water with government funds. Also fueling the bottled-water backlash are environmental concerns.

FIGURE 5.8

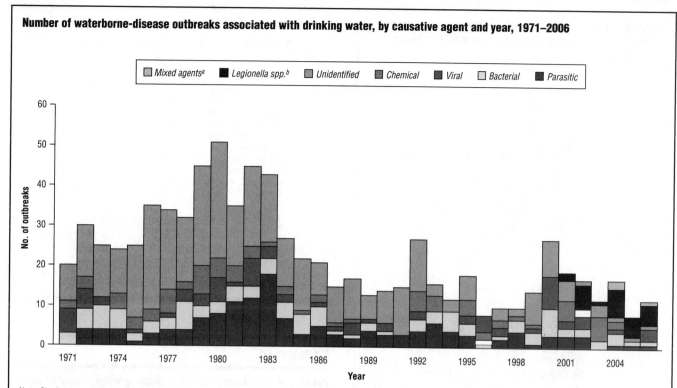

Number of waterborne-disease outbreaks associated with drinking water, by causative agent and year, 1971–2006

Note: Single cases of disease related to drinking water (sample size = 16) have been removed from this figure; therefore, it is not comparable to figures in previous *Surveillance Summaries*.

[a]Beginning in 2003, mixed agents of more than one causative agent type were included in the surveillance system. However, the first observation is a previously unreported outbreak in 2002.

[b]Beginning in 2001, Legionnaires' disease was added to the surveillance system, and *Legionella* species were classified separately in this figure.

SOURCE: Jonathan Yoder et al., "Figure 3. Number of Waterborne-Disease Outbreaks Associated with Drinking Water (n = 814), by Year and Etiologic Agent—United States, 1971–2006," in "Surveillance for Waterborne Disease and Outbreaks Associated with Drinking Water and Water Not Intended for Drinking—United States, 2005–2006," *Morbidity and Mortality Weekly Report, Surveillance Summaries*, vol. 57, no. SS-9, September 12, 2008, http://www.cdc.gov/mmwr/PDF/ss/ss5709.pdf (accessed March 10, 2009).

Meghan O'Rourke reports in "Water, Water Everywhere and Not a Drop to Drink" (*Slate,* April 21, 2008) that Americans dispose of approximately 30 billion empty water bottles each year, recycling only a small fraction of them. Not only do these bottles clog the nation's landfills but also their annual production requires more than 17 million barrels of oil. However, consumers appear to be paying more attention to the environment regarding their bottled water consumption. In the press release "2009 Greendex Survey of 17 Countries Finds Increase in Green Consumer Behavior Worldwide" (May 13, 2009, http://www.eurekalert.org/pub_releases/2009-05/ngs-2gs051309.php), the National Geographic Society indicates that consumers in the United States and six other countries decreased their consumption of bottled water in 2008.

DRINKING WATER SOURCE PROTECTION AND CONSERVATION

Because good sources of drinking water are a limited resource, the cost of developing and treating new sources is expected to rise. In addition, existing water suppliers are faced with the need to provide water to expanding service areas. As a result, the water industry is looking for cost-effective alternatives and is evaluating water conservation and reuse practices, as well as removing salt from seawater (desalinization) to create drinking water. Some water suppliers offer customers rebates for using water-efficient toilets and showers, and in a few areas are limiting the amount that can be used for lawn and landscape watering or car washing. In some locations municipal and county water departments are promoting the reuse of treated waste-water for irrigation and lawn watering instead of using precious drinking water.

WATER IN THE THIRD WORLD— A DEADLY DRINK

Water quality varies greatly in developing nations, as poverty often results in inadequate distribution of resources, including food and water, and sanitation practices are generally poor. The United Nations (UN) notes in *The United Nations World Water Development Report 3: Water in a Changing World* (March 2009, http://www.unesco.org/water/wwap/wwdr/wwdr3/pdf/WWDR3_Water_in_a _Changing_World.pdf) that access to water and sanitation

FIGURE 5.9

Percentage of waterborne-disease outbreaks associated with drinking water, by causative agent, water system, and water source, 2005–06

Etiologic agent (n = 20)

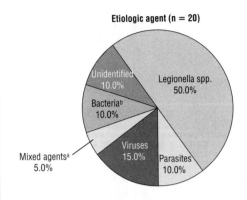

Water system (n = eight)[c]

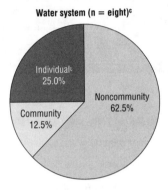

Water source (n = eight)

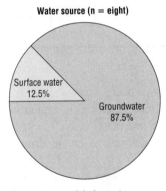

[a]Each WBDO involves more than one etiologic agent.
[b]Other than *Legionella* spp.
[c]Does not include commercially bottled water, therefore, not comparable to summaries before 2003–2004.

SOURCE: Jonathan Yoder et al., "Figure 6. Percentage of Waterborne-Disease Outbreaks (WBDOs) Associated with Drinking Water, by Etiologic Agent, Water System, and Water Source—United States, 2005–2006," in "Surveillance for Waterborne Disease and Outbreaks Associated with Drinking Water and Water Not Intended for Drinking—United States, 2005–2006," *Morbidity and Mortality Weekly Report, Surveillance Summaries*, vol. 57, no. SS-9, September 12, 2008, http://www.cdc.gov/mmwr/PDF/ss/ss5709.pdf (accessed March 10, 2009)

TABLE 5.9

Public opinion on environmental worries, March 2007

[Based on the percentage saying they worry a "great deal" about each problem]

	%
Pollution of drinking water	58
Pollution of rivers, lakes, and reservoirs	53
Contamination of soil and water by toxic waste	52
Maintenance of the nation's supply of fresh water for household needs	51
Air pollution	46
Damage to the earth's ozone layer	43
The loss of tropical rain forests	43
The "greenhouse effect" or global warming	41
Extinction of plant and animal species	39
Acid rain	25

SOURCE: Joseph Carroll, "Environmental Worries," in *Polluted Drinking Water Is Public's Top Environmental Concern*, The Gallup Organization, April 20, 2007, http://www.gallup.com/poll/27274/Polluted-Drinking-Water-Publics-Top-Environmental-Concern.aspx (accessed March 17, 2009). Copyright © 2007 by The Gallup Organization. Reproduced by permission of The Gallup Organization.

TABLE 5.10

Public concern about pollution of drinking water, selected years 1990–2009

I'M GOING TO READ YOU A LIST OF ENVIRONMENTAL PROBLEMS. AS I READ EACH ONE, PLEASE TELL ME IF YOU PERSONALLY WORRY ABOUT THIS PROBLEM A GREAT DEAL, A FAIR AMOUNT, ONLY A LITTLE, OR NOT AT ALL. FIRST, HOW MUCH DO YOU PERSONALLY WORRY ABOUT POLLUTION OF DRINKING WATER?

	Great deal %	Fair amount %	Only a little %	Not at all %	No opinion %
2009 Mar 5–8	59	25	11	5	*
2008 Mar 6–9	53	28	13	6	*
2007 Mar 11–14	58	24	12	5	*
2006 Mar 13–16	54	27	12	7	*
2004 Mar 8–11	53	24	17	6	*
2003 Mar 3–5	54	25	15	6	—
2002 Mar 4–7	57	25	13	5	*
2001 Mar 5–7	64	24	9	3	*
2000 Apr 3–9	72	20	6	2	*
1999 Apr 13–14	68	22	7	3	*
1991 Apr 11–4	67	19	10	3	1
1990 Apr 5–8	65	22	9	4	*

*Less than 0.5%

SOURCE: "I'm Going to Read You a List of Environmental Problems. As I Read Each One, Please Tell Me If You Personally Worry about This Problem a Great Deal, A Fair Amount, Only a Little, or Not at All. First, How Much Do You Personally Worry about—Pollution of Drinking Water?" in *Gallup's Pulse of Democracy: The Environment*, The Gallup Organization, 2009, http://www.gallup.com/poll/1615/ Environment.aspx#1 (accessed March 23, 2009). Copyright © 2009 by The Gallup Organization. Reproduced by permission of The Gallup Organization.

without access to an improved (safe and/or treated) water supply and 2.6 billion lack improved sanitation.

According to the UN, in *The 1st UN World Water Development Report: Water for People, Water for Life* (March 2003, http://www.unesco.org/water/wwap/wwdr/wwdr1/table_contents/index.shtml), as many as 7 billion

rises with income. In *Water—A Shared Responsibility: World Water Development Report 2* (March 2006, http://unesdoc.unesco.org/images/0014/001444/144409E.pdf), the UN estimates that 1.1 billion people around the world are

people in 60 countries could face water shortages by 2050. The UN also suggests that pollution is a major problem, with 50% of the population in developing countries exposed to polluted water. A key goal, the UN report states, is to reduce by 50% the proportion of people who lack access to clean water by 2015.

Adequate quantities of safe water for drinking and for use in promoting personal hygiene are complementary measures for protecting public health. The lack of improved domestic water supply in the home leads to disease through two principal transmission routes: fecal-oral transmission and water-washed transmission.

In the fecal-oral transmission route, water contaminated with fecal material (sewage) is drunk without being treated or boiled, or food is prepared using this contaminated water, and waterborne disease occurs. Diseases transmitted by the fecal-oral route include typhoid, cholera, diarrhea, viral hepatitis A, dysentery, and dracunculiasis (guinea worm disease).

Water-washed transmission, the second route, is caused by a lack of sufficient quantities of clean water for washing and personal hygiene. People cannot keep their hands, bodies, and home environments clean and hygienic when there is not enough safe water available. The quantity of water that people use depends on their access to it. When water is available through a hose or house connection, people will use large quantities for hygiene. When water has to be hauled for more than a few minutes from source to home, the use drops significantly. Without enough clean water for good personal hygiene, skin and eye infections are easily spread, as are the fecal-oral transmission diseases.

The impact of poor water supply on human lives in developing and undeveloped countries is staggering. In *Ecosystems and Human Well-Being: Health Synthesis* (2005, http://www.who.int/globalchange/ecosystems/ecosysbegin.pdf), the World Health Organization states these statistics: "Water-associated infectious diseases claim up to 3.2 million lives each year, approximately 6% of all deaths globally. The burden of disease from inadequate water, sanitation and hygiene totals 1.7 million deaths and the loss of more than 54 million healthy life years." Good drinking water, improved personal hygiene, and better sanitation practices would reduce this worldwide disease burden dramatically.

CHAPTER 6
OCEANS AND ESTUARIES

THE OCEAN

A view of Earth from a satellite shows an azure planet composed almost entirely of water. According to Tom S. Garrison, in *Oceanography: An Invitation to Marine Science* (2007), the ocean covers over two-thirds of Earth's surface to an average depth of 12,451 feet (3,795 m). The U.S. Geological Survey (USGS) notes in *Where Is Earth's Water Located?* (March 4, 2009, http://ga.water.usgs.gov/edu/earthwherewater.html) that the oceans contain 97% of the planet's water. It has a profound influence on Earth's environment.

The terms *ocean* and *sea* are sometimes used interchangeably, but they are terms used out of tradition. According to Garrison, the ocean is "the vast body of saline water that occupies the depressions of the Earth's surface" and includes all the oceans and seas. For convenience's sake, the ocean is subdivided into artificial compartments and given names that include the Atlantic, Pacific, and Indian oceans and the Mediterranean, Red, and Black seas.

Origin of the Ocean

Research suggests that the ocean is about 4.5 billion years old and that both the atmosphere on Earth and the ocean were formed through a process called outgassing of Earth's deep interior. According to this scientific theory, the ocean originated from the escape of water vapor from the melted rocks of the early Earth. The vapor rose to form clouds surrounding the cooling planet. After Earth's temperature had cooled to a point below the boiling point of water, rain began to fall and continued falling for millions of years. As this water drained into the huge hollows of the planet's cracked surface, the oceans were formed. The force of gravity kept this water on Earth. The oceans are still forming in the 21st century at an extremely slow pace with water from deep within Earth. Hydrothermal vents (underwater geysers) are one source of this water. According to Garrison, about 0.03 cubic miles (0.13 cubic km) is added to the ocean each year.

Why Is the Ocean So Salty?

The salinity (saltiness) of the ocean is due to the presence of a high concentration of dissolved inorganic solids in water, primarily sodium and chloride (the components of table salt). Table 6.1 shows the principal constituents of ocean water and compares them to river (fresh) water. Early in the life of the planet, the ocean probably contained little of these substances. However, since the first rains descended on the young Earth billions of years ago and ran over the land, the rain has eroded the soil and rocks, dissolving them and transporting their inorganic solids to the ocean. Rivers and streams also carry dissolved inorganic solids and sediments and discharge them into the ocean. In *Why Is the Ocean Salty?* (1993, http://www.palomar.edu/oceanography/salty_ocean.htm), Herbert Swenson estimates that U.S. rivers and streams discharge 225 million tons (204.1 million t) of dissolved solids (salts) and 513 million tons (465.4 million t) of suspended sediment into the ocean each year. Throughout the world, rivers annually transport about 4 billion tons (3.6 billion t) of dissolved salts to the ocean.

Over billions of years the ocean has become progressively more salty. The activity of the hydrological cycle concentrates the ocean salts as the sun's heat evaporates water from the surface of the ocean, leaving the salts behind. (See Figure 6.1.) According to Swenson, there is so much salt in the ocean that if it could be taken out and spread evenly over Earth's entire land surface, it would form a layer more than 500 feet (152.4 meters) thick—about the height of a 40-story building.

Swenson notes that the salinity of the ocean is currently about 35 pounds per thousand pounds of ocean water, or 35 parts per thousand (ppt). This is similar to a teaspoon of salt in a glass of drinking water. By contrast, the Office of Naval Research indicates in *Ocean Water: Salinity* (September 10, 2008, http://www.onr.navy.mil/Focus/ocean/water/salinity1.htm) that freshwater has

TABLE 6.1

Comparison between ocean water and river water

Chemical constituent	Percent of total salt content	
	Ocean water	River water
Silica (SiO$_2$)	—	14.51
Iron (Fe)	—	0.74
Calcium (Ca)	1.19	16.62
Magnesium (Mg)	3.72	4.54
Sodium (Na)	30.53	6.98
Potassium (K)	1.11	2.55
Bicarbonate (HCO$_3$)	0.42	31.90
Sulfate (SO$_4$)	7.67	12.41
Chloride (Cl)	55.16	8.64
Nitrate (NO$_3$)	—	1.11
Bromide (Br)	0.20	—
Total	**100.00**	**100.00**

SOURCE: Herbert Swenson, "Comparison between Ocean Water and River Water," in *Why Is the Ocean Salty?* U.S. Geological Survey, 1993, http://eric.ed.gov/ERICDocs/data/ericdocs2sql/content_storage_01/0000019b/80/3f/44/0c.pdf (accessed March 18, 2009)

FIGURE 6.1

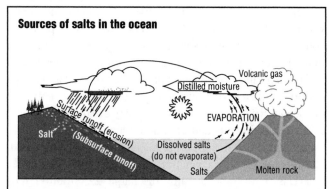

Sources of salts in the ocean

SOURCE: Herbert Swenson, "Sources of Salts in the Ocean," in *Why Is the Ocean Salty?* U.S. Geological Survey, 1993, http://eric.ed.gov/ERICDocs/data/ericdocs2sql/content_storage_01/0000019b/80/3f/44/0c.pdf (accessed March 18, 2009)

less than 0.5 ppt. Salinity in estuaries varies from slightly brackish (0.5 to 5 ppt) at the freshwater end to moderately brackish (5 to 18 ppt), to highly saline (19 ppt or more) near the ocean. An estuary is a body of water where a river meets the ocean and fresh- and saltwater mix.

Ocean as Controller of Earth's Climate

The ocean plays a major role in Earth's weather and long-term climate change. It has a huge capacity to store heat and can affect the concentration of atmospheric gases that control the planet's temperature. In *Environmental Health: Ecological Perspectives* (2005), Kathryn Hilgenkamp indicates that the top 8 feet (2.4 m) of the ocean hold as much heat as the entire atmosphere, making the ocean's ability to distribute heat an important factor in climate changes. For example, the occurrence

of a southward-flowing current of warm water off the coast of western South America (El Niño), which is caused by a breakdown of trade wind circulation (steady winds blowing from east to west above and below the equator), can disrupt global weather patterns.

The ocean plays a crucial role in the cycle of carbon dioxide, a process affecting global warming. For example, the National Oceanic and Atmospheric Administration (NOAA) reports in "After Two Large Annual Gains, Rate of Atmospheric CO2 Increase Returns to Average, NOAA Reports" (*NOAA Magazine*, March 31, 2005) that the ocean stores some of the 7 billion tons (6.4 billion t) of carbon dioxide added each year to the atmosphere by natural sources and humankind's burning of fossil fuels. The ocean, trees, plants, and soil serve as reservoirs for about half of all the human-produced carbon dioxide emitted each year since the Industrial Revolution, whereas the other half is accumulating in the atmosphere.

COASTAL POPULATIONS

According to Liz Creel for the Population Reference Bureau, in *Ripple Effects: Population and Coastal Regions* (2003, http://www.prb.org/pdf/RippleEffects_Eng.pdf), approximately 3 billion people worldwide, about half the world's population, lived within 200 kilometers (124.3 miles) of a coastline in 2003. This living preference places huge segments of the world population at risk from coastal hazards, such as hurricanes, tidal waves, and flooding, and increases pollution of both the ocean and estuaries.

In *Population Trends along the Coastal United States: 1980–2008* (September 2004, http://oceanservice.noaa.gov/programs/mb/pdfs/coastal_pop_trends_complete.pdf), Kristen M. Crossett et al. state that in 2003 an estimated 53% of the U.S. population lived in coastal counties. From 1980 to 2003 the total coastal population of the United States increased by 28%, which is consistent with the nation's rate of increase as a whole. Figure 6.2 shows this increase in coastal populations from 1980 to 2003 and projections to 2008.

Figure 6.3 shows the regional distribution of the nation's coastal population in 2003. The northeast coast had the highest percentage of the coastal population (34%) and the West Coast had the second highest percentage (25%) in 2003. However, Crossett et al. indicate that California had the greatest number of people move into the state between 1980 and 2003 (9.9 million people; 47% increase), but Florida had the highest percentage growth (75% increase; 7.1 million people). Representing the northeast coast, New Hampshire was seventh in growth, with its population increasing 46% from 1980 to 2003.

Coastal Storms

The most common coastal hazard is the threat of the huge ocean storms that come ashore, generally during the

FIGURE 6.2

Coastal population growth, 1980–2003

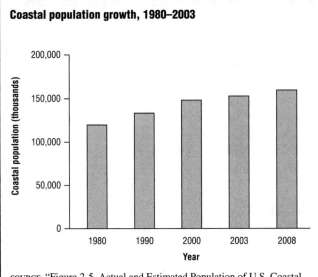

SOURCE: "Figure 2-5. Actual and Estimated Population of U.S. Coastal Counties, 1980–2008," in *National Coastal Condition Report III*, U.S. Environmental Protection Agency, Office of Water and Office of Research and Development, December 2008, http://www.epa.gov/owow/oceans/nccr3/pdf/nccr3_entire.pdf (accessed March 11, 2009)

FIGURE 6.3

Regional distribution of the coastal population, 2003

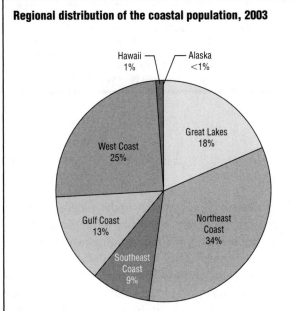

SOURCE: "Figure 2-6. Regional Distribution of the Nation's Coastal Population in 2003," in *National Coastal Condition Report III*, U.S. Environmental Protection Agency, Office of Water and Office of Research and Development, December 2008, http://www.epa.gov/owow/oceans/nccr3/pdf/nccr3_entire.pdf (accessed March 11, 2009).

warmer months of the year, and cause devastating damage to property and human life. These storms go by different names in different parts of the world. They are called hurricanes or tropical storms in the North Atlantic, the eastern North Pacific, and the western South Pacific. Typhoon is used for storms in the China Sea and the

TABLE 6.2

Saffir-Simpson Hurricane scale

Category	Winds	Effects
One	74–95 mph	No real damage to building structures. Damage primarily to unanchored mobile homes, shrubbery, and trees. Also, some coastal road flooding and minor pier damage
Two	96–110 mph	Some roofing material, door, and window damage to buildings. Considerable damage to vegetation, mobile homes, and piers. Coastal and low-lying escape routes flood 2–4 hours before arrival of center. Small craft in unprotected anchorages break moorings.
Three	111–130 mph	Some structural damage to small residences and utility buildings with a minor amount of curtain wall failures. Mobile homes are destroyed. Flooding near the coast destroys smaller structures with larger structures damaged by floating debris. Terrain continuously lower than 5 feet above sea level may be flooded inland 8 miles or more.
Four	131–155 mph	More extensive curtain wall failures with some complete roof structure failure on small residences. Major erosion of beach. Major damage to lower floors of structures near the shore. Terrain continuously lower than 10 feet above sea level may be flooded requiring massive evacuation of residential areas inland as far as 6 miles.
Five	greater than 155 mph	Complete roof failure on many residences and industrial buildings. Some complete building failures with small utility buildings blown over or away. Major damage to lower floors of all structures located less than 15 feet above sea level and within 500 yards of the shoreline. Massive evacuation of residential areas on low ground within 5 to 10 miles of the shoreline may be required.

SOURCE: "Saffir-Simpson Hurricane Scale," National Oceanic and Atmospheric Administration, Atlantic Oceanographic and Meteorological Laboratories, undated, http://www.aoml.noaa.gov/general/lib/laescae.html (accessed March 18, 2009)

western North Pacific, whereas cyclone is used for storms in the Arabian Sea, the Bay of Bengal, and the South Indian Ocean.

Table 6.2 shows the Saffir-Simpson Hurricane Scale. Developed in 1969 by the engineer Herbert Saffir (1917–2007) and Robert H. Simpson (1912–), the director of the National Hurricane Center, the scale categorizes hurricanes into one of five levels of wind speed and potential effects. This scale helps predict the destructiveness of impending storms for emergency preparedness. Hurricanes higher on the scale do not always cause more destruction and loss of life than hurricanes lower on the scale, however. Factors such as where and when a hurricane hits and the population, geography, and circumstances of that area all affect the outcome.

In August 2005 Hurricane Katrina hit the U.S. Gulf Coast, causing widespread devastation in cities such as New Orleans, Louisiana; Mobile, Alabama; and Gulfport, Mississippi. As a category three hurricane with sustained winds during landfall of 125 miles per hour (201.2 km

TABLE 6.3

The deadliest mainland United States hurricanes, 1851–2006

Rank	Hurricane	Year	Category	Deaths
1	TX (Galveston)	1900	4	8000[a]
2	FL (SE/Lake Okeechobee)	1928	4	2500[b]
3	*Katrina* (SE LA/MS)	2005	3	1500
4	LA (Cheniere Caminanda)	1893	4	1100–1400[c]
5	SC/GA (Sea Islands)	1893	3	1000–2000[d]
6	GA/SC	1881	2	700
7	*Audrey* (SW LA/N TX)	1957	4	416[h]
8	FL (Keys)	1935	5	408
9	LA (Last Island)	1856	4	400[e]
10	FL (Miami)/MS/AL/Pensacola	1926	4	372
11	LA (Grand Isle)	1909	3	350
12	FL (Keys)/S TX	1919	4	287[j]
13	LA (New Orleans)	1915	4	275[e]
13	TX (Galveston)	1915	4	275
15	New England	1938	3	256
15	*Camille* (MS/SE LA/VA)	1969	5	256
17	*Diane* (NE U.S.)	1955	1	184
18	GA, SC, NC	1898	4	179
19	TX	1875	3	176
20	SE FL	1906	3	164
21	TX (Indianola)	1886	4	150
22	MS/AL/Pensacola	1906	2	134
23	FL, GA, SC	1896	3	130
24	*Agnes* (FL/NE U.S.)	1972	1	122[f]
25	*Hazel* (SC/NC)	1954	4	95
26	*Betsy* (SE FL/SE LA)	1965	3	75
27	Northeast U.S.	1944	3	64[g]
28	*Carol* (NE U.S.)	1954	3	60
29	*Floyd* (Mid Atlantic & NE U.S.)	1999	2	56
30	NC	1883	2	53
31	SE FL/SE LA/MS	1947	4	51
32	NC, SC	1899	3	50[h, i]
32	GA/SC/NC	1940	2	50
32	*Donna* (FL/Eastern U.S.)	1960	4	50
35	LA	1860	2	47[h]
36	NC, VA	1879	3	46[h, i]
36	*Carla* (N & Central TX)	1961	4	46
38	TX (Velasco)	1909	3	41
38	*Allison* (SE TX)	2001	TS[k]	41
40	Mid-Atlantic	1889	none[l]	40[h, i]
40	TX (Freeport)	1932	4	40
40	S TX	1933	3	40
43	*Hilda* (LA)	1964	3	38
44	SW LA	1918	3	34
45	SW FL	1910	3	30
45	*Alberto* (NW FL, GA, AL)	1994	TS[k]	30
47	SC, FL	1893	3	28[m]
48	New England	1878	2	27[h, n]
48	Texas	1886	2	27[h]
50	*Fran* (NC)	1996	3	26
51	LA	1926	3	25
51	*Connie* (NC)	1955	3	25
51	*Ivan* (NW FL, AL)	2004	3	25

TABLE 6.3

The deadliest mainland United States hurricanes, 1851–2006

[CONTINUED]

Rank	Hurricane	Year	Category	Deaths
Addendum (Not Atlantic/Gulf Coast)				
2	Puerto Rico	1899	3	3369[i]
6	P.R., USVI	1867	3	811[f, i]
6	Puerto Rico	1852	1	800[f, o]
12	Puerto Rico (San Felipe)	1928	5	312
17	USVI, Puerto Rico	1932	2	225
25	*Donna* (St. Thomas, VI)	1960	4	107
25	Puerto Rico	1888	1	100[h]
38	Southern California	1939	TS[k]	45
38	*Eloise* (Puerto Rico)	1975	TS[k]	44
48	USVI	1871	3	27[h]

Notes:
[a]Could be as high as 12,000
[b]Could be as high as 3000
[c]Total including offshore losses near 2000
[d]August
[e]Total including offshore losses is 600
[f]No more than
[g]Total including offshore losses is 390
[h]At least
[i]Puerto Rico 1899 and NC, SC 1899 are the same storm
[j]Could include some offshore losses
[k]Only of Tropical Storm intensity.
[l]Remained offshore
[m]Mid-October
[n]Four deaths at shoreline or just offshore
[o]Possibly a total from two hurricanes
USVI = U.S. Virgin Islands. TS = Tropical storm

SOURCE: Eric S. Blake, Edward N. Rappaport, and Christopher W. Landsea, "Table 2. Mainland U.S. Tropical Cyclones Causing 25 or Greater Deaths 1851–2006," in *The Deadliest, Costliest, and Most Intense United States Tropical Cyclones from 1851 to 2006 (and Other Frequently Requested Hurricane Facts)*, National Oceanic and Atmospheric Administration, National Hurricane Center, April 2007, http://www.aoml.noaa.gov/hrd/Landsea/Blakeetal_noaamemoApr2007.pdf (accessed March 18, 2009)

per hour), Katrina was one of the most devastating storms to reach the U.S. coast in the last 100 years. Since 1900, it was the third deadliest hurricane (killing 1,500 people) and was by far the costliest hurricane. (See Table 6.3 and Table 6.4.)

Tsunamis are another coastal threat. A tsunami is an ocean wave produced by a submarine (undersea) earthquake, landslide, or volcanic eruption. A December 2004 tsunami, triggered by a massive earthquake in the Indian Ocean, killed over 200,000 people and caused massive damage in Indonesia, Sri Lanka, India, Thailand, and many small islands in the region. The true death toll from the tsunami may never be known, and the devastation was so overwhelming that it is difficult to attach a dollar figure to it.

Much research is targeted at understanding and predicting coastal storms and tsunamis so that coastal residents can be warned of an impending event. Besides increasing the amount of property at risk, coastal population growth has created potentially life-threatening problems with storm warnings and evacuation. It has become increasingly difficult to ensure that the ever-rising numbers of residents and visitors can be evacuated and transported to adequate shelters during storm events. Sometimes hurricane evacuation decisions must be made well in advance of issuing hurricane warnings to mobilize the appropriate manpower and resources needed for the evacuation. Also, when a significant percentage of the coastal population has not experienced an event such as a hurricane, people are less likely to prepare and respond properly before, during, and after the event. However, following the 2004 tsunami, government officials and scientists began working to create a new tsunami warning system for the region that had been so hard hit.

TABLE 6.4

The costliest U.S. hurricanes, 1900–2006

Rank	Hurricane	Year	Category	Damage (U.S.)
1	*Katrina* (SE FL, SE LA, MS)	2005	3	$81,000,000,000
2	*Andrew* (SE FL/SE LA)	1992	5	26,500,000,000
3	*Wilma* (S FL)	2005	3	20,600,000,000
4	*Charley* (SW FL)	2004	4	15,000,000,000
5	*Ivan* (AL/NW FL)	2004	3	14,200,000,000
6	*Rita* (SW LA, N TX)	2005	3	11,300,000,000
7	*Frances* (FL)	2004	2	8,900,000,000
8	*Hugo* (SC)	1989	4	7,000,000,000
9	*Jeanne* (FL)	2004	3	6,900,000,000
10	*Allison* (N TX)	2001	TS*	5,000,000,000
11	*Floyd* (Mid-Atlantic & NE U.S.)	1999	2	4,500,000,000
12	*Isabel* (Mid-Atlantic)	2003	2	3,370,000,000
13	*Fran* (NC)	1996	3	3,200,000,000
14	*Opal* (NW FL/AL)	1995	3	3,000,000,000
15	*Frederic* (AL/MS)	1979	3	2,300,000,000
16	*Dennis* (NW FL)	2005	3	2,230,000,000
17	*Agnes* (FL/NE U.S.)	1972	1	2,100,000,000
18	*Alicia* (N TX)	1983	3	2,000,000,000
19	*Bob* (NC, NE U.S)	1991	2	1,500,000,000
19	*Juan* (LA)	1985	1	1,500,000,000
21	*Camille* (MS/SE LA/VA)	1969	5	1,420,700,000
22	*Betsy* (SE FL/SE LA)	1965	3	1,420,500,000
23	*Elena* (MS/AL/NW FL)	1985	3	1,250,000,000
24	*Georges* (FL Keys, MS, AL)	1998	2	1,155,000,000
25	*Gloria* (Eastern U.S.)	1985	3	900,000,000
26	*Lili* (SC LA)	2002	1	860,000,000
27	*Diane* (NE U.S.)	1955	1	831,700,000
28	*Bonnie* (NC, VA)	1998	2	720,000,000
29	*Erin* (NW FL)	1998	2	700,000,000
30	*Allison* (N TX)	1989	TS*	500,000,000
30	*Alberto* (NW FL, GA, AL)	1994	TS*	500,000,000
30	*Frances* (TX)	1998	TS*	500,000,000
30	*Ernesto* (FL, NC, VA)	2006	TS*	500,000,000

Addendum (Rank is independent of other events in group)

19	*Georges* (USVI, PR)	1998	3	1,800,000,000
19	*Iniki* (Kauai, HI)	1992	3	1,800,000,000
19	*Marilyn* (USVI, PR)	1995	2	1,500,000,000
25	*Hugo* (USVI, PR)	1989	4	1,000,000,000
30	*Hortense* (PR)	1996	1	500,000,000

Notes: Dollar figures are not adjusted for inflation.
USVI = U.S. Virgin Islands. TS = Tropical storm.
*Only of tropical storm intensity

SOURCE: Eric S. Blake, Edward N. Rappaport, and Christopher W. Landsea, "Table 3a. The Thirty Costliest Mainland United States Tropical Cyclones, 1900–2006 (Not Adjusted for Inflation)," in *The Deadliest, Costliest, and Most Intense United States Tropical Cyclones from 1851 to 2006 (and Other Frequently Requested Hurricane Facts)*, National Oceanic and Atmospheric Administration, National Hurricane Center, April 2007, http://www.aoml.noaa.gov/hrd/Landsea/Blakeetal_noaamemoApr2007.pdf (accessed March 18, 2009)

CORAL REEFS—A SPECIAL OCEAN HABITAT

A coral reef is a submerged ridge near the surface of the water made up not only of colonies of coral animals that secrete hard skeletons but also of other aquatic organisms such as algae, mollusks, and worms. Coral reefs are among the richest marine ecosystems in terms of beauty, species, productivity, biomass (the amount of living matter), and structural complexity. They are dependent on intricate interactions between the coral, which provides the structural framework, and the organisms that live among the coral. Most reefs form as long, narrow ribbons along the edge between shallow and deep waters, and their assets are many: fisheries for food, income from tourism and recreation, materials for new medicines, and shoreline protection from coastal storms.

Coral Reef Structure

Corals are simple, bottom-dwelling organisms related to the sea anemone and jellyfish. The basic building block of coral is a polyp, a tiny animal that has a common opening used to take in food and excrete wastes and is surrounded by a ring of tentacles. The weak stinging cells of the tentacles are used to capture small zooplankton (minute floating aquatic animals) for food. Each polyp sits in its own tiny bowl of calcium carbonate (its skeleton), which the coral constantly builds as it grows up from the ocean floor. Reef-building corals live in large colonies formed by the repeated divisions of genetically identical polyps, although many species of coral animals are represented within the reef. The colonies can take a wide variety of shapes, including branched, leafy, or massive forms, which may grow continuously for thousands of years.

Inside the sac of each coral polyp lives a single-celled algae. The algae give off oxygen and nutrients the coral uses to grow, and the coral gives off carbon dioxide and other substances the algae uses. Such a living situation is called symbiosis—the living together of two dissimilar organisms with mutual benefit.

Because of their dependence on symbiotic algae, coral reefs can grow only under conditions favoring the algae. Coral reefs are confined to tropical waters because the algae require warm, shallow, well-lit waters that are free of turbidity and pollution.

Coral Reefs—Ecosystems at Risk

The proximity of coral reefs to land makes them particularly vulnerable to the effects of human actions. Because they depend on light, coral reefs can be severely damaged by silt, which leads to an overgrowth of seaweed and other factors that reduce water clarity and quality. Sport diving and overfishing for food and the aquarium trade can deplete species and damage coral, resulting in disruption to the intricate interactions among reef species, as well as coral decline. (Overfishing means that so many fish are harvested that the natural breeding stock is depleted.) The introduction of exotic species through human activity can be devastating as the new predators consume the living reefs.

NOAA notes in "Major Reef-Building Coral Diseases" (January 23, 2007, http://www.coris.noaa.gov/about/diseases/) that along with becoming infected by bacteria or developing diseases of unknown causes, corals may respond to stress and damage with a condition known as coral bleaching. The coral expels the microscopic algae that normally live within its cells and provide the coral with its color, its ability to rapidly grow skeleton, and much of its food. The bleached coral turns pale, transparent, or unusual colors and then starves because it is unable to feed or reproduce. Increased bleaching is an early warning sign of deteriorating health and can be caused by extremes of light, temperature, or salinity.

Natural events, such as hurricanes, can also damage coral reefs. Healthy reefs generally recover from such damage, but unhealthy reefs often do not. In "Hazards to Coral Reefs" (January 23, 2007, http://www.coris .noaa.gov/about/hazards/), NOAA warns, "Current estimates note that 10 percent of all coral reefs are degraded beyond recovery. Thirty percent are in critical condition and may die within 10 to 20 years. Experts predict that if current pressures are allowed to continue unabated, 60 percent of the world's coral reefs may die completely by 2050."

Coral Reefs in the United States

The U.S. Environmental Protection Agency (EPA) explains in *2000 National Water Quality Inventory* (August 2002, http://www.epa.gov/305b/2000report/) that coral reefs are found in only three places in the United States: Florida (primarily in the Florida Keys), throughout the Hawaiian archipelago, and in the offshore Flower Gardens of Texas. The Florida reef system is part of the Caribbean reef system, the third largest barrier-reef ecosystem in the world. Five U.S. territories—American Samoa, Guam, the Northern Mariana Islands, Puerto Rico, and the U.S. Virgin

Islands—also have lush reef areas. However, the northwestern Hawaiian Islands make up 69% of the country's coral reef areas, and the main Hawaiian islands make up 15%—a total of 84% of all the reef areas of the United States and its territories.

Many U.S. coral reefs have been designated as marine sanctuaries with varying degrees of protection. The full extent and condition of most of these coral reefs is only beginning to be studied as a special area of focus.

Jeannette E. Waddell and Alicia M. Clarke of NOAA note in *The State of Coral Reef Ecosystems of the United States and Pacific Freely Associated States: 2008* (April 2008, http://ccma.nos.noaa.gov/ecosystems/coralreef/coral 2008/pdf/CoralReport2008.pdf) that the United States and the Pacific Freely Associated States have 15 jurisdictions that contain coral reef ecosystems: the U.S. Virgin Islands, Puerto Rico, Navassa Island, southeast Florida, the Florida Keys, Flower Gardens Banks, the main Hawaiian Islands, the northwestern Hawaiian Islands, American Samoa, Pacific remote island areas, the Republic of the Marshall Islands, the Federated States of Micronesia, the Commonwealth of Northern Mariana Islands, Guam, and the Republic of Palau.

Table 6.5 and Table 6.6 show the number of the 15 jurisdictions reporting on the condition of the resources and threats to the coral reefs in their area, rating the condition or threats as "decreasing," "about the same," or "increasing." Table 6.5 reflects trends in the condition

TABLE 6.5

Trends in the condition of resources and threats to coral reef ecosystems, 2005–07

	Decreasing	About the same	Increasing	Unknown	Overall
Resources					
Water quality	5	8	1	1	Decreasing
Living coral cover	5	8	2	0	Same
Reef fish populations	5	10	0	0	Decreasing
Harvested reef fish and macroinvertebrates	5	8	0	0	Decreasing
Threats					
Climate change and coral bleaching	8	6	0	1	Increasing
Coral disease	7	7	0	1	Increasing
Tropical storms	3	12	0	0	Same
Coastal development	8	2	4	0	Increasing
Tourism and recreation	8	6	0	1	ncreasing
Commercial fishing	5	7	1	2	Increasing
Subsistence and recreational fishing	8	5	0	2	Increasing
Vessel damage	3	11	0	0	Increasing
Marine debris	5	9	0	1	Increasing
Aquatic invasive species	8	7	0	0	Increasing

Notes: Overall trends were determined by averaging the responses in each row, based on the values decreasing = −1, about the same = 0, increasing = 1. Average values between −0.2 and 0.2 were considered about the same. Unknown responses were not included in the average.

SOURCE: Jeannette E. Waddell and Alicia M. Clarke (eds.), "Table 17.4. Number of the 15 Jurisdictions Reporting a Trend in the Condition of Resources or Threats over the Past 3 Years," in *The State of Coral Reef Ecosystems of the United States and Pacific Freely Associated States: 2008,* National Oceanic and Atmospheric Administration, National Ocean Service, Center for Costal Monitoring and Assessment, Biogeography Branch, April 2008, http://ccma.nos.noaa .gov/ecosystems/coralreef/coral2008/pdf/NationalSumm.pdf (accessed March 18, 2009)

TABLE 6.6

Trends in the condition of resources and threats to coral reef ecosystems, 1982–2007

	Decreasing	About the same	Increasing	Unknown	Overall
Resources					
Water quality	8	4	0	3	Decreasing
Living coral cover	10	3	1	1	Decreasing
Reef fish populations	8	6	0	1	Decreasing
Harvested reef fish and macroinvertebrates	10	3	0	1	Decreasing
Threats					
Climate change and coral bleaching	13	0	0	2	Increasing
Coral disease	11	1	0	3	Increasing
Tropical storms	4	11	0	0	Increasing
Coastal development	9	3	2	0	Increasing
Tourism and recreation	12	1	1	1	Increasing
Commercial fishing	5	5	3	2	Same
Subsistence and recreational fishing	11	1	1	2	Increasing
Vessel damage	6	7	1	0	Increasing
Marine debris	11	2	0	2	Increasing
Aquatic invasive species	8	4	0	3	Increasing

Notes: Overall trends were determined by averaging the responses in each row, based on the values decreasing = −1, about the same = 0, increasing = 1. Average values between −0.2 and 0.2 were considered about the same. Unknown responses were not included in the average.

SOURCE: Jeannette E. Waddell and Alicia M. Clarke (eds.), "Table 17.4. Number of the 15 Jurisdictions Reporting a Trend in the Condition of Resources or Threats over the Past 10–25 Years," in *The State of Coral Reef Ecosystems of the United States and Pacific Freely Associated States: 2008*, National Oceanic and Atmospheric Administration, National Ocean Service, Center for Costal Monitoring and Assessment, Biogeography Branch, April 2008, http://ccma.nos .noaa.gov/ecosystems/coralreef/coral2008/pdf/NationalSumm.pdf (accessed March 18, 2009)

of resources and threats over the past 3 years, and Table 6.6 reflects trends over the past 10 to 25 years.

Over the three years from 2005–2007, one-third of the jurisdictions reported that the condition of the resources of their coral reefs, such as water quality, living coral cover, and reef fish populations, were decreasing. (See Table 6.5.) About two-thirds rated resources as "about the same" in the past three years. Nonetheless, these ratings resulted in overall ratings of "decreasing" for all coral reef resources except living coral cover. Table 6.6 shows that the condition of these resources had decreased during the preceding 10 to 25 years as well, including the condition of the living coral cover.

From 2005 to 2007, one-third to one-half of the 15 jurisdictions reported that most threats to their coral reefs, such as climate change, coral bleaching, and coral disease, have increased. (See Table 6.5.) A similar range of jurisdictions rates threats as being "about the same." These ratings resulted in an overall rating of "increasing" for all coral reef threats except tropical storms in these three years. Table 6.6 shows that these threats, except for commercial fishing, had increased during the preceding 10 to 25 years as well.

NEARSHORE WATERS

Nearshore waters are shallow waters a short distance from the shore in lakes, rivers, estuaries, and the ocean. Depending on the size of the water body, the nearshore waters may be minimal in size (a small lake) or large (the coastal waters of the Atlantic Ocean). They reflect the conditions and activities within the watershed. A watershed is an area in which water, sediments, and dissolved materials drain to a common outlet, such as a lake, river, estuary, or the ocean.

Whether marine, estuarine, or fresh, nearshore waters serve a variety of functions. They are the prime recreational waters, providing opportunities for swimming, boating, diving, surfing, snorkeling, and fishing. Nearshore waters are intimately linked with wetlands and sea grasses and provide a unique habitat for a variety of plants and animals. According to the EPA, in "Nearshore Waters and Your Coastal Watershed" (August 30, 2007, http://www.epa .gov/owow/oceans/factsheets/fact3.html), these waters are the source of food and shelter for many species of fish and shellfish and provide habitat for 80% of the fish species in the United States. Nearshore waters also provide many opportunities for education and research for students, naturalists, and scientists.

Because of their proximity to the shoreline, nearshore waters are particularly vulnerable to pollution. As a result, water quality in most confined waters and some nearshore waters is deteriorating, which in turn affects the plant and animal life. Besides pollution, nearshore waters are vulnerable to the everyday (and to all appearances, harmless) activities of people. For example, swimming has been restricted in some shallow lagoons with coral reefs and beautiful beaches because heavy use by swimmers resulted in chemical concentrations of suntan oil and sunblock lotion in the water that was high enough to kill or impair the coral reefs. Wakes from recreational powerboats in high-use areas have been shown to increase wave action, resulting in increased shoreline erosion. Increased pollutant levels from boat paints, spills during refueling, and leaks of gas and oil from recreational boat engines in areas of high recreational use affect both plants and animals. Private pier and boathouse construction result in the shading of water, which contributes to sea grass decline. Balancing the need to accommodate the public's desire to enjoy water-related activities and ownership of waterfront property and the need to protect nearshore waters is a difficult management issue.

Estuaries

Estuaries are places of transition, where rivers meet the sea. An estuary is a partially enclosed body of water formed where freshwater from rivers flows into the ocean, mixing with the salty seawater. As mentioned earlier, salinity in estuaries is a continuum, varying from slightly brackish (0.5 to 5 ppt) at the freshwater end to moderately brackish (5 to 18 ppt), to highly saline (19 ppt or more) near the ocean. Although influenced by the tides, estuaries are protected from the full force of ocean waves, winds, and storms by reefs, barrier islands, or fingers of land, mud, or sand that make up their seaward boundary. Estuaries come in all shapes and sizes. Examples include the Chesapeake Bay, Puget Sound, Boston Harbor, San Francisco Bay, and Tampa Bay.

The tidal sheltered waters of estuaries support unique communities of plants and animals that are specially adapted for life under a wide range of conditions. Estuarine environments are incredibly productive, producing more organic matter annually than any equal-sized area of forest (including rain forests), grassland, or cropland. A wide range of habitats exists around and in estuaries, including shallow open water, tidal pools, sandy beaches, mud and sand flats, freshwater and salt marshes, rocky shores, oyster reefs, mangrove forests, river deltas, wooded swamps, and kelp and sea grass beds.

NATIONAL ESTUARY PROGRAM. The Water Quality Act of 1987 created the National Estuary Program (NEP) to help achieve long-term protection of living resources and water quality (the basic "fishable/swimmable" goal of the Clean Water Act) in estuaries. To improve an estuary, the NEP brings together community members to define program goals and objectives, identify estuary problems, and design action plans to prevent or control pollution, while restoring habitats and living resources such as shellfish. This integrated watershed-based, stakeholder-oriented, water resource management approach results in the adoption of a comprehensive conservation and management

plan for implementation in each estuary. The estuaries in the program and links to the profiles of each are discussed in detail in "NEP Profiles" (April 14, 2009, http://www.epa .gov/owow/estuaries/profiles.html).

In "Success Stories" (April 16, 2009, http://www.epa .gov/nep/success.html), the EPA mentions several NEP successes. Two examples of environmental improvement resulting from the NEP can be found in the Galveston Bay and Long Island Sound projects. In Galveston Bay, a highly populated and industrialized area, businesses voluntarily joined a program to reduce their waste and the resultant pollution of the bay. Other Galveston Bay NEP projects used coal combustion by-products (primarily fly ash and bottom ash) to develop oyster reefs, and named Christmas Bay and Armand Bayou as preserves to help ensure that their resources were protected. In Long Island Sound sewage treatment plants that discharged processed wastewater into the sound modified their processes to remove greater amounts of nitrogen from the water. Nitrogen levels had increased, resulting in fish and lobster kills from the low levels of dissolved oxygen present in deep waters.

CHESAPEAKE BAY PROGRAM. According to the Chesapeake Bay Program, in *Bay Barometer: A Health and Restoration Assessment of the Chesapeake Bay and Watershed in 2008* (March 2009, http://www.chesapeakebay.net/ content/publications/cbp_34915.pdf), the Chesapeake Bay is the largest estuary in North America. It has a 64,000-square-mile (166,000-square-km) watershed that encompasses 6 states and the District of Columbia. Its watershed is home to nearly 17 million people and 3,600 species of plants and animals. The Bay has over 11,684 miles (18,804 km) of shoreline and averages 21 feet (6.4 m) deep, with hundreds of thousands of acres of shallow water. It is 200 miles (322 km) long and 35 miles (56 km) wide at its widest point.

The first estuary in the United States to be targeted for restoration and protection, the Bay is protected under its own federally mandated program, separate from the NEP. The Chesapeake Bay Program (2009, http://www .chesapeakebay.net/) began in 1983 with a meeting of the governors of Maryland, Pennsylvania, and Virginia; the mayor of the District of Columbia; and the EPA administrator. These individuals signed the Chesapeake Bay Agreement committing their states and the District of Columbia to prepare plans for protecting and improving water quality and living resources in the Chesapeake Bay. The Chesapeake Bay Program evolved as the institutional mechanism to restore the Bay and to meet the goals of the Chesapeake Bay Agreement.

Even though progress has been made in the Chesapeake Bay restoration, its health remained poor as of 2008 after a serious decline in 2003. That year was extremely wet, and as a result excess sediment and nutrients had washed into the Bay from the land. In *Chesapeake Bay*

Report Card 2008 (2009, http://ian.umces.edu/pdfs/eco check_newsletter_20090326150713.pdf), the University of Maryland Center for Environmental Science (UMCES) and EcoCheck, an alliance between NOAA and the UMCES, rate the Bay's health as "moderate poor" in 2008. The determination was made by assessing water quality and various biotic factors, such as the variety, numbers, and types of living organisms in the Bay. "Very poor" health is considered to have an index value of 0%, and "very good" health an index value of 100%. In 2002 the Chesapeake Bay had an index value of 55%. In 2003 the index value declined to 36%. By 2008 the index had increased to 43%, but it was still far below the 2002 index value.

The Chesapeake Bay Program releases its own evaluation annually of the health of the Bay and uses its own health index percentage system. This evaluation is the *Bay Barometer*. According to the report, in 2008 the Chesapeake Bay was unhealthy. The report sums up conditions in the Bay and the reasons for those conditions:

> The Chesapeake Bay and its tributaries are unhealthy primarily because of pollution from excess nitrogen, phosphorus and sediment entering the water. The main sources of these pollutants are agriculture, urban and suburban runoff, wastewater, and airborne contaminants.

> Despite small successes in certain parts of the ecosystem and specific geographic areas, the overall health of the Chesapeake Bay did not improve in 2008. The Bay continues to have poor water quality, degraded habitats and low populations of many species of fish and shellfish. Based on these three areas, the overall health averaged 38 percent, with 100 percent representing a fully restored ecosystem.

Both the *Chesapeake Bay Report Card 2008* and the *Bay Barometer* suggest that many measures must be put in place to improve the health of the Bay. For example, one measure is to reduce pollution by modifying wastewater treatment processes in facilities that discharge treated wastewater into the Bay, strengthening storm water regulations, and regulating emissions from cars, industries, and power plants. Another measure is to revive habitats by planting bay grasses and restoring oyster reefs and wetlands.

CONDITION OF THE NATION'S ESTUARIES. There are three major EPA reports that include information on the state of American estuaries: the *National Coastal Condition Report III* (December 2008, http://www.epa.gov/ owow/oceans/nccr3/pdf/nccr3_entire.pdf), the *National Estuary Program Coastal Condition Report* (June 2007, http://www.epa.gov/owow/oceans/nepccr/index.html), and the *National Water Quality Inventory: Report to Congress, 2004 Reporting Cycle* (January 2009, http://www.epa.gov/ owow/305b/2004report/2004_305Breport.pdf).

The EPA, NOAA, the USGS, the U.S. Fish and Wildlife Service, coastal states, and the NEP coordinate efforts to produce the *National Coastal Condition Report*, which describes the ecological and environmental conditions in U.S. coastal waters, including estuaries. As of mid-2009, the most recent report was the *National Coastal Condition Report III*. Figure 6.4 is a summary graphic from this report and shows the overall national and regional coastal condition, including estuaries, based on data collected primarily between 2001 and 2002. Data collected after 2002 will be included in the *National Coastal Condition Report IV*, which is scheduled to be released in 2011.

The *National Coastal Condition Report III* uses five indices (indicators) of coastal condition, shown in Figure 6.4 as ecological health. The coastal habitat index is an assessment of the loss of wetland areas (where the land meets the water) of estuary ecosystems. Thus, the coastal habitat index provides a measure of the health of estuaries. Figure 6.4 shows the coastal habitat index rated as poor overall, which means significant loss of wetland areas. This index was found to be the best (the healthiest with little wetland loss) on the northeast coast, approaching a condition of good.

The *National Estuary Program Coastal Condition Report* discusses the overall condition of the 28 NEP estuaries using the 5 indices of ecological health, which include the coastal habitat index. This report does not, however, look at that index exclusively.

The *National Estuary Program Coastal Condition Report* states that "the overall condition of the NEP estuaries of the United States is rated fair, with the water quality index, benthic index, and fish tissue contaminants index each rated fair and the sediment quality index rated fair to poor at the national level." As Figure 6.5 shows, the overall condition of the NEP estuaries in the Southeast is the best, approaching a rating of good. The NEP estuaries in other regions are rated less than fair to poor. The NEP estuaries in the Northeast and Puerto Rico have poorer water quality conditions than those in other regions of the country.

Even though the *National Estuary Program Coastal Condition Report* rates the national estuaries as being in somewhat better condition than is reported in the coastal habitat index of the *National Coastal Condition Report III*, the latter report is only assessing estuaries in the NEP, which have been involved in the program to improve their health. There are some regional assessment differences as well.

The EPA also produces a report on the nation's waterways called the *National Water Quality Inventory*. Following the publication of the *2000 National Water Quality Inventory*, the EPA entered a transition period in the gathering and analysis of water quality data to produce nationally consistent, statistically valid assessment reports. Its

FIGURE 6.4

Overall national and regional coastal condition, 2001–02

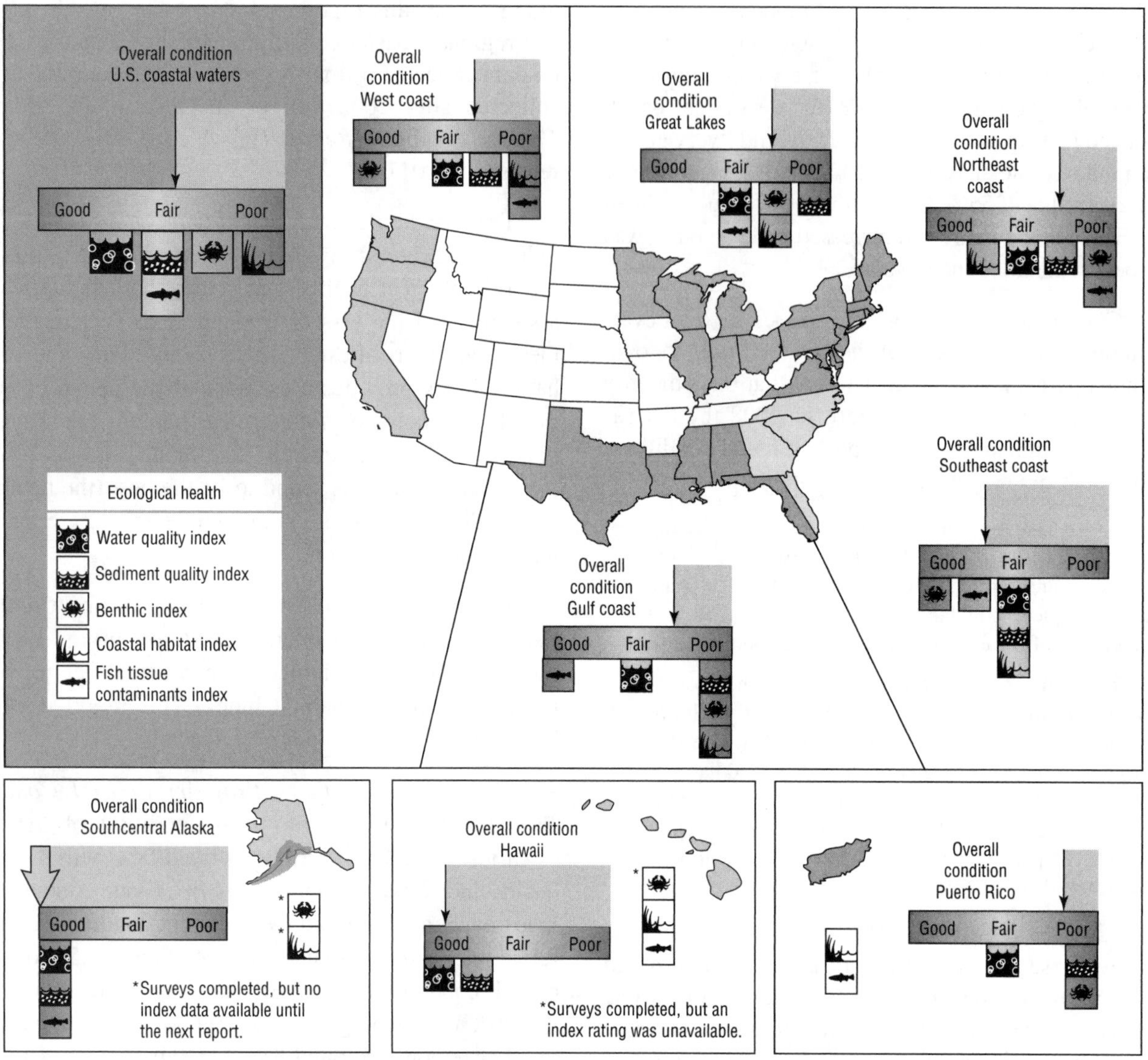

Overall condition
U.S. coastal waters

Good Fair Poor

Overall condition
West coast

Good Fair Poor

Overall condition
Great Lakes

Good Fair Poor

Overall condition
Northeast coast

Good Fair Poor

Ecological health

Water quality index

Sediment quality index

Benthic index

Coastal habitat index

Fish tissue contaminants index

Overall condition
Southeast coast

Good Fair Poor

Overall condition
Gulf coast

Good Fair Poor

Overall condition
Southcentral Alaska

Good Fair Poor

*Surveys completed, but no index data available until the next report.

Overall condition
Hawaii

Good Fair Poor

*Surveys completed, but an index rating was unavailable.

Overall condition
Puerto Rico

Good Fair Poor

SOURCE: "Figure ES-1. Overall National and Regional Coastal Condition Based on Data Collected Primarily between 2001 and 2002," in *National Coastal Condition Report III*, U.S. Environmental Protection Agency, Office of Water and Office of Research and Development, December 2008, http://www.epa .gov/owow/oceans/nccr3/pdf/nccr3_entire.pdf (accessed March 11, 2009)

reports had been plagued by inconsistent and incomplete data provided by the states. The EPA details in "Schedule for Statistically Valid Surveys of the Nation's Waters" (December 5, 2005, http://www.epa.gov/owow/monitoring/ guide.pdf) its new reporting schedule.

The *National Water Quality Inventory: Report to Congress, 2004 Reporting Cycle* summarizes water quality reports submitted by 44 states, 2 territories, and the District of Columbia. Even though states have made progress in providing data that are more consistent nationally, the EPA notes that "states are working to strengthen their water monitoring and assessment programs." Thus, data from this

report do not appear to be as reliable nationally as the data from the two previously mentioned reports. Additionally, the EPA notes in its report that "this information is for a relatively small subset of the nation's total waters which may not be representative of the waters that were not assessed."

Figure 6.6 shows the state-reported water quality in the *National Water Quality Inventory* for assessed bay and estuary square miles. Of a total 87,791 square miles (227,378 square km) of bays and estuaries, 25,399 square miles (65,783 square km; 29%) were assessed in 2004. Of the assessed waters, 30% were found to be impaired and 70% supported all designated uses.

FIGURE 6.5

Overall condition of NEP estuaries, 1999–2001

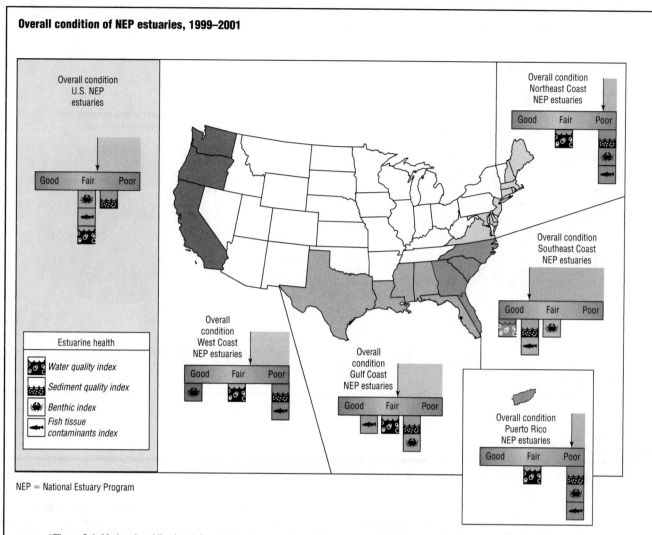

SOURCE: "Figure 2-1. National and Regional Overall Condition Ratings for the Nation's NEP Estuaries," in *National Estuary Program Coastal Condition Report*, U.S. Environmental Protection Agency, Office of Water, June 2007, http://www.epa.gov/owow/oceans/nepccr/pdf/nepccr_natchap.pdf (accessed March 19, 2009)

Table 6.7 shows the top three designated uses of bays and estuaries, the number of square miles of estuarine waters assessed for each designated use, and the percentage of assessed waters that supported that use. Waters rated as good supported their designated use, whereas waters rated impaired did not. Of the estuarine waters assessed in 2004, 73% supported the protection and propagation of fish, shellfish, and wildlife; 81% supported fishing; and 87% supported recreational uses, such as swimming and boating.

A variety of causes impair estuary and bay waters, resulting in their not being able to support their designated uses. Figure 6.7 shows the top ten causes of impairment in assessed bays and estuaries in 2004. Pathogens (disease-causing organisms, usually bacteria) top the list, affecting about 37% of impaired estuary square miles. Organic enrichment (waste materials) and low levels of oxygen were the number-two cause of impaired estuary waters, affecting about 28% of impaired estuary square

miles. Other leading causes of impairment were mercury, toxic organics, nutrients, pesticides, and metals.

The sources of these impairments were also listed in the state assessments. The number-one source of impairment in assessed bays and estuaries in 2004 was atmospheric deposition—that is, substances that were deposited in the water from the air. (See Figure 6.8.) Pollutants such as mercury are released into the air from industrial sources and end up not only on the land but also in surface waters. Atmospheric deposition was a source of impairment for approximately 43% of impaired estuary square miles. Sewage from septic systems and treatment plants was the next most important known source of impairment, affecting about 33% of impaired estuary square miles.

The Overall National Coastal Condition

The *National Coastal Condition Report III* takes a broad look at the health of the national coastal ocean

FIGURE 6.6

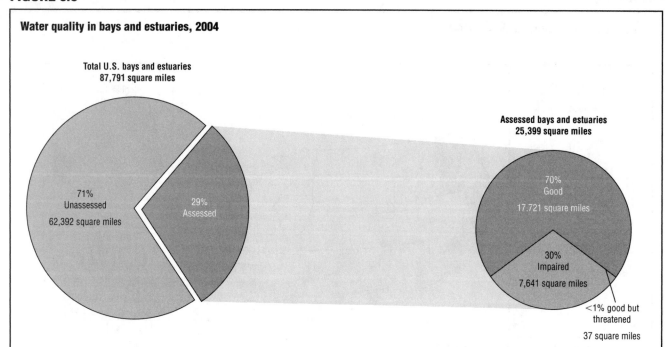

Water quality in bays and estuaries, 2004

Total U.S. bays and estuaries
87,791 square miles

71%
Unassessed
62,392 square miles

29%
Assessed

Assessed bays and estuaries
25,399 square miles

70%
Good
17,721 square miles

30%
Impaired
7,641 square miles

<1% good but
threatened
37 square miles

SOURCE: "Figure 7. Water Quality in Assessed Bay and Estuary Square Miles," in *National Water Quality Inventory: Report to Congress, 2004 Reporting Cycle*, U.S. Environmental Protection Agency, Office of Water, January 2009, http://www.epa.gov/owow/305b/2004report/2004_305Breport.pdf (accessed March 8, 2009)

TABLE 6.7

Percentage of estuary and bay waters that support designated uses, 2004

Designated use	Square miles assessed	Percentage of total U.S. estuarine miles	Percentage of waters assessed		
			Good	Threatened	Impaired
Fish, shellfish, and wildlife protection/propagation	24,338	28%	73%	<1%	27%
Aquatic life harvesting	11,004	13%	81%	<1%	19%
Recreation	9,322	11%	87%	<1%	13%

Note: Waterbodies can have multiple designated uses, resulting in an overlap of square miles assessed.

SOURCE: "Table 5. Individual Use Support in Assessed Bay and Estuary Square Miles," in *National Water Quality Inventory: Report to Congress, 2004 Reporting Cycle*, U.S. Environmental Protection Agency, Office of Water, January 2009, http://www.epa.gov/owow/305b/2004report/2004_305Breport.pdf (accessed March 8, 2009)

waters, which not only include estuaries but also bays, sounds, wetlands, coral reefs, and intertidal zones. Five indices of coastal condition are evaluated in the report: water quality, sediment quality, benthic life, coastal habitats, and fish tissue contaminants. These indices are evaluated for each region of the United States that has a coast on either the ocean or the Great Lakes, and for the nation as a whole. The regions are the West Coast, Great Lakes, Northeast Coast, Southeast Coast, Gulf Coast, Southcentral Alaska, Hawaii, and Puerto Rico.

Figure 6.4 shows that the overall condition of U.S. coastal waters was rated as fair. Hawaii and Southcentral Alaska had the healthiest coastal ocean waters, which

were rated as good, but no data were available for some of their categories of ecological health. Puerto Rico had the least healthy coastal waters, which were rated as poor.

Figure 6.9 expands on four of the five indices of ecological health of the coastal waters. The water quality index consists of indicators such as nitrogen and phosphorus levels, water clarity, and level of dissolved oxygen. The sediment quality index refers to the level of contamination of the sediment with toxic chemicals. The benthic index refers to organisms that live in the substrate at the bottom of coastal waters. A good benthic index is one in which a wide variety of benthic species are found, of which there are few pollution-tolerant species and

FIGURE 6.7

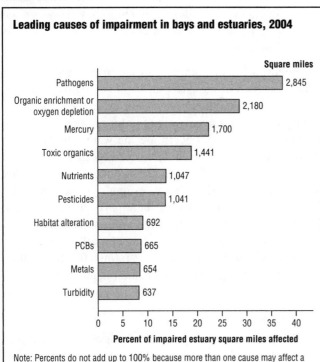

Leading causes of impairment in bays and estuaries, 2004

Square miles

Pathogens	2,845
Organic enrichment or oxygen depletion	2,180
Mercury	1,700
Toxic organics	1,441
Nutrients	1,047
Pesticides	1,041
Habitat alteration	692
PCBs	665
Metals	654
Turbidity	637

Percent of impaired estuary square miles affected
(0 5 10 15 20 25 30 35 40)

Note: Percents do not add up to 100% because more than one cause may affect a waterbody. PCB = Polychlorinated Biphenyls.

SOURCE: "Figure 8. Top 10 Causes of Impairment in Assessed Bays and Estuaries," in *National Water Quality Inventory: Report to Congress, 2004 Reporting Cycle*, U.S. Environmental Protection Agency, Office of Water, January 2009, http://www.epa.gov/owow/305b/2004report/ 2004_305Breport.pdf (accessed March 8, 2009)

FIGURE 6.8

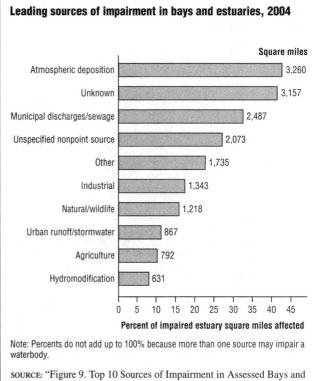

Leading sources of impairment in bays and estuaries, 2004

Square miles

Atmospheric deposition	3,260
Unknown	3,157
Municipal discharges/sewage	2,487
Unspecified nonpoint source	2,073
Other	1,735
Industrial	1,343
Natural/wildlife	1,218
Urban runoff/stormwater	867
Agriculture	792
Hydromodification	631

Percent of impaired estuary square miles affected
(0 5 10 15 20 25 30 35 40 45)

Note: Percents do not add up to 100% because more than one source may impair a waterbody.

SOURCE: "Figure 9. Top 10 Sources of Impairment in Assessed Bays and Estuaries," in *National Water Quality Inventory: Report to Congress, 2004 Reporting Cycle*, U.S. Environmental Protection Agency, Office of Water, January 2009, http://www.epa.gov/owow/305b/2004report/ 2004_305Breport.pdf (accessed March 8, 2009)

several pollution-sensitive species. The coastal habitat index is an assessment of the long-term loss of wetland areas of estuary ecosystems. Small losses would produce a rating of good and large losses a rating of poor. The fish tissue index refers to levels of chemical contaminants within fish.

The bars in Figure 6.9 show the percent of the coastal area rated either good, fair, poor, or missing for each index and the component indicators that make up each index. The water quality index bar shows that 57% of the nation's coastal waters had a water quality index rating of good, 34% had a rating of fair, and 6% a rating of poor. The five component indicators that make up this rating were levels of the dissolved nutrients nitrogen and phosphorus, the concentrations of chlorophyll *a* (indicating plant growth), water clarity, and levels of dissolved oxygen.

High levels of nitrogen and phosphorus result in low ratings because they lead to the overgrowth of plant material, which blocks the light in the water and kills other plants. Bacteria feed on the dead plants and use oxygen, lowering oxygen levels that fish and other aquatic organisms need. Figure 6.9 shows that high levels of dissolved phosphorus were more often the problem in coastal waters than were high levels of dissolved nitrogen. Thus, a higher percentage of coastal waters were

rated good for levels of dissolved nitrogen than for levels of dissolved phosphorus.

The concentration of chlorophyll *a* in water indicates the level of algal growth. High levels of chlorophyll *a* indicate the overgrowth of algae. Approximately 70% of the nation's coastal waters had a chlorophyll *a* rating of good. (See Figure 6.9.)

Water clarity is important for aesthetics and the recreational use of water, but it is also important to the ecological health of the water. Turbidity, which is a measure of the relative clarity of water, is caused by suspended matter or other impurities that make the water look cloudy. These impurities may include clay, silt, finely divided organic and inorganic matter, plankton (floating microscopic plants), and other microscopic organisms. It interferes with the transmission of light to underwater grasses and other plant life in need of this light. If the transmission of light is reduced because of heavy silt in the water, this can smother bottom-dwelling organisms such as oysters. In addition, the plant life is used by marine animals for food, shelter, and reproductive sites. When these plants die, not only are they unavailable for the uses mentioned but also bacteria feed on them, proliferate, and deplete the oxygen in the water needed for the survival of animals, such as fish and marine invertebrates. Figure 6.9 shows that the water clarity was

FIGURE 6.9

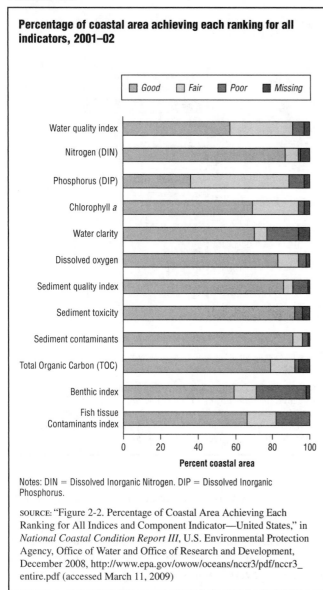

Percentage of coastal area achieving each ranking for all indicators, 2001–02

Legend: □ Good □ Fair ▨ Poor ■ Missing

(Indicators, top to bottom)
Water quality index
Nitrogen (DIN)
Phosphorus (DIP)
Chlorophyll a
Water clarity
Dissolved oxygen
Sediment quality index
Sediment toxicity
Sediment contaminants
Total Organic Carbon (TOC)
Benthic index
Fish tissue Contaminants index

X-axis: 0 20 40 60 80 100
Percent coastal area

Notes: DIN = Dissolved Inorganic Nitrogen. DIP = Dissolved Inorganic Phosphorus.

SOURCE: "Figure 2-2. Percentage of Coastal Area Achieving Each Ranking for All Indices and Component Indicator—United States," in *National Coastal Condition Report III*, U.S. Environmental Protection Agency, Office of Water and Office of Research and Development, December 2008, http://www.epa.gov/owow/oceans/nccr3/pdf/nccr3_entire.pdf (accessed March 11, 2009)

rated as good in about three-fourths of the nation's coastal waters. Dissolved oxygen was rated good in over 80% of assessed coastal waters.

In like manner to the water quality index, Figure 6.9 shows the percent of the coastal waters rated good, fair, poor, or missing for the sediment quality index and its component indicators, which are sediment toxicity, sediment contaminants, and total organic carbon. Sediment is the material that has settled to the bottom of the water. Sediment toxicity rates to what extent substances in the sediment poison and kill organisms. Sediment contaminants are a measure of the concentration of pollutants present, and the total organic carbon (TOC) measures the organic material available on which bacteria can feed. Even though these nutrients also feed certain benthic organisms, these benthic species are often more pollution-tolerant. Thus, a high TOC level results in a

rating of poor, and a low TOC level in a rating of good. The sediment quality index shown in Figure 6.9 was rated good for most of the nation's coastal waters as were its component indicators.

Figure 6.10 is a summary of the overall and regional ratings for each of the five indices of ecological health of coastal waters and their component indicators. The water quality index was rated good to fair for regions throughout the nation. Areas of concern are the water clarity on the West Coast and levels of chlorophyll *a* in Puerto Rico, each with a rating of poor. The sediment quality index rating is not as good as the water quality index, with the Gulf Coast and Great Lakes regions rated poor overall. The West Coast, with poor sediment toxicity, barely rises above a poor rating for the sediment quality index. The Southeast Coast garnered the best ratings for the benthic, coastal habitat, and fish tissue contaminants indices.

BEACHES

Beach closings take place hundreds of times each year to protect the public from possible exposure to pathogens. The bacteria that cause the closings are generally harmless, but they are present in large numbers in human and animal sewage. Their presence indicates the possible presence of disease-causing organisms.

The most common problem caused by swimming in contaminated water is gastroenteritis, which is contracted by swallowing water while swimming and can result in diarrhea, nausea, vomiting, and cramps. Even though gastroenteritis is generally not harmful to healthy adults, it can cause serious illness in children, the elderly, people with autoimmune diseases, and people diagnosed with the human immunodeficiency virus (HIV) or the acquired immunodeficiency syndrome (AIDS).

The EPA established the Beaches Environmental Assessment and Coastal Health (BEACH) Program in 1997 to help reduce the risk of waterborne illness at the nation's beaches and recreational waters through improvements in water protection programs and risk communication. Three years later, the BEACH Act of 2000 was signed into law. This law was an amendment to the Clean Water Act and required:

1. The EPA to issue new or revised water quality criteria for pathogens and pathogen indicators.

2. Coastal states to adopt these new or revised water quality standards.

3. The EPA to award grants to states and local governments to develop and implement beach monitoring and assessment programs.

The BEACH Act also required the EPA to prepare a progress report for Congress every four years. The first report was *Implementing the BEACH Act of 2000: Report*

FIGURE 6.10

Detailed overall national and regional coastal condition, 2001–02

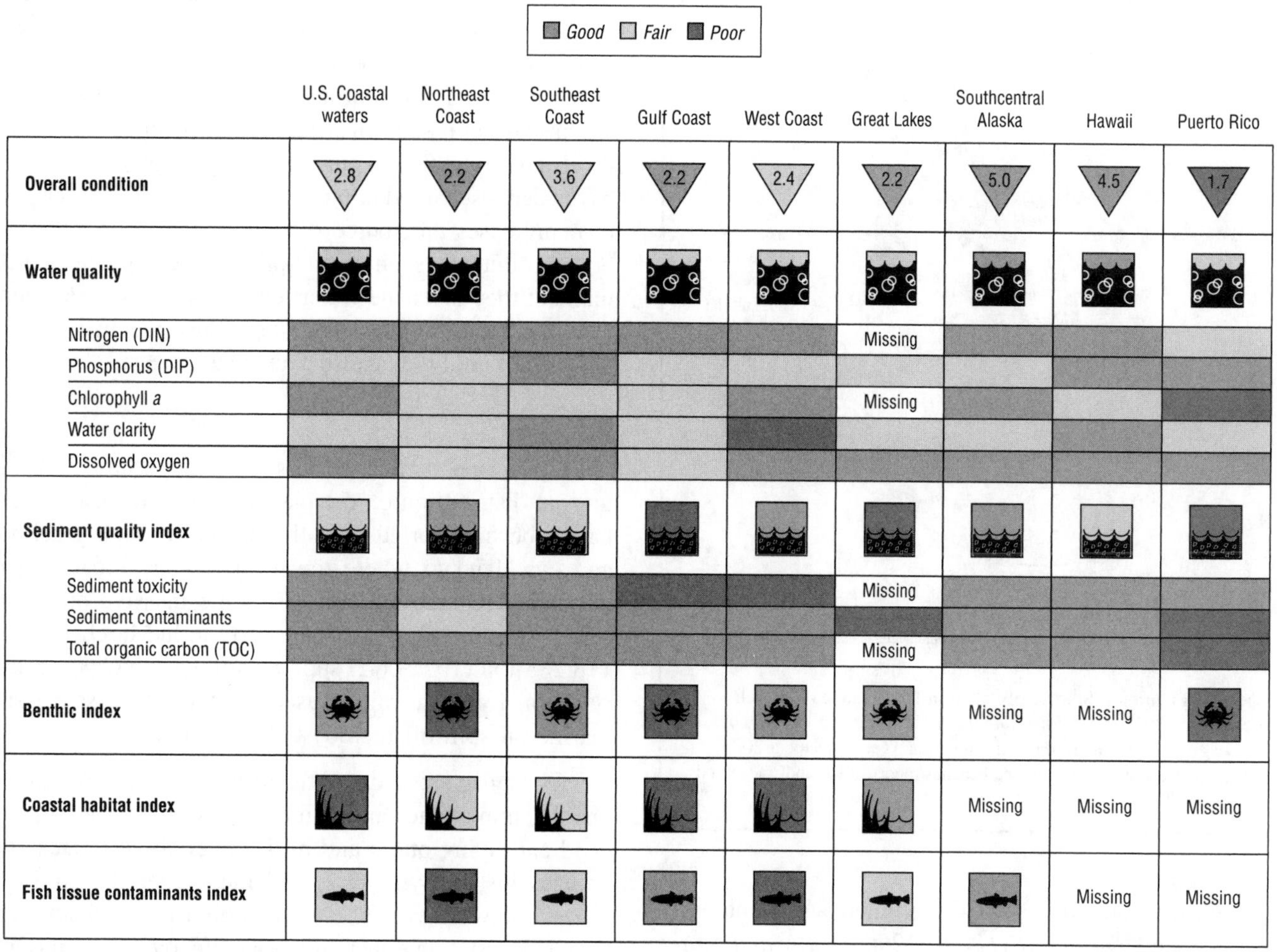

Legend: ☐ Good ☐ Fair ■ Poor

	U.S. Coastal waters	Northeast Coast	Southeast Coast	Gulf Coast	West Coast	Great Lakes	Southcentral Alaska	Hawaii	Puerto Rico
Overall condition	2.8	2.2	3.6	2.2	2.4	2.2	5.0	4.5	1.7
Water quality									
Nitrogen (DIN)						Missing			
Phosphorus (DIP)									
Chlorophyll *a*						Missing			
Water clarity									
Dissolved oxygen									
Sediment quality index									
Sediment toxicity						Missing			
Sediment contaminants									
Total organic carbon (TOC)						Missing			
Benthic index							Missing	Missing	
Coastal habitat index							Missing	Missing	Missing
Fish tissue contaminants index								Missing	Missing

Notes: DIN = Dissolved Inorganic Nitrogen. DIP = Dissolved Inorganic Phosphorus.

SOURCE: "Figure 2-4. Overall National and Regional Coastal Condition, 2001–2002," in *National Coastal Condition Report III*, U.S. Environmental Protection Agency, Office of Water and Office of Research and Development, December 2008, http://www.epa.gov/owow/oceans/nccr3/pdf/nccr3_entire.pdf (accessed March 11, 2009).

---

to Congress (October 2006. http://www.epa.gov/water science/beaches/report/full-rtc.pdf). The second report will be published in late 2010.

In *Implementing the BEACH Act of 2000*, the EPA determines that the major pollution sources responsible for beach closings and advisories in 2002 included runoff of storm water following rainfall (21%), sewage spills or overflows from various sources (13%), and unknown sources (43%). (See Figure 6.11.)

The *National Coastal Condition Report III* reports the percentages of beaches with advisories or closures by coastal state in 2003. Figure 6.12 shows the states that not only had coastal or Great Lakes beaches but also reported their advisories/closures. The percentages reflect the number of beaches with advisories/closures in a state out of all the beaches in that state that were monitored.

Of the reporting states, Pennsylvania was the only state with no beach advisories or closures in 2003. The Great Lakes states of Wisconsin, Ohio, Indiana, and Illinois and the Gulf state of Mississippi had the highest percentages of beaches with advisories/closures that year.

In *National Summary: 2007 Swimming Season Update* (May 2008, http://www.epa.gov/waterscience/beaches/sea sons/2007/pdf/2007fs.pdf), the EPA reports on the number of beaches surveyed for closings and advisories from 1997 to 2007. The number of beaches surveyed by the states grew voluntarily from 1,021 in 1997 to 3,647 in 2007. Beginning in 2003, however, coastal states were required to report beach information to the EPA. Thus, the number of surveyed beaches grew from 1,857 in 2003 to 3,574 in 2004. From 1997 through 2007, 21% to 32% of U.S. beaches were affected by advisories or closings.

FIGURE 6.11

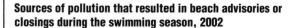

Sources of pollution that resulted in beach advisories or closings during the swimming season, 2002

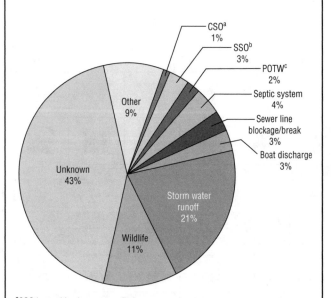

[a]CSO is combined sewer overflow.
[b]SSO is sanitary sewer overflows.
[c]POTW is publicly owned treatment works; a wastewater treatment facility that is owned by a state or municipality.

SOURCE: "Figure 3.1. Sources of Pollution That Resulted in Beach Actions in 2002," in *Implementing the BEACH Act of 2000: Report to Congress*, U.S. Environmental Protection Agency, October 2006 http://www.epa.gov/waterscience/beaches/report/full-rtc.pdf (accessed March 18, 2009)

In July 2007 the U.S. Government Accountability Office issued *The BEACH Act of 2000: EPA and States Have Made Progress Implementing the Act, but Further Actions Could Increase Public Health Protection* (http://www.gao.gov/new.items/d071073t.pdf). The GAO notes that even though water quality monitoring has increased since the implementation of the BEACH Act, some deficiencies in the system should be addressed to improve the protection of the public's health. For example, the sources of identified contamination were not known in many cases. The GAO implies that the low percentage of state officials who had taken action to deal with the contamination stemmed from the fact of not knowing the source. In addition, the GAO suggests that the frequency of monitoring beaches should be increased for some beaches and that increased funding for beach monitoring and notification would provide for a better implementation of the system.

As a result of the BEACH Act and the GAO report, the EPA has improved its Web site "BEACON—Beach Advisory and Closing On-line Notification" (http://iaspub.epa.gov/waters10/beacon_national_page.main), which provides data to the public on beach advisories and closings. Along with collecting more comprehensive data and strengthening

water quality standards, the EPA is also working to improve pollution control efforts at the nation's beaches.

OCEAN POLLUTANTS—SOURCES AND EFFECTS

Any number of human-made materials or excessive amounts of naturally occurring substances can adversely affect marine and estuarine waters and their inhabitants. Because water is such an effective solvent and dispersant, it is difficult to track and quantify many pollutants known to have been discharged into marine and estuarine waters, and in many cases the source of pollution may be unknown. Some pollutants, such as oil spills, are easily detected the moment they enter the water. Others, such as toxic chemicals, are less obvious, and their presence may remain undetected until they cause extensive damage.

Oil Spills

Oil is one of the world's most important fuels. Its uneven distribution on the planet, however, means that it has to be transported over the ocean, through pipelines, and over land to where the refineries are located. This inevitably results in accidents, some massive and some small, during drilling and transporting. In March 1967 the 118,285-ton (107,306-t) supertanker *Torrey Canyon*, carrying oil from Kuwait, caused the world's first massive marine oil spill off the coast of England.

Oil spills are a dramatic form of water pollution—visible, immediate, and sometimes severe. The sight of dead and dying otters and birds covered with black film arouses instant sympathy, and the bigger the spill, the more newsworthy it is. Even though it is true that oil can have a devastating effect on marine life, the size of the spill itself is often not the determining factor in the amount of damage it causes. Other factors include the amount and type of marine life in the area and weather conditions that can disperse the oil. Despite the drama that tanker spills create, worldwide pollution from them is a relatively minor source of marine pollution. Tanker spills represent a small fraction of the oil released to the environment worldwide when compared with industry sources, nontanker shipping releases, and oil seepage from natural sources.

According to the EPA, in "Emergency Management" (March 17, 2009, http://www.epa.gov/emergencies/content/learning/exxon.htm), when the supertanker *Exxon Valdez* ran into a reef in Prince William Sound, Alaska, in March 1989, more than 11 million gallons (41.6 million L) of oil spilled into one of the richest and most ecologically sensitive areas in North America. The *Exxon Valdez* Oil Spill Trustee Council (2009, http://www.evostc.state.ak.us/facts/qanda.cfm) equates the amount of oil spilled to 125 Olympic-sized swimming pools. The council also provides an estimate of wildlife killed from the spill: 250,000 seabirds, 2,800 sea otters, 300 harbor seals, 250 bald eagles, up to 22 orcas, and billions of salmon and herring eggs. Besides this devastating

FIGURE 6.12

Percentages of beaches with advisories/closures by coastal state, 2003

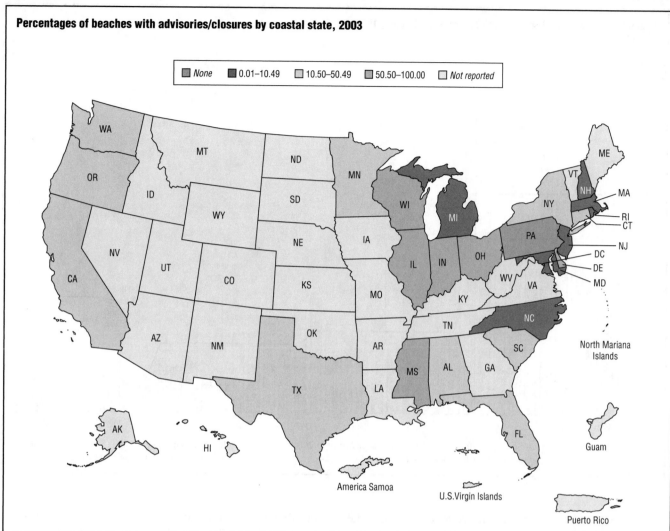

SOURCE: "Figure ES-5. Percentages of Beaches with Advisories/Closures by Coastal State in 2003," in *National Coastal Condition Report III*, U.S. Environmental Protection Agency, Office of Water and Office of Research and Development, December 2008, http://www.epa.gov/owow/oceans/nccr3/pdf/nccr3_entire.pdf (accessed March 11, 2009)

loss of wildlife, the oil is expected to take centuries to disappear completely. Nonetheless, this disaster spurred legislation that took steps to help avoid future oil spills.

OCEAN POLLUTION ACT OF 1990. In response to the *Exxon Valdez* disaster, Congress passed the Oil Pollution Act (OPA) of 1990. Most of the OPA provisions were targeted at reducing the number of spills and reducing the quantity of oil spilled. Among its provisions were the creation of a $1 billion cleanup-damage fund (the money comes from a tax on the petroleum industry), advance planning for controlling spills, stricter crew standards, and the requirement that new tankers have double hulls. When the exterior hull of a double-hulled tanker is punctured, the interior hull holding the oil may still remain intact. (The *Exxon Valdez* was not double-hulled.) The law required older tankers to be fitted with double hulls by 2010. The OPA also:

- Compelled the use of escort tugboats in certain harbors to assist tankers.

- Required standards for tank levels and pressure-monitoring devices to detect leaks in cargo tanks.

- Required the U.S. Coast Guard to establish minimum standards for overfill devices to prevent overfill oil spills. (An overfill oil spill is the result of too much oil being pumped into a tanker during a transfer from a facility to a tanker or between two tankers. On occasion, overfill spills can involve large quantities of oil.)

DECLINES IN OIL SPILLS. In "Guarding against Another Exxon Valdez" (*Anchorage Daily News*, March 23, 2009), which recognizes the 20th anniversary of the *Exxon Valdez* disaster, Wesley Loy summarizes progress that has been made to avoid such catastrophes in the future. In 2009, 14 out of 15 tankers that regularly loaded at Port Valdez had double hulls; the *Exxon Valdez* and most oil tankers of its day had a single hull. Two tugboats escort tankers into and out of Port Valdez through Valdez Narrows, whereas decades earlier one tugboat did the job;

FIGURE 6.13

Number of worldwide oil spills over 700 tonnes (772 tons), 1970–2008

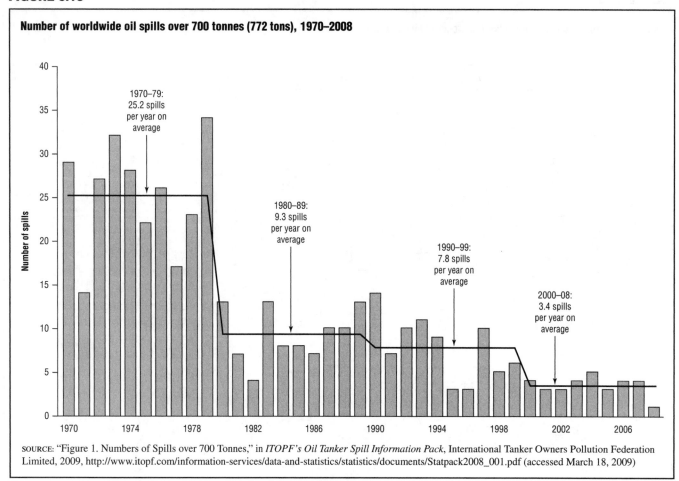

SOURCE: "Figure 1. Numbers of Spills over 700 Tonnes," in *ITOPF's Oil Tanker Spill Information Pack*, International Tanker Owners Pollution Federation Limited, 2009, http://www.itopf.com/information-services/data-and-statistics/statistics/documents/Statpack2008_001.pdf (accessed March 18, 2009)

the *Exxon Valdez* had been left alone to navigate the waters near Bligh Reef, where it ran aground. Prince William Sound is well equipped to respond to a spill disaster instantly; it was ill equipped 20 years prior.

Declines in oil spills are being seen on a global scale. The International Tanker Owners Pollution Federation reports that between 1970 and 1979 the average incident rate for large spills (over 700 metric tons [772 tons]) from the worldwide tanker industry was 25.2 spills per year. (See Figure 6.13.) Between 1980 and 1989 the average rate dropped to 9.3 spills per year. From 1990 to 1999 the global spill rate declined further to 7.8 spills per year and from 2000 through 2008 to 3.4 spills per year. Larger spills, such as these, are most often caused by collisions and groundings. Smaller spills most often occur because of routine operations, such as loading in ports or at oil terminals.

Oil tanker spills are highly visible cases of pollution entering the ocean, but the U.S. Department of the Interior's Minerals Management Service reports in *OCS Oil Spill Facts* (September 2002, http://www.mms.gov/stats/PDFs/2002OilSpillFacts.pdf) that the largest input of oil into marine environments is natural seepage (naturally occurring oil in the ground that moves through the soil and into the water). In North America natural seepage

contributes 63% of the total marine oil input. Twenty-two percent of the oil found in the marine waters off the coast of North America is due to municipal and industrial waste and runoff. Marine transportation is responsible for only 3%, although worldwide it is responsible for 33%. As of mid-2009, these were the most updated statistics on this phenomenon from the Department of the Interior.

Marine Debris

NOAA (August 8, 2007, http://marinedebris.noaa.gov/whatis/welcome.html) defines marine debris as "any man-made object discarded, disposed of, or abandoned that enters the coastal or marine environment. It may enter directly from a ship, or indirectly when washed out to sea via rivers, streams and storm drains." The effects of marine debris can be both costly to coastal communities and dangerous to humans and aquatic life.

The problem of marine debris is significant. To illustrate, the article "7M Pounds of Debris Picked from World's Waterways" (*Gloucester Daily Times* [Massachusetts], April 14, 2009) states that in just one day volunteers picked up nearly 7 million pounds (3.2 million kg) of marine debris from 17,000 miles (27,359 km) of coastline, river bottoms, and ocean floors during the Ocean Conservancy's 23rd International Coastal Cleanup. Certain types of marine debris, such as broken glass and medical waste, can pose a serious threat to public health, causing beach closures and swimming advisories and robbing coastal communities of significant tourism dollars.

In December 2006 the Marine Debris Research, Prevention, and Reduction Act became law. The purpose of the act was to create a Marine Debris Research, Prevention, and Reduction Program within NOAA and the Coast Guard to help identify, determine sources of, and reduce or prevent marine debris and its adverse impacts on the marine environment and navigation safety. According to NOAA, in "Marine Debris Projects" (February 20, 2009, http://marinedebris.noaa.gov/projects/welcome.html), the agency was working nationwide on several large-scale projects in 2009.

CRUISE SHIP WASTE. In "Cruise Ship Discharges" (March 18, 2009, http://www.epa.gov/owow/oceans/cruise_ships/), the EPA reports that there are more than 230 cruise ships operating worldwide. Feeding and housing thousands of people on each of these vessels means that a great deal of waste is generated while at sea. The EPA notes that "some of the waste streams generated by cruise ships include bilge water (water that collects in the lowest part of the ship's hull and may contain oil, grease, and other contaminants), sewage, graywater (wastewater from showers, sinks, laundries, and kitchens), ballast water (water taken onboard or discharged from a vessel to maintain its stability), and solid waste (food waste and garbage)."

During the 1990s many high-profile incidents occurred in which cruise ships illegally polluted marine waters. Laurie Asseo reports in "Cruise Line Fined Millions for Dumping" (Associated Press, July 22, 1999) that in 1999 Royal Caribbean, one of the world's largest cruise lines, pled guilty in federal court to dumping oil and hazardous chemicals in U.S. waters and lying about it to the Coast Guard. It agreed to pay a record $18 million fine for polluting waters. This was besides the $9 million in criminal fines the company agreed to pay in a previous plea agreement. Asseo notes that six other cruise lines had pled guilty to illegal waste dumping between 1993 and 1999 and had paid fines of up to $1 million.

One difficulty of regulating the cruise line industry is that most major ships sailing out of U.S. ports are registered in foreign countries. Nonetheless, international agreements exist relevant to cruise ship pollution. One of the major international agreements is the International Convention for the Prevention of Pollution from Ships, or MARPOL (which stands for *Marine Pollution*). All ships bearing flags of countries that have signed onto MARPOL are bound by the agreement wherever they sail. The Act to Prevent Pollution from Ships (APPS) is the U.S. law that implements the MARPOL agreement in the United States. Infractions of MARPOL and APPS were

the grounds on which cruise ships were fined during the 1990s.

In March 2000 the Bluewater Network, an environmental advocacy group made up of 53 environmental organizations, petitioned the EPA to assess and take measures to reduce the pollution created by cruise ships. The EPA responded by investigating the problem and publishing its findings in *Cruise Ship Discharge Assessment Report* (December 29, 2008, http://www.epa.gov/owow/oceans/cruise_ships/pdf/0812cruiseshipdischarge assess.pdf). The EPA identifies a wide range of options to address cruise ship waste, including establishing a nationwide monitoring program, conducting a review of the cruise industry, researching promising cruise ship waste treatment technologies, enforcing existing laws more consistently, hiring marine engineers to observe ship waste treatment practices while under way, and establishing an interagency Cruise Ship Pollution Prevention and Enforcement Program.

PLASTICS. Plastics such as bags, containers, bottles, and bottle caps are dumped daily from oceangoing vessels, commercial and recreational fishing boats, offshore oil and gas platforms, and military ships. Other types of plastic debris—factory wastes, sewer overflows, illegal garbage dumping, and human littering—come from land sources. Thousands of seabirds and marine animals die each year as a result of ingesting or becoming entangled in this plastic.

Another concern is commercial fishing nets. Once made of natural materials, these nets are now made mainly of durable, nondegradable plastic. When they are lost or discarded in the ocean, they pose a floating hazard to seals, dolphins, whales, and diving birds, which can become entangled in the nets. In 1988, 31 nations ratified an agreement making it illegal for their ships to dump plastic debris, including fishing nets, into the ocean. As part of that agreement, the United States enacted the Marine Plastics Pollution Research and Control Act, which went into effect in 1989. Among other regulations, the act imposes a $25,000 fine for each violation.

Plastic pellets are the raw materials that are melted and molded to create plastic products. According to Paul Watson, in "The Plastic Sea" (July 24, 2006, http://www.seashepherd.org/editorials/editorial_060724_1.html), 60 billion pounds (27.2 billion kg) of resin pellets are manufactured in the United States annually. The two primary ways that these pellets enter the ocean are direct spills during cargo handling operations at ports or spills at sea, and storm water discharges that carry the pellets from industrial sites. Plastic pellets may persist in the water environment for years, depending on the resin type, the amount and types of pellet additives, and how the pellets react to sunlight, wave action, and weathering. Even though pellets have been found in the stomachs of wildlife, primarily seabirds and sea turtles, their effects have not been clearly demonstrated to be harmful.

Since 1991 the Society of Plastics Industries (SPI), the major national trade association for manufacturers who make plastic products in the United States, has been working with the EPA to identify and minimize the sources of plastic pellet entry into the ocean. In July 1991 the SPI instituted Operation Clean Sweep (http://www.opclean sweep.org/), an industry-wide education campaign to encourage members to adopt the SPI 1991 Pellet Retention Environmental Code and the 1992 Processor's Pledge aimed at committing the U.S. plastics industry to total pellet containment. The group publishes *Operation Clean Sweep Pellet Handling Manual* (2009, http://www.opclean sweep.org/manual/OCSmanual.pdf).

GHOST FISHING. Another important problem is ghost fishing. This is the entrapment of fish and marine mammals by lost or abandoned nets, pots, fishing line, bottles, and other discarded objects. When marine creatures are entangled in old six-pack beverage binders or caught in abandoned fishing nets, they suffer and may die. In 2008 initiatives in both California and Massachusetts targeted, among other items, the cleanup of abandoned fishing nets, lobster traps, and plastic fishing line to help reduce the problem of ghost fishing off their coastlines.

Ocean Dumping

In 1972 Congress enacted the Marine Protection, Research, and Sanctuaries Act (also known as the Ocean Dumping Act) to prohibit the ocean dumping of material that would unreasonably degrade or endanger human health or the marine environment. The act applies to waters within 200 miles (322 km) of the U.S. coast and was amended in 1988 to prohibit dumping industrial waste and sewage sludge into the ocean. As a result, the only ocean dumping allowed (with permit) as of 2009 was dredged material from the bottom of water bodies to maintain navigation channels and berthing areas, human remains, fish wastes, and vessels.

ALGAL BLOOMS

Algae are plantlike organisms that manufacture their own food via photosynthesis. Most algal species in U.S. coastal waters are not harmful and serve as the energy producers at the base of the food chain. However, sometimes algae may grow fast and bloom, creating dense, visible patches near the water surface. Red tide is a common name for events in which certain algae containing reddish pigments bloom so that the water appears to be red. Often, these particular species are toxic to humans and wildlife, but not all species of algae are toxic, nor do all species impart color to the water during blooms.

Eutrophication and Hypoxia

Algal blooms often occur because an abundance of plant nutrients, such as nitrates and phosphates, have entered the water. Thick layers of algae block the sunlight from reaching the algae and other plant life below, so those organisms die. (See Figure 6.14.) When the nutrients run out, much of the rest of the algae die. Bacteria and other decomposers feed on the dead algae, using oxygen in the water as they break down the tissues. This process, in which an overenrichment of a water body with nutrients results in an excessive growth of organisms and a resultant depletion of oxygen concentration, is called eutrophication. The deficiency of oxygen in the water is called hypoxia, and it is a condition that can have severe effects on local ecosystems.

FIGURE 6.14

Eutrophication and hypoxia in a body of water

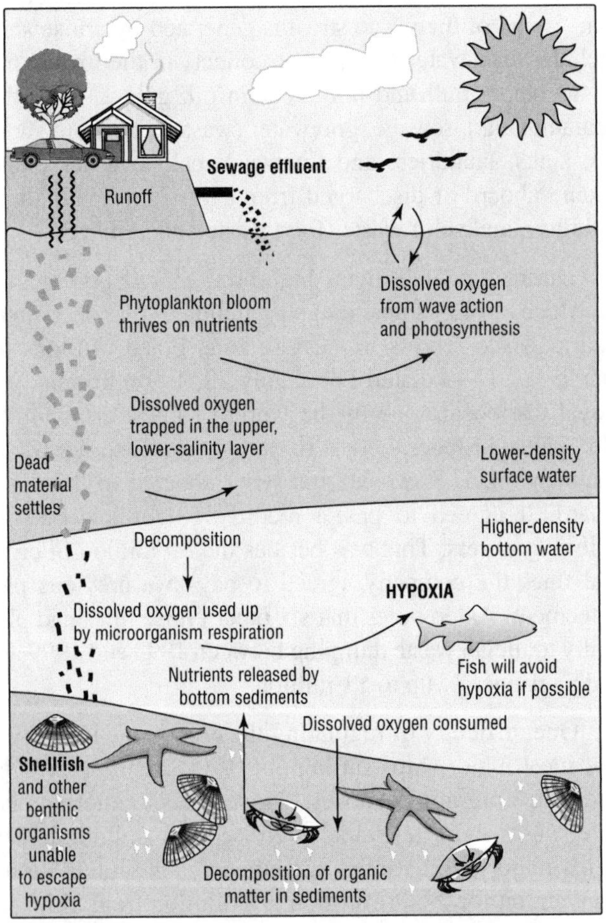

SOURCE: "Figure 1-3. Eutrophication Can Occur When the Concentration of Available Nutrients Increases above Normal Levels," in *National Coastal Condition Report III*, U.S. Environmental Protection Agency, Office of Water and Office of Research and Development, December 2008, http://www.epa.gov/owow/oceans/nccr3/pdf/nccr3_entire.pdf (accessed March 11, 2009)

Hypoxia kills most of the sessile (permanently attached) bottom-dwelling benthic organisms in a body of water, such as oysters and clams; aquatic animals that swim or crawl, such as fish, shrimp, and crabs, either leave the area or die. (See Figure 6.14.) For this reason, areas where hypoxic conditions exist are frequently referred to as dead zones. Hypoxia is a worldwide problem that often occurs where rivers carrying large amounts of agricultural runoff empty into lakes, estuaries, and the ocean.

In 1998 Congress passed the Harmful Algal Bloom and Hypoxia Research Act. The act requires the formation of a federal multiagency task force to investigate the problem and report back to Congress with a plan and recommendations to address harmful algal blooms and hypoxia. The Harmful Algal Bloom and Hypoxia Amendments Act of 2004 reauthorized the 1998 act. NOAA reports in the fact sheet "Harmful Algal Bloom and Hypoxia Research and Control Act" (March 2006, http://www.cop.noaa.gov/stressors/extremeevents/hab/habhrca/HABHRCA_fact_03-06.pdf) that the funding from this act allowed scientific research and assessment on this problem to proceed. The Center for Sponsored Coastal Ocean Research (http://www.cop.noaa.gov/stressors/extremeevents/hab/current/reports.html) publishes a variety of reports on the results of this research and assessment. The Harmful Algal Bloom and Hypoxia Amendments Act of 2008 was introduced in the U.S. Senate in June 2008, but no action was taken. As of mid-2009, the act had not been reauthorized.

EUTROPHICATION AND HYPOXIA IN THE GULF OF MEXICO. One location in the United States where hypoxia occurs is the Gulf of Mexico, off the Louisiana coast. According to the USGS, in the fact sheet "Restoring Life to the Dead Zone: Addressing Gulf Hypoxia, a National Problem" (August 12, 2008, http://www.nwrc.usgs.gov/factshts/016-00/016-00.htm), the Gulf's hypoxic zone is comparable to the largest hypoxic areas in the world, such as those in the Black and Baltic seas. The Gulf of Mexico hypoxic zone is approximately 6,000 to 7,000 square miles (15,540 to 18,130 square km) of water where the oxygen level is below 2 ppm. Under normal conditions, dissolved oxygen levels are 5 to 6 ppm.

The zone is caused by harmful algal blooms that are believed to be the result of the discharge of nutrients from the Mississippi River watershed into the Gulf of Mexico. The nutrients (nitrogen and phosphorus) come from fertilizers, animal waste, and domestic sewage. The nitrate-nitrogen level in the main stem of the Mississippi River, which drains 31 states, has doubled since the 1950s. Figure 6.15 shows the Mississippi Basin watershed and the states whose rivers drain into it.

To correct the situation and as a requirement of the Harmful Algal Bloom and Hypoxia Research Act, the EPA, six other federal agencies, nine states, and two Native American tribes developed in January 2001 an action plan to reduce nutrient loads reaching the Gulf: the Action Plan for Reducing, Mitigating, and Controlling Hypoxia in the Northern Gulf of Mexico. In 2008 the EPA released *Gulf Hypoxia Action Plan 2008* (http://www.epa.gov/msbasin/pdf/ghap2008_update082608.pdf), a report on the progress of this action plan and an updated action plan.

The 2001 action plan has a goal of reducing the size of the hypoxic zone to 1,900 square miles (4,920 square km), a decrease of over 68%, no later than 2015. The 2008 report notes that the zone varies in size each year, depending on conditions. The five-year average from 2003 to 2007 was 5,600 square miles (14,505 square km). Thus, the zone was still much larger than the goal size.

The 2001 plan also calls for the implementation of nutrient management strategies to achieve a 30% reduction in the amount of nutrients reaching the Gulf of Mexico. Reducing nutrients in the water, particularly nitrogen and phosphorus, will help reverse the hypoxia. This is accomplished primarily by implementing farming practices that reduce fertilizer runoff and restoring wetland areas and riverbanks.

The 2008 report notes, "Overall, total annual loads to the Gulf from 2001–2005 show a 21% decline in nitrogen load and a 12% increase in phosphorus load when compared to the average from the 1980–1996 period." It also states that "during the spring period (April, May, and June) most of the reduction in total nitrogen load was from nitrogen forms other than nitrate, an important form fueling the primary production that leads to hypoxia development in the spring." Nonetheless, the report is still positive, noting that of the 11 actions planned in 2001, several have made significant progress. These actions include establishing subbasin committees; issuing monitoring, modeling, and research strategies; and conducting additional monitoring of the hypoxic zone.

EXOTIC/INVASIVE SPECIES

Exotic species are plants, animals, and microbes that have been carried from one geographic region to another, either intentionally or unintentionally. Unintentional introduction includes transport in ballast water of ships or as pests on imported fruits, vegetables, and animals or animal products. Before modern times, movement from one geographical region to another was infrequent and slow, allowing time for the ecology to absorb and counterbalance the newcomers.

However, because of rapid transport, organisms can now move across continents in a matter of hours or days. Once removed from their natural ecological system—where eons of evolution have established predator-prey relationships, competitive species, and other devices that maintain balance—exotic species may reproduce unchecked in their

FIGURE 6.15

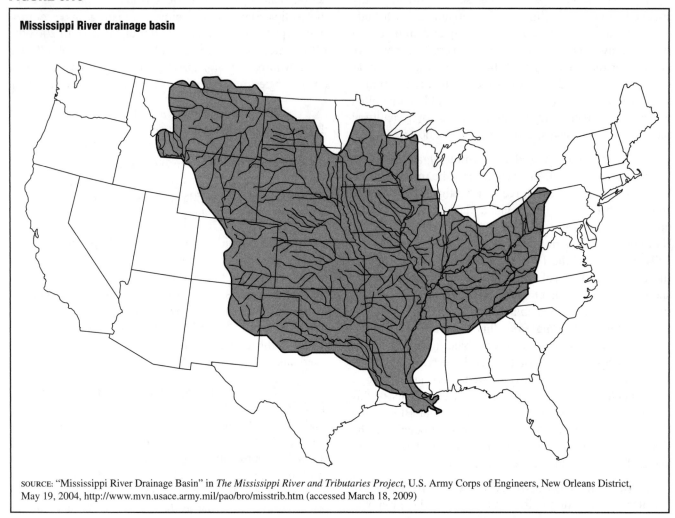

Mississippi River drainage basin

SOURCE: "Mississippi River Drainage Basin" in *The Mississippi River and Tributaries Project*, U.S. Army Corps of Engineers, New Orleans District, May 19, 2004, http://www.mvn.usace.army.mil/pao/bro/misstrib.htm (accessed March 18, 2009)

new locations because they have no natural competitors or predators.

Both estuarine and ocean habitats have suffered from exotic species introduction. In the Chesapeake Bay, MSX (*Haplosporidium nelsoni*) and Dermo (*Perkinsus marinus*), two organisms that ravage oyster populations, came to the Bay with oysters introduced from other regions. In the Northern Mariana Islands the coral reefs are being decimated by the introduction of the crown-of-thorns starfish. From the Baltic Sea to the shores of New England the green crab is believed to be eating young scallops and other valuable seafood.

Passage of the Nonindigenous Aquatic Nuisance Prevention and Control Act of 1990 was a first step in attempting to prevent species migration. This legislation authorized the Fish and Wildlife Service and NOAA to adopt regulations to prevent the unintentional introduction of aquatic nuisance species. In 1999 the Invasive

Species Council was created by presidential executive order to oversee efforts to control unwanted exotic species. The council is chaired jointly by the secretaries of interior, agriculture, and commerce. Council members include the secretaries of state, treasury, and transportation, and the administrator of the EPA.

The problem of invasive species is complex. In "The Unintended Consequences of Changing Nature's Balance" (*New York Times*, February 16, 2009), Elizabeth Svoboda explains that the introduced species become intricately linked with other species within an ecosystem, and sometimes eradicating the invaders upsets the ecological balance in unforeseen ways. A variety of laws have been enacted and legislation has been introduced to help research this problem and find ways to abate and control it. The Northeast Midwest Institute, a nonprofit research organization, maintains the Web site "Biological Pollution" (http://www.nemw.org/biopollute.htm), which provides a listing of proposed and enacted legislation.

CHAPTER 7
WETLANDS

WHAT ARE WETLANDS?

Wetlands are transition zones between land and aquatic systems where the water table is usually near or at the surface, or the land is covered by shallow water. Wetlands range in size from less than 1 acre (0.4 ha) to thousands of acres and can take many forms, some of which are immediately recognizable as "wet." Other wetlands appear more like dry land and are wet during only certain seasons of the year, or at several year intervals.

Some of the more commonly recognized types of wetlands are marshes, bogs, and swamps. Marshes are low-lying wetlands with grassy vegetation. Bogs are wetlands that accumulate wet, spongy, acidic, dead plant material called peat. Shrubs, mosses, and stunted trees may also grow in bogs. Swamps are low-lying wetlands that are seasonally flooded; they have more woody plants than marshes and better drainage than bogs.

According to Thomas E. Dahl of the U.S. Fish and Wildlife Service (USFWS), in *Status and Trends of Wetlands in the Conterminous United States 1998 to 2004* (2006, http://www.fws.gov/wetlands/_documents/gSandT/ NationalReports/StatusTrendsWetlandsConterminousUS 1998to2004.pdf), there were an estimated 107.7 million acres (43.6 million ha) of wetlands in the 48 conterminous states in 2004. These 107.7 million acres of wetlands constituted about 5.5% of the total land area of the conterminous states, whereas deepwater (rivers and lakes) constituted 1% and upland (dry land) constituted most of the total land area at 93.5%. (See Figure 7.1.) Of the wetland areas, 95% were freshwater and 5% were estuarine (coastal saltwater). (See Figure 7.2.) Dahl does not include data on Alaska and Hawaii, but the U.S. Environmental Protection Agency (EPA) notes in "Status and Trends" (January 12, 2009, http://www.epa.gov/OWOW/wetlands/vital/status .html) that in the 1980s an estimated 170 million to 200 million acres (69 million to 81 million ha) of wet-lands existed in Alaska—covering slightly more than half of the state—and Hawaii had 52,000 acres (21,000 ha).

Hydrology and Wetland Formation

Wetlands are distributed unevenly, but occur in nearly every state and U.S. territory. (See Table 7.1.) They are found wherever climate and landscape cause groundwater to discharge to the land surface or prevent rapid drainage from the land surface so that soils are saturated for some time.

In wetlands, when the soil is flooded or saturated, the oxygen used by the microbes and other decomposers in the water is slowly replaced by oxygen in the air, because oxygen moves through water about 10,000 times slower than through air. Thus, all wetlands have one common trait: hydric (oxygen-poor) soils. As a result, plants that live in wetlands have genetic adaptations in which they are able to survive temporarily without oxygen in their roots, or they are able to transfer oxygen from the leaves or stem to the roots. This anaerobic (without oxygen) condition causes wetland soils to have the sulfurous odor of rotten eggs.

Local hydrology (the pattern of water flow through an area) is the primary determinant of wetlands. Wetlands can receive groundwater in-flow, recharge groundwater, or experience both inflow and outflow at different locations. Figure 7.3 illustrates water movement in several different wetland situations. Part A in Figure 7.3 shows how wetlands do not always occupy low points and depressions in the landscape. They can occur in flat areas that have complex underground water flow.

Part B in Figure 7.3 shows a fen, which is a type of wetland that accumulates peat deposits like bogs do. Fens, however, are less acidic than bogs and receive most of their water from groundwater rich in calcium and magnesium. As part B shows, fens occur on slopes at groundwater seepage faces and are subject to a continuous supply of the chemicals that are dissolved in the groundwater.

FIGURE 7.1

FIGURE 7.2

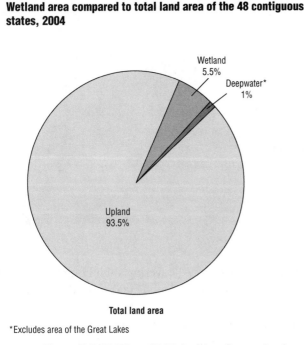

Wetland area compared to total land area of the 48 contiguous states, 2004

Total land area

*Excludes area of the Great Lakes

SOURCE: Thomas E. Dahl, "Figure 22. Wetland Area Compared to the Total Land Area of the Conterminous United States, 2004," in *Status and Trends of Wetlands in the Conterminous United States 1998 to 2004*, U.S. Department of the Interior, Fish and Wildlife Service, 2006, http://www.fws.gov/wetlands/_documents/gSandT/NationalReports/StatusTrendsWetlandsConterminousUS1998to2004.pdf (accessed March 9, 2009)

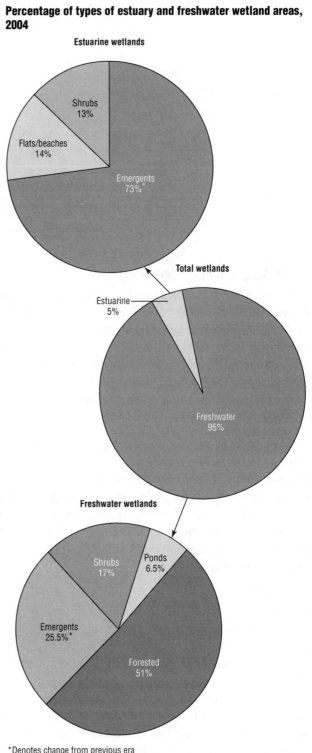

Percentage of types of estuary and freshwater wetland areas, 2004

Estuarine wetlands

Total wetlands

Freshwater wetlands

*Denotes change from previous era

SOURCE: Thomas E. Dahl, "Figure 24. Percentage of Estimated Estuarine and Freshwater Wetland Area and Covertypes, 2004," in *Status and Trends of Wetlands in the Conterminous United States 1998 to 2004*, U.S. Department of the Interior, Fish and Wildlife Service, 2006, http://www.fws.gov/wetlands/_documents/gSandT/NationalReports/StatusTrendsWetlandsConterminousUS1998to2004.pdf (accessed March 19, 2009)

Land along the sides of streams or rivers receives a continuous water supply and is ideal for wetland growth. It may also receive some groundwater discharge, as shown in part C in Figure 7.3. Bogs, shown in part D, are wetlands normally found on uplands or extensive flatlands. Most of their water and chemistry comes from precipitation.

Riverine (areas along streams, rivers, and irrigation canals) and coastal area wetlands are subject to periodic water level changes. Coastal area wetlands, for example, are affected by predictable tidal cycles. Other coastal and riverine wetlands are highly dependent on flooding and seasonal water level changes. Some examples are the floodplains of the Illinois and Missouri rivers.

TYPES OF WETLANDS

A wide variety of wetlands exist across the United States because of regional and local differences in hydrology, water chemistry, vegetation, soils, topography, and other factors. There are two large groups of wetlands: estuarine (coastal) and freshwater (inland). (See Figure 7.2.) Estuarine wetlands are linked to estuaries and oceans, and are places where fresh- and saltwater mix, such as a bay or where a river enters the ocean. The environment in estuaries is one of ever-changing salinity

TABLE 7.1

Location of various wetland types

Wetland type	Primary regions	States
Inland freshwater marsh	Dakota-Minnesota drift and lake bed; Upper Midwest; and Gulf Coastal Flats	North Dakota, South Dakota, Nebraska, Minnesota, Florida
Inland saline marshes	Intermontane; Pacific Mountains	Oregon, Nevada, Utah, California
Bogs	Upper Midwest; Gulf-Atlantic Rolling Plain; Gulf Coastal Flat; Atlantic Coastal Flats	Wisconsin, Minnesota, Michigan, Maine, Florida, North Carolina
Tundra	Central Highland and Basin; Arctic Lowland; and Pacific Mountains	Alaska
Shrub swamps	Upper Midwest; Gulf Coastal Flats	Minnesota, Wisconsin, Michigan, Florida, Georgia, South Carolina, North Carolina, Louisiana
Wooded swamps	Upper Midwest; Gulf Coastal Flats; Atlantic Coastal Flats; and Lower Mississippi Alluvial Plain	Minnesota, Wisconsin, Michigan, Florida, Georgia, South Georgia, South Carolina, North Carolina, Louisiana
Bottom land hardwood	Lower Mississippi Alluvial Plain; Atlantic Coastal Flats; Gulf-Atlantic Rolling Plain; and Gulf Coastal Flats	Louisiana, Mississippi, Arkansas, Missouri, Tennessee, Alabama, Florida, Georgia, South Carolina, North Carolina, Texas
Coastal salt marshes	Atlantic Coastal Zone; Gulf Coastal Zone; Eastern Highlands; Pacific Moutains	All Coastal states, but particularly the Mid- and South Atlantic and Gulf Coast states
Mangrove swamps	Gulf Coastal Zone	Florida and Louisiana
Tidal freshwater wetlands	Atlantic Coastal Zone and Flats; Gulf Coastal Zone and Flats	Louisiana, Texas, North Carolina, Virginia, Maryland, Delaware, New Jersey, Georgia, South Carolina

SOURCE: "Table 3. Locations of Various Wetland Types in the United States," in *Wetlands: Their Use and Regulation*, U.S. Congress, Office of Technology Assessment, March 1984, http://govinfo.library.unt.edu/ota/Ota_4/DATA/1984/8433.PDF (accessed March 19, 2009)

FIGURE 7.3

Examples of water sources for wetlands

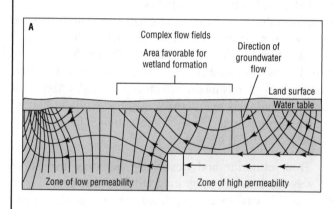
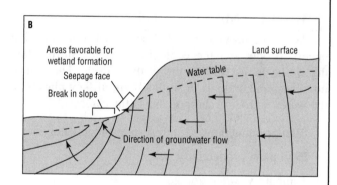
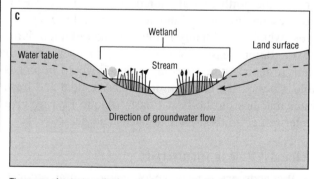
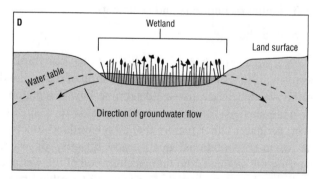

The source of water to wetlands can be from groundwater discharge where the land surface is underlain by complex groundwater flow fields (A), from groundwater discharge at seepage faces and at breaks in slope of the water table (B), from streams (C), and from precipitation in cases where wetlands have no stream inflow and groundwater gradients slope away from the wetland (D).

SOURCE: Thomas C. Winter et al., "Figure 17," in *Ground Water and Surface Water: A Single Resource*, U.S. Department of the Interior, U.S. Geological Survey, 1998, http://pubs.usgs.gov/circ/circ1139/pdf/circ1139.pdf (accessed March 19, 2009)

and temperature. The water level fluctuates in response to wind and tide. Examples of estuarine wetlands are salt-water marshes and mangrove swamps.

Freshwater wetlands are commonly located on the floodplains of rivers and streams, the margins of lakes and ponds, and isolated depressions surrounded by dry land. Some examples of inland wetlands are the Florida Everglades, wet meadows, swamps, fens, bogs, prairie potholes, playa lakes, and wet tundra.

Wetlands are further divided by their vegetation. Emergent wetlands (marshes and wet meadows) are dominated by grasses, sedges, and other herbaceous (nonwoody) plants. Emergent wetlands account for 73% of estuarine wetlands, even though they represent only 25.5% of freshwater wetlands. (See Figure 7.2.) Shrub wetlands (including shrub swamps and bogs), which are characterized by low-to-medium-height woody plants, make up 13% of estuarine wetlands and account for 17% of freshwater wetlands. Forested wetlands, mostly wooded swamps and bottomland hardwood forests, are dominated by trees and account for 51% of freshwater wetlands. (Bottomland hardwood forests are generally found along the edges of lakes and rivers and in sinkholes.)

HOW WETLANDS FUNCTION

Wetlands provide essential ecological functions that benefit people and the ecological systems surrounding the wetlands, as well as the wetland itself. The plants, microbes, and animals in wetlands are all key players in the water, nitrogen, carbon, and sulfur cycles.

Wetland functions fit into several broad categories:

- High plant productivity
- Temporary water storage
- Trapping of nutrients and sediments
- Soil anchoring

Not all wetlands perform all functions, nor do they perform all functions equally. The location of the wetland in the watershed and its size determine how it functions. (A watershed is the land area that drains to a stream, river, or lake.) Other factors that affect wetland function are weather conditions, quality and quantity of water entering the wetland, and human alteration of the wetland or the land surrounding it. The values of wetland functions to human communities depend on the complex relationships between the wetland and the other ecosystems in the watershed. An ecosystem consists of all the organisms in a particular area or region and the environment in which they live. The elements of an ecosystem all interact with each other in some way and depend on each other either directly or indirectly.

Wetlands—Nursery, Pantry, and Way Station

Wetlands are diverse and rich ecosystems that provide food and shelter to many different plants and animals. The combination of shallow water, high nutrient levels, and primary productivity (plant growth and reproduction) is perfect for the development of organisms that form the base of the food chain. The water, dense plants, their root mats, and decaying vegetation are food and shelter for the eggs, larvae, and juveniles of many species. Smaller animals avoid predators by hiding among the vegetation while they wait to prey on still smaller organisms. Fish of all sizes seek the warmer, shallow waters to mate and spawn, leaving their young to grow on the rich diet provided by the wetlands. Food and organic material that is flushed out of wetlands and into streams and rivers during periods of high water flow feed downstream aquatic systems, including commercial and sport fisheries.

Estuarine marshes, for example, are among the most productive natural ecosystems in the world. They produce huge amounts of plant leaves and stems that make up the base of the food chain. When the plants die, decomposers such as bacteria in the water break them down to detritus (small particles of organic material). Algae that grow on plants and detritus are the principal foods for shellfish such as oysters and clams, crustaceans such as crabs and shrimp, and small fish. Small fish are the food for larger commercial species such as striped bass and bluefish. The EPA states in *Wetlands Functions and Values* (September 12, 2008, http://www.epa.gov/watertrain/wetlands/module08.htm) that "the fish and shellfish that depend on wetlands for food or habitat constitute more than 75% of the commercial and 90% of the recreational harvest."

Both estuarine and freshwater wetlands also serve as way stations for migrating birds. For example, the Central Flyway extending from south-central Canada through the north-central United States and into Mexico provides resting places and nourishment for migratory birds (which individually number in the millions) during the migration season. Without this stopover area, the flight to their Arctic breeding grounds would be impossible. Chesapeake Bay with its extensive tidal and freshwater marshes on the East Coast Atlantic Flyway gives winter refuge to thousands of ducks and geese.

Wetlands' Role in Biodiversity

Wetlands are the source of many natural products, including furs, fish and shellfish, timber, wildlife, and wild rice. A wide variety of species of microbes, plants, insects, amphibians, reptiles, fish, birds, and other animals make their homes in or around wetlands because of the availability of water. For others, wetlands provide important temporary seasonal habitats. Physical and chemical features such as landscape shape (topology), climate, and abundance of water help determine which species live in which wetland.

In "Wetlands and People" (January 12, 2009, http://www.epa.gov/owow/wetlands/vital/people.html), the EPA notes that "more than one-third of the United States' threatened and endangered species live only in wetlands." When wetlands are removed from a watershed or are damaged by human activity, the biological health of the watershed declines. Wetland health has a commercial impact as well. Dahl indicates that 75% of the fish and shellfish commercially harvested in the United States and up to 90% of the recreational fish rely directly or indirectly on wetlands for their survival. Dahl also notes that in 2004, 72% of freshwater mussels were imperiled and 39% of native freshwater fish species were at risk of extinction.

Waterfowl are birds such as ducks and geese that spend much of their lives in wetlands, lakes, rivers, and streams. The well-being of waterfowl populations is tied directly to the status and abundance of wetland habitats. According to the USFWS's Division of Bird Habitat Conservation (January 12, 2009, http://www.fws.gov/birdhabitat/NAWMP/index.shtm), waterfowl are the most well-known and economically important group of migratory birds in North America. By 1985 (when waterfowl populations had decreased to record lows), 3.2 million people were spending nearly $1 billion annually to hunt waterfowl. In addition, 18.6 million people spent $2 billion on "waterfowl-watching" activities, such as observing and photographing them.

Measures to preserve and protect the waterfowl population include the North American Waterfowl Management Plan. A joint strategy adopted by the governments of the United States, Canada, and Mexico, the plan established an international committee with six representatives from each of the three countries. Its purpose is to provide a forum for discussion of major, long-term international waterfowl issues and to make recommendations to the directors of the three countries' national wildlife agencies. The Division of Bird Habitat Conservation notes that as of January 2009, $4.5 billion had been invested under the plan to protect, restore, and/or enhance 15.7 million acres (6.4 million ha) of waterfowl habitat. The North American Waterfowl Management Plan projects also target all wetland-associated species in their conservation efforts.

Water Storage

Wetlands absorb water, much like sponges. By temporarily storing runoff and flood waters, wetlands help protect adjacent and downstream property owners from flood damage. Wetland plants slow the flow of water, which contributes to the wetland's ability to store it. The combined effects of storing and slowing the flow of water permit it to percolate through the soil into groundwater, which recharges aquifers, and to move through the watershed with less speed and force.

Wetlands are particularly valuable in urban areas because paved and other impermeable surfaces shed water, increasing the rate, velocity, and volume of runoff so that the risk of flood damage increases. The loss or degradation of wetlands indirectly intensifies flooding by eliminating the absorption of the peak flows and the gradual release of floodwaters.

Nutrient and Sediment Control

Figure 7.4 shows how wetlands improve the quality of water. Wetlands act like natural water filters. When water is stored or slowed down in a wetland by the plants and root masses that grow there, sediment settles out and remains in the wetland so that the water leaving the area is much less cloudy than the water that entered. The loss of cloudiness or turbidity has important consequences for both human health and the ecological health of the watershed. Turbidity has been implicated in disease outbreaks in drinking water. Furthermore, turbid water bearing silt has been responsible for smothering plants and animals in rivers, streams, estuaries, and lakes.

Wetlands can also trap nutrients (phosphorous and nitrogen) that are dissolved in the water or attached to the sediment. These nutrients are either stored in the wetland soil or used by the plants to enhance growth. If too much nutrient material reaches rivers, streams, lakes, and reservoirs, it can cause eutrophication, resulting in the death of many aquatic organisms. (See Figure 6.14 in Chapter 6 and the related discussion.)

Soil Anchoring

Wetlands also play an important role in soil anchoring. The thick mesh of wetland vegetation and roots acts like a net and helps hold soil in place even during periods of relatively high water flow. Removing wetland vegetation that lines a stream or river leads to poorly anchored soil and an increased water flow, which carries away the soil. The result can be severe erosion and changes to the contours of channels, making them deeper and flatter. As a result, aquatic communities at the erosion location are disrupted or eliminated, and downstream aquatic systems are damaged by silt.

Marsh plant fringes in lakes, estuaries, and oceans protect shorelines from erosion in a similar fashion. The plants reduce soil erosion by binding the soil in their root masses. At the same time, the plants and root masses cushion the force of wave action, retarding the scouring of shorelines.

ECONOMIC BENEFITS OF WETLANDS

Appreciation of the economic value of wetlands has undergone a dramatic change since the 1970s. Before that

FIGURE 7.4

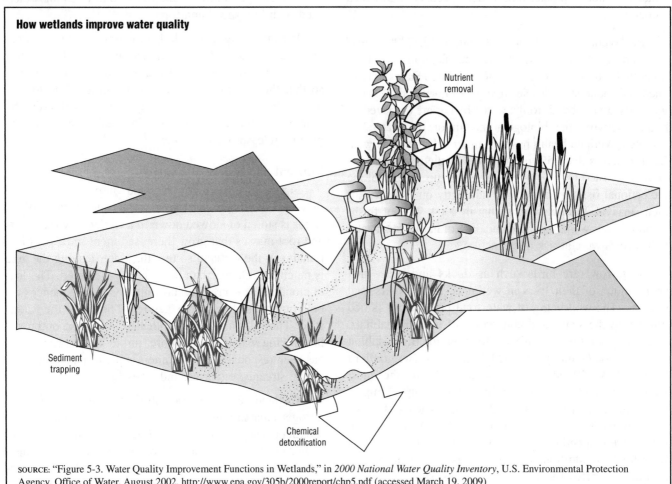

How wetlands improve water quality

SOURCE: "Figure 5-3. Water Quality Improvement Functions in Wetlands," in *2000 National Water Quality Inventory*, U.S. Environmental Protection Agency, Office of Water, August 2002, http://www.epa.gov/305b/2000report/chp5.pdf (accessed March 19, 2009)

time, wetlands were considered useless, good only for taking up space and breeding mosquitoes. The emphasis was on filling and draining wetlands to turn them into productive land for development and agriculture. In the mid-1970s the growing environmental movement with its emphasis on clean water led to a closer examination of wetlands and their role in watersheds and the global ecosystem. Wetlands are now valued not only for their ecological role but also for their contribution to the economy.

Recreation

Some of the most popular recreational activities, including fishing, hunting, and canoeing, occur in and are dependent on healthy wetlands. The EPA notes in the fact sheet "Economic Benefits of Wetlands" (January 12, 2009, http://www.epa.gov/owow/wetlands/facts/fact4.html) that "more than half of all U.S. adults (98 million people) hunt, fish, birdwatch, or photograph wildlife." Figure 7.5 shows that 42% of Americans who observed, fed, or photographed wildlife on trips away from home in 2001 visited wetlands for these activities.

An example of the value of these wetland-related recreational activities can be found in the USFWS's *2006 National*

FIGURE 7.5

Type of site visited for observing, feeding, or photographing wildlife, 2001

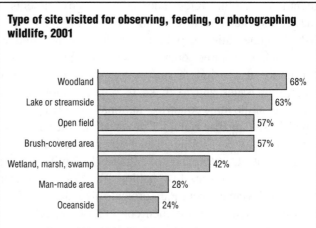

SOURCE: "Type of Site Visited by Nonresidential Participants," in *2001 National Survey of Fishing, Hunting, and Wildlife-Associated Recreation*, U.S. Department of the Interior, Fish and Wildlife Service and U.S. Department of Commerce, U.S. Census Bureau, October 2002, http://www.census.gov/prod/2002pubs/FHW01.pdf (accessed March 19, 2009)

Survey of Fishing, Hunting, and Wildlife-Associated Recreation (October 2007, http://www.census.gov/prod/2008

pubs/fhw06-nat.pdf). The USFWS states that in 2006, 30 million people aged 16 years and older went fishing and spent $42 billion; 25.4 million anglers went freshwater fishing and 7.7 million went saltwater fishing. Overall, anglers spent $17.9 billion in 2006 on fishing trips and $18.8 billion on equipment. Of the money spent on fishing trips, anglers spent $6.3 billion on food and lodging and $5 billion on transportation. They spent nearly $6.6 billion on land-use fees, guide fees, equipment rental, boating expenses, and bait. Camping equipment, binoculars, and special fishing clothing accounted for $779 million in expenditures. Equipment such as boats, vans, and cabins cost $12.6 billion. Anglers spent $4.6 billion on land leasing and ownership and $776 million on magazines, books, membership dues and contributions, licenses, stamps, tags, and permits.

Wetland-related activities are also important to children of all ages. According to the USFWS, 59% of all first-time anglers were aged 6 to 17 in 2005. In addition, 34% of children aged 6 to 15 participated in wildlife-watching activities.

Commercial Fisheries

The National Marine Fisheries Service notes in *Fisheries of the United States 2007* (July 2008, http://www.st.nmfs.noaa.gov/st1/fus/fus07/fus_2007.pdf) that the value of the U.S. commercial fish landings (the part of the fish catch that is put ashore) in 2007 was $4.1 billion. Nearly 10% of the value of U.S. finfish landings was from salmon alone—only one of the many species that are dependent on near-coastal waters and their wetlands for breeding and spawning. The EPA estimates in *National Coastal Condition Report II (2005)* (December 2004, http://www.epa.gov/owow/oceans/nccr/2005/downloads.html) that "95% of commercial fish and 85% of sport fish spend a portion of their life cycles in coastal wetland and estuarine habitats. Adult stocks of commercially harvested shrimp, blue crabs, oysters, and other species throughout the United States are directly related to wetland quality and quantity."

Flood Control

Because wetlands function like sponges by absorbing and storing water, they help control flood waters and the resultant loss of life and property. In *Economic Benefits of Wetlands* (May 2006, http://www.epa.gov/OWOW/wetlands/pdf/EconomicBenefits.pdf), the EPA notes that floods in the United States cost about $2 billion annually. However, depending on their size, wetlands can store millions of gallons of water and then release the water slowly after the flood surge has passed, thereby reducing flood damage. Wetlands can also buffer the effects of coastal tropical storms and hurricanes. The EPA suggests that if the Mississippi-Louisiana coastline had more wetland areas, then the effects of Hurricane Katrina would have been lessened.

HISTORY OF WETLANDS USE

Until well into the 20th century wetlands were considered nature's failure, a waste in nature's economy. For this reason, people sought to increase the usefulness of wetlands. In the agricultural economy of that time, land unable to produce crops or timber was considered worthless. Many Americans began to think of draining these lands, an undertaking that required government funds and resources.

Beginning in the 19th century several states passed laws to facilitate the drainage of wetlands by the formation of drainage districts and statutes. In "When Dismal Swamps Became Priceless Wetlands" (*American Heritage Magazine*, vol. 45, no. 3, May–June 1994), William B. Meyer of Clark University explains:

> When a specified number of landowners in an area petitioned for a drainage project, a hearing was held. If the proposed work seemed practicable, a district encompassing the area affected was created with the power to issue bonds, assess the landholders—petitioners and opponents alike—and drain as needed.... With the approval of the courts, lawmakers around the country set about improving and expanding their drainage statutes. Coupled with an agricultural boom and technological improvements, these legal changes launched a fleet of reclamation projects in the late nineteenth and early twentieth centuries... [B]y 1920 state drainage districts in the United States encompassed an area larger than Missouri. The farmland under drainage, most of it originally wetland, doubled between 1905 and 1910 and again between 1910 and 1920.

Early Conservationists

According to Meyer, the earliest effective resistance came from hunters, sportsmen, and naturalist lobbies. Organizations such as the American Game Protective Association, the Audubon Society, and the Izaak Walton League "deplored the destruction by drainage of wildlife habitats. They attributed declines in waterfowl populations to excessive drainage and overhunting, and they began to press for the protection of wetland breeding grounds in the Midwest and elsewhere." Meanwhile, a growing number of Americans were beginning to sympathize with conservationists. Drainage projects were often disappointing—soils had proven to be poorer than expected, and the costs were generally greater than expected.

Reclamation's Failures

Meyer notes that Lower Klamath Lake in Northern California became a prominent example of reclamation's potential for creating wastelands far more desolate than those they replaced. Surrounded by marshes, the shallow lake was established in 1908 as a waterfowl sanctuary by Theodore Roosevelt (1858–1919). Nonetheless, in 1917 the water inflow was cut off to reclaim the land. When the lakebed dried up, it was ravaged by dust storms and the peat in the marsh bottom caught fire. Rather than being a reclaimed area of extraordinary fertility, the former wetlands became an ecological travesty. The USFWS's Klamath Basin National Wildlife Refuges (April 1, 2009, http://www.fws.gov/klamathbasinrefuges/history.html) states that even though time has helped reverse the damage, less than 25% of the historic wetland basin remains. In spite of this, the basin continues to support tremendous bird life on a smaller scale.

Efforts have been made to help the Klamath Basin recover. According to the press release "President Bush to Propose Record-Level $3.9 Billion for Conservation Programs" (January 30, 2003, http://www.usda.gov/), the U.S. Department of Agriculture (USDA) reports that in the budget for fiscal year 2004, President George W. Bush (1946–) proposed setting aside $8 million for water conservation and water quality enhancements in the Klamath Basin. The Karuk Tribe indicates in the press release "Federal Agencies Issue Final Mandates for Klamath Dams" (January 30, 2007, http://www.karuk.us/press/2007/07-01-30%20final%20mandate.pdf) that the U.S. Departments of Interior and Commerce mandated that fishways and fish ladders be operational in the area, making it economically favorable to remove dams that block water to the area, rather than relicensing the dams and providing fishways and ladders using alternative methods. This action led the way toward returning the Klamath River to being a productive salmon river. In 2008 the diverse stakeholders in the Klamath River (environmentalists, Native Americans, anglers, and government agencies) reached consensus on removing the dams.

Similarly, for many years Florida sought to drain the Everglades, a vast wetland region covering much of the southern part of the state. According to Meyers, efforts there resulted in lands prone to flooding and peat fires. Peat fires are particularly dangerous because they burn underground and can flare up without warning long distances from where they were originally ignited. Costs escalated, and the drainage district went broke. Across the nation the gap between the cost and the value of reclaimed land widened even more. The agricultural depression that began in the 1920s increased the growing skepticism as to the value of reclamation. Nonetheless, during the Great Depression (1929–1939) programs such as the Works Progress Administration and the Reconstruction Finance Corporation encouraged wetland conversion as a way to provide work for many unemployed people. By the end of World War II (1939–1945) the total area of drained farmland had increased sharply.

Concern over Property Rights

Dispute over wetlands regulation reflects the nation's ambivalence when private property and public rights intersect, especially because three-fourths of the nation's wetlands are owned by private citizens. Since the latter half of the 20th century, landowners have protested that their property has been devalued because wetlands regulation prevents its development. They argue that efforts to preserve the wetlands have gone too far, citing instances where a small wetland precludes the use of large tracts of land. Many people believe this constitutes taking without just compensation.

The "takings" clause of the U.S. Constitution provides that when private property is taken for public use, the owner has to be paid just compensation. Wetland owners claim that when the government, through its laws, eliminates some uses for their land, its value is decreased, and they believe they should be paid for the loss.

In the 1970s and 1980s state courts and the lower federal courts frequently handed down contradictory rulings on the issue of compensation for wetland-related takings. In 1992 the U.S. Supreme Court, in *Lucas v. South Carolina Coastal Council* (505 U.S. 1003), finally resolved the issue of compensation when land taken for an accepted public good loses significant value.

David Lucas, a homebuilder, bought two residential lots on a South Carolina barrier island in 1986 for $975,000. He planned to build and sell two single-family houses similar to those on nearby lots. At the time he purchased the land, state law allowed house construction on the lots. In 1988 South Carolina passed the Beachfront Management Act to protect the state's beaches from erosion. Lucas's land fell within the area considered in danger of erosion; as a result, Lucas could no longer build the houses.

Lucas went to court, claiming that the Beachfront Management Act had taken his property without just compensation because it no longer had any value if he could not build there. Lucas did not question the right of the state of South Carolina to take his property for the common good. Rather, he claimed the state had to compensate him for the financial loss that resulted from the devaluing of the property.

The Supreme Court said that a state could stop a landowner from building on his or her property only if he or she was using it for a "harmful or noxious" purpose—for example, building a brickyard or a brewery in a residential area. This was not the case. Lucas had planned to build homes, a legitimate purpose that was neither harmful nor noxious. Even though it was possible to define the planned buildings as harmful to South Carolina's ecological resources, this would not be consistent with earlier court interpretations of "harmful." Only by showing that Lucas had intended to do something "harmful or noxious" with the land could the state take his land without compensation. This the state did not do; therefore, it owed him the money. Lucas was awarded $750,000 for each lot and relinquished the titles to the state of South Carolina, which, in a move criticized by the National Audubon Society and other environmental groups, later sold the property to another developer.

Invasive Species

People are not the only ones who have dramatically altered wetlands. Nonnative—also called exotic—species have been as devastating to wetlands as humans by changing the nature of the ecosystem, thereby interfering with its function and the survival of native plants and animals. Plants and animals introduced either accidentally or deliberately can cause unexpected harm by displacing native species from their habitat or by placing stress, such as disease or predation, on a native species.

In 1899 the coypu (*Myocastor coypus*) was introduced into California for the fur-farming trade. The coypu is a beaverlike aquatic South American rodent that is bred for its fur. This introduction was originally viewed as a way to provide economic benefit. Subsequently, state and federal agencies as well as private interests were responsible for introducing the coypu into the wild in 15 states to provide a new fur resource. In coastal states such as Maryland and Louisiana, the results have been disastrous.

Coypu live in fresh, intermediate, and brackish marshes and wetlands and feed on the vegetation. They eat all the vegetation in an area, changing a marsh to a barren mudflat. Coypu feed on the base of plant stems and dig for roots and rhizomes in the winter. Their grazing strips large patches of marsh, and their digging turns over the upper peat layer. This conversion of marsh to open water destroys valuable habitat for muskrat, wading birds, amphibians, reptiles, ducks, fish, crabs, and a host of other species; furthermore, it causes erosion and siltation.

Invasive plant species can be as harmful as invasive animal species. Eurasian water milfoil, phragmites (common reed grass), hydrilla, and purple loosestrife are introduced species that have disrupted wetland systems. Purple loosestrife (*Lythrum salicaria*) is a good example. It is a perennial herb with reddish-purple flowers that may reach 6 feet (1.8 m) in height under the right conditions. It was an important medicinal herb and ornamental as early as 200 years ago on the East Coast and was probably introduced for this reason. It has no known North American predators and has a high reproductive capacity—up to 300,000 seeds per stalk. Because it can outcompete most native wetland plants, it can change the character and ecological function of a marsh. This is a serious threat because many wetland and other wildlife species are adapted to and depend on specific plants.

LOSS AND GAIN IN WETLAND ACREAGE

When the first Europeans arrived in North America, Thomas E. Dahl and Gregory J. Allord indicate in *History of Wetlands in the Coterminous United States*

(March 7, 1997, http://water.usgs.gov/nwsum/WSP2425/history.html) that there were an estimated 221 million acres (89.4 million ha) of wetlands in the lower 48 states. In *Status and Trends of Wetlands in the Conterminous United States 1998 to 2004*, Dahl notes that in 2004 there were an estimated 107.7 million acres (43.6 million ha). In the intervening years, more than 50% of the wetlands in the lower 48 states were lost. Wetlands had been drained, dredged, filled, leveled, and flooded to meet human needs. Even though natural forces such as erosion, sedimentation, and a rise or drop in sea level may erase wetlands over time, most wetland losses have been caused by humans. Many of the nation's older cities—such as New York City, New York; Baltimore, Maryland; Philadelphia, Pennsylvania; New Orleans, Louisiana; and Charleston, South Carolina—are built on filled wetlands.

However, Dahl mentions that after decades of wetland losses there was an annual gain of 32,000 acres (12,900 ha) of wetlands from 1998 to 2004. (See Figure 7.6.) Additionally, the loss of wetlands over time shrank from 458,000 acres (185,000 ha) in the 1950s and 1970s to 290,000 acres (117,000 ha) in the 1970s and 1980s, which is a decrease of 37%. By the 1980s and 1990s the annual wetland loss had declined to 58,500 acres (about 23,700 ha), which is an 80% decrease from the 1970s and 1980s.

Dahl details the reasons for wetlands losses during the 1998–2004 period. Figure 7.7 shows that the highest acre-

FIGURE 7.6

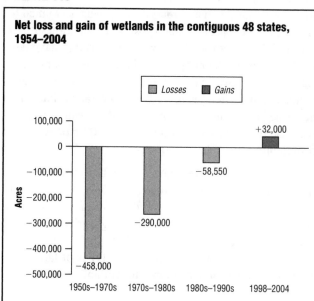

Net loss and gain of wetlands in the contiguous 48 states, 1954–2004

SOURCE: Thomas E. Dahl, "Figure 26. Average Annual Net Loss and Gain Estimates for the Conterminous United States, 1954 to 2004," in *Status and Trends of Wetlands in the Conterminous United States 1998 to 2004*, U.S. Department of the Interior, Fish and Wildlife Service, 2006, http://www.fws.gov/wetlands/_documents/gSandT/National Reports/StatusTrendsWetlandsConterminousUS1998to2004.pdf (accessed March 19, 2009)

FIGURE 7.7

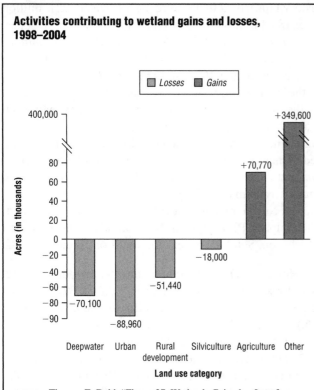

Activities contributing to wetland gains and losses, 1998–2004

SOURCE: Thomas E. Dahl, "Figure 27. Wetlands Gained or Lost from Upland Categories and Deepwater, 1998 to 2004," in *Status and Trends of Wetlands in the Conterminous United States 1998 to 2004*, U.S. Department of the Interior, Fish and Wildlife Service, 2006, http://www.fws.gov/wetlands/_documents/gSandT/NationalReports/StatusTrends WetlandsConterminousUS1998to2004.pdf (accessed March 19, 2009)

age lost annually was because of urban development. Dahl determines that urban and rural development accounted for an estimated 61% of wetland losses. In addition, 70,100 acres (28,400 ha) of wetlands were estimated to have been lost to deepwater habitats. As Dahl describes them, deepwater habitats are "environments where surface water is permanent and often deep, so that water, rather than air, is the principal medium in which the dominant organisms live." Some wetlands (18,000 acres [7,300 ha]) were lost to silviculture (the planting of trees).

Dahl also discusses the reasons for wetland gains. (See Figure 7.7.) Approximately 70,770 acres (28,640 ha) of wetlands were gained from wetland restoration and conservation programs converting agricultural land to wetlands, and 349,600 acres (141,500 ha) were gained from these programs converting other types of land, such as prairie, forest, or scrub land, to wetlands.

WETLAND PROTECTIVE LEGISLATION AND PROGRAMS

Since the early 1970s conservationists have turned to the courts to challenge reclamation projects and protect wetlands. If drainage once seemed to improve the look of the land, beginning in the 1970s it was more likely to be seen as degrading it. Wetlands turned out to be not wastelands, but systems efficient in harnessing the sun's rays to feed the food chain and play an important role in the global cycle of water, nitrogen, carbon, and sulfur.

As the drainage movement once found support in state laws and federal policies, so did the preservation movement. In 1977 President Jimmy Carter (1924–) issued an executive order instructing federal agencies to minimize damage to wetlands. In 1989 the EPA adopted a goal of "no net loss" of wetlands, meaning that where a wetland is developed for other uses, the developer must create a wetland elsewhere to maintain an overall constant amount of wetland acreage.

Clean Water Act

Section 404 of the Federal Water Pollution Control Act of 1972 is commonly called the Clean Water Act (CWA). The goal of the CWA is to "restore and maintain the chemical, physical, and biological integrity of the Nation's water." Wetlands are considered part of the nation's water and are covered by the CWA.

The CWA authorizes the U.S. Army Corps of Engineers to be the primary federal authority for the protection of wetlands. The Corps' jurisdiction encompasses all navigable waters of the United States, plus their tributaries and adjacent wetlands, and includes ocean waters within 3 nautical miles (5.6 km) of the coastline and isolated waters next to navigable waters where the use, degradation, or destruction of these waters could affect interstate commerce or foreign commerce. The Corps evaluates the impact of proposed projects that involve wetlands by considering comments from the EPA, the USFWS, the National Marine Fisheries Service, and the affected states. Regulations established under the CWA require that any project affecting more than 0.3 of an acre (0.1 ha) of wetlands or 500 feet (152.4 m) of streams must be approved by the Corps.

Farm Bill of 1996

The 1996 Farm Bill reauthorized the Conservation Reserve Program and created the Wetlands Reserve Program. The two programs are designed to protect and restore wetlands.

WETLANDS RESERVE PROGRAM. The Wetlands Reserve Program (WRP) is a voluntary USDA program that provides farmers with financial incentives and technical assistance to permanently retire their marginal farmland and restore wetland functions to it. Retiring cropland through the WRP has benefited the recovery of threatened or endangered species and has protected wetlands. According to the Natural Resources Conservation Service (NRCS), in "2008 WRP Cumulative Contract Information" (October 21, 2008, http://www.nrcs.usda.gov/Programs/WRP/2008 _ContractInfo/CumulativeContractInfo2008.html), by the end of 2008 the WRP had been implemented in all 50 states, the Pacific Basin, and Puerto Rico. The NRCS notes that the program had enrolled over 2 million acres (809,000 ha) by the end of 2008, with Louisiana, Arkansas, Florida, and Mississippi retiring the greatest number of acres.

CONSERVATION RESERVE PROGRAM. The Conservation Reserve Program (CRP) was originally authorized in the Farm Bill of 1985 as a soil conservation strategy that included paying farmers to retire marginal cropland from production for 10 years. Under the CRP the Farm Service Agency pays farmers to plant natural vegetation on their land, and after the land's temporary retirement, farmers can resume using the land to plant crops. As a wetland protection and restoration strategy, the program has been successful in terms of the thousands of acres of cropland that have been restored to a natural state, which in many cases includes wetlands. The CRP's political support came from its potential to reduce expensive crop surpluses.

State Wetland Protection Programs

Many states and local governments have enacted their own laws to protect wetlands. These laws may complement or be more stringent than federal regulations. For example, Maryland has had state laws to protect tidal wetlands since the early 1970s. In 1989 Maryland adopted the Nontidal Wetlands Act to provide the same protections to freshwater wetlands.

Besides using their CWA authority, states have included wetland protection in their water quality standards, passed laws protecting ecologically important wetlands such as the Dismal Swamp in Virginia and North Carolina, established mitigation banking, and created public education programs to increase public awareness of the value of wetlands. Several states have set up special funds to buy important wetlands.

WETLAND GAINS

As shown in Figure 7.6, wetland gains have been made in recent years. Figure 7.7 shows the reasons for these gains. Many efforts are ongoing at the private, local, state, and federal levels to protect existing wetlands and to create new ones. Wetland losses can be offset by:

- Wetland restoration—the return of a wetland to a close approximation of its condition before disturbance, including reestablishment of its predisturbance aquatic functions and related physical, chemical, and biological characteristics.

- Creation—the construction of a wetland in an area that was not a wetland within the past 100 to 200 years and is isolated from other wetlands.

- Enhancement—the modification of one or more structural features of an existing wetland to increase one or more functions based on management objectives.

Enhancement, while causing a positive gain in one function, frequently results in a reduction in another function.

- Replacement or reallocation—activities in which most or all of an existing wetland is converted to a different type of wetland and has the same drawback as enhancement.

Private Initiatives

Many of the wetland areas in the United States are privately owned. A number of government programs, both regulatory and voluntary, exist to foster wetland protection, and some foster both restoration and enhancement. Some of the most successful wetland programs and projects are the result of private initiatives. Frequently, private organizations form partnerships with landowners to buy, lease, or create easements paid for with private, or a mix of private and public, funds.

Organizations such as the Audubon Society, the Chesapeake Bay Foundation, Ducks Unlimited (DU), the Nature Conservancy, and hundreds of others are working with private landowners, corporations, local communities, volunteers, and federal and state agencies in innovative projects to protect and restore wetlands. For example, the Nature Conservancy oversees many wetland restoration projects, including two on the Illinois River—Spunky Bottoms (2008, http://www.nature.org/initiatives/freshwater/work/illinoisriver.html) and Emiquon (2009, http://www.nature.org/wherewework/northamerica/states/illinois/preserves/art1112.html)—that aim to return more than 8,500 acres (3,400 ha) of farmed land to their original wetland state.

In another example, DU is working with the NRCS to implement the WRP in the Mississippi Alluvial Valley, which according to DU, in "Mississippi Alluvial Valley (MAV)" (2009, http://www.ducks.org/conservation/initiative21.aspx), historically encompassed 24.7 million acres (10 million ha) of hardwood bottom stretching from southern Illinois to Louisiana. In "Conservation in Mississippi" (2009, http://www.ducks.org/Page1666.aspx), DU reports that it is working to conserve over 250,000 acres (101,000 ha) of waterfowl habitat throughout Mississippi by restoring hydrology and planting bottomland hardwood seedlings.

Constructed Wetlands

Constructed wetlands are marshes that are built to filter contaminated water. They consist of soil and drainage materials (such as gravel), water, plants, and microorganisms. Using constructed wetlands for wastewater treatment is a simple, economical, and environmentally friendly method that is being used more frequently than in the past.

Constructed wetland treatment systems are designed and built to use the natural processes involving wetland soils, vegetation, and their associated microbes to help treat wastewater. They are designed to take advantage of many of the same processes that occur in wetlands but in a more controlled manner. Even though some of these systems are operated solely to treat wastewater, others are designed with the multiple objectives of using treated wastewater as a source of water for the creation or restoration of wetland habitat for wildlife and environmental enhancement. The primary drawback to constructed wetlands for wastewater treatment is that they are land intensive; large land tracts are not always available at affordable prices.

There are two general types of constructed wetland treatments: subsurface flow systems and free water surface systems. Both types are usually built in basins or channels with a natural or human-made subsurface barrier to limit seepage. The subsurface flow systems keep water flowing through soil, sand, gravel, or crushed rock underground to minimize odors and other related problems. (See Figure 7.8.) Subsurface flow systems are also known as rock-reed filters, vegetated submerged bed systems, and root-zone systems. Free water surface systems are designed to simulate natural wetlands, with the water flowing over the soil surface at shallow depths.

The EPA's Office of Water reports in *Constructed Treatment Wetlands* (August 2004, http://www.epa.gov/owow/wetlands/pdf/ConstructedW.pdf) that approximately

5,000 constructed wetland treatment systems have been built in Europe and about 1,000 are operating in the United States.

Marsh construction and wetland rehabilitation as a method of disposing of dredged materials are another growing source of wetland construction. The Army Corps of Engineers has been using dredged material to construct or restore marshes since 1969. Dredged material is placed on shallow bay bottoms to build up elevations to an intertidal level, usually by pumping dredged material to the marsh construction site. If the site is exposed to high wind or wave action, protective structures such as rock or concrete breakwaters are built. Vegetation can be planted or the site may be left to develop naturally. Generally, within two to three years these sites are indistinguishable from natural wetlands in appearance.

Restoration of the Florida Everglades

The Everglades is a premier wetland in the United States. It is designated as an International Biosphere Reserve, a World Heritage Site, and a Wetland of International Importance. Figure 7.9 shows the location of the Everglades and how it has been reduced to about half its former size.

According to the South Florida Ecosystem Restoration Task Force (April 28, 2009, http://www.sfrestore.org/), the Everglades is part of the South Florida Ecosystem, an 18,000-square-mile (47,000-square-km) region extending from the Kissimmee River near Orlando to the Florida Keys. Originally a wide expanse of wetland, pine forests, mangroves, coastal islands, and coral reefs, the Everglades is one of the nation's most highly populated and manipulated regions in the 21st century. Its freshwater supply comes from rainfall in the Kissimmee River Basin and southward, mostly in May through October.

Slow and rain driven, the natural cycle of freshwater circulation feeding the Everglades accumulated in shallow Lake Okeechobee, which currently averages 9 feet (2.7 m) deep and covers about 730 square miles (1,890 square km). Thus began the flow of the wide, shallow "river of grass," as it was called by Native Americans. The lake is 50 miles (80.5 km) wide in places, 1 to 3 feet (0.3 to 0.9 m) deep in the slough's center, and only 6 inches (15.2 cm) deep elsewhere. It flows south at a rate of about 100 feet (30.5 m) per day across the saw grass of the Everglades to the mangrove estuaries on the Gulf of Mexico. A six-month dry season follows this flow. During the dry season water levels gradually drop. The plants and animals of the Everglades are adapted to the alternating wet and dry seasons.

During the past 100 years an elaborate system of dikes, canals, levees, floodgates, and pumps was built to move water to agricultural fields, urban areas, and the

FIGURE 7.8

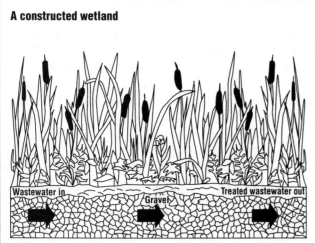

A constructed wetland

Wastewater in — Gravel — Treated wastewater out

Notes: Marsh plants (cattails, reeds, etc.) are grown in beds of soil or gravel through which wastewater flows. Wetlands are useful to further treat wastewater from a lagoon. This is a low-cost system that needs minimal attention from an operator. Periodically, plants need to be checked and sometimes harvested at the end of the growing season. The system requires relatively less land than many land treatment systems. The system may be operated year-round in most climates.

SOURCE: "Figure 2.3. Constructed Wetland," in *Water Pollution: Information on the Use of Alternative Wastewater Treatment Systems*, U.S. General Accounting Office, September 1994, http://archive.gao.gov/t2pbat2/152794.pdf (accessed March 19, 2009)

FIGURE 7.9

The Everglades, past and present

Location of the Everglades.

☐ *Natural areas of the Everglades*

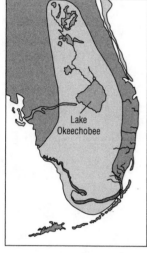

Lake
Okeechobee

Past

Lake
Okeechobee

Present

Historically, the natural areas of the Everglades extended well north of Lake Okeechobee and south to Florida Bay and the Gulf of Mexico.

Today, the bulk of the natural areas remaining in the ecosystem primarily include the Everglades National Park and Big Cypress National Preserve, as well as state water conservation areas.*

*Other smaller natural areas are dispersed throughout southern Florida, such as national wildlife refuges and state, local, or privately owned lands, but are not shown in the figure.

SOURCE: "Figure 23. The Everglades—Past and Present," in *Freshwater Supply: States' Views of How Federal Agencies Could Help Them Meet the Challenges of Expected Shortages*, U.S. General Accounting Office, July 2003, http://www.gao.gov/new.items/d03514 .pdf (accessed March 19, 2009). Data from South Florida Water Management District.

Everglades National Park. Water runoff from agriculture and urban development brought excess nutrients into the Everglades, reducing production of beneficial algae and promoting unnatural growth of other vegetation. Ill-timed human manipulation of the water supply interfered with the natural water cycle, ruining critical spawning, feeding, and nesting conditions for many species.

The Florida legislature has enacted a number of laws to combat the growing water shortage in Florida, including the Everglades. The 1981 Save Our Rivers Act and the 1990 Preservation 2000 Fund authorized the water

management districts to buy property to protect water sources, groundwater recharge, and other natural resources. The South Florida Water Management District (SFWMD; 2009, http://www.evergladesplan.org/pm/progr _land_aquisition.cfm), an agency that oversees flood protection and water supply, has been buying out landowners in the eastern Everglades area in hopes of retaking thousands of acres of agricultural and residential property at an estimated cost of $2.2 billion. The action is aimed at restoring water flow to the Everglades National Park.

In 1998 the Army Corps of Engineers and the SFWMD released their plan for improving Florida's ecological and economic health: the Comprehensive Everglades Restoration Plan (CERP; http://www.evergladesplan.org/index .aspx). This plan covers the entire region and its water problems and focuses on recovering the major characteristics that defined the "river of grass." Specifically, the plan calls for:

- Reducing the freshwater flows into the Caloosahatchee River and the St. Lucie Canal, thereby restoring to the Everglades water now lost to the tide.

- Returning the water flow in the Kissimmee River to its former floodplain to achieve a more meandering river system.

- Restoring 40,000 acres (16,000 ha) of marshes for water storage and filtration to remove nutrients before the water enters the Everglades.

- Modifying water deliveries through improved timing and distribution to mimic historic water conditions.

- Reestablishing historic flows and water levels to sloughs feeding into Florida Bay to restore natural estuarine salinity.

The Water Resources Development Act of 2000 approved the CERP. The SFWMD (2009, http://www .evergladesplan.org/about/about_cerp_brief.aspx) states that this plan will take more than 30 years to carry out and will cost an estimated $9.5 billion. The primary goal of the project is to restore critical water flows to the Everglades and ensure adequate water supplies for cities, communities, and farmers in southern Florida well into the future. The cost of the project will be shared equally between the state of Florida and the federal government.

In *Progress toward Restoring the Everglades: The Second Biennial Review* (2008), the Committee on Independent Scientific Review of Everglades Restoration Progress notes that the restoration process is being hampered by limited federal funding and a complex process. The committee commends the state of Florida on its retaking of Everglades land but states that the Everglades remains heavily polluted with disappearing wildlife habitat. A third independent review of the CERP began in early 2009, and a report to Congress will be published in late 2010.

CHAPTER 8
THE ARID WEST—WHERE WATER IS SCARCE

CLIMATE OF THE AMERICAN WEST

The United States is a nation relatively rich in water resources. Susan S. Hutson et al. of the U.S. Geological Survey (USGS) state in *Estimated Use of Water in the United States in 2000* (2004, http://pubs.usgs.gov/circ/2004/circ1268/pdf/circular1268.pdf), the most recent report available as of mid-2009, that in the lower 48 states the total supply of water in 2000 was about 1.4 trillion gallons (5.3 trillion L) per day.

Nevertheless, even though the nation as a whole is water-rich, this abundance is not spread evenly throughout the country. Some areas have more water than others, whereas some have a higher need than others. Those with the greatest need do not always have adequate water resources, a situation that can lead to serious problems and conflicts.

Much of the U.S. West is arid (characterized by desert land) and semiarid (prairie land), with limited and inconsistent supplies of water. The West includes Washington, Oregon, and California (the Pacific states); and Idaho, Montana, Wyoming, Colorado, Utah, Nevada, New Mexico, and Arizona (the Mountain states). From the Rocky Mountains, which form the Continental Divide, to the shores of California, lay the dry basins and deserts of this vast western region of the country.

According to the U.S. Census Bureau, in "State & Country QuickFacts" (May 5, 2009, http://quickfacts.census.gov/qfd/states/00000.html), the 50 United States encompass 3.5 million square miles (9.2 million square km) of land. The rain and snow that falls on this land is unevenly distributed. The USGS reports in "Rain, a Valuable Resource" (November 7, 2008, http://ga.water.usgs.gov/edu/earthrain.html) that Mt. Waialeale, Hawaii, gets the most rainfall of any U.S. location, where it averages about 450 inches (1,143 cm) per year. In contrast, the Weather Channel (May 2009, http://www.weather.com/) reports that Flagstaff, Arizona, receives 23 inches (58.4 cm)

of precipitation a year, but in Phoenix and Tucson, where most of Arizona's people live and most of the agriculture is located, the yearly rainfall averages between 9 and 12 inches (22.9 and 30.5 cm), respectively. The reason for this is the North Pacific high pressure system. This is a massive zone of high atmospheric pressure that is the characteristic weather pattern for the Pacific Ocean off the coast of North America. The North Pacific high pressure system pushes most precipitation toward the north.

No resource is as vital to the West's urban centers, agriculture, industry, recreation, scenic beauty, and environmental preservation as water. Throughout the history of the West, especially in California, battles have raged over who gets how much of this precious resource. The fundamental controversy is one of distribution, combined with conflicts between competing interests over the use of available supplies.

POPULATION GROWTH IN THE WEST

Even though the climate is arid and semiarid in much of the West, and water is a necessary and less available resource than in other parts of the United States, the population of the West is booming. According to data from the Census Bureau, population growth exploded in the West between 1990 and 2000. Figure 8.1 and Figure 8.2 show that from 2000 to 2008 growth in the United States was focused in the West and Southeast. The maps show that in terms of numbers of people, states in the West and Southeast, along with Texas and New York, had the greatest rise. Louisiana and North Dakota had population declines. In terms of percent change, three western states—Nevada, Utah, and Arizona—had the highest growth rate.

The Census Bureau projects that the two highest percentages of population growth from 2000 to 2030 will be in the West (45.8%) and the South (42.9%). (See Table 8.1.) The top-five states with the projected highest percentage

FIGURE 8.1

Percent change in population for states and Puerto Rico, April 1, 2000–July 1, 2008

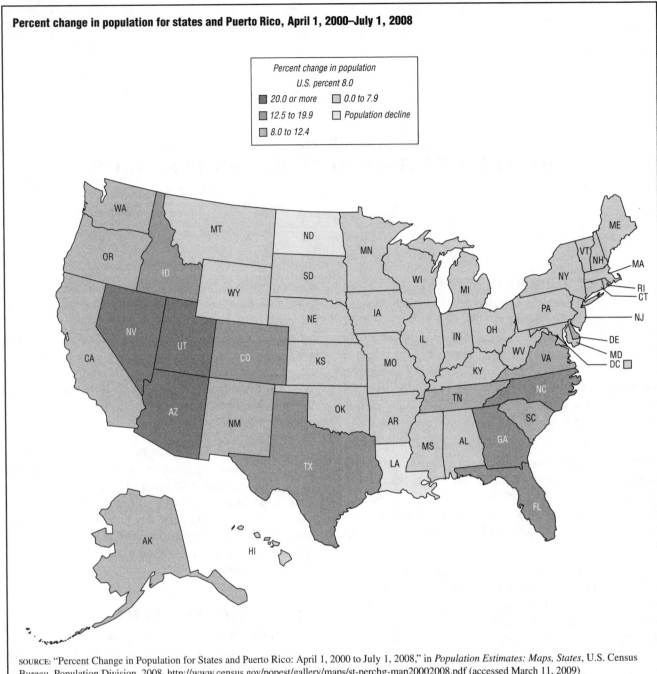

SOURCE: "Percent Change in Population for States and Puerto Rico: April 1, 2000 to July 1, 2008," in *Population Estimates: Maps, States*, U.S. Census Bureau, Population Division, 2008, http://www.census.gov/popest/gallery/maps/st-perchg-map20002008.pdf (accessed March 11, 2009)

gains will be Nevada (114.3%), Arizona (108.8%), Florida (79.5), Texas (59.8%), and Idaho (52.2%).

Table 8.2 shows population growth in metropolitan areas (at least one urbanized area of 50,000 or more people), micropolitan areas (at least one urbanized area of 10,000 to 49,999 people), and areas outside either (often called rural areas). The highest growth rate in metropolitan areas from 2000 to 2007 was in the Mountain states of the West, at 20.4%. The highest growth rate in micropolitan areas from 2000 to 2007 was also in the Mountain states of

the West, at 8.4%. Outside these metropolitan and micropolitan areas, populations were diminishing; that is, people were moving out of rural areas.

SOURCES OF WESTERN WATER SUPPLIES

Precipitation (rain, snow, and sleet) is the main source of essentially all freshwater supplies in the West, largely controlling the availability of surface and groundwater. In the arid regions of the West, much of the available precipitation evaporates shortly after the rains stop. For

FIGURE 8.2

Numeric change in population for states and Puerto Rico, April 1, 2000–July 1, 2008

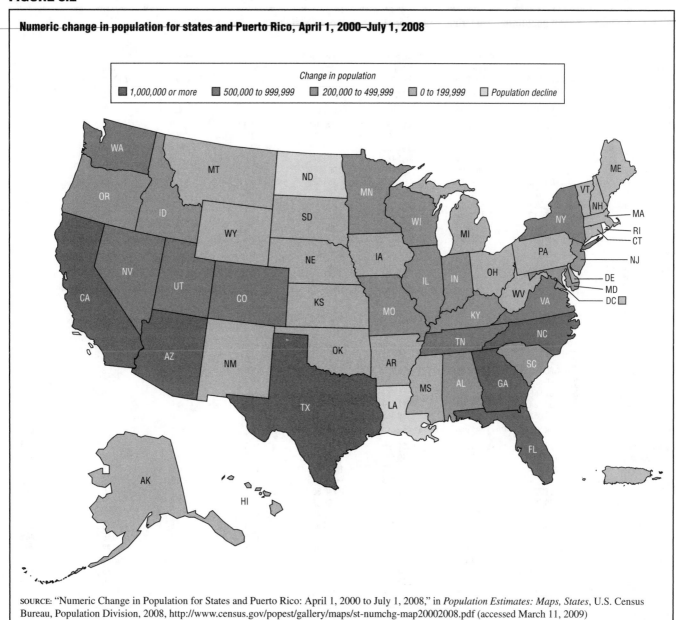

SOURCE: "Numeric Change in Population for States and Puerto Rico: April 1, 2000 to July 1, 2008," in *Population Estimates: Maps, States*, U.S. Census Bureau, Population Division, 2008, http://www.census.gov/popest/gallery/maps/st-numchg-map20002008.pdf (accessed March 11, 2009)

example, Tucson receives most of its annual rainfall from heavy thunderstorms during the hottest months of the year—between July and September—when much of that rainfall is lost through evaporation.

Runoff refers to water that is not immediately absorbed into the ground during a rain storm and runs off into lower-lying areas or surrounding lakes and streams. Runoff is the primary measure of a region's water supply. Besides rain, a large share of the West's runoff comes from the melting of mountain snowpacks, which are essentially huge reservoirs of frozen water that slowly release their supplies during the spring and summer. Much of western agriculture depends on this meltwater becoming available during the growing season.

Changes in climate can adversely affect the volume of snowpacks. The U.S. Climate Change Science Program (CCSP) reports in *The Effects of Climate Change on Agriculture, Land, Resources, Water Resources, and Biodiversity in the United States* (May 2008, http://www.climatescience.gov/Library/sap/sap4-3/final-report/sap4.3-final-all.pdf) that the snowpack of the West's mountain ranges is decreasing, with global warming seen as a factor in this decrease. The CCSP suggests that in the coming years more precipitation will fall as rain (rather than as snow) and that snowpack will develop later and melt earlier. As a result, peak stream flows will likely come earlier in the spring, and summer flows will be reduced. The change in the timing of runoff from snow-melt is likely to have implications for water management, flood protection, irrigation, and planning.

TABLE 8.1

Projected change in total population, numerical and percent, for regions, divisions, and states, 2000–30

Region, division, and state	Numerical change 2000 to 2010	Numerical change 2010 to 2020	Numerical change 2020 to 2030	Numerical change 2000 to 2030	Percent change 2000 to 2010	Percent change 2010 to 2020	Percent change 2020 to 2030	Percent change 2000 to 2030
United States	27,513,675	26,868,965	27,779,889	82,162,529	9.8	8.7	8.3	29.2
Northeast	2,190,801	1,350,258	535,631	4,076,690	4.1	2.4	0.9	7.6
New England	816,272	570,739	313,487	1,700,498	5.9	3.9	2.0	12.2
Maine	82,211	51,531	2,432	136,174	6.4	3.8	0.2	10.7
New Hampshire	149,774	139,191	121,720	410,685	12.1	10.0	8.0	33.2
Vermont	43,685	38,174	21,181	103,040	7.2	5.9	3.1	16.9
Massachusetts	300,344	206,105	156,463	662,912	4.7	3.1	2.3	10.4
Rhode Island	68,333	37,578	−1,289	104,622	6.5	3.4	−0.1	10.0
Connecticut	171,925	98,160	12,980	283,065	5.0	2.7	0.4	8.3
Middle Atlantic	1,374,529	779,519	222,144	2,376,192	3.5	1.9	0.5	6.0
New York	467,215	133,248	−99,491	500,972	2.5	0.7	−0.5	2.6
New Jersey	603,881	443,404	340,805	1,388,090	7.2	4.9	3.6	16.5
Pennsylvania	303,433	202,867	−19,170	487,130	2.5	1.6	−0.1	4.0
Midwest	2,998,657	2,063,742	1,042,123	6,104,522	4.7	3.1	1.5	9.5
East North Central	1,886,286	1,167,410	429,731	3,483,427	4.2	2.5	0.9	7.7
Ohio	223,041	67,877	−93,530	197,388	2.0	0.6	−0.8	1.7
Indiana	311,654	234,869	183,100	729,623	5.1	3.7	2.8	12.0
Illinois	497,601	319,826	196,172	1,013,599	4.0	2.5	1.5	8.2
Michigan	490,239	267,310	−1,821	755,728	4.9	2.6	0.0	7.6
Wisconsin	363,751	277,528	145,810	787,089	6.8	4.8	2.4	14.7
West North Central	1,112,371	896,332	612,392	2,621,095	5.8	4.4	2.9	13.6
Minnesota	501,157	480,133	405,361	1,386,651	10.2	8.9	6.9	28.2
Iowa	83,583	10,589	−65,324	28,848	2.9	0.4	−2.2	1.0
Missouri	326,867	277,804	230,291	834,962	5.8	4.7	3.7	14.9
North Dakota	−5,577	−6,511	−23,546	−35,634	−0.9	−1.0	−3.7	−5.5
South Dakota	31,555	15,540	−1,477	45,618	4.2	2.0	−0.2	6.0
Nebraska	57,734	33,681	17,569	108,984	3.4	1.9	1.0	6.4
Kansas	117,052	85,096	49,518	251,666	4.4	3.0	1.7	9.4
South	13,346,794	13,987,205	15,698,518	43,032,517	13.3	12.3	12.3	42.9
South Atlantic	8,022,621	8,650,245	9,651,190	26,324,056	15.5	14.5	14.1	50.8
Delaware	100,742	78,867	49,449	229,058	12.9	8.9	5.1	29.2
Maryland	608,484	592,656	524,625	1,725,765	11.5	10.0	8.1	32.6
District of Columbia	−42,274	−49,245	−47,126	−138,645	−7.4	−9.3	−9.8	−24.2
Virginia	931,730	907,150	907,624	2,746,504	13.2	11.3	10.2	38.8
West Virginia	20,797	−28,029	−81,153	−88,385	1.2	−1.5	−4.5	−4.9
North Carolina	1,296,510	1,363,466	1,518,450	4,178,426	16.1	14.6	14.2	51.9
South Carolina	434,692	375,873	325,992	1,136,557	10.8	8.5	6.8	28.3
Georgia	1,402,627	1,254,673	1,174,085	3,831,385	17.1	13.1	10.8	46.8
Florida	3,269,313	4,154,834	5,279,244	12,703,391	20.5	21.6	22.6	79.5
East South Central	1,040,901	915,117	923,457	2,879,475	6.1	5.1	4.9	16.9
Kentucky	223,348	159,314	130,567	513,229	5.5	3.7	3.0	12.7
Tennessee	541,569	549,818	599,964	1,691,351	9.5	8.8	8.8	29.7
Alabama	149,230	132,585	145,328	427,143	3.4	2.9	3.1	9.6
Mississippi	126,754	73,400	47,598	247,752	4.5	2.5	1.6	8.7
West South Central	4,283,272	4,421,843	5,123,871	13,828,986	13.6	12.4	12.8	44.0
Arkansas	201,639	185,180	179,989	566,808	7.5	6.4	5.9	21.2
Louisiana	143,703	106,481	83,473	333,657	3.2	2.3	1.8	7.5
Oklahoma	140,862	144,174	177,561	462,597	4.1	4.0	4.8	13.4
Texas	3,797,068	3,986,008	4,682,848	12,465,924	18.2	16.2	16.4	59.8
West	8,977,423	9,467,760	10,503,617	28,948,800	14.2	13.1	12.9	45.8
Mountain	3,568,184	3,816,570	4,352,383	11,737,137	19.6	17.6	17.0	64.6
Montana	66,403	54,137	22,163	142,703	7.4	5.6	2.2	15.8
Idaho	223,338	224,042	228,291	675,671	17.3	14.8	13.1	52.2
Wyoming	26,104	11,062	−7,969	29,197	5.3	2.1	−1.5	5.9
Colorado	530,293	447,313	513,490	1,491,096	12.3	9.3	9.7	34.7
New Mexico	161,179	104,116	15,367	280,662	8.9	5.3	0.7	15.4
Arizona	1,506,749	1,819,067	2,255,949	5,581,765	29.4	27.4	26.7	108.8
Utah	361,844	395,081	495,273	1,252,198	16.2	15.2	16.6	56.1
Nevada	692,274	761,752	829,819	2,283,845	34.6	28.3	24.0	114.3

Surface Water

The Colorado River is a major source of water for many western states: Arizona, California, Colorado, Nevada, New Mexico, Utah, and Wyoming. (See Figure 8.3.) The Colorado River Basin is the land area that drains into the Colorado River and its tributaries. In *2008 Review: Water Quality Standards for Salinity, Colorado River System* (October 2008, http://www.coloradoriversalinity.org/docs/2008%20Review.pdf), the Colorado River Basin Salinity Control Forum indicates that this

TABLE 8.1

Projected change in total population, numerical and percent, for regions, divisions, and states, 2000–30 [CONTINUED]

Region, division, and state	Numerical change 2000 to 2010	Numerical change 2010 to 2020	Numerical change 2020 to 2030	Numerical change 2000 to 2030	Percent change 2000 to 2010	Percent change 2010 to 2020	Percent change 2020 to 2030	Percent change 2000 to 2030
Pacific	5,409,239	5,651,190	6,151,234	17,211,663	12.0	11.2	11.0	38.2
Washington	647,842	890,173	1,192,665	2,730,680	11.0	13.6	16.0	46.3
Oregon	369,597	469,397	573,525	1,412,519	10.8	12.4	13.5	41.3
California	4,195,486	4,139,609	4,238,118	12,573,213	12.4	10.9	10.0	37.1
Alaska	67,177	80,312	93,253	240,742	10.7	11.6	12.0	38.4
Hawaii	129,137	71,699	53,673	254,509	10.7	5.3	3.8	21.0

SOURCE: "Table 7. Interim Projections: Change in Total Population for Regions, Divisions, and States: 2000 to 2030," in *State Interim Population Projections by Age and Sex: 2004–2030*, U.S. Census Bureau, Population Division, April 21, 2005, http://www.census.gov/population/www/projections/projectionsagesex .html (accessed March 19, 2009)

TABLE 8.2

Population change in metropolitan areas in the U.S., 2000–07

	Change, April 1, 2000 estimates base to July 1, 2007							
	Total		Metropolitan		Micropolitan		Outside CBSAs	
Geographic area	Number	Percent	Number	Percent	Number	Percent	Number	Percent
United States	20,196,555	7.2	19,095,472	8.2	1,039,738	3.5	61,345	0.3
Northeast Region	1,085,844	2.0	1,019,812	2.1	55,385	1.4	10,647	0.7
New England Division	341,625	2.5	282,241	2.3	45,713	4.1	13,671	2.2
Middle Atlantic Division	744,219	1.9	737,571	2.0	9,672	0.4	−3,024	−0.4
Midwest Region	1,993,595	3.1	2,060,427	4.2	67,791	0.8	−134,623	−2.1
East North Central Division	1,182,706	2.6	1,172,282	3.2	21,393	0.4	−10,969	−0.4
West North Central Division	810,889	4.2	888,145	7.2	46,398	1.4	−123,654	−3.5
South Region	10,218,933	10.2	9,512,798	12.1	591,181	4.8	114,954	1.3
South Atlantic Division	6,092,766	11.8	5,599,299	12.9	370,040	7.3	123,427	3.6
East South Central Division	921,279	5.4	794,642	7.4	127,477	3.6	−840	0.0
West South Central Division	3,204,888	10.2	3,118,857	12.5	93,664	2.6	−7,633	−0.3
West Region	6,898,183	10.9	6,502,435	11.5	325,381	7.6	70,367	3.1
Mountain Division	3,187,922	17.5	2,961,386	20.4	181,121	8.4	45,415	3.1
Pacific Division	3,710,261	8.2	3,541,049	8.4	144,260	6.8	24,952	3.3

Note: Metropolitan areas contain at least one urbanized area of 50,000 or more people. Micropolitan areas contain at least one urbanized area of 10,000 to 49,999 people. Together these areas are called core based statistical areas (CBSAs). Territory not included as either is called "outside CBSAs."

SOURCE: "Table 12. Population Change by Core Based Statistical Area (CBSA) Status for the United States, Regions, and Divisions: 2000–2007," in *Metropolitan and Micropolitan Statistical Area Estimates: Population and Population Change by CBSA Status*, U.S. Census Bureau, Population Division, March 27, 2008, http://www.census.gov/popest/metro/CBSA-est2007-CBSAstatus.html (accessed March 19, 2009)

river supplies water to about 7.5 million people within the basin area and another 25.4 million people outside the basin area in the states mentioned previously. The forum explains, "The river provides irrigation water to about 4.0 million acres within the United States. Hydroelectric power facilities along the River and its tributaries generate approximately 12 billion kilowatt-hours annually which is used both inside and outside of the Basin. The River also serves about 3 million people and 500,000 irrigated acres in Mexico."

The Colorado River is managed and operated under guidelines called the Law of the River. This law is actually a collection of federal laws, state compacts, court decisions, and regulatory guidelines. Under the Law of the River, the Colorado River is apportioned among the seven basin states and Mexico, into which the Colorado River flows. (See Figure 8.3.) The legal right for a state to use a certain amount of water from the Colorado River over a given period is called a water entitlement. Aqueducts, which are artificial water channels, bring water from the river to the general area where it is needed. It is distributed to users from that point.

Along with the Colorado River, another major source of water for California is the Sacramento and San Joaquin rivers. These rivers come together at the Sacramento–San Joaquin Delta and then flow into the northern arm of San

FIGURE 8.3

Colorado River and river basin states

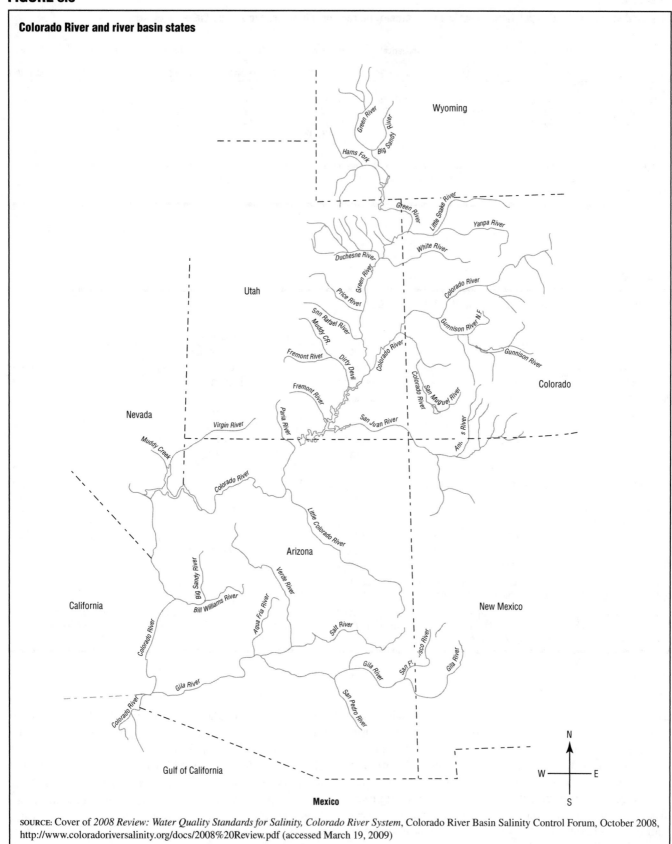

SOURCE: Cover of *2008 Review: Water Quality Standards for Salinity, Colorado River System*, Colorado River Basin Salinity Control Forum, October 2008, http://www.coloradoriversalinity.org/docs/2008%20Review.pdf (accessed March 19, 2009)

Francisco Bay. The rivers, the delta, and their location within the state are shown in Figure 8.4. Jay Lund et al. note in *Comparing Futures for the Sacramento–San Joaquin Delta* (2008, http://www.ppic.org/content/pubs/report/R_708EHR .pdf) that the delta, which is used as a transit point for water, is considered the hub of the state's water supply.

FIGURE 8.4

The Sacramento-San Joaquin Delta

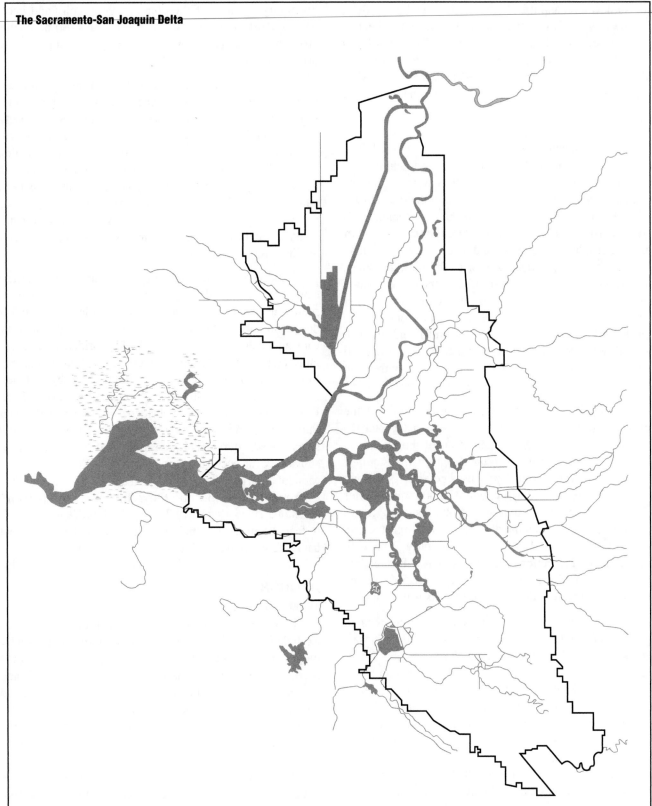

SOURCE: Jay Lund et al., "Figure 1.1. The Sacramento-San Joaquin Delta," in *Envisioning Futures for the Sacramento-San Joaquin Delta*, Public Policy Institute of California, 2007, http://www.ppic.org/content/pubs/report/R_207JLR.pdf (accessed March 19, 2009)

The term *transit point* suggests that the water is traveling somewhere, and it is. In the southern end of the delta near the city of Tracy, the California Aqueduct begins. (See Figure 8.4.) This 444-mile-long (714.5-km-long) artificial channel carries water from Northern to Southern California. Much of the time the water flows by gravity, but pumps are used in certain places along the way.

Groundwater

The other source of water in the West is groundwater (underground supplies). Most groundwater is found in aquifers (underground saturated zones full of water within the spaces between soil and rocks) and within the rocks themselves. These saturated zones are recharged (replenished) primarily from rainfall percolating through the soil. Water from streams, lakes, wetlands, and other water bodies may also seep into the saturated zones. In the saturated zone, water is under pressure that is higher than atmospheric pressure. When a well is dug into the saturated zone, water flows from the area of higher pressure (in the ground) to the area of lower pressure (in the hollow well), and the well fills with water to the level of the existing groundwater. If the pressure is strong enough, the water will flow freely to the surface; otherwise the water must be pumped.

The Ogallala or High Plains Aquifer is one of the world's largest aquifers. (See Figure 4.4 in Chapter 4.) According to Peter B. McMahon et al. of the USGS, in *Water-Quality Assessment of the High Plains Aquifer, 1999–2004* (2007, http://pubs.usgs.gov/pp/1749/down loads/pdf/P1749front.pdf), it covers 174,000 square miles (451,000 square km), stretching from southern South Dakota to the Texas panhandle, and is the largest single source of underground water in the country. The U.S. Environmental Protection Agency designates the Ogallala a sole-source aquifer, meaning that at least 50% of the population in the area depends on it for its water supply.

The Ogallala Aquifer provides water to portions of eight western and midwestern states: Colorado, Kansas, Nebraska, New Mexico, Oklahoma, South Dakota, Texas, and Wyoming. The southern portion of the aquifer is the largest source of groundwater for the western interior plains of the United States. Like many aquifers in the West, this once plentiful source of underground water is being depleted rapidly because its water supply is being extracted by thousands of wells at a faster rate than can be replenished through annual rainfall. Falling water tables invariably signal that the withdrawal of groundwater is exceeding the rate of replacement and that, eventually, the source of water could disappear.

Besides the southern Ogallala Aquifer as a groundwater source to some western states, groundwater is available in the southwestern desert basins. The desert basins are the valleys that lie between mountain ranges. Most of these valleys contain groundwater in layers of gravel, sand, silt, and clay, although groundwater conditions vary because of the complex geography and geology of California and other western states. Some of this groundwater is used for irrigation, public supply, and private wells.

Desert basin aquifers are recharged by rainfall and snowmelt runoff from the mountains. However, the groundwater levels are also affected by short- and long-term climatic conditions and by groundwater withdrawals, irrigation returns, and other factors. Complicating the situation is the climate: the arid and semiarid climate found in much of the West results in slow natural replenishment of aquifer water. Slow replenishment coupled with large-scale removal of groundwater results in loss of springs, streams, wetlands, and their associated habitats; degradation of water quality; and land subsidence.

Land subsidence is the sinking of the ground surface caused by the slow drainage of water from the clay and silt sediments in and next to aquifers. As water levels in aquifers decline and the water is drained from the soil, it compacts, causing the land surface to drop. Land subsidence can cause large cracks and holes in the ground, resulting in damage to roads, pipelines, buildings, canals and drainage ditches, railroads, and other structures. Stanley A. Leake of the USGS reports in "Land Subsidence from Ground-Water Pumping" (January 6, 2004, http://geochange.er.usgs.gov/sw/changes/anthropogenic/subside/) that significant land subsidence is occurring throughout the West, such as in Mendota (29 feet [8.8 m] in depth) and Santa Clara Valley, California (12 feet [3.7 m]); Eloy, Arizona (15 feet [4.6 m]); Houston, Texas (9 feet [2.7 m]); and Las Vegas, Nevada (6 feet [1.8 m]). As of mid-2009, these were the most recent data offered by the USGS.

DROUGHT
What Is Drought?

Drought is a deficiency of precipitation over an extended period, typically a season or more, and is usually judged relative to a long-term average condition in a particular area. Drought is also related to the timing and the effectiveness of the precipitation. Timing refers to factors such as the period when drought is the most likely to occur, delays in the start of the rainy season, and the occurrence of rain in relation to principal crop growth. Precipitation effectiveness refers to the duration, intensity, and frequency of rains or other precipitation events. In many regions of the United States and the world, high temperature, high winds, and low relative humidity are also associated with drought, increasing its severity. In normally arid and semiarid regions, drought refers to dryness over and above the conditions of usual dry seasons.

Figure 8.5 shows drought severity across the 48 contiguous states, Alaska, Hawaii, and Puerto Rico for the week ending March 17, 2009. The National Drought

FIGURE 8.5

Drought conditions, March 2009

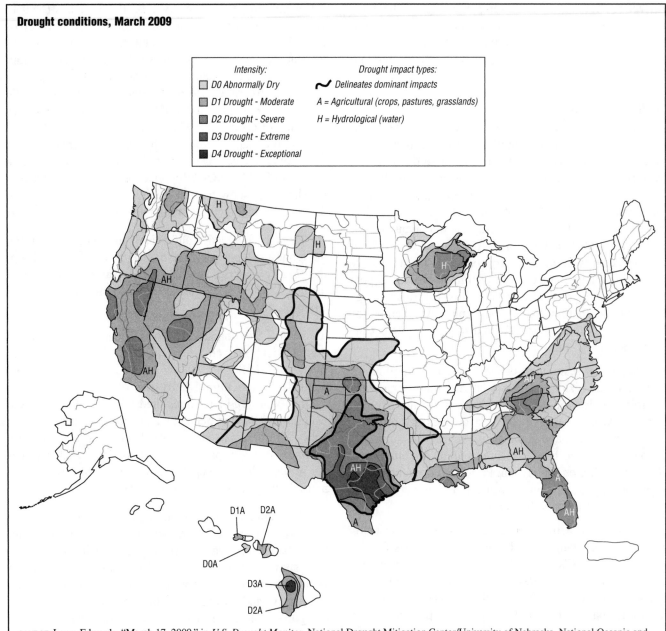

SOURCE: Laura Edwards, "March 17, 2009," in *U.S. Drought Monitor*, National Drought Mitigation Center/University of Nebraska, National Oceanic and Atmospheric Administration, and U.S. Department of Agriculture, March 19, 2009, http://www.drought.unl.edu/dm/monitor.html (accessed March 19, 2009)

Mitigation Center (NDMC) quantifies the drought conditions shown on the map at "Drought Conditions (Percent Area): United States Archive" (May 12, 2009, http://www.drought.unl.edu/dm/DM_tables.htm?archive). Its tables show that over half (54.7%) of the country was not experiencing drought or abnormally dry conditions at that time. Of the 45.3% of the country that was experiencing either drought or abnormally dry conditions, 20.5% were experiencing drought. Nearly 7% of the country was experiencing severe to exceptional drought conditions.

The map shows that normal conditions prevailed in the Northeast and areas south and west of the Great

Lakes, except for Wisconsin and a portion of Minnesota. Much of the southeastern, middle, and western portions of the country were experiencing abnormally dry to moderate drought conditions. Portions of southern Texas were experiencing the most widespread severe, extreme, and exceptional drought conditions in the country, but severe drought was also prevalent in the West.

The interaction between drought, a natural event, and the demand that people place on water supply can worsen a drought's impact. Changes in land use, land degradation, and the construction of dams all affect the characteristics of a water basin (the land area drained by a particular river and its tributaries), and as a result, the pattern and volume of river or stream flow. For example, changes in land use upstream may alter the rates at which water filters into the ground or runs off the ground, causing more variable stream flow and a higher frequency of water shortage downstream.

Predicting Drought

Anyone can predict with absolute certainty that drought will occur somewhere on the planet, because inevitably it will. It is the how, when, where, and for what duration that are difficult to predict. Drought is never the result of a single cause, but comes from the interaction, and sometimes compounding, of the effects of many causes. On the largest scale, global weather systems play an important part in explaining global and regional weather patterns. These patterns occur with enough frequency and similar characteristics over a sufficient length of time to provide opportunities to strengthen scientists' ability to predict long-range climate, particularly in the tropics. An example of these global systems is El Niño, a disruption of the ocean-atmosphere system in the tropical Pacific Ocean.

On a lesser scale, high-pressure systems inhibit cloud formation and result in lower relative humidity and less precipitation. Regions that are under the influence of high-pressure systems most of the year are generally deserts such as the Sahara and Kalahari in Africa. Most climatic regions experience high-pressure systems at some time, often depending on the season. Prolonged droughts occur when the large-scale deviations in atmospheric circulation patterns persist for months, seasons, or years.

The CCSP is actively working to promote understanding of climate change and the implications it has for the United States. In *Effects of Climate Change on Agriculture, Land Resources, Water Resources, and Biodiversity in the United States*, the CCSP notes that advances in climate science are paving the way for scientists to project climate changes at the regional scale, allowing them to identify regional vulnerabilities and to assess potential regional effects. For example, the CCSP suggests that Earth's climate has changed in the past and that even greater climate change is likely to occur during the 21st century. It also suggests that reduced summer runoff, increased winter runoff, and increased water demands are likely to compound current stresses on water supplies and flood management, particularly in the western United States.

DROUGHT MANAGEMENT
California and the 1986–93 Drought

California is located in a climatic high-pressure zone that hovers off its coast, causing rainfall to be diverted northward. The rain that does fall in California is not evenly distributed. According to regional climate data of California's Department of Water Resources (January 14,

2009, http://www.water.ca.gov/floodmgmt/hafoo/csc/), the northern one-third receives 22 to 41 inches (55.9 to 104.1 cm) of rain per year, the central portion receives 21 inches per year (53.3 cm), and the southern region of the state receives 4 to 20 inches (10.1 to 50.8 cm) of rain per year (based on data from 1971 through 2000). Even though Northern California provides two-thirds of the state's water supply, much of the state's population lives in Southern California, which has little water of its own. Population maps developed by the California Department of Finance (December 2008, http://www.dof.ca.gov/html/DEMOGRAP/ReportsPapers/documents/CountyEstMaps.pdf) show that the central and lower portions of the state contain the largest numbers of people.

Drought plagued California from 1986 until 1993, the longest dry period in nearly 100 years of record keeping. Water supplies dwindled and water rationing was instituted. Many asked the governor to proclaim a state of emergency.

In the San Joaquin Valley the earth dropped more than 1 foot (30.5 cm) from land subsidence, damaging roads and buildings. Water resource authorities suspended the agricultural deliveries of water. Crops such as grapevines and fruit trees died because of insufficient water. Farmers who planted water-intensive crops such as cotton, alfalfa, and rice were the hardest hit. Grocery shoppers in every part of the country paid higher prices for some fruits and vegetables because California is the nation's largest agricultural producer.

Throughout the drought, many cities and towns in California instituted severe penalties for excessive water use. Water conservation efforts included installing low-flow showerheads and toilets; not washing cars or filling swimming pools and hot tubs; using dishwashers less frequently; and letting lawns become brown. Water was categorized either as clear (direct from the tap), gray (recycled water from showers, bathtubs, sinks, and washing machines), or black (toilet wastewater). The gray water was reused to water vegetable gardens or plants. Some Californians switched to paper plates to avoid using dishwashers. Others turned off the tap water while brushing their teeth or did not wait for hot water when taking showers. As water rationing became increasingly serious, code enforcers watched for violators and issued citations with fines.

The area's wildlife and vegetation required years to recover from the effects of the drought. The drought years also had a significant impact on trees. Because of the dryness, fire officials continually battled forest fires. In 1990 wildfires forced the closing of Yosemite National Park for the first time in history. Many expensive homes were destroyed as wildfires roared through the canyons. With water from rivers and reservoirs severely limited, helicopters were fitted with large buckets that enabled them to scoop water from swimming pools, if necessary.

Western Water Policy Review Act

Partially as a response to this severe drought and at the recommendation of the Western Governors' Association, Congress adopted the Western Water Policy Review Act of 1992, which directed a comprehensive review of federal activities affecting the allocation and use of water in 19 western states. The Western Water Policy Review Advisory Commission was appointed and chartered in 1995.

The commission released its findings and recommendations in 1997. In the arid West, providing adequate water supplies to meet future demands remained a top priority. Besides the need for more supplies to meet growing water demands, the commission recognized that a need existed to overhaul the existing water infrastructure (irrigation canals and ditches, water piping, and water storage devices). The commission also recognized that there were legal and institutional conflicts that needed to be addressed at the federal-state level, between states, and among various water users. The commission recommended the development and implementation of an integrated, coordinated federal policy for federal activities affecting the allocation and use of water in the 19 western states. The policy was to be developed with the full involvement of the affected states.

National Drought Policy Act

As a result of the Western Water Policy Review Advisory Commission's report, Congress passed the National Drought Policy Act of 1998. The new law established a National Drought Policy Commission to make recommendations concerning the creation and development of an integrated, coordinated federal drought policy. The commission was to seek public input on recommendations for legislative and administrative actions to help prepare for and alleviate droughts' adverse economic, social, health, and environmental effects.

In May 2000 the commission released *Preparing for Drought in the 21st Century* (http://govinfo.library.unt.edu/ drought/finalreport/fullreport/pdf/reportfull.pdf). The commission recommended the following national policy:

> National drought policy should use the resources of the federal government to support but not supplant nor interfere with state, tribal, regional, local, and individual efforts to reduce drought impacts. The guiding principles of national drought policy should be:
>
> 1. Favor preparedness over insurance, insurance over relief, and incentives over regulation.
>
> 2. Set research priorities based on the potential of the research results to reduce drought impacts.

> 3. Coordinate the delivery of federal services through cooperation and collaboration with non-federal entities.

The approach of this policy was a marked shift from emphasis on drought relief to that of proactive stance of working to reduce the effects of drought. The commission stated that preparedness was the key to successful drought management and that information and research were needed to support and achieve preparedness. In addition, the commission recommended that the federal government should develop a national drought policy with preparedness at its core and that federal resources should be dedicated to this goal. The commission provided specific recommendations as to how this should be done and urged Congress to pass a National Drought Preparedness Act to achieve the implementation of the recommended policy.

National Drought Preparedness Acts were introduced into Congress in 2002, 2003, and 2005 to establish a National Drought Council within the U.S. Department of Agriculture and to improve national drought preparedness, mitigation, and response efforts. None of these bills became law. As of mid-2009, another such bill had not been introduced into Congress.

Environmental Quality Incentive Program

Even though a National Drought Preparedness Act has not been passed, the federal government does play a role in assisting farmers to implement technologies and practices to conserve water and to lessen the long-term effects of drought. The Department of Agriculture's Environmental Quality Incentive Program (EQIP) is one such effort. Reauthorized in the Farm Security and Rural Investment Act of 2002 and again in the Food, Conservation, and Energy Act of 2008 (2008 Farm Bill), the EQIP provides payments to the states to implement conservation practices, paying up to 75% of the cost of certain conservation practices. The Natural Resources Conservation Service indicates in "Farm Bill 2008 at a Glance: Environmental Quality Incentives Program" (May 2008, http://www.nrcs.usda.gov/programs/farmbill/2008/pdfs/ EQIP_At_A_Glance_062608final.pdf) that one of the national priorities of the EQIP is "water conservation or irrigation efficiency applications that will reduce water use or where the producer agrees not to use any associated water savings to bring new land under irrigation production." Figure 8.6 shows that a large share of EQIP dollars goes to western and midwestern states.

Water Policies—States Lead the Way

Water shortfalls are first and foremost a local and regional problem. Because of the lack of a cohesive federal water policy, states have become important innova-

FIGURE 8.6

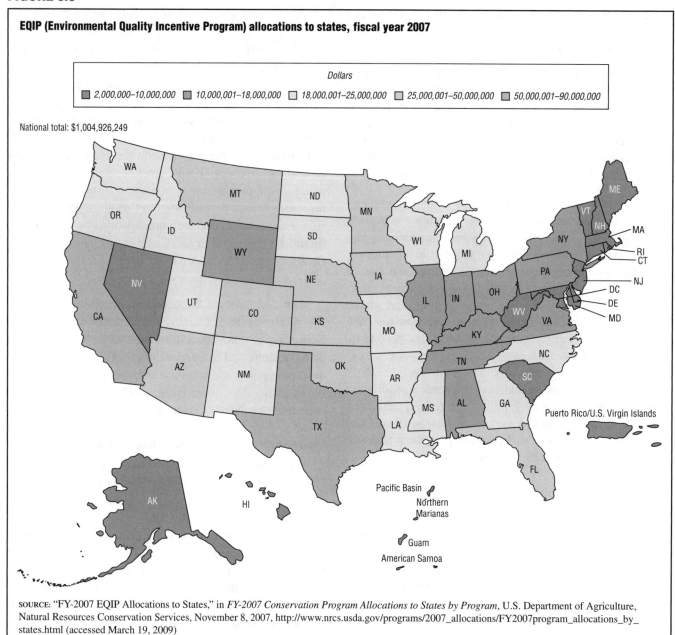

EQIP (Environmental Quality Incentive Program) allocations to states, fiscal year 2007

Dollars

☐ 2,000,000–10,000,000   ☐ 10,000,001–18,000,000   ☐ 18,000,001–25,000,000   ☐ 25,000,001–50,000,000   ☐ 50,000,001–90,000,000

National total: $1,004,926,249

SOURCE: "FY-2007 EQIP Allocations to States," in *FY-2007 Conservation Program Allocations to States by Program*, U.S. Department of Agriculture, Natural Resources Conservation Services, November 8, 2007, http://www.nrcs.usda.gov/programs/2007_allocations/FY2007program_allocations_by_states.html (accessed March 19, 2009)

tors in devising ways to reduce long-term vulnerability to drought. During a widespread drought from 1976 to 1977, no state had a drought plan. In 1982 only three states had them. According to the NDMC, in "Planning for Drought: State Drought Plans and Related Documents" (2008, http://drought.unl.edu/plan/stateplans.htm), by the end of 2008, 41 states had drought plans.

In "Mitigating Drought: The Status of State Drought Plans" (2007, http://drought.unl.edu/mitigate/status.htm), the NDMC indicates that most state plans do not meet all the goals of its recommended planning process. Twenty-nine of the plans address response to droughts rather than mitigation (lessening) of droughts by defining the basic

linkages between local, state, and federal entities for coordinated planning and response efforts.

HISTORY OF WATER RIGHTS IN THE WEST

With water scarce in many parts of the arid and semiarid western United States, finding water, bringing it to where it was needed, and obtaining rights to use the water were extremely important aspects of survival. Two important events in the process of settling the West led to laws for the allocation of the scarce water supplies: the discovery of gold and silver in the western mountain regions and the widespread use of irrigation for crop production.

Miners searching for gold and silver diverted stream water into pipes. As a result, an informal code of water regulations started in the mining camps. The first person to file a claim to a gold or silver mine was allowed priority in getting water over any later claims. To remain the owner of a mining claim, the individual had to mark it off, take possession of it, and work the claim productively. This informal water law, conceived well over 100 years ago, was called the prior appropriation doctrine.

This legal practice was then adopted by farmers, who needed water for irrigation. The "first in time, first in right" priority system gave the first farmers guaranteed water supplies in times of drought, which were frequent. This right to use water by both the miners and the farmers, who were the first nonnative settlers of the West, was exclusive and absolute. However, the prior appropriation and "first in time, first in right" practices used in the West were different from the system of riparian rights (the right to use water, such as a stream or lake, that abuts one's property) used in the East. Riparian rights could not be sold or transferred, whereas water rights governed by the doctrine of prior appropriation could.

As the western population expanded and states began to write down their laws and arrange them into an organized legal system, the rules for water rights and use changed. The concept of beneficial use became the basis for a landowner's rights to water. Beneficial use has two components: the nature or purpose of the use and the efficient or nonwasteful use of water. State constitutions, statutes, or case law may define the beneficial uses of water. The uses may be different in each state, and the definitions of what uses are beneficial may change over time. The right to use water established under state law may be lost if the beneficial use is discontinued for a prescribed period, frequently summarized as "use it or lose it." Abandonment requires intent to permanently give up the right. Forfeiture results from the failure to use the water in the manner described in state statutes. Both require a finding by the state resource agency that a water right has been abandoned or forfeited.

Priority determines the order of rank of the rights to use the water in a system—that is, the person first using the water for a beneficial purpose has a right superior to those who begin to use the water at a later date. Priority becomes important when the quantity of available water is insufficient to meet the needs of all those having rights to use water from a common source. Under a priority system, water shortages are not shared as they are under a riparian water rights system. Some western state statutes contain priority or preference categories of water use under which higher-priority uses (such as domestic water supply) have first right to water in times of shortage, regardless of the priority date. There may also be constraints against changes or transfers involving these priority uses.

Federal Water Laws and Projects

The federal government played a role in both encouraging the economic growth and settlement of the West and developing water laws and projects. The Reclamation Act of 1902 began many years of federal involvement in constructing and subsidizing water projects in the West. The act was designed to provide subsidized water for small farmers who owned up to 320 acres (129.5 ha). Over the years farmers and corporations have used subsidized water to farm thousands of acres by entering into arrangements in which they lease (but do not own) farms.

Based on the existence of irrigated farmland guaranteed by federal subsidies, the West grew rapidly. Cities sprang up in the deserts, attracting a large array of support industries as people from the East and Midwest moved to the Southwest to enjoy the warm, dry climate, stark beauty, and sunshine.

UNANTICIPATED CONSEQUENCES OF IRRIGATION. Because of the composition of the land in much of the West, irrigation practices created some unforeseen problems. Millions of acres of irrigated land overlie a shallow and impermeable clay layer that is sometimes only a few feet below the surface. Significant changes in the land can be caused by the interaction of irrigation water and the clay. During the irrigation season temperatures in much of the desert fluctuate between 90 and 110° Fahrenheit (32.2 and 43.3° Celsius), and some irrigation water is lost to evaporation. When the water evaporates, it leaves behind chemicals called salts that accumulate in the soil.

The water that is retained in the soil seeps downward, carrying the salts with it, until it hits the impermeable clay layer. Because the water has nowhere to go, it and the dissolved salts rise back up into the plant root zone. The high salt concentration in the water can interfere with crop growth. Generally, high salt concentrations hinder the germination of plants and impede their absorption of nutrients. In some cases high salt concentrations in soils have rendered them unable to grow crops. The salts accumulate in the soil as irrigation continues. Eventually, the salts become visible on the ground.

To stop excessive buildup of the salts in the soil, extra irrigation water is required to flush out the salts, generally into surface drainage or groundwater. In locations where these dissolved substances reach high concentrations, the quality of the surface and groundwater in the area can be harmed. In severe cases the increased salinity renders surface and groundwater useless for irrigation or drinking and contributes to degraded aquatic habitats.

Buying and Selling Water Rights

Before the mid-1980s the preferred method of getting water was to develop a new supply. As new supplies became less accessible and environmental regulations made supply development more difficult and expensive, creating mechanisms for voluntary water reallocation by buying and selling water rights became more important. Western cities and industries began looking to the agricultural community for water.

Agriculture has traditionally claimed the lion's share of the West's water supplies. However, if farmers or ranchers could earn more money selling water to a nearby city than spraying it on their crops or watering their stock, shifting the water from farm to city would be in their economic best interest. If buying water saves a city from damming a local river to increase supplies or depleting an aquifer, it also benefits the environment.

Advocates of the sale of water rights maintain that a free market will allow for more efficient distribution of a source that is often subsidized and just as often squandered. Conservative politicians favor it because it reduces the federal government's role in developing new water supplies. Liberal politicians also like it because more efficient use of water could benefit the environment by lessening the need for dams, which are often environmentally harmful. Since 1981 western state legislatures have been slowly changing the old laws dealing with water rights to make water right transfers more flexible.

Opponents to the sale of water rights maintain that the sales are draining the life from small, rural communities and can cause irreparable damage to the environment in the long run as the now waterless land is left to crack, bake, and turn into dust. The farmers and ranchers who have refused to sell their water rights are concerned about not only their own water supplies but also the surrounding weeds, dust, and barren land. Once water rights are sold, the use of the land for farming is over.

Water Banks

Not all water right transfers require that water be shifted permanently away from agriculture. Voluntary market transactions can reallocate water on a temporary, long-term, or permanent basis. A water bank (a clearinghouse between the buyers and sellers of water), acting as a water broker and usually subsidized by the state, can be authorized to spend money to buy water from farmers or other sellers who are willing to temporarily or permanently reduce their own use. The bank then resells the water to drinking water suppliers, farmers, ranchers, and industries that need the water.

In *Analysis of Water Banks in the Western States* (July 2004, http://www.ecy.wa.gov/pubs/0411011.pdf), Peggy Clifford, Clay Landry, and Andrea Larsen-Hayden for the Washington Department of Ecology note that water banks exist in almost every western state and are "emerging as an important management tool to meet growing and changing water demands throughout the United States."

Arizona, California, and Idaho have water banks with a high level of activity.

DESALINATION—A GROWING WATER SUPPLY SOURCE

Desalination plants convert seawater, brackish water (a mixture of seawater and freshwater), and wastewater to freshwater suitable for a variety of purposes. According to Heather Cooley, Peter H. Gleick, and Gary Wolff of the Pacific Institute, in *Desalination, with a Grain of Salt: A California Perspective* (June 2006, http://www.pacinst.org/reports/desalination/desalination_report.pdf), 56% of global desalination plants are designed to process seawater, 24% can process brackish water, and the remaining desalinate other kinds of water, such as wastewater.

In *Desalination: A National Perspective* (2008), the National Research Council assesses the state of desalination and what the future of desalination technologies might hold for helping ease water shortages in the United States. The committee concludes that a definitive answer cannot be given because many factors affect the feasibility of desalination in any particular locale. The committee does note, however, that desalination capacity worldwide has doubled since 1995 and continues to grow, with nearly half the desalination capacity located in the Middle East. Global Water Intelligence (2009, http://www.globalwaterintel.com/), a company that analyzes worldwide water data, reports that in 2007 the global online capacity of desalination plants was over 5 million cubic meters (about 1.3 billion gallons [5 billion L]) per day.

According to the Saudi Arabia Market Information Resource, in "Desalination" (April 20, 2009, http://saudinf.com/main/a541.htm), Saudi Arabia is a country heavily invested in this technology; it has 27 desalination plants that provide 70% of the country's drinking water. However, Cooley, Gleick, and Wolff report that worldwide, desalination plants in service in 2005 had the capacity to provide only 0.3% of the freshwater used globally.

In the United States desalination has become a rapidly growing alternative to water scarcity. With population growth and the threat of drought throughout the United States—particularly in the western states and Florida—desalination, once considered too expensive, is becoming more attractive.

Desalination Processes

Desalination is the removal of dissolved minerals (including, but not limited to, salts) from seawater, brackish water, or treated wastewater. A number of technologies have been developed for desalination. In the United States desalination research is directed by the Bureau of Reclamation, which is a branch of the U.S. Department of the Interior.

There are two major types of desalination processes:

- Reverse osmosis—filtered water is pumped at high pressure through permeable membranes, which hold back the salts but allow the water to pass.

- Distillation—water is heated and then evaporated to separate out the salts.

Concerning distillation, there are four basic types of process:

- Multistage flash distillation, in which the water is heated and the pressure lowered so that the water flashes into a vapor that is drawn off and cooled to provide desalted water.

- Multiple effect distillation, in which the water passes through a number of evaporators in a series with the vapor from one series being used to evaporate the water in the next series.

- Vapor compression, in which the water is evaporated and the vapor compressed; the heated compressed vapor is used to evaporate additional water.

- Electrodialysis—electric current is applied to brackish water, causing positive and negative ions of dissolved salt to split apart.

The two most common desalination processes worldwide are multistage flash distillation and reverse osmosis. Even though waters of different qualities, including seawater, brackish water, or impure industrial wastewater, can be desalinated, seawater and brackish water are the most common water sources worldwide.

Desalination Plants in the United States

Buckeye, Arizona, became the first town in the United States to have all its water supplied by its own electrodialysis-desalting plant. Starting in 1962 the plant provided about 650,000 gallons (2.5 million L) of water daily at a cost of about $1 per 1,670 gallons (6,322 L).

In 1967 Key West, Florida, opened a flash-distillation plant and became the first city in the United States to draw its freshwater from the sea. Cynthia Barnett notes in "Desalination: Salty Solution?" (*Florida Trend Magazine*, May 1, 2007) that in 2007 Florida became the home to the largest desalination plant of the 250 operating in the United States: the Tampa Bay Seawater Desalination Facility. As of 2007, Florida also led the nation in having the most desalination plants, at 120; Texas had 38; and California had 33.

Unlike the Key West plant, the Tampa plant uses a reverse osmosis process, but like the Key West plant it draws its water from the sea. Figure 8.7 shows a schematic of the reverse osmosis process as carried out in the Tampa Bay plant, which provides Tampa Bay–area residents with 6 million gallons (22.7 million L) of fresh drinking water per day, as noted by Barnett. Figure 8.7 is annotated, explaining the reverse osmosis desalination process beginning at the intake canal at Tampa Bay. Reverse osmosis is one of the last processes to take place, after the water has been screened and filtered.

Advantages and Disadvantages of Desalination

One of the most important factors determining whether desalination is a viable way to provide water to consumers is cost. Desalinated water is expensive, and even though the long-term trend in desalination costs has been downward, in recent years prices have increased due to rising energy and construction costs. Nonetheless, desalination can provide a reliable source of water independent of the weather and can serve as an additional source of water to those already in place. The desalination process also removes water impurities. However, water quality must be monitored to ensure that contaminants are not added during the desalination process or that essential minerals are not removed.

WATER REUSE

Wastewater from sewage treatment plants is one of the largest potential sources of freshwater where supplies are limited. After it has been treated to kill pathogens (disease-causing organisms) and remove contaminants, it can be reused for irrigation and industrial use and to maintain stream flow.

Indirect reuse of treated municipal wastewater (reclaimed water) is becoming increasingly attractive to many municipalities, especially in the West. For example, the Orange County Water District in California has implemented the Green Acres Project, which uses reclaimed water for landscape irrigation at parks and schools, as well as for various industrial uses. According to the district (2008, http://www.ocwd.com/ca-168.aspx), the project can purify up to 7.5 million gallons (28.4 million L) per day of reclaimed water from the Orange County Sanitation District. Using a newly built reservoir, the project can store up to 350 million gallons (1.3 billion L) of this recycled water per year.

WATER 2025

Problems in the West, including explosive population growth, existing water shortages, conflicts over water, aging water facilities, and ineffective crisis management, prompted the Bureau of Reclamation to publish *Water 2025: Preventing Crises and Conflict in the West* (August 2005, http://www.sustainca.org/files/WPuUSA-USBR_2005 .pdf), which was designed to assist communities in addressing these needs. The bureau calls for concentrating existing federal financial and technical resources in key western watersheds and in critical research and development, such

FIGURE 8.7

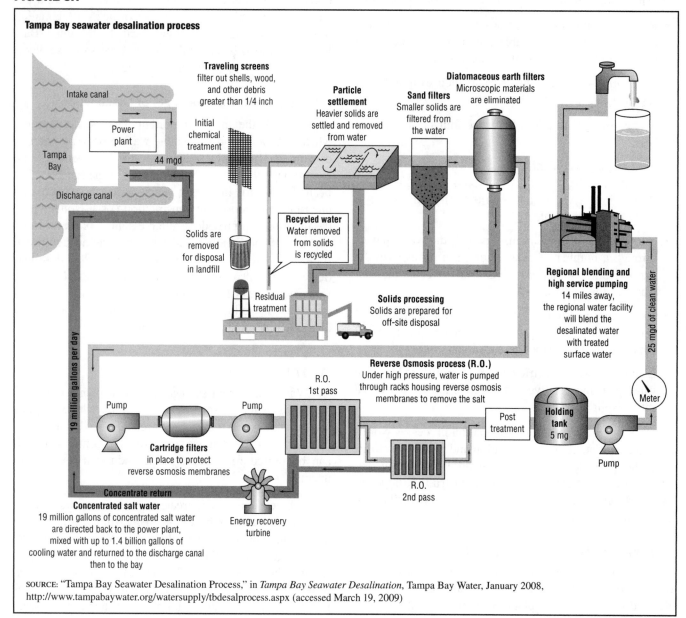

Tampa Bay seawater desalination process

SOURCE: "Tampa Bay Seawater Desalination Process," in *Tampa Bay Seawater Desalination*, Tampa Bay Water, January 2008, http://www.tampabaywater.org/watersupply/tbdesalprocess.aspx (accessed March 19, 2009)

as water conservation and desalinization, that would help predict, prevent, and alleviate water supply conflicts.

Water 2025 is a departure from previous plans in that it focuses on strategies and measures that can be put in place before events such as drought bring further divisiveness to communities in the West. The Bureau of Reclamation believes conflict can be minimized or avoided when potential water supply crises are addressed in advance by local and regional communities. Figure 8.8 shows the areas *Water 2025* identifies as having potential water supply crises by 2025.

Water 2025 is an important initiative for water conservation and has become part of the Water for America initiative. In the fact sheet "Water for America: Leadership to Address Changing Water Realities" (June 22, 2004, http://www.usbr.gov/newsroom/presskit/factsheet/factsheetdetail.cfm?recordid=3), the Bureau of Reclamation explains the goal of this initiative: "To address the impending confluence of three factors threatening to overwhelm our current ability to provide water to the arid West: increased water demands, aging infrastructure, and decreased or altered availability of water supplies. This initiative will incorporate and build upon the successes of the Water 2025 Program by expanding the scope and placing renewed emphasis on responding to the changing water realities of the 21st century. *Water for America* will focus on three strategies: Plan for our Nation's Water Future, Enhance Our Nation's Water Knowledge, and Expand, Protect, and Conserve Our Nation's Water Resources."

As a primary part of the first two strategies, the Bureau of Reclamation is conducting studies in locales

FIGURE 8.8

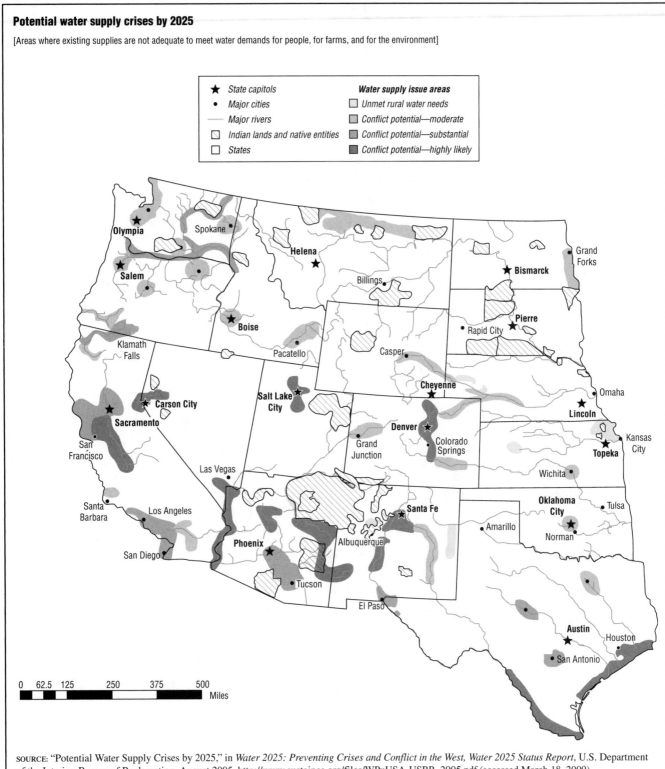

Potential water supply crises by 2025

[Areas where existing supplies are not adequate to meet water demands for people, for farms, and for the environment]

★ State capitols
• Major cities
— Major rivers
▨ Indian lands and native entities
☐ States

Water supply issue areas
☐ Unmet rural water needs
▨ Conflict potential—moderate
▨ Conflict potential—substantial
▨ Conflict potential—highly likely

SOURCE: "Potential Water Supply Crises by 2025," in *Water 2025: Preventing Crises and Conflict in the West, Water 2025 Status Report*, U.S. Department of the Interior, Bureau of Reclamation, August 2005, http://www.sustainca.org/files/WPuUSA-USBR_2005.pdf (accessed March 18, 2009)

where it projects high water demand and water access issues. The studies will result in recommendations to meet these challenges. As a primary part of the third strategy, the bureau is administering a Challenge Grant program. This program seeks proposals from irrigation and water districts to partner with the bureau to develop plans and technologies to conserve, recycle, and desalt water. The bureau notes in "Water for America Initiative: Addressing 21st Century Water Challenges" (April 8, 2009, http://www.usbr.gov/wfa/) that the 2009 funding opportunities were funded under the American Recovery and Investment Act of 2009.

IMPORTANT NAMES
AND ADDRESSES

American Ground Water Trust
50 Pleasant St.
Concord, NH 03301
(603) 228-5444
FAX: (603) 228-6557
E-mail: trustinfo@agwt.org
URL: http://www.agwt.org/

American Petroleum Institute
1220 L St. NW
Washington, DC 20005-4070
(202) 682-8000
URL: http://www.api.org/

**American Water Works
Association**
6666 W. Quincy Ave.
Denver, CO 80235
(303) 794-7711
1-800-926-7337
FAX: (303) 347-0804
URL: http://www.awwa.org/

**Association of State Drinking Water
Administrators**
1401 Wilson Blvd., Ste. 1225
Arlington, VA 22209
(703) 812-9505
FAX: (703) 812-9506
URL: http://www.asdwa.org/

Bureau of Land Management
1849 C St. NW, Rm. 5665
Washington, DC 20240
(202) 208-3801
FAX: (202) 208-5242
URL: http://www.blm.gov/

**Centers for Disease Control and
Prevention**
1600 Clifton Rd.
Atlanta, GA 30333
1-800-232-4636
URL: http://www.cdc.gov/

Chesapeake Bay Program
410 Severn Ave., Ste. 109
Annapolis, MD 21403
1-800-YOUR BAY
FAX: (410) 267-5777
URL: http://www.chesapeakebay.net/

Ducks Unlimited
One Waterfowl Way
Memphis, TN 38120
(901) 758-3825
1-800-45-DUCKS
URL: http://www.ducks.org/

**International Bottled Water
Association**
1700 Diagonal Rd., Ste. 650
Alexandria, VA 22314
(703) 683-5213
FAX: (703) 683-4074
E-mail: ibwainfo@bottledwater.org
URL: http://www.bottledwater.org/

**National Drought Mitigation Center
University of Nebraska, Lincoln**
819 Hardin Hall
3310 Holdrege St.
PO Box 830988
Lincoln, NE 68583-0988
(402) 472-6707
FAX: (402) 472-2946
E-mail: ndmc@unl.edu
URL: http://www.drought.unl.edu/

**National Oceanic and Atmospheric
Administration**
1401 Constitution Ave. NW, Rm. 5128
Washington, DC 20230
URL: http://www.noaa.gov/

National Wildlife Federation
11100 Wildlife Center Dr.
Reston, VA 20190-5362
1-800-822-9919
URL: http://www.nwf.org/

**Natural Resources Conservation
Service**
Attn: Public Affairs Division
PO Box 2890
Washington, DC 20013
URL: http://www.nrcs.usda.gov/

Nature Conservancy
4245 N. Fairfax Dr., Ste. 100
Arlington, VA 22203-1606
(703) 841-5300
URL: http://www.nature.org/

Soil and Water Conservation Society
945 SW Ankeny Rd.
Ankeny, IA 50023-9723
(515) 289-2331
FAX: (515) 289-1227
URL: http://www.swcs.org/

**U.S. Environmental Protection
Agency**
Ariel Rios Bldg.
1200 Pennsylvania Ave. NW
Washington, DC 20460
(202) 272-0167
URL: http://www.epa.gov/

U.S. Fish and Wildlife Service
1849 C St. NW
Washington, DC 20240
1-800-344-WILD
URL: http://www.fws.gov/

U.S. Geological Survey
12201 Sunrise Valley Dr.
Reston, VA 20192
(703) 648-4000
URL: http://www.usgs.gov/

U.S. Government Accountability Office
441 G St. NW
Washington, DC 20548
(202) 512-3000
FAX: (202) 512-8546
E-mail: contact@gao.gov
URL: http://www.gao.gov/

U.S. Water News
230 Main St.
Halstead, KS 67056
(316) 835-2222
1-800-251-0046
FAX: (316) 835-2223
URL: http://www.uswaternews.com/

Water Environment Federation
601 Wythe St.
Alexandria, VA 22314-1994
1-800-666-0206
FAX: (703) 684-2492
URL: http://www.wef.org/

RESOURCES

Responsibility for the protection, management, and use of water is spread across many federal agencies. The U.S. Geological Survey (USGS), a branch of the U.S. Department of the Interior, has the principal responsibility within the federal government for appraising the nation's resources and providing hydrological information. The USGS publications consulted for this edition include *Ground-Water Availability in the United States* (2008, Thomas E. Reilly et al.), *Water-Quality Assessment of the High Plains Aquifer, 1999–2004* (2007, Peter B. McMahon et al.), *Estimated Use of Water in the United States in 2000* (2004, Susan S. Hutson et al.), *Where Is Earth's Water Located?* (March 2009), *Analysis of Water Use in the Piscataqua River and Coastal Watersheds, Southeastern New Hampshire* (2006), and *The Quality of Our Nation's Waters: Volatile Organic Compounds in the Nation's Ground Water and Drinking-Water Supply Wells* (2006, John S. Zogorski et al.).

The U.S. Environmental Protection Agency (EPA) is the federal regulatory agency charged with, among other things, protection of both surface and groundwater quality, overseeing the states' management of drinking water protection programs, the development of water quality standards, and the enforcement of laws addressing water quality. The EPA published the *National Water Quality Inventory: Report to Congress, 2004 Reporting Cycle* (January 2009), *National Estuary Program Coastal Condition Report* (June 2007), *National Listing of Fish Advisories Technical Fact Sheet: 2005/06 National Listing* (July 2007), *National Coastal Condition Report III* (December 2008), and *The Wadeable Streams Assessment: A Collaborative Survey of the Nation's Streams* (December 2006).

The U.S. Government Accountability Office, the investigative arm of Congress, was an excellent source for many graphics from archival documents.

The National Oceanic and Atmospheric Administration (NOAA), a branch of the U.S. Department of Commerce, has the principal responsibility within the federal government for appraising and protecting the nation's aquatic resources, managing its fisheries, and predicting weather and climate. NOAA documents and publications used for this book include the "Saffir-Simpson Hurricane Scale," *The Deadliest, Costliest, and Most Intense United States Tropical Cyclones from 1851 to 2006 (and Other Frequently Requested Hurricane Facts)* (April 2007, Eric S. Blake, Edward N. Rappaport, and Christopher W. Landsea), and *The State of Coral Reef Ecosystems of the United States and Pacific Freely Associated States: 2008* (April 2008, Jeannette E. Waddell and Alicia M. Clarke).

The U.S. Fish and Wildlife Service (USFWS), a branch of the Department of the Interior, is charged with protection of living resources. USFWS documents used in this edition include *2006 National Survey of Fishing, Hunting, and Wildlife-Associated Recreation* (October 2007) and *Status and Trends of Wetlands in the Conterminous United States 1998 to 2004* (2006, Thomas E. Dahl).

The U.S. Department of Agriculture (USDA) provides national leadership on natural resources. USDA documents and publications consulted for this edition include *FY-2007 Conservation Program Allocations to States by Program* (November 2007) and *National Resources Inventory 2003 Annual NRI* (May 2006).

The Centers for Disease Control and Prevention (CDC) is part of the U.S. Department of Health and Human Services. CDC documents used in this book include "Surveillance for Waterborne Disease and Outbreaks Associated with Drinking Water and Water Not Intended for Drinking—United States, 2005–2006" (September 2008, Jonathan Yoder et al.) and "Surveillance for Waterborne Disease and Outbreaks Associated with Recreational Water Use and Other Aquatic Facility–Associated Health Events—United States, 2005–2006" (Jonathan S. Yoder et al.,

September 2008). Both documents are published in the CDC's periodical *Morbidity and Mortality Weekly Update*.

Additional important publications about water include the South Florida Water Management District's *2009 South Florida Environmental Report* (March 2009) and the United Nations' *The United Nations World Water Develop-* *ment Report 3: Water in a Changing World* (March 2009). Gallup provided Americans' opinions on water issues in three documents: *Gallup's Pulse of Democracy: Environment* (2009), *Polluted Drinking Water Is Public's Top Environmental Concern* (March 2007, Joseph Carroll), and *Are Americans Financially Prepared for Disaster?* (October 2005, Dennis Jacobe).

INDEX